HANSON

Alex Brummer has edited the *Guardian's* Finance and Economics pages since 1989, where he writes a daily column. He was previously the paper's foreign editor and from 1979 to 1989 the paper's Washington correspondent. In 1988 he received the prestigious Overseas Press Club award as best US foreign correspondent. He has a degree in economics and politics from Southampton University and an MBA from Bradford University Management Centre.

Roger Cowe joined the *Guardian's* financial staff in 1987. In that year he founded the Outlook column of company comment and analysis to which he continues to contribute. Previously he was deputy editor at *Accountancy Age*. He is a member of the Chartered Institute of Management Accountants and has an MBA from Manchester Business School. He is the editor of *The Guardian Guide to the UK's Top Companies 1995*, also published by Fourth Estate.

HANSON

The rise and rise of Britain's most buccaneering businessman

Alex Brummer
and Roger Cowe

FOURTH ESTATE · *London*

This paperback edition first published 1995

First published in Great Britain in 1994 by
Fourth Estate Limited
6 Salem Road
London W2 4BU

2 4 6 8 10 9 7 5 3 1

A catalogue record for this book is available from the British Library.

ISBN 1–85702–351–X

Printed by Cox & Wyman Ltd, Reading, Berks

Contents

Preface and Acknowledgements

The first major story this author (Alex Brummer) ever wrote for a national newspaper focused on the proposed merger of James Hanson's emerging industrial group Hanson Trust with Malcolm Horsman's Bowater in the summer of 1973. One knew very little about James Hanson or, for that matter, Malcolm Horsman at that time, except that both the companies they chaired, while independently successful, were viewed by the investment community as being run by a new generation of financially orientated industrialists with strong connections to Jim Slater's investment group: Slater Walker Securities. The Hanson–Bowater link-up never took place because of the intervention of the Monopolies Commission but, over the last two decades, one rarely lost sight of the tall, elegant business leader from Huddersfield.

As a financial correspondent in London and later as a foreign correspondent in Washington I never ceased to be curious as to how James Hanson had managed to break away from the Slater stable, build a transatlantic empire and add a Conservative peerage to the controversial knighthood bestowed upon him by a Labour prime minister. So when, in the spring of 1991, James Hanson became embroiled in what would potentially be the biggest takeover in UK financial history, the siege of ICI, I became determined to know more about this very private financier, his political connections and his driving ambitions.

When first approached by Giles O'Bryen, then of Fourth Estate, about a possible biography of Hanson I was initially sceptical. Even though, as an incumbent financial editor, I had a useful relationship with Lord Hanson, he had never shown any interest in cooperating on a biography. Nevertheless, the seed of an idea had been planted. With the encouragement of a former colleague and old friend Stewart

Fleming, formerly of the *Financial Times*, who was particularly interested in the parallels between Hanson's business and political career, the idea of a biography was re-awakened. Armed with the enthusiastic support and trust of Clive Priddle, who had taken over from Giles as an editor at Fourth Estate, Roger Cowe was recruited to the project as co-author. Roger's shrewd understanding of accounting practices provided a sensible balance, in a biography which is as much about James Hanson's corporate growth as his personal and political development.

Our first approaches to Lord Hanson, on the possibility of him cooperating with a biography, were generally negative although unfailingly courteous, but we discovered fairly quickly that several people who had worked with Lord Hanson over the years were pleased to have the opportunity to talk about the experience. Lord Hanson, while still cool to the project, never allowed this to get in the way of the normal discourse which goes on between financial journalists and their targets, and was to include me at lunch on Brompton Road even as the biography to which he was opposed was getting under way.

Moreover, when we requested from Hanson plc a complete run of the company's annual reports – dating back to the first days as public company in the 1960s – they were sent round by messenger almost immediately, even though there was only a limited number of full sets available.

There were, however, more serious hiccups. When Debbie Gordon, a researcher, was dispatched to Huddersfield to look into the origins of the Hanson family she placed a notice in the *Huddersfield Daily Examiner* asking anyone with memories of the Hanson family and their businesses to contact her. The letters and phone calls, many of them from former employees of the Hanson family and Hanson companies, came flooding into her hotel. Within days, however, Lord Hanson in a front-page interview with the *Huddersfield Daily Examiner* distanced himself from the biography. He told the *Examiner*'s readers:

When I am dead, if people decide there is something worth writing about, that's OK; while I'm alive it's a different matter. First of all, my private life is just that and I am sure that the people of Huddersfield respect an individual's right to privacy. Secondly, I feel that most biographies of industrialists like me are largely 'ego trips' and one which I would not want my fellow townspeople to endure.

Despite this setback Debbie Gordon (now with the *Independent*) bravely persevered with her research. Without her diligence in the Registrars' Offices and the local historical archives, the early chapters of this book would have been an insurmountable task. The relationship between the authors and Lord Hanson was becoming rather turbulent. Having agreed to talk with us informally in the autumn of 1993, he abruptly cancelled the arrangements after I had paid a visit to the Hanson-owned Peabody coalmines in Kentucky, which were on strike. In a personal handwritten note Lord Hanson criticised the reporting from there, arguing that 'a reporter of your standing is supposed to present both sides!'

Regardless of this he agreed to further informal meetings in the New Year. Several hours of background discussions with Lord Hanson and his long-standing vice-chairman Derek Rosling took place in the spring of 1994 as the extensive accounting and other research was being analysed. Through his public-relations adviser Aviva Geshuny-Roth, Lord Hanson provided us with further supporting material including a full run of the share offer documents for the dozens of takeovers and mergers over the years: invaluable source material. Without these documents and without Lord Hanson's forbearance and a supply of coffee and sweets during our visits, the task of this biography would have been much more difficult.

As with any serious probe of a business empire, reliance solely upon interviews, however good the sources, is seldom enough. The inner workings of a corporate empire are to be found in the trail of paper it leaves behind. This includes the information circulated to shareholders, such as annual reports and bid documents, together with the tens of thousands of uncirculated papers and accounts which lie beneath the surface at Companies House, at the Securities & Exchange Commission in the United States, in registered offices in Panama and in court records. It is in these dry financial archives, rather than the glossy brochures that a company such as Hanson plc provides to its stakeholders, that its real nature is to be found.

Carefully researched financial archaeology is critical to the understanding of how James Hanson and his corporate empire work.

A significant element of the research for this book has concerned James Hanson's main business, now known as Hanson plc, and the growth of that business through the 1960s, 1970s and 1980s. The main source for material on this aspect of his life comes from the company itself, largely in formal public reports.

Companies such as Hanson plc which are quoted on the stock exchange are required to publish 'preliminary' results, together with a brief commentary, as soon as practicable after the end of their financial year. Hanson, whose financial year-end since 1969 has been 30 September, has normally published its preliminary figures early in December. It is at this point that the results are commented on in the press, and this is the primary source of financial information and comment about the company. Public companies are also required to publish 'interim' results at the half-way stage of the year, which form another source of information and comment about the progress of the company, although in its early days Hanson Trust was not sufficiently noteworthy to merit much comment even at the end of the financial year and certainly not for its interim figures. Companies must also call annual general meetings of shareholders, the main formal purpose of which is to approve the annual accounts and to re-elect directors. This is another opportunity for the company chairman to comment on progress and prospects, and for large companies such as Hanson has become the annual meeting is an important public-relations vehicle.

The full annual accounts that are presented for shareholders' approval at such events also include a wealth of technical information, however, which can offer important insights into the company's development. The minutiae of the full accounting statements include important detail which is not available at the time of the preliminary results, and which is therefore not generally commented on in the press. Such matters include capital investment, the directors' pay, details of the tax charge, political and charitable donations and the number of employees.

The raw data from these annual filings has provided important information on, for example, pay levels. Of even greater use has been the ability to dissect the figures using the Datastream database. This offers the possibility not only of manipulating figures for Hanson plc, but also making comparisons with thousands of other companies. Thus it is possible, using Datastream, to compare Hanson's tax charge with that of other leading UK companies, as well as to track ratios and key statistics for the company itself. To make cross-company comparisons meaningful, Datastream adjust published figures to ensure as far as possible that comparisons are on a similar basis. In some cases, therefore, figures extracted from the Datastream database are not the same as those published by Hanson plc.

Since 1985, when Hanson shares were first traded in the form of American Depository Receipts (ADRs) in the US, it has also been required to file information with the Securities and Exchange Commission (SEC). The annual Form 20-F includes similar information to the annual report published in the UK, but goes further. For example, the SEC requires more information about the group's history and developments during the period, greater disclosure about directors and senior officers, and especially about transactions they have been involved in during the year. These documents have been vital additional sources, amplifying the material available from UK filings and revealing other information as well.

Just as US annual reports contain more detail than their UK equivalent, so do US takeover documents. In the UK, circulars explaining Hanson's offers for target companies' shares reveal important details that would not otherwise be available, such as share dealings. In the equivalent US documents, even more information is required, including a detailed report of contacts between the two companies. These documents have been helpful in determining aspects of Hanson's voluminous takeover activity.

All these source documents provide crucial raw data. In many cases that raw material has required extensive manipulation and analysis to explore the full facts of Hanson plc's development. Of course, a large, public, highly active company such as Hanson has constantly been thoroughly analysed by experts working for major stockbrokers. And the results of their deliberations have been reported in the press over the years. But such analysis has inevitably focused primarily on the prospects for Hanson's shares, which is what stockbrokers' analysts are paid to understand and explain. For the purposes of this book some further analysis has been necessary. This has been carried out by the authors from the data available in public documents and in some cases the analysis has been confirmed with accounting experts. We are grateful to them, as well as to the analysts whose public reports have shed light on the company, but ultimately, of course, we are responsible for the conclusions contained in these pages.

Inevitably, some of the accounting and tax detail is rather complex. The statistical appendix has been included to help illustrate some of the financial issues described in the text. The charts and tables are not intended to provide comprehensive coverage, but to highlight some issues and illustrate them in a form which complements the description in the text. Some of the inclusions, such as the charts of sales and earnings, give an overview of the growth of Hanson plc, others show important details, such as the financial results of subsidiaries in the late 1970s and early 1980s. And the table of bids and deals is intended to help readers follow the vigorous corporate development of Hanson plc.

No book of this kind could have even have been contemplated without a great deal of assistance. Special thanks to the *Guardian*'s editor-in-chief Peter Preston who allowed us some long absences from the office to complete the writing. Imperial Chemical Industries kindly provided us with an extensive media archive covering the period of the siege at Millbank in 1991–92. We have conducted numerous interviews with eminent industrial, political and City figures. In keeping with the traditions of lobby and City journalism many of those who have cooperated have preferred to remain anonymous and we have respected that. Those who made no such requests for anonymity are quoted and referenced throughout the book. In addition, a great deal of help has been received from newspaper libraries and colleagues. Among those who were particularly helpful was the *Guardian*'s industrial editor Simon Beavis. Special thanks go to Geoffrey Lumb of Huddersfield who opened up his personal transport archive to us; to Mary Batten who gave us access to the *Financial Times* library; to Maryvonne Grellier in the *Guardian* library who spent many hours digging out the relevant cuttings; to Nick Pandya in the *Guardian* financial library who has brought his expertise to bear in many areas; to Nick Richmond of the *Guardian*'s picture desk who was responsible for much of the picture research; to James Nicholson for his work in the *Daily Mirror* library;

to Mark Tran in New York who tracked down the SCM court records and to Carol Keefer in the *Guardian* Washington office who was so helpful on Peabody files and in obtaining SEC records. Last, but by no means least, thanks must go to the *Guardian*'s City office secretary Primrose Williamson whose calmness, telephone skills and letter writing helped to make all of this possible. It goes without saying that the research effort was theirs, the mistakes are ours.

Finally, a word about our respective spouses Tricia and Christine and our offspring Jessica, Justin and Gabriel Brummer, and Tim, Robbie and baby Gabriel Cowe. We know full well that this has been an all-consuming project, which has kept us up late, ruined many a weekend and made our behaviour at home intolerable. We apologise for that. But without your support and good humour this study would never have happened. So thank you all very much.

Alex Brummer and Roger Cowe
London, 12 July 1994.

CHAPTER 1

The Private Potentate

Seated in his light and spacious seventh-floor office, with a glorious view over the winged Angel of Victory at Hyde Park Corner and the stately brick walls of Buckingham Palace, James Hanson exudes corporate power. At 73 years old Hanson still cuts an elegant figure. His stance is ramrod straight, his grip is firm, he wears a light midwinter tan and his carefully groomed hair is sleekly brushed back. Hanson patrols his offices in shirt-sleeves, favouring monogrammed deep blue shirts with double cuffs and generous down-pointing collars, reminiscent of a grander era. His trousers are closely tailored and pulled high above his well-cushioned girth. The gold cufflinks, glistening belt buckle, slim gilt bracelet on his wrist, and the distinctive signet ring betray a faint air of the dandy.

The fastidious attention to his own appearance is a reflection of how James Hanson judges those who work with him. He cares passionately about his employees' outward appearance, demanding the same high standards of them as he does of himself. Hanson employs a leading trichologist, Philip Kingsley, at the company's Knightsbridge premises, on the look-out for tell-tale signs of dandruff on the collar or a thinning crown among Hanson executives. The more senior the executive the more access allowed to the lotions and creams of Philip Kingsley, who counts actresses Candice Bergen and Kathleen Turner among his clients. But Lord Hanson is also concerned with the inner self: he requires regular reports on employees' cholesterol count. Some of the senior people who have worked closely with Hanson go as far as to suggest that he relishes the influence he exercises over the lifestyles of those he employs.

The quarters James Hanson inhabits feel more like a drawing-room than the high-tech offices of the 1990s: the walls, window-sills and shelves behind his large mahogany desk are decorated with dozens of photographs of Hanson himself, his family and his close business friends like Lord King, President of British Airways. The tycoon has an enduring leisure interest in photography and photographic images. So enamoured is he of filmic reproduction that he has even been known to make a judgement about companies he wants to buy on the basis of the pictorial quality of their annual reports.

Among the portraits behind Hanson's desk is a strikingly powerful image of the thick-set and pugnacious patriarch of the dynasty: his father, the Yorkshireman Robert 'Bob' Hanson, at whose knee James learnt takeover techniques and the art of bank borrowing. There are also pictures of James Hanson's dashing younger brother Bill – once the family's heir apparent – whose brilliant career was cut short so tragically. All the pictures are immaculately framed in gleaming silver. Highly polished decorated silver bowls, cups and objects are interspersed around the room along with the 'tombstones' – the encased souvenirs of done deals provided by the investment bankers. These are potent symbols of Hanson's ability to put together loans to the value of billions of pounds and dollars on the capital markets on both sides of the Atlantic. There is always a generous display of freshly cut flowers, on occasion the palest shaded orchids brought directly from his California home by the tycoon himself. In the foyer to his suite of offices a middle-aged woman in overalls fusses around an empty desk, in the manner of the babushka who might guard the offices of an important Russian official.

The only obvious concession to modernity in this timeless setting is a lonely, switched-off computer screen, at the side of Hanson's large, antique desk, and a facsimile machine. This is not the designer, advanced processing office that one has come to associate with tycoons from the movies of the 1980s like Oliver Stone's *Wall Street* or from the images which flicker across our television screens each time there is turbulence on the financial markets. Nor is there any shade of the frugality which is seen as a virtue in the hundreds of companies that Hanson has taken over and stripped to the core over the decades –

literally removing the oil paintings from the walls. There is an atmosphere of business conducted with old-style courtesy, of tea and coffee drunk from bone-china cups. There is little sense of the hive of activity and urgency that one might associate with the corporate headquarters of an empire capitalised at around £15,000 million – almost twice the total wealth of a small industrialised economy such as Luxembourg – with scores of subsidiaries dotted around the globe and employing worldwide some 80,000 people. It is in this decept-ively peaceful room, known as 'the furnace' to his business associates, that James Hanson will, if the occasion demands, turn his fearsome temper in uninhibitedly direct language on those profligate with company funds or those who have, in some way, offended Hanson's sense of how his corporation should be perceived in the outside world. Senior executives recount tales of leaving Hanson's office shaking like a leaf after an angry encounter with the chairman.

Hanson is an intensely private person who will go to great lengths to ensure his confidentiality and that of his family is protected. Having lived the life of a playboy until his fourth decade, before which 'Jimmy' Hanson, as the Press styled him, was featured constantly in the gossip columns, he built a defensive wall around himself and his family after his marriage to American divorcee Geraldine Kaelin in 1959. Although a good communicator, a technique learned as an army broadcaster in the 1940s, Hanson rarely gives interviews except in the most tightly controlled circumstances, when he can be most sure of the outcome. When he does make himself available he normally insists on vetting or scrutinising the quotations. He has, nevertheless, a winning manner which can instantly charm those allowed into his inner sanctum, as long as they avoid asking questions which force him to look backwards or pry into his personal affairs. The chairman's close associates at Hanson headquarters know little of his early history including his educational and military service background. Hanson will go to great lengths to block unauthorised access to friends and family. Even his own son Robert, a bright, Oxford-educated, merchant banker in the image of his father – who was elevated to the main board of Hanson plc at just 31 years of age – is protected from public glare when he might be expected to be more available. Like a character in an F. Scott Fitzgerald novel, James

Hanson enjoys the life of luxury but prefers to seclude himself and his family from public scrutiny except on his own terms.

In many ways the impression one gains from Hanson's surroundings – of a multi-billion-dollar business run on the lines of a family concern – is accurate. It is more than three decades since James Hanson moved his business interests from the relative obscurity of Huddersfield, where the Hanson family had been in the transport business since the mid-nineteenth century hauling worsteds across the Pennines in horse-drawn wagons, to the much more cosmopolitan arena of the London and New York stock exchanges. Yet many of the values and structures which James Hanson brought with him from Huddersfield to London, New York and Palm Springs still live on. It is as if his father, the tough, blunt-speaking Robert Hanson – who nursed the family business back from disaster in 1919 into a multi-million-pound empire by the time it was nationalised in 1948 – were still looking down upon his elder son James, reminding him not to forget his Yorkshire roots, despite the grandeur of the contemporary Hanson.

The essence of the modern Hanson empire is that even though it straddles the globe encompassing branded products from Player's cigarettes to Seven Seas vitamins and Jacuzzi to natural resources from aggregates to coal and forestry, it remains a family concern. Although Hanson plc is a large public company the lines of control are very similar to those found in a smaller private company. Decisions are taken informally, a high premium is placed on loyalty, and members of the family and intimate friends like Gordon White are accorded unusual privileges and respect. The complex business and personal relationship between Hanson and White intriguingly mirrors that between Bob Hanson of Huddersfield and his Halifax business partner Charlie Holdsworth in an earlier generation. But the Hanson–White relationship runs deeper than that. Although the company carries the Hanson name it is Gordon White who in some respects has been the surrogate brother – the intelligent sophisticate, who has carried the more prudent and less instinctive James Hanson along with him. White, first a close friend of Hanson's younger brother Bill, is a fast-talking free spirit with a huge appetite for life who delights in the company of beautiful women. Consequently James Hanson has delighted in White's company, his quick wit, his taste in starlets and his lively mind, always looking to the next opportunity and the next deal. In many ways business is a game to White who would have been just as happy freebooting on his own rather than being part of a vast conglomerate. It was Hanson who brought the discipline and organisation to what might otherwise have been a chaotic relationship yet, at crucial moments such as takeovers, Gordon White often appeared to be more in control.

James Hanson is, too, the consummate politician. Although Hanson plc always has been a large contributor to Conservative causes, James Hanson also recognised that companies have to work amiably, with whichever government is in power. In many ways the spectacular growth of Hanson in Britain has mirrored the swings in the nation's political fortunes. As a businessman James Hanson first came to the fore in the 1960s, developing a good working relationship with that other famous Huddersfield son Harold Wilson. For somebody who was to become so close to the Conservatives in the 1980s the Hanson–Wilson connection is something of an enigma. But in the world of Yorkshire politics their lives are unexpectedly intertwined. When in 1989 Huddersfield contemplated building a statue of the industrialist as the centrepiece of a £1.5 million town centre redevelopment, Hanson wrote to the *Huddersfield Examiner* putting forward Wilson's name instead. 'There is no doubt that a statue, if there should be any, should be of Lord Wilson,' the Tory tycoon wrote. 'The greatest honour a town could have is for one of its sons to become Prime Minister.'[1] Hanson, who was honoured by Wilson in 1976 and maintains contact with the former Labour Prime Minister and his family even today, was also to join that small band of Margaret Thatcher's favourite businessmen. James Hanson qualified for this privilege on several grounds: his company was to become the second largest corporate benefactor to Conservative causes; he exemplified a Northern value system embedded in Mrs Thatcher's bones by her father, 'the keeper of the corner store in Grantham',[2] and as his many photographs testify he was tall, dashing and courtly – the kind of man who made Margaret Thatcher's eye twinkle. At the peak of their powers in the mid-1980s when they were in each other's company 'you could almost see the love in their eyes', according to a senior Hanson plc insider.[3] As Prime Minister, Mrs Thatcher would enjoy nothing more than a Friday afternoon whisky with one of her favourite businessmen like Hanson or his close friend John King of British Airways, before she set off with her husband Denis for her official country residence at Chequers. Mrs Thatcher thought of Hanson, like King, as a self-made man. He had in fact remade himself as a London-based financier, having been born into the wealth of Huddersfield's merchant elite.

Lord Hanson and Lord White represent a swashbuckling, entrepreneurial strain in the business world in which many of the most significant decisions are based upon instinct rather than complex Harvard Business School models. 'Gordon was the buyer', James Hanson has reflected. 'Gordon was the one who sniffed out the possibilities and then went on to conduct the takeovers. He's certainly the brightest person I've ever met in that way. He can sense a business. He can feel absolutely and he can sell you on an idea of it because he knows he is going to be right. But he's also the quickest one to throw his own ideas out of the window.'[4]

This highly personal approach, within a major public corporation, has been both a source of strength and of weakness. In the heat of a takeover battle, particularly in the laissez-faire atmosphere on both sides of the Atlantic in the 1980s, it made Hanson plc a formidable machine. Whereas its opponents in bid battles were constantly required to check each step in a complex bid process with the board of directors and a panoply of experts and financial advisers, the Hanson–White partnership was able to move at the speed of Concorde. Typically, according to a senior Hanson financial adviser for more than a decade, the company would seek to 'dominate the market'. It would wade into takeovers on both sides of the Atlantic with all guns blazing, picking up shares from wherever it could, conducting a blitzkrieg against its target, so that they were so confused they never quite knew where the next shots were coming from.

When on a war footing the critical decisions were taken between Hanson and White across the transatlantic telephone, on the basis of faxes, in the cab ride between John F. Kennedy airport and Hanson Industries headquarters on Park Avenue and sometimes on the most flimsy of evidence. In many cases the extensive accounting and legal checks, and visits to subsidiaries, which are part of the takeover game, were skipped in favour of the personalised, family-style, instinctive approach.

Just how unusual this is, particularly in the United States where boards of the larger quoted companies are seen as inviolable, was evident from Hanson's most bitterly contested takeover in that country – the $930 million takeover in 1985 of the chemicals, coatings and typewriter group SCM Corporation. Counsel for SCM Corporation, which sought to fight the bid in the United States District Court, showed astonishment at the crude information gathering and communications process used by the Hanson group, which was nothing like anything they had encountered before. The assessment of the bid in this case was simply based upon a set of accounts. Lord Hanson testified that his interest in SCM came as a result of a phone call with Gordon White.

'"I would like you to see the accounts because they are very well photographed" and since I take personal responsibility for our accounts Sir Gordon felt there was something to be learned from that document in addition to investment potential,' Lord Hanson told counsel.[5] This was not the kind of corporate arrangement described in case studies, but one in which decisions were based on codes spoken between friends of 35 years. It is not a concept which the legalistic American business community easily comes to terms with.

The sense that Hanson is a family business, rather than one controlled by vast, anonymous institutional shareholders on both sides of the Atlantic, pervades all aspects of the way that Hanson is governed. There is no organisational chart which accurately describes where decisions are taken and how the company is run – although American firms of stockbrokers, in a vain attempt to explain the sources of power to investors, have tried to draw them up. Rather, Hanson prefers a personal style in which he is the centre of the web. He executes his authority through direct contact with his fellow executive directors, some of whom dread the moment when his voice booms down the telephone or when he wanders into their office. He communicates most frequently by means of his secretaries who are his all-important link to the rest of the group and for that matter the rest of the world: there is one secretary who deals with group matters, another deals with broadly political and other issues and a third with his personal interests including the totally separate family business in Huddersfield, Hanson Transport.

Inside the Hanson headquarters the mark of a successful year at Christmas or a job well done is a neat, silver-framed portrait of the boss. Lord Hanson doesn't take portraiture lightly. The photographic opportunities at the company's annual meetings are carefully posed, with backcloths, backlighting and special props including the high chrome stools used at the 1992 meeting. The small picture, taken for the 1993 annual report and accounts was photographed by Sally Soames who has been the group's official photographer since 1967.

In many public corporations there is a clear concern about employing family members, especially when the chairman owns less than one per cent of the outstanding shares. But Hanson as a family-style business does not share these worries. The current acquisition team at Hanson includes James's son the Hon. Robert Hanson, a former merchant banker at N. M. Rothschild. He works in a team with Lord Hanson's nephew (by marriage), the former National Hunt jockey Chris Collins who was taken on to the board for his entrepreneurial value. Even the designated successor to Lord Hanson, deputy chairman and chief executive Derek Bonham, has a spouse inside the net: Karen B. Levy, described in the Securities & Exchange Commission filings as a non-executive associate director of the Hanson group. However talented the individuals, this represents an unusual degree of family penetration at senior levels. Even though Hanson has striven to build the reputation of Derek Bonham and anointed him as his successor he has still chosen to put his greatest trust in his son, whom he consults on all major personnel and public relations decisions.

Board meetings in the Hanson organisation have often seen Lord Hanson using his immense allure, having begun the proceedings by 'gladhanding' his fellow directors, in the manner of a member of the royal family visiting a national institution, and leaving little room for detailed discussion of strategy. Occasionally, the chairman will announce something out of the blue, such as the decision to buy and operate Melody Radio, which was partly inspired by the wishes of himself and Lady Hanson for some easier listening while they worked. In conversations with directors and former directors of Hanson there emerges the distinct impression that there is some disquiet that, in the transformation of the group from the small investment vehicle of three decades ago to an unassailable Anglo-American conglomerate, the highly personalised, family-style management has never really changed. Moreover, the stylish transatlantic lives of Lords Hanson and White are supported at some expense by an array of facilities ranging from corporate jets and helicopters, to Concorde travel, high salaries, California houses, which serve as offices, a fleet of planes and helicopters owned by Air Hanson (which cost up to £1 million a year to run) not to mention distinctive black Rolls-Royce cars with customised number plates. The accoutrements of the wealthy private individual have been adopted in the context of the public company.

The issue of private versus public was brought into sharp relief by the ICI siege of 1991, which saw Hanson and White – the two master predators – driven from the field of battle. But they have never conceded that the way they conduct their businesses, including the mystery surrounding Gordon White's emoluments may be wrong. He, like Hanson, retains a proprietorial attitude towards the business, as if the shareholders (who after all provided the capital) owe them a personal debt of gratitude.

This cult of personality in business sits uncomfortably with the 1990s and the focus on improved corporate governance on both sides of the Atlantic. In the years of Margaret Thatcher and Ronald Reagan, all that mattered in the boardrooms of Britain and the United States was the flow of earnings and dividends, not how the companies were organised. The manner in which companies were run, the enormous salaries paid to executives, the lax disclosure rules and the unbalanced way in which boards were structured came under close scrutiny in the new era. The Cadbury Committee, which was to set new rules as to how companies should be governed in Britain, was established in May 1991 – just as Lords Hanson and White were making their tilt at ICI. The prevailing order in Britain's boardrooms and the quality of protection offered by auditors to shareholders were seen to be failing in the wake of a series of scandals. These culminated with the collapse of Robert Maxwell's media and communications empire.

The interest in corporate governance was an unfortunate piece of timing for Hanson since it focused attention on the peculiarities of its governance too, from the family presence on the board to unsatisfactory disclosure in the accounts to the weakness of the non-executive directors who, at Hanson, appeared to consist of business friends and retired diplomats. By the time that the final Cadbury report was published in May 1992 Hanson's titanic effort to merge his corporation with ICI had ended in failure. Lord Hanson, like many other self-made executives, was coming to terms with the need to reshape his board to include more non-executives and a greater degree of disclosure to meet the Cadbury standards, although there was a sense that Hanson embraced this without much enthusiasm.

In keeping with the atmosphere of the 1990s, Hanson plc – while still run in a highly personalised way – has moved to reform itself. At 73 Hanson formally recognises that the baton of power will eventually have to pass from him to an executive chairman in the shape of Derek Bonham, still a relatively unknown figure on the national business scene. The board has been strengthened to include a cadre of non-executive directors, although within this group Hanson could not resist the appointment of Thatcher political loyalist and former chairman of the Conservative Party Kenneth Baker. Perhaps as much as any industrialist in Britain, James Hanson recognised the importance of political alliances and what they can bring in terms of prestige and profit. In the United States Hanson Industries and its coal-mining subsidiary Peabody Corporation have been active lobbyists on Capitol Hill. The Hanson companies also have funnelled funds to local and national political campaigns through their own political action committees. The need to establish personal rapport with politicians is part of the charm-led style of conducting commercial relations which James Hanson learned from his father.

Like many businessmen, James Hanson saw the election of Harold Wilson in 1964 as a break with the dull and ineffectual Toryism of the Harold Macmillan era. Harold Wilson's 'Hundred Days of Dynamic Action', as he called it, in emulation of John F. Kennedy in the United States, was a period of excitement in which business, for that moment at least, saw expansion opportunities on the back of Wilson's promises to encourage productivity and efficiency and to ensure that scientific methods would in the future be applied to industrial production.[6]

For the young James Hanson, still embroiled in the family businesses in Huddersfield, the Wilson era provided the opportunity to break loose from the provincial yoke and aim for broader horizons. The opportunity came in 1965 when Hanson, together with a successful printing entrepreneur and family friend from Hull, Gordon White, joined forces with an ascendant Slater Walker Securities to buy into a publicly quoted vehicle, the Wiles Group. By the time Harold Wilson had left Downing Street in 1970, to make way for the three-year interregnum of Edward Heath, the Wiles Group had become Hanson Trust Limited and was taking the first tentative steps to more permanent success from the unlikely setting of a mews house on Pont Street, just behind the Harrods store in Knightsbridge. Even in the 1990s the mews house with its supply of leggy secretaries remains the quiet, secluded nerve centre of the Hanson businesses.

The Hanson Trust had begun to establish its credentials with the Conservative Party in the 1970s. As the Wiles Group it had made a small political donation of £550 in 1968; this had almost doubled to £1000 in 1970, the year that Edward Heath surprised the pollsters and the political world by sweeping into Downing Street. The cautious stewardship of Roy Jenkins as Chancellor of the Exchequer gave way to an unseemly dash for growth executed by the new Chancellor Anthony Barber, which was to become known as the Barber boom.

In September 1971 the Bank of England, with the support of the Treasury, unveiled its new, more flexible financial strategy in the City, known as Competition and Credit Control. The result was disastrous. The storm clouds over the economy began to gather and the go-getting world of Slater-Walker, which had enriched the Prime Minister Ted Heath himself through the management of his savings while he was in Opposition,[7] began to implode. Credit was tightened, the three-day week – as the Heath government confronted the unions – brought growth to a halt and the stock market and property values collapsed. Hanson Trust's share price languished along with all the other companies which had been associated with the Slater–Walker phenomenon.

Economic and political disillusion set in on the Hanson Trust board, as the recurrent problems of the British economy clouded its ambitions. Gordon White, ever impatient and unimpressed by the business opportunities in his own country, packed his suitcase and headed for New York's exclusive Pierre Hotel in 1973, with just the $3000 that exchange controls allowed. The financial and technological promise of the 1960s had given way to the spectacular failure of the 1970s and the frustrations had driven Hanson Trust into the arms of rampant US capitalism; it was, in many ways, the making of James Hanson and his Anglo-American conglomerate.

The Hanson Trust was a ready-made vehicle for the 1980s. It had put down business roots on both sides of the Atlantic and come through Britain's turmoil of the previous decade. The turn of the decade brought a conservative revolution on both sides of the Atlantic. In May 1979 Margaret Thatcher was swept into Downing Street; on the other side of the Atlantic, another conservative, Ronald Reagan, was moving up the polls as the US voters punished President Jimmy Carter for his failure to deal with US hostages held in Iran and for chaotic management of the economy. In November 1980 the former Hollywood actor, Governor Reagan of California, was swept into office in a landslide which temporarily put the Republicans in control of the Senate too.

Both Thatcher and Reagan were committed to broad economic reforms. Mrs Thatcher's government sought to create a business environment in which takeovers were acceptable, free from government interference on public interest grounds; where entrepreneurship was properly rewarded and in which big boardroom salaries on a par with the UK's industrial competitors were acceptable and not a cause for attacking capitalism from the dispatch box, as her Conservative predecessor Ted Heath fatefully had done. Sir James Hanson, the businessman knighted by Harold Wilson, moved swiftly to back the Conservative government. Hanson funds were made available to support the Centre for Policy Studies, the right-wing think-tank established by Sir Keith Joseph, and the birthplace of many of the intellectual ideas which fuelled what came to be known as the Thatcher revolution. Similarly, as Hanson grew in size, and allies at Conservative Central Office became more important, the political contributions to the Tories began to surge reaching £117,000 in 1987, an election year, making Hanson the second largest corporate donor to the Conservatives.

James Hanson, who was elevated to the House of Lords by Mrs Thatcher in 1983, had joined the inner ranks of the Conservative Party. In March 1986 he was to be found lunching with Deputy Prime Minister Willie Whitelaw at Dorneywood, letting his hair down and exchanging expletives with the former Defence Minister Alan Clark, before 'clattering off in his helicopter'.[8] In fact, whenever there was an industrial problem for the government Lord Hanson was quickly on the scene. Hanson has argued that his known role as strong financial supporter of the Conservative Party made it more difficult for him to do business with the government because of the need to retain an arm's length relationship. Yet the record of the 1980s suggests that it not only produced the right climate for him to transform Hanson plc into a multi-billion-pound enterprise, it brought him close to power and enabled him to secure a peerage for his American alter ego, Gordon White, who had been 'flying the flag'[9] for Britain in the United States.

In many ways Britain's entry into the European Exchange Rate mechanism on 5 October 1990, marked the beginning of the end of the Thatcher era. The move re-opened deep wounds in the Conservative Party over Europe and just over a month later, after a fiercely contested leadership challenge, Mrs Thatcher was forced from power. Mrs Thatcher's friends, including Lord Hanson, felt that she had been betrayed. There was frustration that the only British political figure viewed as a statesperson in the United States, where Hanson spent so much time, had so rapidly become a non-person in Britain who was barely listened to. The passing of the Thatcher era in Britain also meant changes for business.

The circumstances which heralded John Major's arrival at Downing Street exposed the deep divisions in the Conservative ranks over Europe, symbolic of the fratricide between the hard right of the party and its more moderate wing. Despite wearing the mantle of Mrs Thatcher's favoured successor, the new prime minister demonstrated a determination to stamp his own, less doctrinaire, identity on the party, encapsulated in the notion of a classless society. The years 1990–92 were characterised by deep recession and rising unemployment, which climbed above three million, the highest level in the post-second-world-war period. In the City the markets were destabilised by a series of financial scandals and a raft of billion-pound receiverships as several icons of the previous decade – including Asil Nadir's Polly Peck and the ambitious docklands development at Canary Wharf – collapsed. The 'can do' culture which was so central to Hanson plc's success in the 1980s had given way to an atmosphere of vacillation and uncertainty causing widespread economic and political dissonance and social disturbances. Against this backdrop an image-conscious James Hanson, reaching for the final deal which would seal Hanson plc as Britain's most influential company, launched the fateful assault on Imperial Chemical Industries in a move which would spotlight his own corporation's structural frailties.

In the aftermath of the ICI bid signs appeared that Hanson and White had given serious thought to their retirements and to the structure of the group under new leadership. Even if Hanson retained the looks and vigour of a much younger man his company, compared to some of its rivals, had evidently become as bloated as the sleepy companies over the years that had fed its expansion. Some inventive post-modern advertising was produced to bolster the group; it emphasised the breadth of the group's businesses rather than the name or image of its chairman. The most extraordinary advertisement was a pastiche of Orson Welles's *Citizen Kane*, in which the name on the lips of the dying industrial competitor was not 'Rosebud' but 'Hanson'. It is hard, though, not to see the parallel between Kane and Hanson himself: driven, acquisitive, larger-than-life personalities determined to dominate their particular worlds. Kane's final word is a harking back to the sledge from his childhood – a more precious memory than all his wealth and celebrity have showered upon him. Hanson too has strong memories of his youth: of pastoral outings with his mother, visiting the transport depots with his father and of a brilliant younger brother Bill, struck down by illness in his prime. It is the memory of Bill and the slights that James must have felt in his youth, that shaped both his relationship with business partner Gordon White and a restless ambition for success and recognition. As he approaches retirement Hanson has sought to cultivate the image of a more permanent corporate legacy deeply rooted in basic industries like bricks, coal and chemicals with the resilience necessary to remain competitive, however turbulent the economic and financial conditions outside. In effect he has re-created for himself the certainties of his Huddersfield youth.

CHAPTER 2

Packhorses, Charabancs and Trucking

It was in the early hours of the morning of Monday, 18 August 1919 that the residents of Milnsbridge, a small woollen community in Colne Valley on the fringes of Huddersfield, were awoken by choking smoke, a series of loud explosions and the flicker of flames leaping into the chill night air. The Huddersfield Fire Brigade under the command of Inspector Wharfe, proudly driving the town's new motorised fire apparatus, arrived at the scene at 1.25 a.m. to be greeted by one of the largest blazes in the history of the West Riding. Terrified residents gathered in knots on street corners to watch the conflagration, which had been whipped up by gale-force winds, while others, fearing that the fire might spread to nearby buildings, had secured a hose and a water line from the nearby woollen mill of C. & J. Hirst, in an effort to douse the flames.

Some eleven firemen and dozens of helpers battled the fire at Joseph Hanson & Son's furniture depository and the adjoining shed, but the flames were so fierce and the series of blasts, from petrol drums stockpiled in the shed, so severe that the crew quickly began to realise the warehouse could not be saved. As the warehouse roof collapsed with a loud crash, the main objective of the firefighters was to control the intense heat and to prevent the flames from leaping to the nearby Longwood gasholder just ten yards away from the burning warehouse. Eyewitnesses said 'never had such a blaze been seen in

Milnsbridge, and one could have read a newspaper quite distinctly at 'Crosland Hill – away across the valley'.[1]

By the time the blaze was over, the two-storey warehouse, covering an area 39 feet by 90 feet, and the adjoining shed, occupying much the same kind of space, were smouldering wrecks. The flames had consumed some 130 van-loads of furniture stored in what had been described by the proprietors as a fireproof warehouse. Among the contents was at least one valuable oil painting worth £800. Also destroyed by the intense heat and fire were Joseph Hanson & Son's steam-driven vans and several motorised coaches. Most of the telephone lines to the Milnsbridge area of Huddersfield were burnt out by the intense heat. The scale of the loss was large: first estimates put it at £25,000, but within twenty-four hours of the fire, after a full inspection of the damage by insurance assessors, this was raised to £50,000 – an enormous sum in 1919 and the equivalent of just under £1 million today. The warehouse, the shed and the motor vehicles had been properly insured by Joseph Hanson & Son. But under the storage agreements, which customers had signed with Hanson's, it was the clients' responsibility to insure their own chattels.

Despite the epic nature of the destruction the warehouse owners appeared undaunted. The same entrepreneurial spirit that led Mary Hanson to expand her transport business in 1846 – when she began to haul wool and other goods across the Pennines to Manchester on packhorses – pulsed through the veins of her great-grandsons. Robert Hanson, aged 27, and his younger brother Donald, 22, had been forced to take over the family business from their elder brother, Joseph, who had died of influenza just a few months earlier. The indefatigable Robert 'Bob' Hanson was of resilient and pugnacious Yorkshire stock. Within four days of the blaze he had placed large advertisements in the *Colne Valley Guardian* declaring that it would be business as usual for his family firm.

'Joseph Hanson & Son, Removal, Storage and Motor Haulage Contractors. We wish to inform our Customers that our Removal and Haulage Departments are carrying on as usual', it boldly declared. 'We have been successful in obtaining immediate delivery of STEAM WAGGON and PETROL LURRIES, and by SATURDAY, our fleet will be up to its normal strength.' Moreover, the company announced that with a few exceptions its 'Charabancs' would be on the road next week and its telephone booking service at Milnsbridge (where the lines had been destroyed by fire) was now back in order.[2] This was clearly a remarkable manifesto for the future, from a remarkable man. The ability of Bob Hanson to pick himself and the business up in such short order suggests a speed of action and a skill in financial manoeuvring – attributes which would certainly be passed to the next generation of Hansons.

The smart resumption of normal service did not, however, mean that the incident was behind Robert Hanson. What was to follow, in the West Riding Assizes at Leeds, would have a profound effect on his character and left an indelible impression on a family that to this day is conscious to the point of obsession about its reputation, privacy, image and respect.

Almost a year after the great fire at Milnsbridge, on 30 July 1920, Mrs Minerva Fox of London, the recent widow of a travelling salesman, went to court in Leeds and charged Robert Hanson, as proprietor of Joseph Hanson & Son, of negligence and trespass in regard to the depository blaze in which she lost furniture worth £683. The essence of Mrs Fox's case was that it was wrong for Joseph Hanson to have been storing furniture adjacent to a flimsy wooden garage containing large quantities of petrol; that the firm had never properly accounted for her loss; that some of the furniture may have been removed from the warehouse before the fire; and that the insurance was in any case inadequate because of the sharp rise in the price of furniture – partly caused by shortages in the wake of the Great War in Europe.

The testimony of the Superintendent of the Huddersfield Fire Brigade, who had inspected the area after the fire, was devastating for the owners of Joseph Hanson & Son. He told the Leeds Assize that five windows in the warehouse had opened on to the lean-to wooden garage. The draught of the flames through these windows, together with the storage of large quantities of petrol in drums, had caused the fire to spread more rapidly than anyone could cope with. Another witness, an expert on furniture prices, pointed out that the figures in Mrs Fox's claim were well below the current price of new furniture. The judge, Mr Shearman, said he was 'astonished' that so much inflammable material had been left so close to the depository.[3] The following day he awarded Mrs Fox £400 of damages in respect of the furniture destroyed and a further £100 for the furniture which had gone walkabout. Robert Hanson was ordered to pay £200 forthwith and given three weeks to pay the remainder.

The judgment, in that it sustained the allegation of negligence and also recognised the rise in furniture values, was a disaster for Joseph Hanson & Son. The firm was soon inundated with claims from other furniture owners seeking similar compensation to Mrs Fox. With the claims pouring in, Joseph Hanson & Son moved with some haste to sell off the company's remaining assets and to sue for bankruptcy. On 21 August 1920, a year to the day after the Milnsbridge fire, auction announcements in the *Huddersfield Examiner* listed a sale of assets which included a valuable storage warehouse, a garage, dwelling-houses, stables and a fleet of motor vehicles including a charabanc, Commer and Leyland petrol wagons, four furniture vans, trailer wagons, coal carts, stable equipment, a typewriter and filing cabinets. All the lots were sold and some £11,000 raised. [4]

This sale of assets was to haunt Robert Hanson for seven years – perhaps even for the rest of his life. At a bankruptcy hearing in the Huddersfield County Court on 29 December 1920, the Official Receiver assessed the deficiency in the business of Joseph Hanson & Son to be some £22,741. In a series of damning 'observations' on the case he expressed dissatisfaction with the way in which Mr Hanson had conducted his affairs. The court noted that the assets had been bought by a consortium of Hanson's friends, business associates, even family: Bob Hanson's younger brother Donald had received a £1700 loan from his bankrupt elder brother to become part of the deal. Moreover, the syndicate had registered itself as a new limited company, J. Hanson & Son Ltd, and was now employing Robert Hanson at a salary of £7 per week. While the bankrupt had paid off trade creditors, he had essentially ignored the claims of those who had lost their furniture.

Donald Hanson was to all intents and purposes running a separate business as an Auctioneer and Valuer from 34 King William Street, Huddersfield after the fire. Much of his business, however, seemed to involve selling off surplus Hanson assets including transport plant and charabancs. His city centre address in Huddersfield, from which he also operated a charabanc service and later Hanson buses, was also an address used by Joseph Hanson & Son. The separation of the two brothers' businesses seems to have been more of a legal convenience than representative of the reality of the situation. Donald Hanson maintained this role until he died on 30 September 1951 at the age of 56 years.

The smell of scandal refused to lift from Robert Hanson. When he appeared before the Huddersfield County Court in 1924, in an effort to be discharged from the disgrace of bankruptcy, he was reminded of his sharp dealings. 'Everybody was liable to be unfortunate, and no man could avoid at times, getting into a position that he could not pay 20 shillings in the pound', the judge told him. But Hanson, he declared, had gone beyond the rules: he had traded when insolvent and not treated all the creditors equally. Thus the discharge he had hoped for would be postponed for another three years until 1927 – some eight years after the Milnsbridge fire. [5]

The fire and subsequent bankruptcy were a searing experience for Robert Hanson. Throughout the crisis he was to demonstrate an inner strength and determination to carry on in the haulage business whatever the consequences; to give up an enterprise which was so intertwined with family interests was unthinkable. But it also demonstrated to Robert Hanson that no business, however successful, could stand alone. The link with the Holdsworth family of Halifax which was forged in the aftermath of the Leeds Assize judgment against the firm would be enduring, with the Holdsworth and Hanson companies closely entwined up to, and beyond, the nationalisation of their jointly owned transport interests by the Attlee government in 1948. It was an adventurous alliance which, among other things, saw the birth of the Jet cut-price petrol franchise, which still survives in different ownership. It can be no coincidence that the relationship between two powerful Yorkshiremen in the inter-war and post-war years, Charlie Holdsworth and Robert Hanson, provided a fine model for the extraordinary bond which would develop in a later era between another Yorkshireman, Gordon White from Hull, and James Hanson.

As importantly, the bankruptcy was reflected in Bob Hanson's abrasive personality and in a determination to throw off the stigma and establish his family in the top echelon of Huddersfield's merchant classes. This would enable Robert himself to put disgrace behind him, and ensure there was enough wealth and standing in the family to prevent any future humiliation. He determined that his family would be brought up in prosperity, be well trained and that there would be enough resources to indulge the family passion for horses, from cart-horses to showjumping, hunting and breeding, which had been part of the Hanson makeup since the early nineteenth century.

It was James Hanson's great-grandmother Mary, in an age when women were not generally given much latitude in business, who had started the family's association with both haulage and horses. Lord Hanson – and his two sons, John Brook and Robert William – remain closely involved in Hanson Transport, with its undistinguished modern headquarters on Woodland Road in Huddersfield. Lord Hanson still personally negotiates the major contract for Hanson Transport, which is with ICI at Kirklees. A threat to cancel the ICI contract was among the weapons used by the chemical company in its titanic effort to fend off a Hanson bid in the summer of 1991. Even today James Hanson regards the private family company as among his most important interests, jesting that it is his own money, not that of public shareholders, which is at stake. Each year he goes through the ritual of a lunch with ICI's chief executive to shake hands personally on the Kirklees contract under which Hanson Transport tankers carry chemicals in trucks painted in ICI's livery.

The horse connection has also provided a notable thread in the Hanson family lives. James Hanson's late brother Bill was an extremely talented showjumper, and for many years the family supported the stables of another Yorkshire showjumper, Harvey Smith. Chris Collins, Hanson's nephew by marriage and a former national hunt jockey, sits on the board of Hanson plc. In the late 1980s, unbeknownst to most shareholders, since no mention was made of it in the annual reports, Hanson plc owned a loss-making string of bloodstock. Lord Hanson still maintains several retired hunters at his 26-acre estate, Kimber Cottage, near Newbury, and employed a full-time groom, until she was unfairly dismissed, with a flurry of publicity, in February 1994.[6] James's son Robert Hanson, has an expensive polo habit and has been known to use the Hanson corporation private jet to fly friends from the English national polo team across the United States.

Mary Hanson started the horse-drawn haulage business in the 1830s to supplement the income of her husband Joseph, who was a farmer in Yorkshire's fertile Colne Valley. Initially trade was local, carrying textiles along the valley from the cobbled streets of Longwood to the Cherry Tree Inn in Huddersfield, at 3 p.m. every Tuesday, Thursday and Saturday. The local service became so popular that by 1846 the matriarch of the family had moved into longer-distance transport, hauling textiles, ore and other goods across the Pennines to Manchester, and north-east to Leeds, three times a week. Milnsbridge, which was to become the centre of the Hanson operations, had developed as a ford across one of the wider sections of the Colne Valley and administratively fell within three separate boroughs: Huddersfield, Golcar and Longwood. The mid-nineteenth century, as Hanson haulage was starting to build, was a time of great industrial expansion in the West Riding which saw Milnsbridge swamped by woollen mills and workers' cottages.

In 1845 there were more than forty water wheels working along the Colne Valley, providing power to the mills. As the demand for wool and cloth expanded, the mill-owners built rows of terraced back-to-back housing. By 1860 the Longwood gasworks had been built, with an uncovered coke stack, to power the mill boilers. With the mills belching dark smoke, the countryside was blackened with soot and waste deposits and the once-clean waters of the Colne ran red and blue with dyestuffs and effluents from the Leitch's and the Thornton Brothers' dyeworks on the Colne Road. Britain ruled the world's textile markets and the Crowther's Mill in Milnsbridge alone employed 2000 people by the time of the great fire at the Hanson warehouse in 1919.[7]

Having put down the roots of the Hanson transport businesses, Mary Hanson died on 5 September 1854, at the age of 63, passing the business to her eldest son, Joseph Hanson, whose name would remain on the letterhead of the firm until it was nationalised in 1948. With the woollen and finished clothing industries flourishing in the Hudders-field area, Joseph was able to build and expand the company. In 1880 he moved to Bothan Hall Farm and for a while combined the haulage business with farming. The clothing boom continued, however, and Joseph Hanson had to expand to meet demand, and so in 1896 he constructed stables under the sturdy, vaulting railway arches which ran through the Colne Valley at Milnsbridge.

Joseph's elder son, Buckley Hanson, took over the family farm from his father while the younger son, James William, inherited the more challenging haulage business. It would not be the only time in the Hanson family that a sharper younger brother would be preferred to an elder sibling to take on the more difficult task: this is exactly what Robert Hanson had in mind for his brilliant younger son Bill, two generations on.

By this stage the firm had some 14 horses stabled under the arches and had added a removals business to the general haulage; at first this was conducted in open wagons but in 1898 the firm acquired its first 'tunnel van'. Although the business was still horse-driven, the records show that Joseph Hanson's firm conducted removals right across the country to towns which included Grantham, Scarborough, Blackpool, Southport, Liverpool and even as far as Llandudno – a distance of 120 miles from Huddersfield.

Nevertheless, the carriage of textiles was the mainstay of the business. It was while James William Hanson was in charge that the company became the first in the region to develop equipment which allowed it to move cloth looms from mill to plant without having to dismantle them – a costly and time-consuming exercise. To make the journey easy on the looms, Hanson's developed a primitive suspension system which allowed the horse-drawn lorries to carry up to 14 tons of textile machinery.

When James William Hanson died in 1911, he handed on a sizeable enterprise to his still youthful sons, Joseph, aged 21, and his younger brother, Robert, 18. J. W. Hanson also left behind a legacy of public service. He was a stout Wesleyan, who held several senior offices in the Church, and a great educationalist who played no small part in the foundation of the Crow Lane School at Milnsbridge, which would be attended by several generations of Hansons. In the long tradition of the progressive politics of the Colne Valley, he was a staunch Liberal who was often to preside over meetings of the local executive. In this respect J.W. Hanson was effectively the first of the line to recognise the importance to business of maintaining good political relations. Although the haulage business prospered under J.W. Hanson's leadership, the Hansons were still struggling to lift themselves up the social scale at the time of his death.

It was Lord Hanson's father, Robert, who found himself in the driving seat at Joseph Hanson & Son after the death of his elder brother in 1919, who successfully lifted the family from its modest commercial status, in which it all but lived over the stables, into Huddersfield's élite with all the trappings which came with it: large houses, a butler, servants, tennis courts, public school education for his children and membership of the Rockwood Hunt. Robert Hanson, like many of his generation, attended the Crow Lane School in Longwood. Whereas most of the children in his class left to begin full-time work as young as 12 years old, the school records show that Robert Hanson was among the few who moved on to a college, to gain a higher grade certificate of education.

The better schooling, together with sharp business acumen, would be necessary to take over a business which expanded steadily in the years leading up to the First World War. The number of horses in service had been increased to 32 after the firm had won the contract to move coal to the Longwood gasworks and to remove the coke afterwards. But it also had developed an important sideline in supplying horses to the army, a job which allowed it to add the warrant 'Contractors to H.M. Government' to its letterhead.[8] At the outbreak of the First World War the Hansons supplied some 40 horses together with harnesses and vehicles to the local battalion of the Territorial Army. This was but the start of a hugely profitable contract under which the Hansons would supply 20 horses a week to the armed forces. As the war progressed as many as 3200 horses a year were being shipped to the forces, and Robert Hanson would travel personally to the annual spring fairs in Ireland to make the purchases.

The years of the First World War were financially successful for Joseph Hanson & Son. The horse sales to the army proved a useful source of cash for the firm and allowed it to invest in its first mechanised vehicles. As the war progressed the Hanson fleet expanded to six steam wagons and three petrol trucks, and the furniture depository and garage at Milnsbridge were constructed. The company continued to show great flair for expansion and started to fit charabanc bodies to its steam wagons and to organise day-trips from the mills to Blackpool. Three years after the end of the First

World War, on 9 October 1921, Joseph Hanson & Son decided to treat its own employees – mainly charabanc and bus drivers, operating in and around the West Riding – to their own trip to Blackpool. The excursion, which was organised by Bob Hanson, is thought to have given rise to the popular expression 'a busman's holiday'.[9]

Soon Hanson's was moving into passenger transport and its first local bus services, later to be known as Hanson's Buses, were developed. Despite the fire of 1919 and the subsequent bankruptcy, Robert Hanson, with his new partners, pressed on by moving into the livery business for weddings and funerals. By 1928, the year he was discharged from bankruptcy, Robert Hanson had enough resources to acquire several Rolls-Royces to replace the livery at Hanson funeral services. But he still retained the common touch, riding in a Rolls to buy his fish and chips. The haulage side of the company was also expanding and diversifying to carry all manner of goods. Premises were opened in London and the first overnight services began.

In much the same way as Robert Hanson had become the dominant haulier one side of the ridge which divides Huddersfield from Halifax, Charles 'Charlie' Holdsworth was the main haulier on the other side of the divide. The businesses were very similar including the supply of horses to the Territorial Army. Holdsworth also owned livery stables and, again like the Hanson family, had a fleet of Rolls-Royce cars for weddings, funerals and so on.

There was a kind of gentleman's agreement to divide up territories and to look after each other. Charlie Holdsworth and Robert Hanson became firm buddies and it was Holdsworth who bailed Hanson out of the bankruptcy. A letter dated February 1931 on the headed paper of I.W. Holdsworth Limited (the main Holdsworth company) suggests a close relationship. The typed letter starts 'Dear Robert', goes on to announce the cancellation of an overdraft agreement between the two companies and then adds, 'should you at any time require a little help in this direction, you can rely on us doing our best . . . We trust that J. Hanson & Son Ltd will go on from strength to strength, and that you will be blessed with good health to make it all that you desire.'

While developing the business Bob Hanson also began to work on his family life. In 1916 he married a local woman, Louisa Ann Rogers, who had been brought up in the small West Yorkshire village of

Linthwaite, south-west of Huddersfield. The daughter of a master butcher, she came from much the same respectable commercial background. As Bob was fighting for the survival of the Hanson businesses after the Milnsbridge blaze and bankruptcy, Louisa Hanson, described by those who knew her as simply a housewife, was producing a family. The first child to arrive was a daughter, Muriel, born in September 1918, followed on 20 January 1922 by James Edward, the future Lord Hanson. Their youngest child, Robert William, 'Bill' as he was known, was born in 1925.

In a family driven by a need to over-achieve, it was James's mother Louisa who brought an air of normality to the Hanson homes. James remembers her affectionately as the warm, loving and tender member of the family who was always there for her children even after they had gone away to boarding school or the forces. Hanson considers his mother's role in the family as broadly similar to that of his own wife Geraldine today: work was the most important part of her husband's life and it was therefore best to let him get on with it. This, James believes, made for a happier home, an almost idyllic childhood. In part Louisa's domesticity offset the strong and stern personality of Bob Hanson, a businessman feared throughout the West Riding. Bob Hanson was a man who very much enjoyed life to the full, showing up at the works, in his hunting gear, at the end of the day to make sure the lorries were being loaded correctly. He was the sort of man who saw no problem in mixing business with pleasure.

But James's mother was different. Unlike the rest of the family, she was much less interested in horses than her husband and her three children, who were born with jodhpurs on. But she would, nevertheless, always be there, dragging along the picnic basket whenever the family went on holiday, or working around the home. She was also personally generous – a trait that James has developed in dealing with family, friends and close business associates, to whom he can be enormously kind. Like Bob Hanson, however, James's mother always assumed that he and his younger brother Bill would go into the family business, so she had no need to protect the boys from the strong influence of her husband. Even as toddlers James and Bill were routinely taken to the works and depots during weekends and school holidays, and the possibility of James doing anything other than going into the haulage game was never really discussed in the family.

The Hanson family home in the 1920s was an unprepossessing terraced house, Woodbank, on Scarr Lane in Golcar, a short distance from the railway arches where the Hanson shires were stabled. The Hansons liked children and were good neighbours who enjoyed taking a stroll with the pram, parading young James. By the time that Bill Hanson was born the family had moved on from the belching chimneys of Milnsbridge to the suburbs, first to a semi-detached house at 19 Beech Street in Paddock, and then in 1928 to a more substantial pebble-dashed home at Le Marchant Avenue in Lindley.

The prosperity and success which old Bob Hanson, as he is known around Huddersfield, craved was some time in coming. Although the business had been brought back from the brink by some early financial engineering, it would be 15 years after the blaze before Bob would be able to lift his family from among the tradesmen to the élite of the West Riding's merchant classes. In 1934, when James was 11 years old, the Hansons moved to a mansion in Egerton, in what is known locally as 'mill-owners' quarters' on a ridge high above the town on the old Halifax Road. Norwood Grange would be home to the Hanson family until James's mother Louisa died in 1982. The Hansons' new home was a solid Victorian structure, built of York stone with striking mullioned windows. The L-shaped mansion, with its own gatehouse, was reached by a long, curving 300-yard driveway, with neatly planted herbaceous borders. The house had its own tennis court and the main reception room looked over a bowling green lawn beyond. By now the family was cared for by servants and Bob would be driven into town or to Halifax, to meet with his pal Charlie Holdsworth, by chauffeur.

In the 1930s Bob Hanson began to recognise the value of takeovers in expanding the business. Working closely with the Holdsworths – with each family retaining control over their respective businesses – haulage firms were acquired across the United Kingdom, including companies as far afield as Glasgow. In 1935 the Hanson–Holdsworth partnership took a leap forward when it negotiated the purchase of the Oswald Tillotson business of Burnley – one of the country's largest transport concerns which would later play a significant role in the building of James Hanson's business empire. Tillotson would become the public vehicle used to buy into the Wiles Group, which in turn would become Hanson plc. Bob Hanson was regarded as a shrewd financial manager who knew how to convince his bank managers of the need to finance expansion – even in the depth of the 1930s depression, which hit the Huddersfield worsted trade hard.

'One of the important things I learnt from my father', Lord Hanson has observed,

> was the importance of very simple effective financial controls. To him profit was a yardstick of success. He taught me how to go to a bank and borrow money. He was good at it and would take me along so I got the confidence to do it. His technique was always pay them off more quickly than expected so he could go back and borrow a bit more than the previous time.[10]

In parallel with the expansion of his haulage businesses Bob Hanson also aggressively pursued bus routes and franchises in the West Riding, which he perceived as a licence to print money because of the cash they would generate for other business activities. Between 1932 and 1935 old Bob was in almost constant battle with the Huddersfield local authorities as he applied to the traffic commissioners for new routes and services. At the same time he bought out many of the local, privately owned coach and charabanc services, putting all the company's passenger transport services into a separate company – Hanson's Buses Ltd. The drive to become the dominant force in West Riding transport caused the Hanson companies to become a thorn in the side of the local authorities.

Bob Hanson recognised very early on, before the sophisticated world of public relations, lobbyists and parliamentary advisers developed, that political pressure could be an extremely useful tool in achieving a business end: another powerful message he passed on to his son. From December 1935 to July 1936 Hanson, via its Huddersfield-based solicitors Eaton Smith & Downey, engaged in a prolonged campaign in the Commons and the Lords to try and prevent the spread of trolley buses, a clear threat to Hanson's private-sector services in Huddersfield. Hanson told MPs that the new Bill being sought by Huddersfield Corporation would create 'an unfair advantage in relation to the carrying of passengers over certain of the Corporation's tramway routes', [11] that is, those already run by Hanson. As part of the effort, leading counsel was engaged to oppose the Bill and petitions were laid before both the Lords and the Commons. The cost to Hanson's Buses Ltd of this not inconsiderable early exercise of political lobbying techniques was £775 17s 5d.

Having seen the writing on the wall, as far as private bus services were concerned, Bob Hanson then sought to sell Hanson's Buses to the Huddersfield Joint Omnibus Committee. But he withdrew from the negotiations after failing to receive the price he wanted. The willingness of Bob Hanson to sell off carefully constructed and long-established businesses, if the price was right, is a principle which was to play an important part in later Hanson-run businesses.

Until the move to Norwood Grange Bob Hanson's family followed a relatively modest lifestyle, including a state education. Young James briefly attended his father's school, Crow Lane, of which his grandfather had been a founder. He then moved on to the Waverly School before attending what was then Elland Grammar School (now Brooksbank School), an elegant early Victorian building with spacious windows, wrought-iron gates and gardens surrounded by shrubbery. Elland was a grammar school of average standards which was generally open to clever children from the better social backgrounds. There were entrance scholarships for brighter children from less well-off families as well as fee places for the better off. Elland was a co-educational establishment, with a boys' entrance on the left and girls' entrance on the right, and surrounded by large green playing fields. The young James was among an entry of around sixty in his year and could, if his parents had so wished, have remained there right up until the sixth form.

Bob Hanson had grander plans for his sons, however. It was intended that James, a bright, if not brilliant boy, would go on to a more prestigious establishment, and a place had been reserved for him at Uppingham, the Leicestershire public school founded by Robert Johnson in 1584 which lies in some 56 acres of grounds with generous sports facilities. But around the age of 11, as he was due to go to Uppingham, James became ill and this interrupted educational plans. One tradesman, cleaning the windows at Norwood Grange, by then the Hanson seat, recalls coming across young Jimmy as he lay ill in bed. He asked the lad what he was doing lying down on such a bright Yorkshire morning. The boy, who 'looked long faced', replied as quick as a flash, 'I'm minding my own business.' The workman thought that James's reply had been a little cheeky. The incident, nevertheless, made a lasting impression on the tradesman because he did not expect anyone in the Hanson household to be lying around in bed. 'I think he was a bit poorly. The Hansons were always up and ready. They were not people who laid around doing nothing. They were workers,' he recalls.[12] A contemporary remembers Hanson as being 'an ordinary ginger-haired lad with no special charisma'.

The illness was serious enough for James's parents to rethink their plans. Uppingham, where many of James's friends from Huddersfield's mill-owning class were sent, was seen as too large and too challenging, both academically and physically, for a child who had been sickly. His parents cast around for a more suitable alternative for an 'away school' for their son, and through the family's connections in the horse-breeding world discovered a smaller public school founded by the Joel family, who were bloodstock owners. The school, Merlegh, near Reading, took its name from the Joel estate after the school moved from Sutton Courtney near Paignborne to its Berkshire location. It was a relatively small school with less than 200 pupils and has since gone out of business. By all accounts the young Jimmy Hanson had a good time at Merlegh, but the old school tie connections, so much part of the public school ethos, passed him by, and he has only the most occasional contact with any former schoolmates – never really coming across them in business.

Although Hanson now likes to nurture the image of the homespun, self-made Huddersfield lad with some blunt Yorkshire still in his accent, he plainly regrets having left Elland Grammar, which he enjoyed greatly, and moving to a school which provided little of the academic or social distinction which is generally expected from a public school education. When he eventually left Merlegh, to train as an accountant, he had a school certificate, but had been cut off from his social peers who had gone to Uppingham and the like. Hanson remains sensitive to the point of being defensive on the subject of his education, preferring to emphasise his other achievements. When he does speak of schooling he would generally rather talk about the success of his brilliant younger brother Bill at Oundle – the sixteenth-century school near Peterborough – than his own less memorable schooldays.

Despite the shortcomings of his own education, Hanson has been a benefactor to schools in Huddersfield and when he addresses them his words are filled with the simple work ethic inherited from Bob Hanson. 'When I speak to children, when I do prizegivings at speech days, the one thing I say is that anything can be done but you must first of all want to do it,' Hanson asserts.

A lot of people believe they have ambition but they are not really serious about it. What they mean is that they would like to make a lot of money. They would like a comfortable life. That's never been my upbringing. My upbringing was to get the job done, enjoy it and really want to do it. My father was a great example of that.[13]

With the approach of the Second World War, James Hanson, now a spindly 16-year-old going through a growth spurt, left his boarding school and returned to Huddersfield to prepare for a role in Joseph Hanson & Son Ltd, which by the outbreak of war was among the largest transport groups in the United Kingdom. The business was now far more complicated than when Bob Hanson had taken it over almost two decades earlier and a different range of skills would be required if it was to be developed. In 1938 Bob Hanson arranged for his elder son to become an audit clerk at Smith & Garton, general accountants, one of Huddersfield's most prominent professional firms with offices at 24 John William Street in the centre of the city. In 1970 the Huddersfield-based firm would be absorbed by Ernst & Young, the international chartered accounting practice whose Hull office remains to this day Hanson plc's auditors. At Smith & Garton, James worked on routine accounting tasks in the mornings, but was given the afternoons off to work on a correspondence course for his auditing examinations.

James stood out from the other junior employees. Despite being paid a negligible amount of money, he would sometimes arrive at work in a chauffeur-driven car, from the Hanson fleet of vehicles, and would occasionally drive himself and park outside. At a time when it was unusual for anyone in Huddersfield to travel to London, James would often take the train south at weekends and return to regale his workmates with stories of the women he had met under the bright lights. James was popular with his fellow employees and, despite his academic record, showed genuine aptitude as an accountant – training which would become an essential component of his financially driven approach when he was to acquire his own public company. 'He was a jovial chap, who treated us just like anyone else. A great lad, really good in the office and very down to earth,' notes Wilbert Morris, who worked as an audit clerk with Hanson.[14] His colleagues gained an insight into the increasingly grand Hanson lifestyle when he invited them, in the summer of 1939, to a tennis party at Norwood Grange. For many of those who went the highlight of the day was being waited on by the Hanson family butler after the tennis was over.

Just as James Hanson was settling into his accountancy training and a relaxed lifestyle built around Norwood Grange, regular excursions to London and the Huddersfield horse set, focused on the Rockwood Hunt, his life took another important turn with the outbreak of the Second World War. This brought an abrupt end to his accountancy training in much the same way as illness had interfered with his entrance to Uppingham a few years earlier. Whereas in the First World War his father and uncle served out the war years supplying horses first to the Territorials and then to the army as a whole, in 1940 James and Bill – straight from Oundle – felt it imperative to join the forces. The army was to be the making of Hanson's younger brother Bill. As a star horseman, an athlete and an intellectual, Bill Hanson was to become the youngest officer in the British forces when he was commissioned as a major at the age of just 19.

If being in the forces came naturally to Bill, with his more sophisticated background, it was a nuisance to James. His army days, like his school years, are quickly glossed over in conversation and official company biographies, and have become shrouded in an air of mystery. The entrepreneur's brief *Who's Who* entry blandly records war service 1939–46, without the customary mention of regiments, commission or theatres of service. This reticence is even more curious in that there is no element in this of the young James brooking a challenge. It was at his own accord in April 1939, with the scent of conflict with Hitler's Germany in the air, that James joined the Territorial Army, with which his family had long connections stretching back to before the Great War. Then in September 1939, at the age of 17, Hanson was called up and forced to abandon the audit training to which he was so well adapted. James Hanson's army career began in the 7th Duke of Wellington's regiment (in which his uncle Donald had served in the Great War) based in Yorkshire, where he received his commission, before moving on to another service. He was first stationed near to home but was eventually to spend four of his seven years abroad, playing a part in campaigns in North Africa, Italy and Greece.

The army also kindled Hanson's interest in the airwaves. Towards the end of his military service in 1945–46 Captain James Hanson spent time with the Army Broadcasting Service in Athens which provided entertainment for British and Indian troops in southern Europe. The small station operated from the heart of the Zappion Gardens in the centre of Athens, just a stone's throw from the Greek royal palace. Despite the splendid location the facilities were fairly basic. The broadcasters had the use of one small studio, fitted with a single microphone and ageing twin turntables. There was a larger studio which could cope with concerts. Only one transmitter had been left operative after the retreat of the German army and it was this which was used to broadcast the English-language programmes, when the local Greek service was off the air. Nevertheless, the small station had its successes. Among its first broadcasts was a recording of Winston Churchill and Anthony Eden with the Greek Prime Minister Palstiros and the Regent, from just outside the Old Palace, where Churchill addressed a crowd on his return from Yalta in 1944. Among the volunteers to work at the station was Captain James Hanson, who was seen 'as an expert in swing'.[15] Among other things, James was a participant in the programme 'Radio Rhythm Club' and produced a programme on Artie Shaw.

The combination of his military service in transport – which was like civilian life for a Hanson with its haulage and logistics aspects – followed by the period in broadcasting left James Hanson feeling vaguely dissatisfied with his military service. In his own mind Hanson takes the view that it somehow was not tough enough. He compares his own service to that of his younger brother Bill, who was pitched straight into the far more arduous Burma campaign and had much more of what James views as a 'real' war. Lord Hanson ascribes his unwillingness to talk about his schooldays and the army to his boredom with friends who are always harking back to the past round the dinner table. In his view it is only the future which must count for a businessman – an attitude that is, however, inconsistent with his strong nostalgia and respect for certain aspects of his past, including his Yorkshire origins.

Even though he has luxurious residences on both sides of the Atlantic and has been elevated to the House of Lords, James never totally cut himself off from his Huddersfield roots. He is a regular visitor to his native town and proudly mentions his Hon. DBA from Huddersfield Polytechnic and his membership of Huddersfield Borough, along with Brooks's, in his *Who's Who* entry. He is also unfailingly courteous when he receives correspondence from West Riding residents, former employees and associates. In a 1989 letter from Palm Springs to Mrs Betty Bruce of Otley in West Yorkshire, Hanson wrote: 'I was most interested to receive your letter and be reminded of so many familiar things.' He went on to reminisce with Mrs Bruce about a Hanson home on Beech Street, a pony called Robin as well as the closure of the Hopkinson's mill.[16] This is not the letter of a man seeking to put distant events behind him. It is more the effort of a man to bury those parts of his life that remain distasteful. The strain of living for so many years, through school, the army and in the post-war Hanson transport years in the shadow of a brilliant younger brother almost certainly took its psychological toll on James.

Moreover, the premature death of that younger brother may have left James with some personal guilt as to why was it Bill's life rather than his own which was cut short. This has led James to over-compensate by blotting out certain incidents from his background and, some forty years after Bill's death, still to praise his brother's achievements above his own at every possible opportunity. The Second World War also left James with a wanderlust. His period in the army opened vistas to a world beyond Yorkshire and the hunting set. It also made him determined to reclaim the social life lost during his seven years in the forces. The 1950s were to see James embark on a new career in North America, with the opening of Hanson's Canadian operations and the start of his decades-long friendship with another tall Yorkshireman, Gordon White. It would also see the quiet older brother launch himself into a swashbuckling social life which would

make Jimmy Hanson – with his matinée idol slicked-back hair-style –
the darling of the gossip columnists.

CHAPTER 3

Prosperity, Playboys and Partners

By the time the Second World War had broken out the Hanson family company had become a far more significant enterprise than the local firm of the 1920s that bussed its employees to Blackpool for the day. Together with its partners, the Holdsworth companies, based across the ridge in Halifax, it was the largest road haulage enterprise in Britain with some 1200 trucks in its fleet. It was clear that during the war years such a significant haulier would be of critical importance in the strategic planning and logistics of an economy over which the wartime administration had so much control. With his sons and would-be heirs away in the army, Bob Hanson, James's resourceful father, again showed considerable skill in putting the family firm in an advantageous position.

The Hanson–Holdsworth haulage business came under the control of the Ministry of War with Bob Hanson in a position of considerable power and influence as the North-Eastern Divisional Officer Ministry of War Transport, Road Haulage. In the period 1939–45 the joint Hanson–Holdsworth haulage businesses covered millions of miles, delivering foodstuffs, ammunition and war materials around the country. Throughout the conflict, including the perils of the Battle of Britain, the trunk services ran without a break despite blackouts and air raids. 'Great credit is due to the drivers and mates who have carried on through the trying periods of the blackout, and have often driven through towns during intense air raids,' the magazine *Motor Transport* was to record in an editorial.[1] However, although the vehicles were put at the disposal of the government, Bob Hanson still had control over the company's haulage fleet and this, like the supply of horses to the army in the First World War, provided Hanson–Holdsworth with an abundant cash flow.

This money allowed Hanson to continue expanding the business even in wartime conditions. There were further mergers with smaller haulage firms, such as the Chelmsford Transport Company in 1944. Even as the war was drawing to a close in 1945, Hanson–Holdsworth were buying further trucking companies in Halifax and Yeadon, West Yorkshire, strengthening their hold on the London trunk routes. Hanson's itself retained the management of its own parcels services company and was 'responsible for repairs and maintenance of vehicles in an area designated by the Government'[2] – another useful government contract. Investment in the business carried on apace with the company constructing garages on Woodland Road in Huddersfield and landing its first major contract deal with ICI Dyestuffs, under which Hanson lorries would move dyes between ICI plants and to other companies in trucks wearing the distinctive ICI colours and logo.

During 1946 Bob Hanson's two sons, James and Bill, returned from the forces and, despite their inexperience in business, were immediately parachuted into the family enterprises as joint managing directors of the Hanson and Holdsworth group of companies. The formal education of the brothers had been brought to an abrupt halt by the war, but their father had kept their seats warm waiting for their return. The Britain the brothers were to encounter after demobilisation was already a very different place to the one they had left behind. The war years of central economic planning, symbolised by the War Office's temporary takeover of the Hanson haulage businesses, had given the British people a taste of a different kind of world in which the government was expected to deliver economic and social security, as well as national security.

The changing expectations and aspirations resulted in the return of a Labour government headed by Clement Attlee in July 1945. It was a government with radical plans to reshape the nature of business in Britain through public ownership. The architect of nationalisation was Herbert Morrison, the Lord President of the Council, who had gained experience in the field of public corporations when he merged the London underground and buses into a single authority. As he told the House of Commons in 1946: 'There are going to be public corporations, business concerns, they will buy the necessary brains and technical skill and give them their head.'[3]

In much the same way as President Roosevelt had moved with dramatic speed in the 1930s to reshape America's economic and financial structure in the teeth of depression, so Clement Attlee, with Morrison as his general, did the same for Britain after the Second World War. In rapid succession many of the great privately owned industries from airlines to gas, power, coal and even the Bank of England were brought into public ownership – using a variety of different models. But Morrison's approach was essentially conservative in that it generally allowed those who knew the institutions or industries well – Lord Catto at the Bank of England and Lord Hyndley of the colliery company Powell Duffryn at the National Coal Board – to run the new breed of public corporations.

A shrewd and gutsy operator like Bob Hanson, who had steered his family company through two world wars and dodged bankruptcy in between, could see the writing on the wall for the road haulage industry. It was the Attlee government's intention to develop an integrated national transport system of which the Hanson–Holdsworth trunk network, as the largest in the country, was bound to be an essential component. The Labour transport system, as envisaged, would put together 'the running of the 3800 road hauliers, all road and transport in London, the great harbours of Southampton and Hull which were owned by the railway companies plus several similarly owned hotel chains and Thomas Cook the travel agents for good measure'.[4]

At the end of 1946 Bob Hanson and his two sons embarked on a plan which would result in the family becoming extremely cash-rich. Hanson senior split Joseph Hanson & Son Ltd into two separate enterprises. A new company, Hanson Haulage, was formed, with a capital of £20,000 and with Bob Hanson and his two sons as directors. Hanson Haulage took over the new contract fleet, which had been built up in the war years, the removal and storage interests, and the funeral and car-hire business. Hanson Buses was already a separate company.[5]

Fully aware of Labour's nationalisation plans, Bob Hanson and Charlie Holdsworth demonstrated again that an understanding of politics is a considerable help in business. Instead of waiting to be compulsorily acquired by the newly formed public corporation British Transport Services, the Hanson–Holdsworth companies approached the government about a voluntary sale. There was much speculation in Huddersfield that the Hanson companies were about to sell out. Such rumours were promptly denied by the family – but no one guessed the buyers or the advantageous terms of the deal.

On 18 August 1948 it was announced that Ministry of Transport representatives had taken control of some 18 trucking firms in the Hanson–Holdsworth group, including Joseph Hanson & Son Ltd, Bouts–Tillotson (the jointly owned long trunk haulage company, the forerunner of Oswald Tillotson) and I.W. Holdsworth (Halifax). The Hansons and the Holdsworths were now cash millionaires, after receiving a £2 million draft from the government as the down-payment of a deal estimated, at the time, to be worth £3 million – some £48 million in current money.[6] The actual payment would eventually rise to £4 million.

The Hanson links to the nationalised companies were not, however, cut. Bob Hanson agreed to assist the transition to a national freight company by remaining in charge for at least 12 months. His son James, who was to epitomise Thatcherite business values some 40 years later, suddenly found himself as managing director of a nationalised industry – the Holdsworth and Hanson Group of the British Transport Commission – working for a radical Labour administration. The deal of 1948 was to impress on the young businessman the importance of political alliances in commerce, a lesson he was never to forget. It was the Hansons who found themselves advising Major-General G.N. Russell, chairman of the Road Transport Executive of the British Transport Commission, on how best to integrate and organise the nationalised freight companies the government was still acquiring. Bob Hanson, sporting a bow-tie and with his distinctive chin jutting out, became a spokesman for Labour's cause, an outright advocate of the benefits of the integrated transport opportunity presented by Labour's nationalisation plans.

'Other people in different parts of the country will help the Holdsworth and Hanson group to serve this area,' he explained. 'There will be some snags in the teething stages, but the public will eventually have a better freight service than ever before.'[7]

Bill Hanson returned from Burma a war hero and, encouraged by his family, resumed his equestrian career. Horses were still playing a major part in Hanson family life, but now it was top-class hunters stabled for the Rockwood Harriers Hunt, rather than the shires and working horses stabled under the railway arches at Milnsbridge, which were the focus of their lives. In 1945 Bob Hanson received the social recognition he craved when he took on the Mastership of the Rockwood Harriers Hunt. The Rockwood hunted over the harsh sporting country of the western edge of the West Riding in a triangular area from the Hansons' home town of Huddersfield across green pastures to about five miles from Sheffield to the south-east, then towards Wakefield to the north and back to Huddersfield. Most of the country covered was open, broken only by drystone walls. While Bob Hanson took on the Mastership of the hunt, his elder son James, also a good horseman, took on the more mundane post of hunt secretary. Having achieved the Mastership of the Rockwood, Bob Hanson took advantage of the prestige conferred upon him by his showjumping son Bill, to become joint master, with Bill, of the more genteel Grove and Rufford Hunt at the end of the 1948–49 hunting season.[8]

With his father providing the best hunters that the fortune conferred upon him by the Attlee government allowed, Bill was rapidly moving to the top echelon in British showjumping. By 1951 Bill Hanson had won almost every major award in the hunter classes at the leading shows in the country riding his horse Unique, which was stabled at the family estate of Norwood Grange, and regarded as the best of its kind in the country. 'Unique has won every big show in England, Scotland and Wales,' Bill Hanson told a visitor to the family stables.[9] With his son's success now assured, his father, who had once bought tens of thousands of horses for the British armed forces, acquired the horses which would help to make Bill Hanson the best-known rider in Britain: The Monarch, Snowstorm and Talisman. In 1952 Bill joined the British showjumping team in Dublin and won more individual prizes than anyone else in the competition. Later that year at the Horse of the Year show in Harringay, Bill added the leading showjumper of the year prize to his trophy case. During the following year he travelled to Europe with the Great Britain team and carried off the then premier prize in showjumping, the Grand Prix of Rome, riding his big hunter The Monarch. He was the first rider from Britain to win the coveted trophy and became a national hero overnight.

In October 1953 Bill Hanson joined the British showjumping team tour of the United Sates and Canada as part of a team which included two other great equestrian names, Lt-Col. Harry Llewellyn and Pat Smythe, who later came to be recognised as the face of showjumping in Britain in the post-war period. As the tour drew to a close, with Bill Hanson having taken yet more individual prizes, Llewellyn described Bill Hanson, still only 28 years old, as 'the backbone of the British team'.

Bill Hanson's success in the show ring was matched by that in business and society. He was now Bob's favoured son to take over the business and was given the role of scouting out Canada as a suitable place to transplant the business, following nationalisation. He also played a key role with his father and the Holdsworth family in founding Jet Petroleum. On 11 August 1953 he married Patricia Janet Ann Edge, a member of a leading Anglo-Irish hunting family, in a ceremony at St Patrick's Cathedral in Dublin, watched by more than 3000 finely dressed guests. The match was hailed by the gossip columnists as the society wedding of the year.

But tragedy was soon to strike. Soon after Bill's return from the North American riding tour in 1953 he was taken ill. The next few months were a nightmare for his new wife and family as he underwent a series of major operations to try and deal with what had been diagnosed as cancer of the colon, a particularly virulent strain of cancer in younger people. Louisa Hanson explored every possible way of saving her younger son's life but her efforts enabled her only to cope more easily with the end when it came than the rest of the family. Bill's life could not be saved. The nation's sporting hero died, with his family at his bedside, at the Duke of York Nursing Home in Bradford on 2 October 1954. He was laid to rest at a private funeral at Thoresby Park near the young couple's family home at Ollerton in Nottingham-shire. The sudden death of the brightest Hanson of his generation was a hammer blow to Bob Hanson. He and Bill had been particularly close and he had great ambitions for his youngest offspring. It also meant that Bob Hanson's careful tax planning – he had handed over 50 per cent of the business to James during the war and the rest to Bill three years later – had been wasted. The death duties had to be found and James Hanson's lifelong distrust of the Inland Revenue was fashioned.

The loss of his brother was to prove the most formative event of James Hanson's life. It left scars that still colour his views even today. James, who had never expected to take on the mantle of the family businesses, suddenly found himself the heir apparent. His brother Bill, although younger, was everything James had never been: he was better educated, a top horseman, happily married and settled, and had inherited strong entrepreneurial instincts from his father – while James was essentially an administrator. He was good at making decisions and carrying out other people's ideas, but was not an innovator himself. He was also personally extremely close to his brother: so close in fact that when Bill died he left most of his personal fortune of £328,000 to James and made a relatively small settlement of £20,000 to his 25-year-old widow Patricia. 'James was deeply affected by Bill's death,' records Jean Stead, who was brought up in the same social circles as the Hansons.[10] Even now, some 40 years later, James finds it hard to talk about his own youth without measuring it against the brilliance of his brother. Over the years, in fact, James has left an impression with many of his closest colleagues (not to mention press profiles) that Bill was his older brother and thus Gordon White was the natural, older surrogate who replaced him as a role model. James has developed a tendency over the years to deprecate his own achievements, in comparison to those of his brother as well as Gordon White. This partly reflects his generous nature. But there is also an element of false modesty which does not chime with his fondness for his own photographic image and the sense of self-worth he displays in his public life. The reality is that the young James Hanson, with his reddish-tinged hair, also cut a stylish figure. 'James was less well known than his brother,' one contemporary recalls. 'But he was very impressive, upright, mannered and very confident with girls.'[11]

After the nationalisation of Joseph Hanson & Son it was the two brothers, Bill and James, who pioneered the family's expansion into North America, while Bob Hanson continued on the takeover path at home, seemingly unperturbed by the radical bent of the Attlee administration. The company chosen to spearhead the Hansons' first overseas adventure was Crawford Cartage Ltd, a Canadian haulage firm based in Hamilton, Ontario – an unfashionable steel town on the banks of Lake Ontario, to the south-west of Toronto. Finding the right vehicle was one thing, but making the investment was far harder in the post-war years when sterling was under fierce pressure on the foreign exchange markets and the Bank of England had been required to impose draconian exchange controls, which all but banned the export of capital.

However, the Premier of Ontario, George Drew, was very anxious to attract British businesses to the province and made an arrangement with the UK Treasury, under which part of the interest on Canada's war loan would be made available in foreign exchange for British firms wishing to settle there. The possibilities were brought to the attention of the young James Hanson by the Bank of Nova Scotia, whose manager in London was regarded as exceptionally bright and knew how to make these complex transactions work. It was the Bank of England, then under the governorship of Lord Catto, which gave the Hansons the wherewithal to make their first ever North American investment. It agreed that Hanson could borrow $250,000 in Canada and send a further $250,000 of currency from London. In exchange Hanson agreed to spend twice the amount of the expatriated money, some half-a-million dollars, on buying equipment in the United Kingdom. By coincidence Donald Stokes, then rising up the corporate ladder at UK truck manufacturers Leyland, was seeking to open up the Canadian markets to UK exports – so Hanson and Leyland came to an enduring relationship. Moreover, James has never forgotten the Bank of England's helpful role in facilitating the family's first venture in North America.

James Hanson's decision to leave Britain in 1949, to make a fortune in Canada, was duly recorded in the newspapers, which were beginning to take a strong interest in the high-octane social lives of the Hanson brothers. The young James Hanson's public relations skills were starting to be well honed and he made the departure of talent and capital look like a triumph for Britain. 'Mr James Hanson, 27-year-old bachelor, leaves Huddersfield next month with £100,000 to start a private enterprise road haulage business in Southern Ontario, Canada which he hopes will earn Britain dollars,' the *Sunday Express* trumpeted.[12] The 1949 investment in Crawford Cartage, which was soon to be renamed Hanson Transport Company Ltd, was to give James Hanson his first taste of the possibilities that North America had to offer in terms of a larger canvas for an acquisition-minded company to work upon. Moreover, the Hanson brothers also made the strategic judgement that if the company was to be run as they wanted it, then it could not be done by remote control from headquarters in Huddersfield. The Hansons acquired a residence in Oakville (now home to a large Ford plant), a commuter town between the industrial city of Hamilton and the Canadian showcase of Toronto. James was to spend up to six months of the year there, although he came home to Huddersfield more frequently as Bill became seriously ill.

Under James's stewardship as deputy chairman (Bill was initially chairman) the new Canadian company prospered. The managing director and president of the firm was Harold White, a Canadian who had worked as general manager of Joseph Hanson & Son in Britain, prior to the company being taken over by the Road Haulage Executive. Between 1949, when the Canadian firm was established, and 1957 the size of the Hanson Transport Co. fleet doubled to 340 trucks, including some 25 acquired through the takeover of a Toronto-based carrier, Andrews Freight Lines. Some 60 of the vehicles were Donald Stokes's Leyland Beavers, especially designed for the Canadian market. The company also established a series of new depots in Toronto, London (Ontario) and Niagara Falls. In Hamilton itself it invested some $750,000 in a new office and warehouse complex in the Parkdale area of the city.[13] In addition to handling steel and heavy industrial shipments, the company had expanded into package freight. The path trailed by Hanson in Canada was soon to be followed by other UK transport concerns, including British Electric Traction and the United Transport Company, which also found themselves exiled from British haulage as a result of nationalisation.[14]

The Canadian adventure, which lasted until 1967 when the Hanson family sold out to California-based Consolidated Freightways, was to be a formative experience for the young James Hanson. It would open perspectives for him well beyond Huddersfield and set in motion an interest in North America and a work pattern, with six months on either side of the Atlantic, which he continued within the far larger and more powerful Hanson plc group. At the same time it would demonstrate the possibilities for escaping from the all-powerful presence of his father, Robert Hanson, who was never willing to give up real control of his private companies until he was all but carried from his office in Huddersfield at the age of 82, after working for more than six decades in the family enterprise. It would teach the young Hanson that the only possible way of running a business internationally was being on the ground oneself, or having someone who can be absolutely trusted to handle the parts of the empire furthest from headquarters. This is the role that Gordon White would eventually play in Hanson plc's American investments.

While James was building a Canadian empire for the Hanson family, Bob Hanson was as energetic as ever in his efforts to expand the Huddersfield businesses in the wake of nationalisation. He was determined to rebuild some form of business on the same scale as before its transfer to public ownership. This once again set Hanson on the expansion trail, and showed the first signs of diversification. In 1950 it moved into the travel agency business with the opening of Hanson Travel Services, with a great fanfare and a large shopfront in the centre of Huddersfield. But Bob Hanson was also to use the resources he gained from nationalisation to develop the coaching and haulage businesses. In 1951 he snapped up the coaching activities of J.W. Bottomley of Huddersfield; the haulage and coaching activities of Ivy Coaches would be added in 1953; Sutcliffe's of Leeds was bought out in 1953–54 and in 1954 Hanson's joined with coach operators Wallace Arnold to buy Kia Ora of Morecambe. In addition Robert Hanson, with the assistance of his sons and the Holdsworth family, founded Jet Petroleum, a discount petrol chain which was to operate from the forecourts of Yorkshire Car Hire (one of the Bottomley companies bought in 1951).

In the early years after nationalisation Hanson concentrated on building its contract haulage business, which was outside the scope of nationalisation. As it became clear, however, that the grandiose transport schemes originally envisaged by the government would never come to fruition, Hanson also gradually moved back into the haulage business operating private sector trunks between Huddersfield and London, a competitor to the nationalised companies of which they had been an original part.

Although provincial prosperity and status appeared to be the prime driving force in Bob Hanson, his sons, their lives broadened by 'away school' and the army, wanted more. With his 6 foot 4 inch frame, Savile Row suits, transatlantic commuting and access to any number of fast and expensive cars, as well as helicopters, James Hanson cut something of a dash in the London of the early 1950s. The army had meant that many young men of James Hanson's generation had lost time, and James, his brother Bill and Bill's flamboyant friend from Hull, Gordon White, were making up for lost time as men about town, edging their way into a fast showbusiness crowd. 'I didn't spend all my energy on business, not at all,' Gordon White has explained. 'I'd seen six years of my life disappear on the army so I wanted to play. I suppose you could say we were the playboys of that era. I didn't object to that label, I didn't really care.'[15] Gordon may not have cared then, and still does not appear to care about social appearances, in stark contrast to his friend James. White has been through two divorces, countless very public relationships and is currently wedded to the former model Victoria Tucker, who is no less than 40 years his junior.

James Hanson has been consistently more sensitive about the privacy of his social dealings in the 1950s, when he was often described as Britain's number one playboy. He has clearly been concerned that too much exposure of his social exploits in the 1950s might undermine the image he has sought to cultivate as a member of the establishment and a serious player in the business and political life of Britain. Moreover, although Hanson was always in the gossip columns in this period, much of the coverage was patronising, noting James's failure – despite several attempts – to contract the kind of glamorous marriage he desperately seemed to want. Hanson's first high-profile romance was with the young British actress Jean Simmons, a child star of the silver screen who made a relatively smooth transition to adult roles, becoming one of the top box office attractions in Britain by the time she met the dashing haulage entrepreneur.

Jean Simmons met James Hanson at a party in London, and soon found herself invited to join the businessman at home in Huddersfield – which was to become something of a pattern for the women Hanson romanced. James Hanson's Huddersfield had a great deal to offer in the shape of a grand house and extensive grounds at Norwood Grange, a fleet of luxury cars as well as the best stable of hunters in Britain. One member of the Rockwood Hunt recalls receiving a surprise phone call from Bob Hanson. 'We've got a visitor at our house, Miss Jean Simmons,' Bob Hanson said. 'Do you think you could take her out hacking this afternoon?' An arrangement was made and at 2 p.m. on the dot, Miss Simmons was delivered by chauffeur to Honley Livery Stables and was taken out for an hour's ride. Miss Simmons was questioned by the stables as to her abilities. She described herself as a novice and was taken out on a leading rein. Her companion, a chorus girl, turned out to be a much better rider. The group set off across the moors although the ride was interrupted when Miss Simmons decided she wanted to smoke. At the end of the hack she said that she was very keen to take up riding – but she was never seen at the stables again.[16]

Jean Simmons nevertheless attended the Rufford Hunt Ball in Nottinghamshire in late 1949 as the guest of the Hanson family. In the first few weeks of 1950 James Hanson was still to be seen squiring her around London. Elegantly clad in evening dress, the couple were at the ringside at Earl's Court when Freddie Mills, then world boxing champion, defended his title against Joey Maxim. But by February of the same year, when Miss Simmons celebrated her 21st birthday in London, the relationship with James appeared to be fading. Hanson, who worked at his office from 9 a.m. to 6 p.m. before returning to Norwood Grange for dinner, claimed he could not make it to the party because of his work – the first time he had used this particular explanation in public. As for Jean, her explanation was that 'Jimmy was a bit busy because he is going to America soon.'[17] Despite Jean Simmons's discovery of the Hanson stables, it appeared to be the beginning of the end. It was the actor Stewart Granger who escorted her to the private birthday party and, before the turn of the year,

Granger and Simmons were married and off to Hollywood to pursue their careers.

The Jean Simmons interlude was merely a warm-up for James's more intense involvement with another gamine, up-and-coming actress Audrey Hepburn. Whereas Jean Simmons had an established career when she met the young man from the Huddersfield haulage and horsey set, Audrey Hepburn was barely on her way up the ladder and was the product of a far more exotic background. She had been born Edda van Heemstra Hepburn-Ruston in Brussels on 4 May 1929, and arrived in London, where she met Hanson, only after the lifting of the Nazi occupation of Holland, where her family had lived. Her mother, Ella, 'the Baroness', came from an aristocratic land-owning family, directly descended from the royal family of Holland. She had been twice divorced by the time she met Audrey's father, also a divorcé, the Anglo-Irish banker John Victor Hepburn-Ruston, who managed the Brussels branch of the Bank of England. By the time she was six, Audrey's father with his embarrassing Nazi connections had vanished and the child became an early Euro-commuter, spending her time between the family home in Arnhem (where she would eventually be trapped during the Nazi occupation) and London, where she enrolled in ballet school.[18]

Audrey Hepburn's first screen appearance was in a Dutch comedy *Nederland 7 in Lessen* in 1948 and this was quickly followed by chorus roles on the stage in London in the West End productions of *High Button Shoes* and the Cecil Landau review *Sauce Tartare*, with a slightly bigger role in the follow-up show *Sauce Piquante*. Next came a couple of cameo film roles in *One Wild Oat* and *The Lavender Hill Mob* which brought her to the attention of the cinema world. *Picturegoer* magazine wrote of the young Hepburn:

> God's gift to publicity men is a heart-shattering young woman with a style of her own, no mean ability and a photogenic capacity for making the newspaper pages among the first nighters; the name is Audrey Hepburn; and the fact that some people have been twenty-four times to Ciro's to see her cabaret performance is a good enough start for Elstree (Associated British) to talk of signing her for the screen. [19]

The Ciro's of the early 1950s was an extremely fashionable late-night venue which attracted a highly influential clientele from theatre and films, which came to look at the legs of the chorus girls as well as to search for genuine fresh talent.

Among those who fell for the Hepburn charm, just as she was about to become an international success, was the Huddersfield man-about-town James Hanson, fresh from his flirtation with Jean Simmons. Hanson was plainly seduced by the glamour of showbusiness, which must have made the narrow world of business in the provinces, where social life broadly revolved around the hunting crowd, look fairly tame. 'We met in London at a reception when she was with her agent, the late Jack Dunfee, and I asked her out to lunch,' Hanson recalled in 1993. 'She was a beautiful girl and we were together for two years and became engaged when she was making *Roman Holiday*.'[20] The unlikely alliance between the Huddersfield businessman and the performer on the verge of genuine stardom was badly timed. Although Hanson offered the possibility of the financial and personal security which had never been part of Hepburn's life, becoming seriously involved and married to him would inevitably have meant curtailing her career.

Nevertheless, Audrey Hepburn, like Jean Simmons before her, was brought by James to visit Norwood Grange in August and September 1951, so that he could introduce his latest conquest to his immediate family and friends. The futility of the exercise was recognised early on by Audrey's mother, the Baroness, who was determined that her daughter should pursue her acting career and not settle for second-best: the life of a countrywoman in Yorkshire.

It was while Audrey was making a minor Anglo-French film, *Nous Irons à Monte Carlo/Monte Carlo Baby*, that her career breakthrough came. The actress was filming at the baroque Hôtel de Paris in Monte Carlo when she was spotted by the novelist Colette, who was staying as the guest of Prince Rainier. The novelist thought that Hepburn looked ideal for the Broadway adaptation of her work *Gigi*. The producer of the show, Gilbert Miller, agreed: with one leap the obscure, if talented, performer looked set for the top rung on Broadway. Even as the negotiations about her Broadway appearance were going on, the actress tested for and was offered a part in the film *Roman Holiday*, in which she would play opposite Gregory Peck, after

Hanson's old flame Jean Simmons had dropped out. Hepburn's sudden success meant that her blossoming relationship with James Hanson would be more tortuous: the actress now had an almost impossible schedule. *Gigi* opened at the Fulton Theater in New York on 24 November 1951, with some encouraging notices. Brook Atkinson of the *New York Times* wrote of the production: 'Among other things it introduces us to Audrey Hepburn, a young actress of charm, honesty and talent who ought to be interned in America and trapped into appearing in a fine play.'[21] Soon after the opening of *Gigi*, which was playing to packed houses, James Hanson and Audrey Hepburn became engaged on 4 December 1951, with a formal announcement in *The Times*.[22]

The possibility of a marriage between the young star of *Gigi* and one of England's most eligible bachelors had the British newspapers in a great state of excitement. Barely a day passed without pictures of the couple parting or coming together again at an airport, or without some details of the impending Huddersfield wedding. The actress eschewed any wedding while *Gigi* was showing in New York, preferring to wait until after she had fulfilled her commitment to shoot *Roman Holiday*. It was during the filming in Rome, in which the press insisted on linking her romantically with Gregory Peck (a phenomenon Hanson had been through with Jean Simmons), that the couple announced that they would be married at Huddersfield Parish Church on 30 September 1952, followed by a reception at Norwood Grange. The wedding would be squeezed in after the shooting of *Roman Holiday* and before *Gigi* returned to its New York run. More than 200 guests were invited to the wedding reception and Miss Sharman Douglas, the daughter of the former US Ambassador to the Court of St James (and a later escort of James) was picked by Audrey as one of the bridesmaids. However, the filming of *Roman Holiday* stretched beyond the date expected and the increasingly precarious wedding plans had to be postponed, with the couple now promising a New York wedding. Although James and Audrey flew to New York together from Northolt Airport the bride-to-be, with James standing at her side, sounded anything but sure about matrimony plans: 'I have to go to New York for my play *Gigi*, which is going on a four-month tour of America. Then I have film commitments too, it's all so difficult,' she told waiting reporters.[23] Despite Audrey's crowded schedule the besotted James was still convinced that the wedding would take place within three or four months. But the reality was that the relationship was doomed. Just six weeks later the couple formally announced that the engagement was off. James, by now working at the company's Hamilton office in Ontario, described the breakup as a very hard decision, adding: 'Our work is keeping us more and more apart.'

The 351-day engagement was a traumatising experience for Hanson: the wedding postponements, the denial of rifts and the rumoured romance between his fiancée and Gregory Peck all took their toll. In addition Hepburn's mother bitterly opposed the match and Hanson gave the impression of being a rather lovelorn young man, ready to chase his would-be bride from capital to capital. There was undoubtedly genuine affection between the two, with Audrey regularly writing to Hanson and dreaming of flying off to Canada to visit him, whenever possible. But the conflicting pressures on her from her mother, who disparaged the Huddersfield set, and from Hepburn's own screen and stage ambitions meant that it was never a likely match. Hanson was naïve in not recognising this and in allowing the marriage plans to get ahead of the relationship. He also again displayed a need, even though showbusiness talents were not widely appreciated in Huddersfield, to hold the wedding in the place which was least like Hepburn's own Continental background.

In August 1953 Audrey Hepburn was back in London for the British première of *Roman Holiday*. At a party hosted for her by the photographer Cecil Beaton she was introduced to the intelligent actor and writer–director Mel Ferrer who was to become her first husband; this time her career did not interfere with her nuptial plans.

The backwash of James's break-up with Audrey Hepburn, rapidly succeeded by the death of his brother Bill, put a temporary stop to Hanson's galloping social life. But by the following year the tabloids, which had nicknamed him 'Jimmy All Alone', because of his bad luck in love, were relishing his latest date, the Hollywood starlet Terry Moore, who was best known for having been thrown out of Korea after posing for the US troops in a revealing ermine swimsuit. This particular romance was going nowhere but now Hanson, in partnership with his late brother's best friend Gordon White, was becoming a regular feature on the Californian party circuit, partly helped by

White's imaginative decision to set himself up as Hollywood agent and impresario, a rather more exotic occupation than the development of his family printing business in Hull. White escorted a series of actresses in the mid-1950s, including Ava Gardner, Marilyn Monroe and Grace Kelly, and was using his business card to meet even more actresses including Jane Russell. Hanson and White's taste for tall, beautiful women has never moderated. The executive offices of Hanson plc, particularly the mews house behind Harrods, are still famed for employing tall, stunning women.

Gordon White, at the age of 34, seemed more interested in how many women he could date, rather than becoming seriously involved. 'I'm past the dangerous age. A chap who is going to get wedded usually does it before he is 25 years old,' White explained to an interviewer. 'Why should I marry? I don't need anyone to look after me. I've got a good housekeeper to darn my socks, sew on my buttons and cook my meals.'[24] Even at this early stage of the lifelong White–Hanson relationship it was the slightly worldlier White who, though younger and originally an army friend and flat-mate of Bill's, was the creative side of the partnership with James – including finding possible girlfriends for Hanson. After White himself had given up the chase for starlet Beth Rogan, Jimmy Hanson stepped into the breach, sending her a drawing of a chessboard and the message: 'It's your move now.' Later in the same year Gordon White and James Hanson started to date a couple of young American socialites, again met at a Hollywood party, described as peas-in-the-pod twins. White was soon off on other adventures, but James, who still hankered to settle down, had other ideas. One of the twins, Evelyn Diane Bates, heiress to an American publishing family, soon became his regular date. In September 1956 the couple announced their engagement with the intention of a New York marriage in February 1957. By all accounts Eve's parents were less than happy about their future son-in-law's intention to whisk their daughter off to Huddersfield.

Once again, however, Hanson's desire for marriage seemed greater than his ability to sustain a relationship: in November came the formal disclosure that the wedding was off. With the popular press having a field-day, remembering his series of failed romances, Hanson retired hurt to Canada, maintaining a discreet silence about what had happened. Interviewed in Hamilton, where his father Bob Hanson was visiting the business, James sounded thoroughly dejected, as well he might – despite his wealth and his film-star looks, he continued to find it difficult to persuade a young woman to marry him:

> I don't look for this kind of thing. It just seems to happen to me. Eve and I have just decided that we would not be able to make a go of it. I have no social plans for the future. When I get home I shall have a lot of work to do. But I am not through with the idea of marriage. I can't foretell the future.[25]

Despite the rejections Hanson remained in close touch with his former fiancées: entertaining Audrey Hepburn and her husband Mel Ferrer in London, and writing to Eve Bates in New York. Although plainly the constant media attention had not helped, his less than successful social life had become a source of both embarrassment and irritation.

Hanson became determined that when he did finally marry it would be done well away from the spotlight of publicity. It was in New York, soon after the broken engagement with Evelyn Bates, that James first met Geraldine Kaelin, modestly employed as an office worker, a slightly built, dark-haired American divorcée, who close Hanson acquaintances observed bore an uncanny likeness to Audrey Hepburn. A year later, in December 1958, Hanson was in London at St Margaret's, Westminster to be best man at the wedding of his social and now business partner Gordon White to Elizabeth Kalen, the daughter of a Venezuelan diplomat. James, who had generally been quite successful in avoiding the gossip columns after the failure of his last relationship, quipped: 'I don't feel that I have lost a friend, I feel that I have gained an address book.' Among the guests at the London wedding was Geraldine Kaelin and although few of the guests knew it, James and Geraldine had become seriously involved and intended to marry within a few weeks.

On 31 January 1959 James Hanson wrote a private note to the editor of the *Huddersfield Examiner*, J. Stewart Esq., offering him a worldwide exclusive. Hanson revealed that two days later on Monday, 2 February, *The Times* would carry a brief announcement:

The marriage took place on January 17 between Mr James Hanson, son of Mr & Mrs Robert Hanson of Norwood Grange, Huddersfield, Yorkshire, and Miss Geraldine Kaelin, daughter of Mrs S. Kaelin of 240 East 76th Street, New York, United States.

After all the public humiliations Hanson had pulled off a secret wedding and foiled the popular press. Hanson accompanied the announcement with a brief history of the relationship, noting that they had known each other for nearly two years and had seen each other 'frequently' on trips to the United States. After the wedding they would be spending a great deal of time in the US. Geraldine, he disclosed, had been staying in the Huddersfield area since before Christmas as a guest of friends in Kirkheaton. The wealthy businessman stated: 'Now that I am no longer an eligible bachelor I sincerely hope that my name will fade quietly and permanently from the gossip columns!'[26]

This was, of course, the faintest of hopes. The details of the secret wedding at the Upper Agbrigg Register Office, attended only by immediate family and with Gordon White as best man, soon hit the headlines with Hanson admitting that the clandestine plan almost fell apart. 'A few minutes before the wedding took place a man entered the Register Office with some flowers for the marriage room and appeared to recognise me. I managed to think of just the right thing to say to allay any suspicions he may have had,' Hanson recalled.[27] The gossip columnists clearly felt deprived at being left out of one of the social events of 1959 and punished Hanson for it with some garish headlines. 'Gay bachelor Jimmy Hanson weds so quietly' proclaimed the *Daily Express* with a strapline describing Hanson as 'The man with a star studded list of dates'. There was the now familiar reprise, with pictures, of the glamorous women Hanson had dated or been engaged to, from Jean Simmons through to Evelyn Bates.

The marriage was not quite as simple as it appeared from the announcements. His new bride was divorced, with one child, Karen, which partly explains the Register Office wedding at a time when the Church of England was more severe on partners in a broken marriage. So Hanson, who always had declared he wanted a large family, had a ready-made one. His inherited daughter had already been exposed to the delights of riding on the ridges around Huddersfield. On 2 February, with the tabloids mourning the loss of one of their staple bachelors to marriage, Hanson, 36, and his 25-year-old bride flew to Oakville in Ontario, his Canadian residence.

The newly married couple had more homes to start with than most families have in a lifetime. Separate 'At Home' cards dispatched to friends announced no less than four different addresses from 1 February 1959 onwards: Egerton Grove, James's large house – close to his parents' mansion, Norwood Grange – on a ridge overlooking Huddersfield; a generously built home in Oakville, Ontario; an apartment on the east side of Manhattan at 56th Street; and a flat at 2 Wilton Terrace, close to the centre of London at Hyde Park Corner. The residences in New York, Canada, London and Huddersfield reflected the peripatetic business lifestyle which Hanson had adopted, a feature of his conduct which remains as true in the mid-1990s as it was in 1959. 'It will be like this all the time in our married life,' James said. 'London, New York, Hamilton Ontario: we'll have apartments in all three and divide our time between our three countries.'[28] Now that he was married Hanson was even more anxious to keep his name and that of his wife out of the newspapers. Geraldine, a determined woman with a strong sense of self, was not at all enamoured of the condescending way her husband was written about in the popular press. In the first few months after the wedding the couple would travel separately so that Geraldine could avoid having her name dragged through the newspapers. In April Britain's former two most eligible bachelors, Jimmy Hanson and Gordon White, were to be found vacationing at an old haunt on the Côte d'Azur in France. A year earlier Hanson had been on the Riviera in the company of Joan Collins; this time he and White were accompanied by their respective spouses, Geraldine and Elizabeth.

At the age of 37 James was also now anxious for a son who would continue the long Hanson tradition in haulage. There was not long to wait. Robert William Hanson, named after his powerful grandfather Bob and the late showjumper Bill Hanson, arrived on 3 October 1960. With the birth the Hansons moved to a larger flat in Knightsbridge, overlooking Hyde Park. Geraldine determined that the baby would have a nanny with 'a good English accent'[29] and would also go to a British public school. James, taking no chances in the wake of his own less than satisfactory education, put young Robert's name down for three public schools. He eventually was to settle for the most establishment of them all, Eton. The life of the young Hanson heir would be carefully planned so that after a stint at the merchant bank N.M. Rothschild, following university, he would eventually find himself as the director in charge of acquisitions at his father's public company, Hanson plc. On Robert's birth Geraldine Hanson boldly proclaimed that she wanted three or four children. It was not to be. A second son, John Brook, who now works at Hanson Transport in Huddersfield, was adopted by the Hansons soon after his birth in April 1964.

James Hanson's public search for social adventure may have been tempered by his marriage, but his lust for business adventure was just starting. Having managed to extricate himself from the watchful gaze of his father by managing the expansion into North America, James now started to think more broadly about the best way to develop the family businesses and his own personal enterprise. His first business partnership, outside the family, was inevitably with Gordon White, his surrogate brother.

White had a streak of the rebel or buccaneer about him. He had left school at the age of 16, against his father's wishes, and worked as an office boy in a timber company in Hull. When White's wages as timber clerk failed to rise fast enough he left and joined the army. After being commissioned into the Pioneer Corps, he was sent to India where he was recruited by the Special Operations Executive. After the war White joined his family business and set about converting it into a major printing and publishing enterprise.

It was in the late 1950s, when the Hanson–White playboy days appeared to be slipping away, that the two formed their first joint company, Hanson & White, which hit upon the idea of importing humorous American-style greetings cards to Britain. It was a modest but not outstanding success, although it required Gordon to use his best salesmanship, making 200 cold calls a week, to get the enterprise off the ground. The company was eventually sold, at a profit, in the early 1960s. Hanson & White was to prove more durable than other joint enterprises, including Gordon's stint as a Hollywood agent. It is still operating and was sold on to Pentland Industries – the holding company of another entrepreneur, Stephen Rubin – for £5.75 million in 1989. The greetings-card enterprise would have one long-term effect. It meant that when Hanson and White did, eventually, acquire their own public company, the pairing of names – which should have been over the company door – was unavailable. White was not, at the time, prepared to pay the £10,000 which the new owners wanted for the title.

Greetings cards were no more than a sideline for James, who was still deeply embroiled in family businesses on both sides of the Atlantic. Nationalisation had only made old Bob Hanson even more ambitious than in the past. Although one horse, a nine-year-old bay hunter named Wisdom, remained in the Hanson fleet delivering small parcels around Huddersfield, the company had been transformed into a modern, multi-faceted transport enterprise. In 1962 Hanson Haulage opened a new £100,000 freight terminal on the Leeds Road in Huddersfield. The terminal's 400-foot frontage incorporated air, water and electricity lines along the loading deck, as well as the most modern mechanised handling equipment. The Hanson trunk fleet had grown back to more than 420 vehicles; its contract fleet, which now included articulated vehicles, had become among the largest carriers in the country with depots in Huddersfield, London and Southampton. And James, always on the look-out for a more glamorous side to the transport business, wanted a heliport to be included in the new freight depot; the first step towards the eventual creation of Air Hanson, which now services Hanson Group companies. Just to make the point, the guest for the official opening on 11 April 1962, a former Transport Minister, Lord Brabazon of Tara, was flown by helicopter to the new terminal from the Hanson seat at Norwood Grange just three miles away. Brabazon was well known to the Hanson family. He was chairman of ACV, owners of the lorry-building company AEC which had employed the young accountant Jim Slater before he went off to the City to make real money. In his welcoming speech James noted, to some mirth: 'In 1948 we were nationalised and my brother and I went to Canada leaving our father sitting at home waiting for nationalisation to end – although it had started only a few minutes before. It was purely a temporary arrangement as far as he was concerned!'[30]

But James was frustrated with Yorkshire and the overpowering figure of his father watching over his new depot from a suite of offices built above the glass-walled 'traffic control' nerve centre at the company's new headquarters. James was fully aware of the potential in the world of takeovers – he had learnt about that at Bob Hanson's knee. But private companies, which have only limited ability to raise capital, are largely dependent on their bankers for expansion. The key to success in the 1960s, as Jim Slater was demonstrating, was the takeover business. Cash could be generated from such acquisitions by cutting costs, stripping the business down and selling off the parts surplus to requirements. It became known as asset stripping. James Hanson, however, like his father – who had faced the traumas of bankruptcy, two world wars and nationalisation – was more likely to hang on to the productive assets than to sell them. Gordon White persuaded James that the two of them needed to climb aboard this bandwagon. Quoted companies, White argued, could be used to inject other companies, to gear up through borrowing for further takeovers and to issue paper. It was Gordon White's bright idea. But James knew how to execute it because of his business contacts and his ability to negotiate with bankers.

In 1960 Hanson and White cast around for the right vehicle to fulfil their ambitions. They found it right under their noses in the shape of Oswald Tillotson, a loss-making company which had originally come under the business control, but not the full ownership, of the Robert Hanson–Charlie Holdsworth partnership in the 1930s. The haulage business of Tillotson, like other transport companies, had been nationalised in the late 1940s. James Hanson had taken over as chairman in the 1950s and begun to build the company as a dealer in trucks made by AEC – where Jim Slater was commercial director.

Using their 70 per cent stake in Tillotson as a base and armed with a £1 million loan from Lloyds, and with the support of Slater, who had purchased a 12 per cent holding in the Wiles Group, James Hanson and Gordon White embarked on a 30-year takeover adventure which has made them among the most feared partnerships in corporate history. Ironically, however, their introduction to the world of takeovers came when Tillotson's was itself bought out by the Wiles Group, which in turn became the seed of the Hanson empire.

Hanson and White were called in by Barclays Bank in Burnley, where because of Bob Hanson's shrewd negotiating skills, Tillotson's had been able to borrow for years at the rate of 0.5 per cent above base, the same kind of fine credit costs as enjoyed by BP and Shell. However, the Barclays manager indicated that now that Tillotson was part of the publicly quoted Wiles Group the rate would be 2 per cent above base. As the joint loans were sizeable, James and Gordon were directed to a Mr Barclay in the London office to conclude the deal. James Hanson recalls that he and Gordon were put in a small office where they awaited the arrival of Mr Barclay, who showed up in a morning coat. This scion of the banking family refused to be shifted on the cost of the facility, even though Hanson pointed out that Tillotson had been a ghastly mess when his father had rescued it in the 1930s, thereby saving Barclays' bacon.

Hanson walked out of Barclays and strode across Lombard Street in the City to the headquarters of Lloyds Bank, which got the business and has been Hanson plc's main bankers ever since. Indeed, James Hanson would eventually become a main board director at Lloyds, as well as one of its most valuable clients. 'Of course the worst thing which happened was the nice bank manager in Burnley lost his Rover,' James notes wryly. 'Barclays lost out. It took a long time, by the way, to get in with us. But it was Mr Barclay himself.'[31]

Although James Hanson saw his future as running a London-based public concern, buying and selling industrial assets, the haulage company – which was run by his father Bob until his death in 1972 – is still in business as an independent, family-owned enterprise. The company, now known as the Hanson Transport Group, is chaired by Lord Hanson and the shares are closely held through a series of nominee companies based in St Peter Port, Guernsey, according to records at Companies House. Hanson's two sons, Robert and John Brook, joined the board in 1989, after the resignation of their mother, Lady Hanson. The main activity of the group is contract hire with Phillips Petroleum, Staveley Chemicals and, most recently, the House of Fraser among its main customers, along with ICI. In early 1991 the firm ran up a substantial loss of £570,553 after tax, on turnover of £8.8 million after a large surge in administrative costs including the salary bill and leasing. The continued existence of the family company remains something of an enigma, since James has ensured that its activities are kept entirely separate from the public enterprise. At best it has been a useful bolt-hole for family members and retainers who might find it more difficult to find a role in a public company.

Although, from the moment he left to run the Canadian outpost, James Hanson had determined to escape from the restrictions of his patriarchal Huddersfield roots, even in the 1990s the Huddersfield background remains a critical component of his makeup and character – as the continued existence of the family business so powerfully demonstrates.

CHAPTER 4

The Slater Years: 1964–73

When Harold Wilson walked into 10 Downing Street in October 1964 for his first spell as Labour Prime Minister, his contemporary from Huddersfield, James Hanson, was an anonymous director of a company (the Wiles Group) which few business people had heard of beyond its North of England base and the narrow confines of the motor vehicle distribution and agricultural supplies industries. By the time Wilson returned, in February 1974, for his second period at the head of a Labour government, the Wiles Group had become Hanson Trust and James Hanson had become a well-known financier: one of the few of the 1960s tyros not only to have survived but flourished during the economic and financial chaos of the early 1970s. Curiously, Wilson had also become an admirer of this successful businessman, despite the fact that Hanson made no secret of his sympathy and financial support for the Conservative cause.

That James Hanson and the company which now bore his name had prospered where so many others of a similar type had failed was due in part to the deeply ingrained sense of caution of James and his partner, Gordon White, but also to luck. A combination of the two prevented the group from moving too heavily into the riskiest areas, notably the property market. But luck – and politicians – also played an important part, not only in the 1970s survival, but also in the company's phenomenal growth in the later 1970s and early 1980s which would propel James Hanson to the top echelons of the business world on both sides cf the Atlantic. Without what he saw as political ineptitude and weakness in the United Kingdom, Gordon White might never have gone to the United States – the move which was to lift the group out of a rut of mediocrity and set it on the road to stardom.

In their first ten years as public company bosses, Hanson and White had given little indication that they had anything special to offer which would mark out Hanson Trust as any different from a myriad of other small, ambitious but not particularly well-placed public companies. Apart from haulage, they had not built up any deep knowledge or experience of any particular industry, nor were they skilled in any particular aspect of operating industrial enterprises. The only skills they demonstrated in this period were in buying and selling companies – skills which were later to prove remarkably profitable.

They began promisingly enough. A few small acquisitions set up Wiles Group as an interesting little conglomerate. An association with Jim Slater, the financial guru who built up Slater Walker to become a fashionable financial institution in the 1960s and early 1970s, helped bring in deals and put the company on the business map. James Hanson was seen, and projected, as one of the Slater group of young men who were out to transform British industry. But by the early 1970s the deals started to go wrong. As the Slater empire began to crumble, that association became more of a liability than an asset, and Hanson Trust (as it became in 1969) was seriously lacking in credibility. At that time James Hanson was merely another Slater satellite.

The Wiles Group had been launched on to the stock market in March 1964. It was a small agricultural supplier with sales of less than £2 million and with capital employed of less than £500,000. But its chairman, George Wiles, had ambitions for it to become much more than this. In the form of the publicly quoted company's tradable shares, he had the means to achieve that end, and he wasted little time in pursuing it. By the end of its first year of trading as a public company Wiles Group had acquired Oswald Tillotson, Hanson and White's commercial vehicle company, and Commercial Motors (Hull), a similar company run by Jack Brignall. At the end of that first year, in June 1965, George Wiles resigned from the board, along with his long-serving colleagues Sidney Bays, who was Jack Brignall's father in-law, and John Anderson, who had been finance director of the group. James Hanson became chairman and Gordon White joined the board. Derek Rosling, who had been the Hanson family's accountant and who finally retired from formal executive duties at Hanson in 1994, took over the finances and was acting as company secretary. With the annual report for that first year, shareholders received a circular proposing the acquisition of the White family printing and publishing business, Welbecson, in which James Hanson was also a shareholder. The two men were on their way: following the purchase of Welbecson with Wiles Group shares, Hanson and White owned 41 per cent of a public company with significant assets and, perhaps more importantly, the capacity to issue new shares. By the end of 1969 Wiles Group had become Hanson Trust and had made seven major acquisitions and three significant disposals. Its stock market value had grown from barely £2 million in 1965 to more than £12 million and the group's sales had reached almost £50 million.

This astonishing progress had much to do with the stock market boom of the mid-1960s, but was also the product of a series of lucky accidents. Wiles Group was not the sort of company James Hanson and his friend were looking for as they set out to pursue Gordon White's idea (copied from Jim Slater) of takeover-led growth. James Hanson's wife Geraldine was astonished when she was told that the commercial vehicle company which her husband had been running was merging with a hirer of agricultural sacks. The company Tillotson was keen to take over was Jack Brignall's very similar business in Hull, but the Yorkshire business community was a small world in 1964, and Brignall was also being chased by the business of which his father-in-law was a director, the Wiles Group, which was advised by Jim Slater. James Hanson's legendary parsimony with his company's money would not allow him to match the price offered by Wiles, but his eye for a good deal also left him unable to say no when Wiles offered to buy Tillotson as well, at a price which was too good to refuse. It seemed that the two friends were back where they started, though rather better off, looking for a public company vehicle with which to pursue their takeover targets. They agreed to stay on at Wiles for 12 months to ensure that the acquired companies were effectively absorbed, but began casting around for another vehicle, with the aid of Derek Rosling, who had now been tempted from his private accountancy practice and employed in the Hanson family business empire.

But in the summer of 1965, while Rosling was holidaying in Wales, he received a telegram from James Hanson: 'Wiles wants to sell. How much is it worth?' George Wiles was an excitable, volatile character. He was only in his mid-forties, but he had suddenly decided that he did not like being chairman of a publicly quoted company, and declared that he was going off to New Zealand to become a sheep farmer. James Hanson and Gordon White bought him out and suddenly found themselves back in charge of a public company. (Sheep farming did not work out for George Wiles, but he was saved from penury when his brother died and he inherited a chunk of Hanson Trust shares.)

The trio of Hanson, White and Rosling set up their headquarters in Pont Street, Chelsea, which is still associated with the Hanson group, as a base for Lord White when he is in London. It had been bought in 1963 for £5550 by Hanson Transport (the family business, which still owns it) as James Hanson's London headquarters. It was actually two houses knocked into one, in a quiet mews just a short walk from Harrods to the north and Chelsea's fashionable Kings Road to the south. Pont Street was a rather oddly elegant base for a small Yorkshire company which sold trucks, hired out sacks to farmers and did a variety of printing jobs. But it was very suitable for an ex-playboy who was determined to be part of the London business scene rather than a Yorkshire businessman. It was clear in those early days that Hanson had no intention of remaining merely the boss of a motley collection of northern businesses. Pont Street was the base for an embryonic empire. It was a comfortable location from which to plan operations, somewhere to return to in the evening to discuss the day's events and to mull over new ideas. Even when the group outgrew the place as a corporate headquarters, White and Rosling liked to work from there, so that they did not become embroiled in the day-to-day managerial tasks.

This was something which marked out the Wiles Group from most budding business empires: its top managers did not attempt to become involved in the operating units which the group owned.

They remained aloof, with time to think and to concentrate on acquisitions. The interests and objectives of James Hanson and his partners were in acquiring companies, not in running them. That was left to others.

The acquisition trail began with a sale rather than a purchase. In August 1966 they sold the C. Wiles fertiliser business for £400,000. This was the company which had given the group its name. George Wiles had become a partner in the business following the war,[1] when it was a 'knacker' or, in the more refined business terminology, 'an animal by-products business'. In 1949 it began producing granular fertilisers from inorganic chemicals such as nitrogen and potash, and this activity gradually took over during the 1960s. In 1960 the company acquired Frederick Harker, a hirer of sacks to farmers for the storage of grain, and these two businesses constituted the group which became public in 1964.

James Hanson concluded, however, that C. Wiles could not compete on equal terms with the likes of Fisons and ICI. He told shareholders in his second annual report as chairman that the company was too small to compete in purchasing and marketing and it had proved impossible to buy out competitors to address this problem. But Hargreaves Fertilisers had made an offer for C. Wiles, an offer the board could not refuse. The company had contributed profits of £54,000 before tax in the year to June 1966, so the sale price represented roughly 12 times after-tax earnings – an attractive multiple compared to the Wiles Group's own price/earnings ratio of less than ten and an early illustration of the Hanson–White negotiating skills.

In that same annual report, Hanson laid out the group's strategy. Commenting on the sale, and on how the cash would be used, he wrote:

A definite pattern has now emerged in your company's activities. We have faced up to the problem of being too small a unit in the highly competitive world of fertilisers, and we are concentrating on two main fields of endeavour. Wiles Group invests specifically where your directors have personal knowledge and wide management experience. We shall continue to seek expansion in the general areas of transportation and publishing.

It was not long, however, before it became clear that strategy and James Hanson were only loosely acquainted. As has been seen repeatedly over the years, Hanson and White operate opportunistically. True, the first acquisition was just about in the transport field, but it did not take long for Wiles Group to move beyond the two areas which he had identified, and into businesses which the board knew nothing about.

In February 1967 Wiles Group announced the £655,000 acquisition of Scottish Land Development (SLD), which, despite its name, was mainly a dealer in earth-moving and construction equipment, established by the founder of Blackwood Hodge, Niall Hodge, almost thirty years previously. Acknowledging that these activities were barely describable as 'transportation', SLD was inserted into the group as a separate division, rather than being added to the Commercial Vehicle division.

There were subsequent attempts to expand the motor dealerships before the group abandoned that business altogether in 1970, but the next moves were in surprisingly different areas to the supposed targets of transport and publishing. A rash of deals in December 1968 brought in Nathaniel Lloyd, a maker of various kinds of tape, which was bought from Slater Walker. Dufaylite Developments, which produced honeycomb material for the core of mass-produced doors, was also acquired at this time, as was Butterley, the brick company which was to be the only significant long-term survivor of these early deals, eventually forming the core of Hanson Brick. SLD and Dufaylite remained part of the Hanson Group for many years, despite remaining small and insignificant. They were finally sold as part of a management buyout package at the end of 1993.

Also in 1968, however, Wiles paid £2.8 million for West of England Sack Holdings, extending its interests in the sack hire business which was part of the original Wiles Group, but which had appeared to be unattractive and of diminishing interest to the group. It was a classic Hanson operation, which has been repeated time and again over the years. It took advantage of a company in trouble through poor management, in this case because steps had not been taken to rationalise two companies following a merger. And Wiles Group soon recouped some of its outlay through disposals, another classic Hanson move. James Hanson explained the financial logic of the sale:

West of England Sack had bought a company called Marshall Conveyors. The cost had been £1 million, but when Wiles took over, this part of the business was losing £115,000 a year. We might have been able to pull it round in three years or so, but we didn't really have the expertise. So we sold it for a knock-down price of £400,000 to somebody who really understood it. In one move we cut our large losses and got ourselves cash which will earn us £80,000 a year if wisely invested. That is a £195,000 turnaround in profits. In the business world a company is generally valued at around five times its profits, so by this one move we have improved the value of West of England Sack by £1 million – the amount originally invested. [2]

Wiles also recouped substantial sums by closing two offices in Hull and Bristol, and centralising sack administration in Gloucester. Even the Gloucester building helped cash flow, in a sale and leaseback operation. In the annual report for 1967/8 the chairman of the Agricultural Division pointed out another factor which was important in this acquisition and in many others subsequently. The combination of West of England Sack with Frederick Harker gave Wiles 80 per cent of the market for sacks hired for the 1968 cereal harvest. James Hanson would subsequently always be seen to be happiest dominating markets, so that margins cannot be undermined by vigorous competition.

By 1968, the sack hire market was clearly in terminal decline as bulk storage became a more sensible means of dealing with the harvest. But Hanson was not worried about the volume of sacks hired falling year after year. Most businessmen, finding themselves in such a situation, would have sought to arrest the decline or, failing that, to invest in the alternative technology (in this case, bulk storage) or related activities, which would retain their place in the market. This is partly what West of England Sack had done, with the disastrous results already noted in its conveyor business. James Hanson was not like most businessmen, however. He was not trying to build a business, but a portfolio of interests: a conglomerate. It was not important what the individual businesses were; James Hanson was not interested or involved in them. The only thing that mattered was that they contributed to the aggregate earnings growth which was the objective of the enterprise. This lack of interest in the operating activities was to be extremely important in enabling James Hanson to achieve the dramatic growth which was already beginning. The young conglomerateur could take a more detached, financial view of the situation in the sack business than would have been possible for somebody who was committed specifically to that business.

Wiles Group was also helped by the kind of financial approach it had adopted. It was ahead of many of its peers in recognising that return on capital was more important than the absolute level of profits, and in being aware of the importance of cash as well as profits, especially when expansion and growing inflation were requiring additional working capital. West of England Sack was what consultants and business academics came to call a 'cash cow'. It may have been in decline so far as volumes were concerned, but that meant working capital could be reduced, and since it needed no new investment, the business produced strong cash flows from its operations. Cash flow was further helped by the fact that as it contracted, land and building became surplus to requirements, so could be sold to raise yet more cash. So long as falling profits were matched by falling capital invested in the business, the return on capital ratios remained strong. West of England Sack was a classic Hanson deal: quick returns from sell-offs, a dominant market position leading to high margins, low investment requirements leading to strong cash flow.

These deals took place in the fevered atmosphere of the mid-1960s stock market boom. Following a slump in 1966 after Harold Wilson won his second election victory and continued to struggle vainly to resist devaluation, the All-Share index began to rise from a low of 88 points in November 1966 to 180 points by the beginning of 1969, boosted by the eventual devaluation and undeterred by the government's continuing struggle against inflation and the quagmire of industrial relations. These were the years in which Jim Slater built his reputation for supposedly infallible investment, which earned him the soubriquet of 'The Master' among his most adoring followers. The Slater years were a time when financial wheeler-dealing was briefly respectable, and when the new breed of 'conglomerateurs' seemed to offer hope to Britain's battered industry.

The connection with Jim Slater was highly significant in Hanson's early years, and certainly much more important than Lord Hanson has sometimes been prepared to admit. In fact a company called Hanson Trust was sold to Slater Walker in 1968, apparently cementing the fruitful relationship between the two groups, and Slater Walker was for a while formally Hanson's merchant bank and financial adviser. Slater was instrumental in bringing James Hanson and Gordon White to the Wiles Group, and was also important in bringing them some of the early deals. But, largely through his friendship with White, he was also a key force in shaping the Hanson philosophy of opportunist, deal-based, financially centred corporate growth. Despite the huge swing in fashion away from the Slater style and the conglomerate form after the financial crash of 1973–4, James Hanson stuck with the basic premise throughout the difficult 1970s, and benefited in the 1980s when the political and business climate swung to create another 'Slater era'. With Slater long out of the headlines, however, the 1980s acquisition-mad spree could be described as a 'Hanson era', so effective had Hanson become at applying the Slater techniques.

But while the 'Hanson era' and the stock market fever of the 1980s were part of the Thatcher/Lawson free-market Conservative experiment, the Slater era began under Harold Wilson's first Labour government. This surprising conjunction of free-market capitalism with corporatist social democracy was partly a conjunction of anti-establishment forces. Slater Walker had no truck with socialism. Indeed Peter Walker (the 'Walker' of Slater Walker) was an ambitious young Conservative MP, later to hold several Cabinet posts in the 1970s and 1980s, and to be made a peer in 1992. But Jim Slater, like James Hanson, was a young man in a hurry, impatient with what they both saw as the inadequacies of the business and financial establishment. In that respect they had more in common with the Labour Party than with the Conservative government of the early 1960s.

The Labour Party had won power in 1964 promising to modernise Britain, to sweep away the outdated, class-based attitudes to society which remained after 13 years of Conservative government. The Labour Party was committed to social reforms: to better housing, more equal educational opportunities, support for those in need; but it was also committed to more efficient private industry as well as continuing to run nationalised industries and even take more sectors, such as steel and aerospace, into public ownership. Indeed the party believed that more efficient, more profitable private industry was necessary to pay for the social reforms it espoused. Jim Slater must have seemed just the kind of businessman to deliver what Labour needed. He was from fairly humble origins, although his father owned his own building firm, and had limited formal education, having left school at 16. More importantly, he was somebody who had no time for the niceties of establishment practice, who seemed to be in a hurry to clear out old, ineffective managers and to shake up British business.

What is more, the Labour government was convinced that part of Britain's economic problems stemmed from the difficulty UK companies faced when competing against much larger foreign enterprises, especially US multinationals. It therefore espoused a policy of encouraging mergers, formally through the Industrial Reorganisation Corporation, and less formally through a relaxed attitude to the takeover boom of the mid-1960s. Slater Walker's highly active takeover and investment approach was therefore in step with government industrial policy, at least during the first Wilson government from 1964 to 1970. Ironically, it was during the Heath government that Slater's empire began to crack and his practices began seriously to be questioned.

Slater is widely remembered as a financier, because he became best known for Slater Walker Securities and the associated web of unit trust, investment trust and merchant banking activities, and because his downfall, and the crash of his financial empire, was precipitated by the collapse of London property and share prices. But before moving into the financial arena, Jim Slater had been an industrialist. Indeed, had the lure of financial-dealing not been quite so strong he might well have ended up running British Leyland.

Like James Hanson, Slater joined an accountancy firm after leaving school. But unlike Hanson, Slater qualified as an accountant[3] – in 1953, when James Hanson was already busy in Canada and in the nightclubs of London and New York. Almost immediately he moved into industry, first with a private group owned by a Danish businessman, Svend Dohm, then with Park Royal Vehicles, the West London makers of the famous Routemaster London bus. Unlike many chartered accountants, however, Slater did not take long to move out of the accountancy and company secretarial functions. In 1959, three years after joining Park Royal, he was appointed commercial director of the Associated Equipment Company (AEC), a sister company which made the vehicle chassis, and which was an important supplier of Oswald Tillotson – the UK company which James Hanson was then running. It was at this time that he first met James Hanson and Gordon White, who came to see him to negotiate a discount on a large order they were ready to place on behalf of Tillotson. It was a meeting which was to serve both Slater and Hanson well in later years.

When AEC's parent, Associated Commercial Vehicles (ACV), was acquired by Leyland Motors, Slater became commercial manager of the Leyland group, encompassing Standard Triumph cars as well as Leyland, Albion and Scammell trucks and other heavy vehicles. In 1963 he became deputy sales director to Donald (later Lord) Stokes. But while he had effectively become a general manager, with a heavy orientation towards sales, his thinking retained a strong financial element. Indeed finance remained his main interest.

By the early 1960s Slater had become more interested in the workings of the stock market than the car market. At about the same time that the Wiles Group was becoming a public company, Slater was falling prey to the lure of money and leaving Leyland to turn his part-time hobby dabbling in shares into full-time employment. He was not solely concerned with financial wheeler-dealing, however. The original declared intention was to build an industrial empire, and one arm of his fast-growing empire was the Slater Walker Industrial Group (SWIG), which was created to act as a much more involved shareholder than a purely financial investment manager. SWIG was intended to take large shareholdings in companies; this would allow Slater and his colleagues to influence the management of the companies concerned – a kind of hands-on investment banking operation which stopped short of being a conglomerate because SWIG owned only a minority shareholding in the companies whose performance it was trying to improve.

One of the initial private backers of SWIG, in addition to eminent City banks such as Schroders and Lazards, was George Wiles, who invested in SWIG £300,000[4] of the money he had made when his company went public, through a private investment trust he set up jointly with Slater. Wiles's brother, Leonard, was another Slater client, as was Jack Brignall.

SWIG itself soon gave way to its publicly quoted parent, as Slater realised the benefit of making purchases with shares rather than cash. But one way or another the group set about making a rapid series of investments in industrial companies, which mounted in a crescendo in 1968. During 1967 and 1968 Slater Walker conducted a series of deals that grew in size along with its own soaring share price – which itself allowed the deals to be made. Acquisitions in those two years included the rubber company Greengate & Irwell, a tape maker, Nathaniel Lloyd, window maker Crittal-Hope, and Drages, a holding company owned by Sir Isaac Wolfson of Great Universal Stores – Slater's biggest deal so far at £34 million.

In the summer of 1968 Slater also made a curious investment in a smaller conglomerate: the Wiles Group. Slater Walker became a significant shareholder – the only one apart from the directors to own more than the 10 per cent which at that time was the limit above which disclosure was required. Slater explained the deal as 'a complicated £5.5 million share exchange whereby we acquired a 15 per cent shareholding in Wiles Group and £2.5 million in cash'.[5] He said the deal 'consolidated the already strong business links between James Hanson and myself'. In the Wiles Group accounts the Slater Walker share stake was revealed, but no reference was made to what the Wiles Group received in exchange for the £5.5 million shares and cash. Detailed reading of the accounts around that period reveals that Slater Walker had bought the private company, called Hanson Trust Company Ltd, through which Hanson and White (and White's brother Bernard) owned their 2.3 million share stake in Wiles Group, representing 28 per cent of the shares. Part of the complication was that Hanson and White bought back from Slater Walker half their shareholding in Wiles, then sold some of those shares, so that James Hanson's stake fell below 1 million shares for the first time, representing just 11 per cent of the shares in issue. The remainder of the share exchange was never disclosed.

In fact it was shares in Slater Walker, which were then sold in the stock market, and this deal was largely a tax-driven transaction. Hanson Trust Company had been set up in 1964 to become the vehicle for the Hanson–White expansion plans, after Wiles Group had bought Tillotson, and when it was intended that James Hanson and Gordon White would stay only temporarily. But the introduction of capital gains tax by the new Labour government had destroyed its tax-effectiveness. The deal with Slater enabled them to crystallise gains efficiently – effectively Slater took the tax liability, which he was able to offset elsewhere within his empire.

Wiles Group, soon to become Hanson Trust, had become one of Slater's 'satellites'. These were the collection of associated groups, sometimes run by independent entrepreneurs like Hanson, sometimes by Slater's former lieutenants, the most famous of whom were John Bentley and Malcolm Horsman. (Horsman was to figure significantly in Hanson's affairs during the 1970s.) For Slater, the satellites were ostensibly a means of retaining an association with some of his more impatient young managers, who were eager to create their own empires. Perhaps more importantly, they gave Slater Walker greater flexibility, stretching the web further, since they too had their own share quotations and financial resources, thus spreading the empire's financial capability. Sometimes the satellites also came in handy for offloading businesses which Slater Walker no longer wished to keep. For example, at the end of 1968 Wiles Group issued almost 330,000 shares to Slater Walker in payment for Nathaniel Lloyd.

Jim Slater was even instrumental in the renaming of the group in 1969. 'Wiles Group' made less sense once George Wiles had left, C. Wiles had been sold, and the sack hire business had been overtaken in importance by truck sales and the heavy equipment of SLD. Slater was keen that a change of name should incorporate the two key founders. But the obvious solution, 'Hanson White Ltd', raised an objection from John Millar, the sales manager who had bought the Hanson and White greetings card business from the duo. Mr Millar was prepared to sell the name, but only for £10,000. Gordon White was outraged, so the name of the group had to be just Hanson. Lord Hanson likes to joke that the two men tossed a coin and he lost, but there could have been no doubt about whose name would be chosen. James Hanson was, after all, the chairman and the largest shareholder. He was the well-established businessman, with solid society connections. Gordon White, on the other hand, was at that time little more than a salesman, a fun-loving entrepreneur who, as he once admitted, had always been a playboy at heart[6] and could well have given the whole thing up to concentrate on having fun (as he very nearly did in 1973). James Hanson had been through the playboy era; now he was married with two children of his own, as well as his step-daughter Karen, and he was intent on replicating his father's business success. 'Hanson' it had to be, with Trust added because at that time it was intended to create a web of shareholdings similar to the Slater model.

The Slater link became even stronger. In his report on 1970, Hanson told shareholders that Slater Walker had become the group's financial advisers and merchant bankers, strengthening what he described as 'a long personal and business relationship'. Slater Walker subsequently handled some of Hanson's takeover work, but as part of Slater's move into banking and away from conglomeracy, its 20 per cent shareholding in Hanson Trust was reduced by placing the shares with Slater clients. The rump of the holding was later placed in the poorly regarded Dual Trust, and eventually bought back by James Hanson.

Slater only briefly attempted to build a true industrial conglomerate. He was always heavily involved in purely financial activities: share dealing, investment advice, insurance and property; and by 1970 he was moving towards becoming an investment bank rather than an industrial conglomerate. But James Hanson and Gordon White learned several important lessons from Slater's conglomerate phase, as well as benefiting for a while from an association with the man and the company which for several years in the late 1960s and early 1970s were widely regarded as the most able and most promising in Britain.

The Slater experience had shown how conglomeracy could be made to work in the right circumstances. He had shown that, in many ways, it is easier to please the stock market as a conglomerate than as a more focused company. Crucially a true conglomerate has no interest, other than financial, in the activities or industries in which its subsidiaries operate. This is one of the factors which subsequently made Hanson Trust so successful, while others fell by the wayside. Slater's approach, copied by Hanson, was to buy companies or to make investments on purely financial grounds, just as when buying shares as a private investor. The judgement was made on an assessment of the financial return which might be gained, based on relatively short-term, tactical investment considerations, not on the basis of any fundamental assessment of a company's potential in the markets in which it operated, nor with any intention in most cases to create any operating links between various acquisitions. This contrasts with most conventional business people, who are interested in their industries and committed to the success of the companies they run.

There are several benefits of this 'disinterested' approach. Most obviously, it avoids the need to build existing businesses in order to generate extra profit. Instead, extra profit is acquired, and (as shown in detail in Chapter 9) sometimes 'created' simply by the takeover process. Building a conglomerate also avoids many of the hazards of creating a group of related companies by acquisition or merger. As Slater had seen when ACV was acquired by Leyland Motors, and subsequently with the merger of Leyland and British Motor Corporation, putting two companies together creates all manner of problems: the personal jealousies and ambitions of individual managers, clashes between overlapping product lines, the physical difficulties of co-ordinating or merging production and distribution. When a conglomerate like Hanson buys a new company, on the other hand, none of this is necessary. The new subsidiary usually continues to operate on its own, as it has always done, with little or no reference to other trading members of the group.

The parallel with investing in shares also applies to selling. If a share turns out to perform rather less well than had been expected, or if its prospects suddenly seem about to turn sour, or if a decent offer comes along, a natural solution is to sell the shares and invest the cash in something more promising. Disinterested conglomerates adopt the same approach with companies. If an acquisition turns out not to have been as perceptive as it seemed at the time the deal was done, or indeed if an existing company falls on hard times, the company can simply be sold. Of course any group can do this: even a highly focused business sometimes sells or closes poorly performing subsidiaries. But it is much harder for managers to take such decisions if they are deeply committed to the business they are in, especially if they see some improvement in a few years' time, and harder to justify to shareholders than in a conglomerate which is committed to no particular business.

The conglomerate approach also offers, in addition to the usual business opportunities for making profits, the money-making potential of the market trader: the potential to buy cheap and to sell dear. This is profitable whether the commodity in question is potatoes, shares or companies, although conglomerates have the advantage, like buyers of mixed bags of produce, of being able to split a purchase and make a profit on a sale of just part of what has been acquired. It creates profit for the shareholders, but at the expense of the shareholders who sold the original group, or the company and shareholders who are now buying at an excessive price. As shown in Chapter 10, there is very little evidence, in Hanson's experience or elsewhere, that this kind of activity has the positive effect on managers and companies, by liberating them from the bureaucracy of the parent group, which its supporters, including Lord Hanson, have always claimed. It has nevertheless been highly profitable for Lord Hanson, and has explained a huge part of the growth of his company.

Market trading, whether in greengrocery or companies, requires the resources to buy at the right time, plus the good luck or the skill to spot which items are 'cheap'. So far as public companies are concerned, cheapness refers to the relationship between their share price and their underlying value. There are broadly two ways in which a company can be valued, and therefore two ways in which it can be 'cheap', or undervalued by the stock market: on the basis of assets (the tangible possessions such as land, buildings and equipment); or on the basis of expected future earnings. Slater became famous for spotting what he described as 'asset situations': companies whose asset values were not reflected in their share prices. The subsequent profitable sale of such assets became known as 'asset stripping' and was one of the practices, especially in the hands of Slater's apprentice John Bentley, which gave conglomerates a bad name. Hanson has not engaged in asset stripping, but he has nevertheless made substantial profits over the years from selling superfluous assets out of groups which he has acquired – notably head office buildings. Slater also attempted to find companies whose future earnings potential was similarly unrecognised by stock market traders, although in this he was not nearly so successful as in finding asset situations. And while Gordon White has a reputation for much greater success in this aspect of the conglomerate game, he too has been far from infallible. But he has been skilled in finding value where others have seen none, and avoiding unpromising companies which some other conglomerateurs thought made promising targets.

This 'market-trading' aspect of conglomeracy, while frowned upon by those who feel that business should be about improving underlying operating performance by boosting productivity, developing new products and entering new markets, can at least be described as the legitimate form of profit-making for this kind of company. Asset stripping, unpalatable though it may have been, did generate real profits. The accounting methods which benefited Slater, Hanson and all other acquisitive companies, and which were perfectly legitimate under accounting rules, created improvements in the company's performance on paper which were not reflected in any way by the underlying financial position.

In assembling unrelated businesses, conglomerates lose one of the potential benefits of the business-builder approach: economies of scale. In buying, production, marketing, research and development and finance, economies are at least potentially available to a group which builds a business in one area, or a group of companies in related areas which operate in a co-ordinated fashion. Sometimes those economies are not realised, or are overwhelmed by the additional costs of co-ordination, planning and simply keeping the various parts of the group on the same track. Even where they are realised, however, such operational benefits are frequently hugely over-whelmed by the financial gains which can be made from the wheeler-dealing aspects of conglomerate trading.

In the early days of the group James Hanson was keen to explain his approach to running the company. He was also given the opportunity, outside of the annual report, because the early deals, together with the Slater association, brought Wiles Group plenty of publicity during 1967 and 1968 – the two peak years of Slater's acquisition spree when the stock market was booming and was in love with conglomerates such as Slater Walker and its satellites such as Wiles Group. Hanson seems to have been torn between milking the connection with 'The Master' for all it was worth while the City was so clearly smitten with Slater, and trying to mark out a distinctive position. But he had learned from Slater the usefulness of the free publicity available by courting the press, and the ease with which it was possible to exaggerate a company's prospects. One diarist, rather optimistically, commented that James Hanson was a year behind Jim Slater in terms of profits, but 'armed with an ambition to keep at level pegging, plans to take some of the takeover bites that might be a bit small for his old friend and new business partner'.[7] In fact, Slater Walker's profits for 1969 were £10 million, a level not reached by Hanson until 1974, and then only with the help of the rapid inflation of the early 1970s. In the same article, James Hanson was reported to be contemplating several of the corporate tricks of his new associate: creating a satellite to handle some smaller bids, and spinning off some subsidiaries once they were big enough to be separately quoted companies. Hanson was also quoted as being ready to contemplate a £20 million takeover, although in fact he did not achieve that in the United Kingdom, even in nominal terms, until the acquisition of Lindustries in 1979. In real terms, adjusting for inflation, the controversial purchase of Berec in 1982 was the first to reach that scale. In fact, none of the other manoeuvres forecast in the article came to anything, but the plans made good publicity, helping to maintain investor interest in the company and so to sustain the share price. It turned out that it was not as easy as it sounded to have a network of 'nursery' investments. Each such investment needed monitoring, and usually needed a Hanson representative on the board. But there were few enough people at the Hanson centre, and certainly not enough to go round all these companies and still make a useful contribution to the direction of the company. The idea was quickly abandoned.

Despite these strengthening links, however, and while benefiting from the publicity, Hanson was keen to express a distinctive approach which was different from Slater's. James Hanson explained how he thought Wiles differed from other conglomerates, or 'industrial holding companies' as they were formally described. At this distance his answer is amusing, given his company's subsequent record of managing diversified companies. It illustrates either his limited ambition at the time, or, more plausibly, an understanding that investing fashions were changing away from conglomeracy:

> We do not believe in the concept of trying to manage a great
> number of diversified companies, often hastily put together . . .
> We feel that if we stick to certain specialised lines we shall avoid
> the normal holding company troubles – and by specialised lines I
> mean those activities about which we know a great deal.[8]

Hanson frequently took the opportunity to explain his business
philosophy in his annual report to shareholders, although, as shown
later, he also frequently omitted comment on significant transactions
which had happened during the year. In 1967 he introduced
shareholders to the concept of 'free form management' – relative
autonomy for divisions, free from interference from group directors,
although at that stage he still talked about the group board co-
ordinating these autonomous divisions. It was a concept which was
30 years ahead of its time, and which in the 1990s came to be
described as 'delayering', 'flattening the organisation', 'shortening
lines of communication' and similar expressions. But in fact it was
born of James Hanson's experience in the relatively small family
business. While the business had prospered, money had not been
splashed around. As in most such concerns, the proprietors –
including James – would have been very conscious that every penny
spent was a penny out of their own pockets. Unnecessary managerial
or supervisory posts were therefore avoided at all costs. Furthermore,
given the nature of the transport business, with a series of depots
around the country, it would have been very difficult to maintain
detailed control of operations. Depot managers had to be left to get on
with their jobs, subject to the usual financial disciplines. An early
associate who was instrumental in helping to set up financial control
and incentive schemes in the Wiles Group commented that the small
business, pre-war philosophy marked out the Hanson approach from
others at the time:

> The idea grew from wartime experience that businesses needed
> an army of staff posts and a hierarchy, so companies ended up
> with an array of worthy people who were not doing anything
> useful. Hanson's was the small business approach, keeping
> everything tight, especially cash. It took a lot of nerve to do it,

when the conventional wisdom was that you needed an army of accountants and managers to run companies.[9]

A fuller explanation of the Hanson philosophy was provided in the 1968 annual report:

> We have created a clear distinction in Wiles Group between responsibility for strategy, which is assumed by the parent company board, and for the efficient conduct of operations, which is assumed by the chairmen of the divisions. This is in line with our management concept for success, to which your board has given very detailed study, in consultation with outside experts . . . Our method of operation lies in using the most up-to-date systems of management structure and control. Strict financial supervision is instituted by Wiles Group to ensure prompt implementation of sound business methods, but individual management is given maximum opportunity to act on its own . . . In order to encourage corporate growth and increased profits, management must be left – and motivated – to get on with that job. This leaves the parent board a number of vital functions: to plan favourable financing arrangements and a sound management framework; to be concerned with profit motivation at all levels; to plan strategy and represent your interests in the widest sense.

The message was rammed home again in 1970 as Hanson referred to 'a real understanding of the dynamics of growth', and stressed that divisional management autonomy was subject to control through strategic plans, capital and operating budgets. He claimed that this marked out Hanson Trust as more than merely an acquirer, and justified the description as 'a financially-oriented industrial management company'. While much of this was merely public relations, James Hanson and Derek Rosling, aided by outsiders such as London Business School professor Tony Merrett and consultant George Cyriax, had created a structure and an approach which was quite different from most of British business, including the new entrepreneurs of the 1960s. Acquisitions were restricted to what became known as 'basic industries', with low technology and limited volatility in markets, and it was possible for these to be run on purely financial lines and monitored adequately by remote accountants. The remoteness of central management, and their refusal to get involved in detailed decisions about operating unit performance, could only work if the managers running the operating units performed well enough. That depended partly on finding good people and putting them in the right positions – one of James Hanson's skills – but it also depended on their being motivated to produce the earnings and cash which were the raw materials for the central team to continue building the empire.

Incentive schemes which push managers in the required direction are notoriously difficult to invent, but the Wiles Group managed to create a system which has continued to be effective for decades. The key factor was the link to the group as a whole, by awarding the incentive in the form of shares in the group. The central notion has remained that operating managers should be rewarded in the shares of the group, for performance which furthers the standing of the group. There was a time when this notion was not adhered to rigidly, for example in several cases subsidiaries were not wholly owned and were separately quoted companies, in which case their managers received incentives in the form of shares in those separate companies. That was a copy of the Slater approach but it was eventually recognised to be a mistake because of the inevitable conflict of interest for the managers concerned between the share price of their own company and that of Hanson Trust.

In 1970 Slater Walker shares did not do very well and by 1972 serious doubts about the company's financial methods were aired in the financial press. As Slater fell out of fashion, Hanson distanced himself further and further, and has sometimes denied that there was ever any formal link between the two companies. The need to play down the Slater connection was clear: doubts were growing about Slater's skills, about Slater Walker's prospects, and about Hanson's abilities if cut off from 'The Master'. As one commentator observed at the beginning of 1970: 'whether Mr Hanson can regain the limelight will depend on proof that he can step out of the shadow of others and stand or fall on his own abilities.'[10] There were clearly differences of approach. James Hanson was never tempted into Slater's favourite area of investment advice, which led Slater into unit trusts and eventually investment banking. In that respect, Hanson Trust was much less of a creature of the City and based much more in industry (and agriculture) than was Slater Walker. But Hanson Trust could never be depicted as a group which depended on its performance at operating company level. As shown by the sale of C. Wiles and the West of England Sack deals, profits from trading in companies and assets were important from the earliest days of the group. Nor was James Hanson entirely devoted to the mainstream manufacturing and service activities, as he claimed. While he did eschew financial services at this time, he was tempted, like Slater, by the property market.

In 1970, Hanson Trust bought a 51 per cent shareholding in a property development company, City & St James. Even before the property boom of the early 1970s, Hanson had made a handsome profit on the sale of office buildings from West of England Sack and from the head office of motor distributor Jack Olding (acquired in 1969). As for many another entrepreneur, it must have seemed much easier to make money from property than from manufacturing, especially as the early promise of the free-market 'stand-on-your-own-two feet' Conservative government disappeared in the familiar mist of industrial disputes, rising inflation and balance of payment problems. Over the next couple of years £10 million was invested, mostly in London, in blocks of flats and offices, and James Hanson's enthusiasm for this new venture mounted rapidly. 'We are actively in the market to purchase more property,' he told shareholders in the report on 1970/71. In the following year property operations contributed £1.3 million of the £5.2 million trading profits, more than any other division except the expanding brick operations. The boom was short-lived, however, as the monetary explosion unleashed after the government's economic policy U-turn ran into the mayhem caused by the first oil price crisis in 1973 and the industrial unrest at the tail end of the Heath government. By the time Harold Wilson came to power again in February 1974 the property boom was over. Hanson's investment was being wound down and property profits in 1973/4 had stalled at £1.3 million, while the total for the group had grown to almost £10 million. In the following year property profits had virtually disappeared and nothing more was heard of this supposedly lucrative diversion. It was yet another example of James Hanson's opportunism, which always got the better of whatever strategy his company was supposedly following at the time. But Hanson Trust avoided the fate of many other entrepreneurs whose empires were smashed because of their dependence on property values. And for that they can be thankful largely to Gordon White's prescience and pessimism: 'I insisted we got out of property. You'd see a property sold one day for £1 million, a week later for £1.5 million, two weeks later for £3 million . . . and suddenly you realised that the world had gone mad.'[11] The group survived intact, but property was one of several dead-ends in the early 1970s.

By this stage, however, the Hanson style had been established, and the group's management team, which would take it to the very top of the business tree, was largely in place. Most of the original Wiles Group board left once Tillotson and Commercial Motors (Hull) had been absorbed. The sale of the fertiliser company C. Wiles accounted for the last of the original managers: Bryan Boston-Smith. Jack Brignall, founder of the Hull motor company, had become a director, as had Gordon White's brother Bernard when Welbecson was acquired. Kenneth Osborne, managing director of SLD, had also joined the board. James Hanson also recruited Peter Lorne, a former chairman of advertising agency McCann-Ericson. They joined Hanson and White on the board. One other director from the original Wiles Group board remained, however: John Pattisson, a City financier who had joined the board when the group he worked for (Industrial Finance and Investment Corporation, owner of small merchant bank Dawnay Day) had first injected some capital into the company in 1960. He gave the *ingénus* from Yorkshire first-hand City experience to help them handle the coming flood of acquisitions and disposals. Like many of the other early associates, he has remained on or close to the Hanson board ever since.

The new board did not have long to settle down. In 1967 the directors responsible for operating companies 'retired from the board to devote themselves completely to their divisional responsibilities', as Hanson put it in the annual report that year. Mr Lorne, lauded on his appointment only the year previously as 'a leading international authority on marketing techniques', also left – the first of a series of such 'non-executive', expert directors to have only a brief association with the group. This left a board consisting of just Hanson, White and Pattisson, but they were supplemented in 1969 by Derek Rosling, who had been company secretary since 1967, although continuing to be paid and employed for some time by the private family interests. This quartet saw Hanson through to the mid-1970s, when for a few years they were joined by Douglas Oliphant, who had briefly been financial controller before taking charge of Northern Amalgamated Industries – the hotch-potch of industrial manufacturing companies which became the Industrial Services Division. Oliphant's replacement as financial controller was Brian Hellings, who became a director in 1974 and was primarily responsible for creating the financial control systems which enabled the central management team to maintain their fierce grip on the operating units. Hellings appointed a deputy in 1970: Peter Harper, who did not become a director until 1990 although as early as 1976 he was made an associate director (a peculiar Hanson concept which gives status to senior managers without actually putting them on the board). When Harper went off to run the Construction Equipment Division in 1972, he was replaced as deputy financial controller by Derek Bonham – the man designated in 1993 to take over from Lord Hanson as chairman of the group. Several other key figures joined around this time. Martin Taylor, a company spokesman famed for his stonewalling skills since the early 1970s, took over from Derek Rosling as company secretary in 1969, and handed over two years later to Tony Alexander, the UK chief operating officer who was passed over for the top job in 1992 in favour of Bonham. Also in 1969, Alan Hagdrup joined as solicitor, becoming a director in 1975 and remaining on the board until 1991.

This is a remarkable record of longevity, which testifies to the loyalty inspired by James Hanson but also suggests a worrying level of introspection, a self-reinforcing culture immune to changing standards, for example, of corporate governance. It, too, suggests a subservience of most of the board to Lord Hanson, especially given the absence of powerful non-executives to bring an outside perspective. Of the UK executive directors who were on the board in 1991, only one joined the group later than 1973 – and that was Christopher Collins, James Hanson's nephew by virtue of marriage to his sister's daughter.

*

The team was in place by 1973, and the philosophy of the group was also quite clear. But unfortunately for James Hanson, conditions turned against him, just as they turned against Edward Heath and his government. Wiles Group had done well under Harold Wilson's first Labour government. Indeed, it was the only government the group had known, apart from the last few, directionless months under Sir Alec Douglas Home in the summer of 1964 – the first months of the Wiles Group as a public company. Devaluation did not have a significant impact, since operations were almost entirely within the United Kingdom. (The Canadian companies were part of the family business, not Hanson Trust.) Exports in 1970 were a mere £982,000, out of total sales amounting to more than £47 million. The only overseas operations were those of Henry Sykes Pumps, part of the SLD acquisition, which had a business in Australia and some rental outlets in the United States. The credit squeeze of 1966–67 did not help the motor distribution businesses, but most of the group's interests at that time were in commercial rather than private vehicles, so the impact was not enormous, and was countered by a previous shortage of products, which had resulted in a pent-up demand.

The stock market boom of 1967–68 had certainly been beneficial, especially for Hanson shareholders, both directly and indirectly. Directly, the share price soared, increasing almost tenfold from a low point in 1966 to highs in 1968 and early 1969. That was despite the issue of 3 million new shares to pay for acquisitions and a further rights issue of 600,000 shares to raise cash, which increased the number of shares in issue by more than 80 per cent. Even with this increased number of shares, dividends had also risen, from just over 10 per cent in 1967 to 17.5 per cent in 1970. Indirectly, the stock market boom had enabled Hanson to issue all these shares profitably to make the acquisitions which shot it to prominence and moved it rapidly up the company league table. At one point in 1968, at the peak of the boom, the share price represented 50 times the previous year's earnings, guaranteeing that the takeovers would pay off, since the highly priced shares ensured that the acquisitions would add to the group's earnings per share.

The growth of these early years left Hanson Trust as a sizeable company, well up in the Times 500 listing. In 1970, as Edward Heath began trying to implement his tough, free-market philosophy,

Hanson reported sales of £47 million and capital employed of almost £8 million. The group employed almost 5000 people. With the political atmosphere having shifted to one which could be expected to be even more favourable to the kind of rampant capitalism that Hanson and his peers had pursued with such great effect under Labour, it seemed that there was no limit to what could be achieved in the 1970s. The outcome was very different, however, and the performance of the Heath government so far removed from what Gordon White, in particular, had hoped for, that it almost led to the break-up of the magical partnership between him and James Hanson.

The stock market crash of 1973–74, which saw the share index plummet at one point to its lowest point since the war, was bad news for any acquisitive company which relied on an inflated share price to finance the acquisitions which fed that share price and so allowed the acquisitive growth to continue. At the end of 1973, Hanson shares were trading at under 100p, only six times earnings, and the price slipped further to about 50p, barely three times earnings, by the end of the following year. Had the group contained any really attractive businesses, Hanson itself might well have fallen victim to takeover. But even before these debilitating circumstances arose, Hanson Trust had lost any direction it might have had in the 1960s, and the chairman himself seemed to have lost some of his interest in the company which was now named after him. He dissipated his energies in a variety of ventures both for the company, including helicopters (setting up Air Hanson in 1973), and privately, in television and other manufacturing companies.

James Hanson had been one of the backers of Yorkshire Television when it won the ITV franchise in 1968. As well as being a normal financial investment, the association was part of James Hanson's cultivation of the persona of a 'professional Yorkshireman', as one associate from those days put it. In 1970, Yorkshire merged with its smaller neighbour Tyne-Tees Television, and a new company, Trident, was formed (the name is explained by the fact that Anglia was also supposed to join the new venture, but pulled out at the last minute). Trident needed a non-executive chairman, preferably somebody more useful than the kind of local dignitary who had been chair of Yorkshire. James Hanson was the obvious choice: he was the company's largest shareholder, he was a local boy who had made it in the big time, and he had useful connections in the City, which could come in handy if Trident wanted to extend its interests. Typically, James Hanson was clear that was what the company should do. 'If you have a big stake in television you're going to see good times and bad, so there is a need for additional revenue,' he told the advertising industry magazine *Campaign*.[12] Such expansion did not come, however, and James Hanson remained chairman for only a couple of years, although he remained on the board and returned briefly to the chair to oversee the sale of the group to Pleasurama in 1985.

Trident was not the only foray back into Yorkshire during this period although, unlike the television involvement, what began as a personal interest in two engineering companies quickly came to involve Hanson Trust as well. In March 1972 Hanson picked up a block of shares in a small window-making company, Heywood Williams, and bought 16 per cent of the shares of BHD Engineers. The shares were acquired on behalf of the Hanson family interests, not Hanson Trust.

These two investments illustrate the way in which James Hanson was relaxed about distinguishing between his private interests and the public company of which he was chairman, a weakness which influenced his running of the Hanson board and brought criticisms in the 1990s. BHD was a collection of engineering companies, the most significant of which was Holset Engineering, based in Huddersfield, which made turbochargers, vibration dampers and fan drives for the automotive industry, as well as general engineering products. Hanson joined the board of BHD in March 1972, shortly after buying the share stake. And in September he added the chair of BHD to his public company portfolio. Mr Hanson could not take part in discussions on what must have been the main item on the agenda of his first meeting in that position, because of a conflict of interest: directors had to consider the question of takeover talks with Hanson Trust. In December an agreed deal was announced, with Hanson Trust paying £12 million.

As so often with Hanson Trust in this period, observers were left wondering what the group was up to now. Was this the new direction the group had been searching for? Engineering was certainly not the kind of business which Hanson had ever seemed keen on in the past, but the offer document to BHD shareholders spoke of BHD becoming 'a substantial engineering division' within Hanson. BHD deputy chairman, P.J.F. Croset, told shareholders that the directors had received satisfactory assurances from Hanson that the businesses of BHD would continue to operate autonomously under its present management. In keeping with that expectation, Mr Croset joined the board of Hanson Trust – but not for long. It may have been James Hanson's intention at the time to create an engineering empire, but, ever the opportunist, the bulk of BHD was sold on within nine months. Two of BHD's five operating companies were sold to US firms, for £13 million in cash, leaving a sizeable profit on the original purchase price. This episode emphasised that opportunism was the dominant force in Hanson Trust's development, regardless of what James Hanson might say about strategy and about the logic of the group's interests. It also left Hanson personally with a hefty profit of £200,000 on his £643,000 investment in BHD shares, while other Hanson Trust directors also profited from the deal.

These diversions in the early 1970s did not prevent Hanson Trust from continuing, or trying to continue, along the acquisition trail, which took the group once again into new areas. The 1970s began with the abandonment of what had previously been the group's main business stream – motors. Through Oswald Tillotson and Commercial Motors (Hull) – the two companies which had effectively taken over Wiles Group in 1964 – the group had a sound base in vehicle distribution. SLD added to this the heavy equipment business, while the purchase of Provincial Traction and Jack Olding in 1969 took this a stage further. It was enough to justify Hanson's claim that 'transportation' was one of its main activities, although by 1970 it had been overtaken in profit terms by the loose collection of companies described by Hanson as 'Industrial Services', including Butterley, the pump distribution business of SLD, and Dufaylite.

The sale of the transport interests that had been Hanson's heritage came only after trying to expand the division further, which resulted in Hanson's first contested takeover bid – and its first defeat. Early in May 1970, Hanson Trust stepped in as what would later come to be termed a 'white knight' when the Lex Service Group made an unwelcome offer for Steels Garages, a vehicle distributor in the South-West of England. Steels was not impressed by the approach from Lex, but agreed an alternative, higher, bid from Hanson. Rather than returning with a higher offer, Lex surprisingly withdrew. But not for long. Two weeks later the company was back, not only with a bid for Steels, but having agreed to buy Hanson Trust's vehicle interests as well. So in one bound, Hanson Trust had reversed its strategy, abandoned its main activity, but also transformed its liquidity. It received a total of £4.5 million from Lex. It was another piece of luck: being out of motor sales was no bad thing in the difficult mid-1970s, and the cash began a period of liquidity which accidentally survived for several years, and helped the group through the financial chaos of that period. If James Hanson had not been thwarted in this and various other deals, he may well have struggled with excessive debts as interest rates rose, a position which was fatal for some other 1960s stars. Instead, defeat brought cash, which helped Hanson Trust through.

Amazingly, despite this abrupt reversal, and despite the fact that transport was both James Hanson's heritage and a key part of the group since 1964, the decision merited only passing reference in the annual report, in the context of the cash raised from the sale. Otherwise, the chairman used his statement to laud the prospects for property development. Property also came to nought over the next few years, and so did most of Hanson's other efforts to make that £20 million deal and to leap into the UK's top 100 companies. The only real success was the expansion of the brick business, interestingly by the acquisition of brickworks from the then nationalised British Steel and the National Coal Board, in an early example of Hanson's involvement in a muted form of privatisation. Expansion of brick interests also saw Hanson's first success in a contested takeover bid, for the Newport-based company, National Star Brick and Tile Holdings. Hanson's first bid, handled by Slater Walker as merchant banker in November of 1970, offered loan stock worth only £800,000, and was rejected by National Star. The bid attracted a rival offer from the bigger brickmaker, Ibstock Johnsen, and after both companies had increased their offers, National Star finally accepted Hanson's rather more generous terms, including a large element of cash, which valued the target company at £1.4 million. It was a small victory, but – astonishingly, given the group's reputation for invincibility by the mid-1980s – the only victory in a contested takeover which James Hanson was to have until the end of the 1970s.

This was a relatively small move, however. James Hanson's ambitions had grown well beyond this level of operation by now. He and Gordon White had their sights set on much more prominent acquisitions, not just on a national, but an international scale. Encouraged by their initial ventures in the property field, attracted by the possibility of supporting the group's heady profits with some rather more solid assets and businesses, and seeing a way of internationalising his company at a stroke, James Hanson's next move was a bold attempt to merge the company with Richard Costain, the builder and contractor. The move was encouraged by Jim Slater. Slater Walker had picked up a 10 per cent share stake in Costain from Trafalgar House. Trafalgar's Nigel Broakes was another of the 1960s conglomerateurs and friend of Jim Slater, and had been busy building a property and construction group through the acquisition of Ideal Homes, Trollope, and Colls and Cementation. Perhaps it was a lead which James Hanson decided to follow, especially as Trafalgar's standing in the City was rather higher than that of Hanson Trust. Once Trafalgar had abandoned its interest in Costain, Hanson took up the running. In November 1971 the two companies announced that they were negotiating a merger. The idea was for a new holding company to acquire both Costain and Hanson Trust, creating a group in which the two companies' shareholders would share equally. The idea was barely public, however, before it had been knocked down by the Costain board, which could not accept entering the merger on an equal basis with this upstart company, despite Hanson Trust's higher profits. Costain was much the larger company, on every measure except profits and stock market valuation. It made sales of £108 million in 1970, compared to Hanson Trust's £47 million. Its assets were valued at the equivalent of more than £2 a share, while Hanson Trust's assets were worth merely 52p a share. James Hanson, however, had reported profits of £2.4 million in the previous year, compared to Costain's £1.7 million, which Hanson used to justify its claim to be treated equally in the merger. None the less that was not enough to persuade Costain and talks were called off almost before they had begun.

The affair had focused attention on Hanson Trust's rationale and its prospects, and the greater scrutiny which it brought did not leave the City thinking any better of the group. As the *Financial Times*'s influential Lex column said, commenting on the results for 1970/71, which were published in the middle of the Costain talks: 'the addition of a lump of dealing profits can hardly do much for the quality of earnings . . . it leaves open the question of where Hanson can find consistent earnings growth . . . it is understandable why Hanson hankers after a leap in an asset-rich direction.'[13]

The hankering continued. In the absence of any alternative target, Hanson Trust returned to Costain with a surprise, hostile takeover bid just two months later, a step which James Hanson described as 'a natural progression' following the abandoned merger talks. With Slater Walker having control over almost 20 per cent of Costain's shares, the construction company seemed to be in a difficult position. But its board rejected the bid in no uncertain terms, saying it would not be in the interests of the company, quite apart from the small matter of the price on offer. Chief executive J.P. Sowden declared: 'Our prospects have never been better, why share them with somebody else?' This claim was backed up by financial results showing a strong advance in profits, a leap in property values, and a jump of 40 per cent in the number of houses built in the United Kingdom compared to 1970. James Hanson and his advisers at Slater Walker attempted to pick holes in these optimistic figures but its rumbustious attack failed to dent Costain's stiff resistance. On 10 April, unwilling to raise its offer to match Costain's buoyant share price, James Hanson was forced to admit defeat, although he put a brave face on the setback by claiming that his success lay in never having paid too much.

The Costain episode was unhelpful at the time, because apart from the fact of defeat it also highlighted Hanson's lack of direction, lack of assets and lack of quality earnings. But it was another piece of luck which helped Hanson Trust survive the coming financial onslaught in much better shape than if it had been more heavily involved in property, and in better shape than others of its ilk, notably its merchant banker, Slater Walker. Ironically, one consequence of the bid battle was that Slater Walker decided to keep the shares as an investment, and in September Jim Slater joined the Costain board which his circulars had so roundly rubbished just a few months earlier.

This was a difficult period for James Hanson, and for other Slater satellites which had done well in the booming stock market of the late 1960s but had unexpectedly failed to benefit from the change of government in 1970. The British economy was in trouble, with the Barber boom producing a surge in inflation which the government, in its new interventionist mode, sought to counter with legal controls over prices, incomes and dividends. There was another sterling crisis, with balance of payments problems not helped by a dock strike. Share prices, having soared in the first couple of years of the Conservative government to a peak in the middle of 1972, began to slide back rapidly at the end of that year. A weak stock market was not such bad news for Hanson as for some other conglomerates. Through its fortuitous failure to build its motor interests and failure to merge with Costain, the group was left with strong cash resources, which protected it from the pain of rising interest rates and left it with the option of buying for cash. The property boom was over, however, posing a severe threat to companies like Hanson which had relied heavily on property profits to maintain their growth, including unspecified profits from dealing in properties rather than managing or developing sites.

Malcolm Horsman had faced these issues from a similar perspective to Hanson. He was an even closer associate of Jim Slater's, having joined the nascent Slater Walker organisation in 1965 and become a director two years later. In 1969 he emerged as the most significant of Slater's 'satellites' when he was put in charge of the commodity trader Ralli Brothers, which had been acquired by Slater Walker as part of the acquisition of Drages from Sir Isaac Wolfson. In a classic fit of conglomeracy, the cotton trader Ralli had been merged – with Slater Walker acting as midwife – with the paper company Bowater, Trafalgar House once again losing out as Bowater spurned its alternative offer. The deal made financial sense to Ralli, but there was no pretence that this was anything other than a financial operation – something which was to prove important for the subsequent attempt to merge the new Bowater with Hanson Trust. Bowater was then one of the world's largest paper makers, one of Britain's biggest manufacturing companies, also with large manufacturing interests in the United States. Yet Horsman was planning to turn it into another Slater Walker. The next step would have made even less commercial sense: early in 1973 Slater had tentative discussions with Bowater about incorporating Slater Walker itself into the group. The talks led nowhere, according to Slater,[14] because of fears that the Monopolies Commission would become involved. Instead Slater Walker went on to attempt a merger with the merchant bank Hill Samuel – a merger which passed Monopolies Commission scrutiny but failed when the directors of the merchant bank got cold feet.

Having failed to bring Slater Walker into Bowater, Horsman then turned his attention to Hanson Trust. On 16 June 1973 Bowater announced a £51 million offer, which had been agreed by Hanson. It was a classic financial manoeuvre: Hanson Trust would continue to be run independently as a division of Bowater, although it was possible that Bowater's few interests in building materials would be merged with its new subsidiary. The advantage to Bowater would be Hanson's UK earnings, which would balance Bowater's foreign earnings and so help with the tax bill. The advantage to Hanson Trust was not at all clear. There seemed no prospect of James Hanson having a wider role in the Bowater group: Horsman had only recently been appointed joint managing director and deputy chairman, and was almost ten years James Hanson's junior. Some commentators saw in the deal the invisible hand of Slater himself, 'moving the pieces around the chess board',[15] and were particularly concerned that Slater Walker had sold 2.5 million Bowater shares at about the same time that Horsman and James Hanson had begun discussing the merger. The two men insisted, however, that Slater had only been informed at a much later stage, when Hanson Trust had called in Slater Walker as its adviser on the deal.[16]

The City remained puzzled and dubious. Hanson and Horsman were described as being 'like chalk and cheese'.[17] *The Times*'s financial editor complained in a leader column about the incestuous nature of the deal and its lack of logic:

Coming before the conclusion of the negotiations for the subsequently shelved merger of Hill Samuel and Slater Walker, the timing was doubly unfortunate. For, coincidentally, Hill Samuel advised Bowater on last year's controversial bid for Ralli International. And while Rothschilds are advising Bowater on the present bid, Mr Robert Clark, a deputy chairman of Hill

Samuel, was until earlier this year a member of the Bowater board, and must, therefore, have watched the Hanson deal with interest . . . Hanson does not look like the right company for Bowater. While its management has proved its ability to generate profits, these profits are not of the highest quality . . . The logic at the time of Bowater/Ralli was shaky, and it would look more so in the changed financial climate of today. To carry through the bid for Hanson might exacerbate that situation.[18]

In the end the debate was irrelevant, because on 25 July the government stepped in, referring the bid to the Monopolies Commission as part of the widespread concern about conglomerates, and so effectively scuppering it. Horsman was strong in his condemnation, saying that the six-month delay would be disastrous for two such 'fast-moving' companies, and accusing the Department of Trade and Industry of 'a frightening lack of knowledge of how commerce works'.[19]

On the contrary, the Department of Trade and Industry seemed belatedly to have shown great perception as to how Horsman's kind of commerce worked, as part of the government's new-found interest in industry. Having seen the effects of its hands-off approach in the early years of the government, the DTI – ironically with Peter Walker as Secretary of State from 1972 – was now taking a much more active interest. In December 1972 a Fair Trading Bill had been published, aimed at making sure consumers did not suffer from the power of large corporations. It was made clear that more takeovers than previously would be referred to the Monopolies Commission, and not only for conventional monopoly reasons. The Commission was now charged with protecting 'the public interest', and opinion had now swung away from free-market capitalism so that purely financially motivated business deals were seen as not necessarily being in the public interest. Plans to merge British Match and Wilkinson Sword, and for Tarmac to take over Wolseley-Hughes, had also fallen victim to this logic, and manoeuvres such as the Ralli–Bowater merger had fuelled the feeling that the financial tail was wagging the industrial dog.

Horsman and his style of operation did not last much longer. By 1975 it became apparent that his strategy at Bowater was flawed, and details also emerged of share incentives that should have been disclosed to shareholders. He resigned as an executive director. That was also Jim Slater's last year in the City. He resigned from Slater Walker on 24 October, as investigations into his Singapore activities began to apply increasing pressure, and create increasing danger, for Slater Walker, which was handed into the custody of James Goldsmith by the Bank of England. It was the end of the Slater years, but James Hanson was untouched by the various scandals which emerged. Privately, in characteristically honourable, loyal fashion, he helped his old associate Slater financially. Publicly, he peddled the same story of steady growth from investment in basic industries and services which had been his message since taking the chair at Wiles Group in 1965. And he continued on the deal-making route: adding to the growing brick interests with the purchase of Midland Brick from the National Coal Board in a further example of privatisation even before the term had been invented.

A further attempt at such involvement brought another significant defeat for Hanson, however. In 1973 the government sold Rolls-Royce Motors, the famous manufacturers of luxury cars, which had been part of the Rolls-Royce group and whose rescue – following its crash in 1971 – by the government had marked the beginning of the famous U-turn away from non-intervention in industrial affairs. Despite abandoning motor vehicles only a few years previously, and despite the relatively complex, high-technology nature of car manufacture, which certainly does not fit with the declared target of basic industries, James Hanson saw another opportunity. It was an opportunity to add a prestige name to the nondescript bunch of companies he controlled – a name which would have been used as a brand elsewhere in the group. Hanson Trust joined with financial partners to make a consortium bid for the car-maker. The £34 million tender was higher than the competing bids, but the government decided that it would do better to float the company on the stock market, a precursor of the PowerGen affair 17 years later.

As usual, this failed attempt to change the group's direction was not rated sufficiently interesting or important to appear in the annual report to shareholders, just as the failures to merge with first Costain, then Bowater, were not touched on by the chairman. Instead, Mr Hanson laid out his philosophy, stressed another year of success, and promised further progress based on the notions of decentralisation and 'free-form management', which he said had produced continual growth in profits and earnings. The figures do clearly show that the group managed to churn out higher profits each year, but it is not at all clear that this stemmed from the management of the operating units. Quite apart from the distorting effect on profits of acquisition provisions, it is impossible to assess properly the performance of operating companies, as observers noted at the time, because of continual changes not only in the members of the group but also in its internal organisation. The reported divisional structure changed in 1968, 1969 and 1972 under the impact of acquisitions and disposals. A change of year end in 1969 further confused the picture, as did the inclusion of acquisitions for periods other than 12 months. The figures which were disclosed show some disappointing performances, however. The Commercial Vehicle business remained stuck on profits of just under £300,000 until the addition of Provincial Traction and Jack Olding. Then profits rose to a peak of about £1.1 million in 1969, only to fall back in the following year – the year in which the transport operations were sold. Publishing and printing (the White family business) began with a contribution of roughly £40,000 in 1966 (the reported profits were for a 21-month period), rose to £75,000 then fell back to £69,000 in 1968. After that the figures were not reported separately. Reported profits from 'agricultural services', combining sack hire with agricultural equipment sales, peaked at £1 million in 1970, then remained stuck at £600,000 until 1974, despite rapid inflation during that period and despite the fact that sales kept growing. The brick operations, described as Building Materials division, showed a steady rise in profits in the early 1970s, but much of that must have come from the acquisitions, and after peaking at £4 million in 1973, the contribution fell away to £1.3 million two years later, once again despite rising sales.

The conclusion must be that the reported profits growth for the group as a whole came from the various benefits of acquisitions and disposals, the property spree of the early 1970s, and possibly profits on share dealing. Nevertheless, shareholders had been well looked after. They had been asked to contribute £9.5 million in three rights issues up to the end of 1973, but the total dividends paid out in that period amounted to more than £6 million, and shareholders' funds had grown from virtually nothing to £31 million. Even after allowing for inflation, shareholders had every reason to be happy, as they would continue to be throughout the 1970s and the first half of the 1980s. Hanson Trust had survived the crash in relatively good shape, thanks to Gordon White's instinct about the fragility of the property boom, and ironically because of the various strategic failures of the early 1970s. The sale of the transport business, and the failure to use the receipts because most attempts were blocked, left Hanson Trust with its first cash mountain in 1974 – a feature of the group which was to become familiar in the 1980s. It had been very heavily indebted in the early years, in keeping with the Hanson philosophy of using 'other people's money'. In September 1969, net debt had been £8.6 million, 60 per cent more than shareholders' funds in a 'gearing' ratio which would have alarmed many financiers, although it was made to look more respectable than it was by the early use of convertible loan stock, which could be treated as share capital on the assumption that conversion would eventually take place. The frustrations of the early 1970s helped to reduce this racy level of debt, however, and in 1974 the group ended that year with £5 million of cash in the bank. It was another fortunate accident which left Hanson Trust better able than many to withstand the turbulent years of the mid-1970s.

The early 1970s were dispiriting, however. Deal-maker Gordon White was clearly casting about rather wildly for the quantum leap which James Hanson had promised several years earlier. But they could not achieve it, and their style of operation was fast going out of fashion. Well before Slater Walker's collapse in 1975, conglomerates had earned themselves a bad name. Some of the American examples which had been a model for Slater and his fellow conglomerate builders had begun to hit trouble, while the Monopolies Commission in Britain and a Congressional committee in the United States had reported unfavourably on the conglomerate form.[20] The era of the conglomerate was over, at least temporarily. Most such groups retired quietly from the glare of publicity, attempting to invest some rationality for their disparate operations and to focus on one or two specific industries. But James Hanson stuck with the original idea of building a group by acquisition using other people's money – the idea which came via Gordon White from Jim Slater, and which had first set the two men on the road to becoming directors of a public company.

They attempted to continue as before, but in the UK could not find the deal which would project them up the corporate hierarchy. That £20 million takeover continued to elude James Hanson throughout the 1970s – at least in Britain. In the United States, on the other hand, the story was very different.

CHAPTER 5

Up and Away: 1973–83

Gordon White is a patriot as well as an expatriate. His no-nonsense right-wing views about politics, financial and personal morality are the kind you might expect to find in any expatriate bar from Hong Kong to Harare. He has no time for trade unions, government 'interference' in industry, layabouts and lazy managers. For him, the 1970 general election result seemed to represent a new dawn. Gone was Harold Wilson's technocracy, with its Industrial Reorganisation Corporation, economic planning, Prices and Incomes Board, and talk of worker participation. Instead, White looked forward to government by a modern Conservative Party, with little time for the establishment in industry or anywhere else, bent on taming the trade unions but otherwise leaving business to get on with the task of making money and improving Britain's lot. It was exactly what he wanted from government.

But White, and Britain, were not to get it on a sustained basis until the following decade. Heath did manage to pass the Industrial Relations Act of 1971, but it made precious little difference to the state of industrial relations, except to trigger a series of high-profile confrontations. It failed to prevent disruption in the docks and the railways, long strikes at Ford and in the Post Office. At the beginning of 1972 the miners went on strike for almost two months in pursuit of something more than the £2 a week extra offered by the National Coal Board – and eventually won £6 a week after an inquiry. After this very public defeat and with inflation hitting 9 per cent in 1971 – the highest since the war apart from a brief blip in 1951 – Heath performed his famous U-turn. With the failure of non-intervention at smoothing industrial relations and reducing wage demands, he opted instead for intervention, with a statutory pay and prices policy, which also brought dividend payments into the net of control. Worse was to come, so far as White was concerned. In 1973 Heath coined the 'unacceptable face of capitalism' phrase, following Tiny Rowland's coup that ousted the 'straight eight' directors of Lonrho to give him unfettered control of the mining and trading conglomerate. And the economic boom unleashed in 1972 by Heath's Chancellor, Anthony Barber, was beginning to implode, helped by the Yom Kippur war and the consequent oil crisis. The combination of the oil crisis and industrial action in the mines brought 50 m.p.h. speed limits on motorways and, at the start of 1974, the three-day week, when emergency measures were introduced with a rota under which companies received no power on four days each week.

These national tribulations were supplemented by Hanson Trust's own problems: the failure to build on the motor interests and their eventual abandonment; the failure of the Costain merger plan; the Monopolies Commission's intervention which stopped the Bowater merger; and the failure to acquire Rolls-Royce. To top it all, in November 1973, trade and consumer affairs minister Sir Geoffrey (now Lord) Howe announced that the Monopolies Commission was to investigate the brick industry. Hanson had only 5 per cent of the market at that stage, well behind London Brick's 43 per cent, so was not directly affected, but it was another blow to market forces and industrial independence.

Personally, too, the property crash hit White hard. Prosperous enough to begin with, as boss of the family printing company, he had made £220,000 (worth more than £2 million in 1994 money) by selling the company to the Wiles Group. But the property crash came at precisely the wrong time for White – just as he had completed a dream home, with the aid of a £150,000 mortgage.

White has subsequently rationalised all this as the cause of his departure for the United States:

What had happened was that Mr Barber and Mr Heath had screwed up the whole country. Six and seven generations of money had gone down the tube because of this easy borrowing power and these low interest rates, and most of the people that made those millions [in property] went down the drain. Slater's empire collapsed and there were dozens of others. The lifeboat came out from the Bank of England. And then you had the petrol crisis, at which point the British [stock market] index reached 150. The day after Dunkirk it was 350! So you can imagine the over-compensation for this sudden increase in petrol prices: the whole of Britain collapsed, from a financial point of view. The change of government happened about that time.[1]

In fact Gordon White went to America well before the Labour government returned to power in February 1974, but the disappointment of Heath's U-turn, the economic turmoil and the threat of a Labour government apparently intent on nationalising the country's top 25 companies must have been a powerful incentive to leave. By the time Harold Wilson came to power once again, White had already begun to rescue Hanson Trust by doing in the United States what he had been unable to achieve in Britain over the previous few years: building a highly profitable US arm of the Hanson empire – though he also continued to mastermind deals in the United Kingdom.

Hanson and White had wanted to move beyond the relatively narrow confines of the United Kingdom for some time. It was one of the reasons behind the attempted mergers with Costain and Bowater. This, together with White's personal disillusionment with Britain, created the opportunity to make a transatlantic move, and to make it in the best possible way. Many British companies have attempted a similar expansion, and many have failed because they attempted to run their US operations from the UK, in UK style and with UK managers. Thanks to the fortunate coincidence of corporate and personal desires, Hanson Trust avoided these traps. White became the group's permanent representative in the United States. And thanks to the long-lasting partnership between the two men, he was largely left to do his own thing. Hanson had another advantage over companies invading the US market: its chairman probably knew more about North America than any of his peers. James Hanson had run a business in Canada for ten years. His wife Geraldine was American, and consequently he had owned a house in California for years. Both James Hanson and Gordon White were almost as much at home in New York as they were in London.

Nevertheless the venture could have come to nought. White, who was 50 years old in 1973, had been ready to quit the business, so disillusioned had he become. He wanted to become his own man: a New York based wheeler-dealer, with plenty of time to enjoy the good life with the benefit of a lightly-taxed income – as suggested by his choice of Bermuda for a home when he left Britain. But James Hanson was well aware of how much he and his company needed Gordon White. Instead of waving goodbye to Hanson Trust, White was persuaded to continue their 20-year partnership – but at a price. The details of the agreement took some time to iron out, and only emerged several years later, causing some embarrassment to the group. White later explained his emigration like this:

I left England in 1973 and came out here to start a new business – by myself and for myself. I did not need Hanson Trust. But James and I had been partners for years, and we both felt that while a Labour government ruled in the UK, America was the place to make money . . . I was finished with England – I felt it was the end. I was leveraged up to the eyebrows and technically insolvent. If my agreed loan of £150,000 had been an overdraft, they could have called it in, and I would have gone down. I did not leave England as a tax exile. I left broke, and came here to start on my own. James said: 'Why not do it for Hanson Trust?' and I said OK – but not without equity, so we agreed 10 per cent.[2]

In fact it was not quite as simple as that. When he left, Gordon had agreed with James Hanson a much looser arrangement. He might do some deals on his own account, but if he brought any to Hanson Trust they would share 50:50. In typically buccaneering White fashion, however, he had done the first deals in Hanson Trust's name before the details of his own contract had been hammered out. By the time the lawyers got to work on a proper agreement, it was clear that the scale of the US operation was going to be greater than either side had anticipated. Once the bankers and lawyers had finished, Gordon White's share had been cut down to 10 per cent, as eventually emerged much later. This rankled with White, who has always felt the importance of financial rewards and has been irritated by the feeling that he was largely responsible for making the Hanson group what it is, yet James Hanson, whom he has often treated with disdain despite their long friendship, has received most of the credit. So far as White was concerned, Hanson Trust was not putting any money into the US operation, because of the innovative financing which he was forced to dream up, so 50 per cent of the returns would have been more than fair.

At the time, none of this was made known to shareholders or the outside world, not that there was any requirement to disclose this information. The focus was on Gordon White's and Hanson Trust's new adventure in the United States. White set up camp with an associate, Eddie Collins, in New York's Pierre Hotel. The Pierre is one of New York's plushest and most exclusive hotels, with rates at least double those at the better-known Plaza. It is a favourite of many foreign dignitaries, and in the 1970s was the preferred haunt of Henry Kissinger. The choice illustrates White's and Hanson's fondness for comfortable surroundings, and James Hanson in particular would be keen to be seen at the most exclusive places – despite the cost.

Collins was an old American friend of White's who was not exactly a businessman but knew a lot of people on Wall Street and around the US business scene. Together with Richard Reiss and Gordon Robinson, contacts from James Hanson's Canadian days, they set up Hanson Industries and began looking for companies to buy. They did not have far to look, since New York, even more than London, was awash with deal merchants, such as Peter Bauer Mengelberg, somebody who would cause James Hanson embarrassment more than a decade later when the details of his dealings with the group emerged. But while there were plenty of companies to buy, the means of doing so were not so easy to come by. Britain still operated exchange controls, and there were no friendly connections as when the Hanson brothers went to Canada shortly after the war. In the United States, Hanson Trust was virtually unheard of. Nor was the Slater connection of much use, since Slater was also just building up in the US. White had only $3000 to spend, the maximum he was allowed to take out of the country, and that would just about pay his hotel bill. He had to devise a means of paying for the first acquisitions, and he invented the leveraged buyout, paying for the companies he was buying in what James Hanson has subsequently called 'Gordon White promissory notes'. White would arrange a loan to buy a company using the assets of that company as security, rather than the assets of the Hanson group, as would have been more usual. It was a typically pragmatic solution, but one which was also influenced by the fact that Gordon White was initially acting as much on his own account as he was on behalf of Hanson Trust.

White's other problem, apart from raising the finance, was that the quality of companies on offer was not high. But at least that meant their price was not high, either. His first deal from the Pierre was not a takeover, but merely a stake in a building materials company quoted on the New York stock exchange, Gable Industries. It was not a huge success, but endeared White to Chemical Bank, and therefore secured much easier access to funds for subsequent deals. In the meantime, however, White had no funds to call on, and that influenced both the companies he bought and the way he paid for them. The stake was on offer following pressure on the seller, Mr J.B. Fuqua, from the stock exchange, which did not like his sizeable holding in Gable in addition to chairing his own public company, Fuqua Industries. James Hanson flew in to help negotiate the deal, and they agreed to pay $10.7 million (then equivalent to £4.5 million) for the 534,200 shares Mr Fuqua was selling, representing a stake of 24 per cent. Hanson Trust paid in loan notes issued by Hanson Industries Inc., the US arm of the group, repayable between 1974 and 1979 – in effect, it bought the shares on the never-never, paying in instalments over the next five years.

Simultaneously, White was agreeing to buy a privately-owned fish-processing company, J. Howard Smith, which was available because the family owners wanted to sell out. As he later discovered, it had been hawked up and down Wall Street without success, because the fish oil and protein industry was not terribly attractive; a commodity business subject to the volatility and unpredictability of any agricultural operation. It was not a simple purchase, however, and it illustrated that Gordon White's skills were not restricted to the cut and thrust of takeover battles. It also showed he had that crucial intuitive touch needed to make such a deal-making approach to business a success, and it showed how superficial his approach to acquisitions had been. The shares in J. Howard Smith were held by various members of the Smith family, some of whom were less willing to sell than others. White had to trek up and down New Jersey cajoling the reluctant members of the family; when necessary, White could be surprisingly patient, despite his usual volatility and distractibility. Eventually his careful negotiations were rewarded. The family agreed to a price of $32 million (£14 million), but with little of that up front. On completion of the deal, $7 million was to be paid, but the family agreed to accept loan notes repayable over the following three years for the remainder of the purchase price. That suited the impoverished Hanson Industries, and fortunately it also suited the Smith family, since it deferred their tax liability.

White had got off to a quick start, but the results were mixed. The Gable stake was sold a couple of years later for £1 million less than it had cost. Seacoast, as J. Howard Smith was renamed, lasted rather longer but fared little better. It was sold in 1984 for $32 million – the same as the purchase price in actual dollars, but only about half as much in value after allowing for inflation, although Hanson had, of course, received income from the company in the intervening period. In a huge piece of luck for White and for Hanson Trust, Seacoast's first year was a bonanza, but only because of problems with rival fishmeal from Peru. Seacoast contributed almost $16 million in its first full year in the group (1974/5), equivalent to more than £8 million in those days, but it never reached this level again. Profits were erratic through the rest of the 1970s, and fell steadily in the 1980s. By 1982 Seacoast was making an annual loss of nearly $4 million. It was not an auspicious start to the group's American invasion, but by the time Seacoast had proved that White could make mistakes, it was a minnow among the whales in the Hanson ocean. Seacoast proved a successful purchase for another reason, however: the company had $14 million cash in the bank – a fact which White had neglected to discover when agreeing the purchase.

Hanson's record of continually increased profits was maintained only by White's acquisitive progress in the US. Activity in the UK remained limited, constrained partly by the group's low share price. The Hanson share rating bounced back quite quickly from the trough of the 1974 slump, but after reaching a peak price/earnings ratio of almost 15 early in 1976 on the back of the apparently successful US expansion, the rating swiftly slid back to levels which ruled out using shares to make takeovers. Between that 1976 peak and 1980 the price/earnings ratio was stuck well into single figures and the shares performed poorly in comparison with the All-Share index. Hanson Trust was not quoted in the United States, although that had been the original intention, so the flagging share price meant nothing to White or to the companies he was buying. What mattered was his credit – the standing of the Gordon White promissory notes – and after a shaky start White's standing with New York's bankers grew more substantial.

White later gave a graphic description of what it was like in the beginning:

After I'd bought the company [Seacoast] and the money started coming in I discovered we had $14 million in the bank, and they were banking with Morgan Guaranty. So I asked to go and see somebody there and I arrived at this banking hall down in Wall Street on a bitterly cold day. In front of the door there's all these desks and I sit in front of the first desk in front of the draughty door – so I know I'm actually sitting talking to the fellow who joined the bank *yesterday*.

I wanted to do a back-to-back, but after a couple of minutes I knew this fellow didn't know what I was talking about – that if I put up £10 million in England and we took the exchange risk, would they grant us credit for £10 million here? He said he'd think about it and I said: 'Well, don't think about it, I'd like to see your vice-president.' So I got an appointment for two or three days later. I sent for one of our young accountants from England and we arrived and we again sit outside this door and wait half an hour, and then we're sent for. We go into a nice office and there are three young chaps sitting around.

We pass the time of day and nothing much happens and then this much older man comes in and sits behind the desk and says: 'Now, what can I do for you?' So I said: 'I'd like to know what would happen if we put up £10 million in Britain and we took the exchange risk and you lent us the equivalent of £10 million – what would be your charge?'

So he took our balance sheet – which was not the most impressive sight, this Hanson Trust balance sheet – and starts to go through it. He said: 'I don't like your equity rate here. I'm not at all happy about this.' By then I'd been putting up with this arrogance for quite a long time, and the fact that being British meant that you were an arsehole. So I said: 'Just a minute – would you mind telling me how much we've got on deposit in your bank?' He said: 'You have money here?' I said: 'Yes, we do, would you mind finding out?' So he gets on the telephone, and there's about five minutes of silence. These three young men, my accountant, myself, we sit there, until finally he said: 'You've got $14,150,000 on deposit.'

I said: 'No sir, we *had*. I'm about to close the account.'[3]

And White proceeded to give the Morgan Guaranty banker a lesson in manners and in doing business. But he still didn't have a friendly banker – until he proved his corporate virility in a tussle with trade unions at Gable Industries.

Having established his credentials, White continued on the acquisition trail, though still with very limited success. In 1974 he paid $4.5 million (£1.9 million) for 22 per cent of the shares of United Artists Theater Circuit (UATC). Despite the name, this company no longer had anything to do with United Artists film distributors, the company set up by Charlie Chaplin, Mary Pickford and other early movie stars, although its main asset was a 500-strong cinema chain. UATC also had interests in cable television, drive-in restaurants and shopping centres, and that explained its attraction to White. He saw it as a Slater-style 'asset situation'. Its assets worked out at $18.60 per share, which made the $10.50 paid by Hanson Trust look cheap, despite the shares having traded at only $6.25. UATC was another family business, but this time the deal went wrong. The company had been owned by two sisters and two brothers, and while the sisters had been happy to sell to White, the brothers were not. Despite having talks about extending Hanson's interest and possibly having seats on the board, just before Christmas UATC issued writs, claiming that Hanson's purchase of an additional 90,000 shares infringed stock exchange rules and amounted to a takeover offer, suing James Hanson and Gordon White for $10 million each, and seeking a court order preventing Hanson Trust from voting its present shares and from buying any more. Hanson Trust filed a counter-suit and the lawyers got to work, the outcome being an agreement for UATC to buy back the shares owned by Hanson, in exchange for the cable television stake and four properties. The value of these assets was put at $8.3 million, leaving Hanson with a profit of something like $2.5 million, before legal costs, plus properties which were leased back to UATC to bring in income of $860,000 a year. It is no wonder the bankers were happy to keep lending White millions of dollars, if he could make a profit of almost 50 per cent in less than a year, although some might say this was an early example of 'greenmail' – the practice of taking threatening stakes in companies and effectively forcing them into buying back the stakes at an exorbitant price.

So Gordon White's first three ventures into the US acquisition business were far from auspicious: Seacoast started well but faded fast, the stakes in Gable and UATC came to nothing. But with a Labour government now firmly ensconced in Britain after a second general election in October 1974, and with Hanson Trust going nowhere in the UK, there was no incentive to abandon the experiment and head back home. White and Collins therefore moved out of the Pierre – under threat of legal action because they had been tying up the switchboard using their suite as an office – and set up an office on Park Avenue. It was another typical White move – to one of New York's best addresses, where he also established a personal base with his own apartment. And 1975 proved to be rather more fruitful, even if the two purchases that year once again cast doubt on White's famed ability to spot a bargain.

In July Hanson Trust announced it was buying the speciality textile operations of a Dutch-owned US conglomerate called Indian Head. This was a sizeable business, employing 4000 people in 15 factories, making a variety of textile products ranging from needlecraft and knitting yarns to netting. Its sales in 1974 had been $170 million (£78 million) – slightly more than the entire Hanson Trust group managed in 1974. Indian Head had fallen on hard times, however, with profit sliding to just $6 million in 1974, well below the level of the previous few years. With that background, White managed to negotiate a purchase price of a mere $36 million (£16 million) which was only about four-fifths of the value of the assets. Indian Head was renamed Carisbrook after the takeover. At the same time, White was talking to several other targets, and in November agreed to take a 27 per cent stake in a publicly quoted meat-processing company: Hygrade Food Products. This time, unlike in the Gable and UATC cases, the initial investment did lead to something more. In February 1976 Hanson offered to buy the rest of the shares and Hygrade duly became a subsidiary, at a total cost of $28 million. White continued picking up this kind of undistinguished, small quoted company when he bought Interstate United, a contract catering and gaming machine business which provided meals through vending machines and directly in institutions such as hospitals and schools, and to business canteens and sports stadiums.[4] At $30 million, the price was very similar to the cost of Seacoast, Carisbrook and Hygrade, as was the performance in its first few years in the group.

These purchases proved rather more successful than Seacoast, although Interstate brought its own problems of a rather different nature, which would subsequently be used by James Hanson's enemies. There were allegations of Mafia involvement and corruption among senior Interstate executives.[5] In 1977 it was investigated by a federal grand jury looking into illegal trade union links. After an investigation by external auditors, Interstate filed a report with the Securities and Exchange Commission, admitting that it had made secret payments to union officials, and had received kickbacks from beer and milk suppliers. Peter Tullio, who was president of Interstate in the mid-1970s, was initially found guilty in 1978 of authorising a $30,000 payment to a trade union official in exchange for a 'sweetheart' labour contract.[6] Tullio was later acquitted when a judge ruled that the prosecution had not proved that he had criminal intent when he approved the payments. These legal problems referred to events before Interstate was acquired, but nevertheless did not help Hanson Trust's image when they were publicised in the British press.[7]

None of these acquisitions was the goldmine which Hanson needed to shake the group out of its rut. The picture as reported in the group's annual accounts was difficult to interpret because the US company results were reported in sterling. But the figures in dollars present a contrast to the notion of Hanson Trust's industrial management skills transforming these companies. Hygrade, the frankfurter and meat-processing company, produced $11 million profit in 1976/7, its first full year with Hanson Trust. The figure fell to just over $7 million in the following year, but returned to $11.4 million in 1978/9. That was the highest profit it ever reported, however. In the early 1980s it only just managed to beat $10 million annual profit. The textile operations grouped in Carisbrook showed a slightly better trend, but the trend is confused by the addition of a Lindustries subsidiary in 1979. Even so, profits peaked at $23 million in 1980/1, and fell to just $17.5 million two years later. Interstate, the vending business, was also uninspiring. In its first year it made more than $12 million, but only once, in 1981/2, was that figure bettered. These figures ignore the impact of disposals, which affected each company to some extent, but they also ignore the impact of inflation in pushing up the reported profit figure. Assuming those influences do balance each other out, it is clear that Hanson's ownership of these companies did not result in the boost to performance which could have been expected if the group really did have the invigorating effect on its targets that has always been claimed. James Hanson was only able to report continuing growth in profit from his supposedly hugely successful US empire because of the addition of new acquisitions.

In fact, as was common throughout the group's early years, the acquisitions continued to be run by their previous managers. It was only later, once Hanson began acquiring much larger conglomerates such as Imperial Group, that the idea grew of liberating middle managers from the bureaucratic, remote tyranny of their incompetent board members. The most significant asset acquired with Seacoast was David Clarke, one of the original family owners, the man who was running it and who, in 1992, long after Seacoast was sold, was named as White's heir-apparent as deputy chairman and chief executive of Hanson Industries. Similarly, Newton Glekel, the chairman of Hygrade before it was acquired by Hanson, was still running the meat company when it was sold in 1989.

Interstate completed a quartet of purchases which put Hanson on the map in the United States, and gave it an active profile in Britain so far as investors were concerned. In 1976 they also put Hanson Trust into the UK's top 100 companies. But as attention was focused more firmly on the group's US activities, the progenitor of Hanson Industries – Gordon White – also came under scrutiny, as his curious relationship to the parent group came into the open. White had been deputy chairman since 1966, when the original Wiles Group directors departed. He was joined in that position in 1973 by Derek Rosling, and in the following year, after his departure for the US, White stopped being a director. A brief comment in James Hanson's chairman's report said merely that White had left the board 'in order to concentrate exclusively on responsibility for our overseas interests, in particular our very healthy activities in North America'. What was not mentioned in this statement was that White had left the company, but was still tied to it by various financial arrangements.

The existence of a 10 per cent shareholder first appeared in Hanson Trust's half-year results statement for 1974/5. The document detailing the Carisbrook purchase explained to shareholders that the 10 per cent of Hanson Industries had been sold to this minority participant on a very partly paid basis: just 0.1 per cent of the value had been paid, in fact. Now the Hygrade circular revealed that the owner of the 10 per cent stake was none other than Gordon White. In a footnote to the annual report for 1974/5, James Hanson gave an explanation of the arrangement with White, and stated that negotiations were underway to buy out his partner:

The White investment [in Hanson Industries] was made on the understanding that it would be retained for up to five years in anticipation of a public flotation by the end of that time. Our overseas growth and success, due to a large extent to Gordon White, has been remarkable and with our continuing expansion the value of the minority is becoming increasingly relevant. Since there is no immediate intention to obtain a local quotation, we are actively considering the purchase of this interest, and, when an acceptable formula is found, the necessary approvals will be sought.

In effect, the deal was an early form of 'golden handcuff incentive' – 10 per cent of a company whose growth was almost entirely dependent on White's acquisition skills, which would have crystallised when the US company was floated. This arrangement would be unusual even today, and it was certainly unusual in the 1970s; it brought critical, though muted, comment. The influential Lex column in the *Financial Times* pointed out that it had not been necessary to divulge the shareholding, since White had resigned as a director, but wondered nevertheless whether the arrangement was not so special that shareholders should have been informed. 'On balance', Lex concluded, 'the answer would probably be that it is [so special]'.[8] But the writer was not too perturbed, noting that US practice was rather different to that in Britain, and that White had done remarkably well in building up the US business. Lex was not quite so understanding when Hanson's annual report was published at the end of 1976. This time Lex worked out that White had paid the equivalent of just £265 (the 0.1 per cent paid-up element) for a stake which was by then worth £1.6 million.[9] It also recognised a potential conflict of interest, since the growth of the US arm had been financed largely by debt which was backed to some extent by Hanson Trust. Hanson Industries was not therefore an independent entity, and White was faced with balancing what was best for Industries, and his own 10 per cent, against what was best for the group as a whole. This was precisely the conflict of interest which had led the group to abandon the Slater notion of having associated companies which were themselves quoted on the stock exchange in the United Kingdom. Lex also pointed out that the US business had a relatively short record, most of which coincided with an economic upturn. Before negotiating to buy out the minority, it suggested, Hanson should wait to see how Industries performed in a downturn. The negotiations did drag on as advisers worried about how to value the business which White was owed 10 per cent of. The matter was eventually settled in 1979, when an extraordinary meeting of shareholders approved the issue of 4.3 million shares in Hanson Trust in exchange for the 10 per cent stake. That was worth some $12 million, but shareholders and commentators reckoned it was a fair price for what seemed to be an outstanding performance from the ace acquirer. Apart from the question of the money and the nature of the arrangement, however, the affair had raised the issue of Gordon White's position in the group. If he was so crucial to its development, why was he not a director? That was a question which would haunt James Hanson years later, although one which he has always insisted is irrelevant.

There was also an undercurrent to this issue: was White going to carry on? In his 1975 footnote, Hanson said that White was 'currently exploring further expansion possibilities in Europe'. And it was suggested that if the group was lucky it might manage to keep him on in some consultancy capacity. This harked back to White's original departure for America in 1973. He had then been ready to leave the group, and it seemed that, with the prospect of a separate US company now disappearing, he was restless again. Perhaps, influenced by his old friend and francophile Sir James Goldsmith, and always a one for good living, he fancied whiling away his fifties in the congenial surroundings of Paris. His attempt to replicate the US experience on the continent was doomed, however; French bankers would be even more sniffy about a British predator nosing around their companies than White had found Morgan Guaranty to be in New York. He tried the same approach, taking a suite in a hotel and looking for deals, but after several months the operation was called off. The uncertainty over White's future continued for some time, however, until 1982, when Hanson told shareholders:

> I am very pleased to report that Sir Gordon White KBE has accepted our offer to become chairman and chief executive of Hanson Industries Inc., our US holding company . . . This important new appointment adds greatly to our confidence in the continuing growth of Hanson Trust in the USA, which was the major contributor to our 1982 profit.

Shareholders might well have been confused by this statement since there had never been any indication – apart from the reference to his sojourn in Europe – that White had ever reduced his commitment or involvement in the United States or in the group. Indeed, in his report the previous year, Hanson had paid special tribute to White, as part of his persistent attempt to boost his partner's profile in public perception, so as to offset any possible irritation on White's part at the publicity attracted by the company chairman. Although David Clarke had been appointed chief executive of the US operations, and president of Hanson Industries, in 1978, and despite the fact that there was no mention of White in the annual reports from 1977 to 1981, there was never any suggestion, formal or informal, official or unofficial, that White had lessened his involvement in or importance to Hanson Industries.

In fact, as official US documents filed with the SEC show, he had technically been 'an independent consultant', prior to his appointment as chairman of Hanson Industries in 1983. Despite his power and authority, up to that point he had not been an employee of any Hanson company since leaving Britain. Nor, it later emerged, was he at all involved in running the US operation. That was David Clarke's job. White's role was simply to find companies to buy and do the deals – a role he performed from his own office on Park Avenue, not from the company's offices in New Jersey, just as in England he had liked to work from Pont Street, not from the corporate headquarters in Teddington, and later Knightsbridge. It was an anomalous position which would come back to haunt Hanson.

While Gordon White had been buying up whatever nondescript US companies he could lay his hands on, back in the United Kingdom Hanson Trust continued to meander with little apparent purpose and to little effect, despite Sir James's public assurances that everything was continuing according to plan. Notwithstanding this lack of direction, however, the 1970s saw Hanson gaining a wider appreciation in the financial press and the City. This process was helped by the apparent successes in the United States, and by James Hanson's growing outspokenness on political matters. His increasingly vigorous denunciations of socialism sat oddly with the surprise award of a knighthood in Harold Wilson's retirement honours list in 1976, but his award was overshadowed by the knighthood given to his more prominent friend, James Goldsmith. It certainly did not harm his growing reputation, which gradually projected him as a businessman in his own right as the Slater era receded, rather than as just another Slater hanger-on.

As the financial community struggled to come to terms with the stock market, property and fringe bank crash of 1973–74, Hanson Trust had emerged as something more solid to hold on to than many of the erstwhile stock market stars, and more solid than many sceptics had expected when it was seen as just another Slater satellite. 'If survival is the game, then Hanson Trust looks better equipped than many,' commented *The Times*, approving of the group's strong cash position.[10] The *Daily Telegraph* drew a contrast with other Slater acolytes: 'James Hanson must be just about the only survivor of the late sixties generation of whiz-kids to weather the bleak days of the bear market and keep his reputation – if not share price – intact.'[11]

The share price was a problem. The stock market index did climb back from the worst depths of its slump following Wilson's second victory in October 1974, but it took another three years before it returned to 1972 levels in actual terms, during which time Britain suffered rampant inflation. As Hanson came to be recognised as safer and more promising than many other fashionable stocks of the late 1960s, its shares performed well in the early part of this recovery period. But that appreciation only lasted until early in 1976, after which followed a long period of underperformance as investors looked for something more than mere survival and solidity. Only when Mrs Thatcher came to power and the takeover bandwagon began to roll in earnest once again in the United Kingdom did the group's shares begin to outperform the FT All-Share index again, beginning a long run of amazing returns for Hanson shareholders.

The low share price meant that it was financially difficult to justify issuing new shares during this period, although Hanson did raise £8.7 million in 1975. This rights issue was seen, however, as a means of bypassing the government's 10 per cent limit on dividend increases that was part of the prices and incomes policy directed at cutting inflation, which reached 25 per cent during that year as a result of the government's relaxed financial policy prior to the second general election of 1974. It was a typically audacious – though not entirely original – piece of skill by the financial wizards who worked at Hanson Trust's headquarters on the Brompton Road. The income from the issue also added to the group's resources and improved the balance sheet ratios, which helped White persuade the sceptical US bankers that Hanson Trust was a viable lending proposition. And it left some spare cash for Hanson to try to develop the UK side of the empire. This was a useful move but it was no substitute for highly rated shares, which make acquisitions much cheaper than if the shares are languishing below the stock market average. James Hanson therefore embarked on a campaign to raise the group's status and reputation. Having outlasted the Slater era, it was now time to become more than just a survivor. It was time that the company's progress over the past ten years became properly recognised, and that James Hanson's position in the pantheon of industrialists was made as prominent as he felt it should have been. The knighthood in 1976 was extremely helpful in this respect. It added credibility to Hanson personally, despite the tainted nature of the tinted list. But it was not enough. Sir James, as he had become, was tireless in his personal efforts at projecting the image of Hanson Trust in the mid to late 1970s. For example, one executive who worked there at the time recalls that Sir James would cultivate leading businessmen whenever possible: 'He would go up to people on Concorde and introduce himself, and invite them to lunch at the office with the team. Then after they had been in we would sit around discussing whether they were any good.'[12] Sir James was also a prolific letter-writer. He was in the habit of writing to company chairmen to comment on their annual reports. The general tenor would be complimentary, but he would also usually find some small criticism. The point was to make himself better known, and to encourage people to take Hanson Trust more seriously.

The publicity campaign also had a more formal dimension. In 1977 Hanson embarked on a corporate advertising campaign – one of several which have brought the group to the attention of a wider public. Using the theme that people, and especially managers, were the group's 'Principal Assets', Hanson Trust took out expensive advertisements in the business press projecting an image of a sound but rapidly growing, well-managed business. The advertisements were dominated by a soaring graph showing earnings per share between 1967 and 1976, annotated by quotations emphasising changing perceptions of the company. Beginning with: 'Never heard of them', the line advanced through: 'Hanson Trust are a crew of entrepreneurial opportunists', to: 'I've always said you could rely on Hanson Trust for a respectable earnings record.' The accompanying copy explained the philosophy of diversified investment in basic industries. The copy stressed that diversified interests protected the group against a downturn in one industry, that central management was there to help subsidiaries to perform better, and that better operating performance was the route to better earnings – both for managers and shareholders. It also sought to counter the view of conglomerates such as Hanson Trust as asset strippers or traders in companies: 'We believe the earnings we look for can only come through good management and careful housekeeping . . . We are not interested in buying companies to sell (a destructive policy that has emasculated many sound management teams).' The campaign also featured a revamp for the annual report in 1978, which had kept the same basic format since 1967. In fact early attempts at including magazine-style colour photography (by the photographer Sally Soames, who was still doing work for James Hanson in the 1990s) had been abandoned in 1974 in favour of a more austere production. But now, under the personal direction of James Hanson, Hanson Trust leapt into the glossy age with a 48-page annual report that included a separate magazine section devoted to an exposition of the group's many activities. The front cover featured the now-famous bow combining the British and American flags, which continues to be the group's corporate logo and which was dreamed up by UK operating chief Tony Alexander. Inside, Sir James took up the themes which had been stressed in the corporate advertising campaign. Under the heading 'Objectives', the chairman's report included a fulsome discourse on the Hanson philosophy and style. The chairman explained that large investors probably understood the group's aims and objectives, but it might be worth setting these out for the general public, to whom Hanson Trust's rationale perhaps remained a mystery. Sir James also suggested that the group's willingness 'to make bold moves into areas sometimes new to us' was responsible for Hanson's low stock market rating – a situation he found understandable but frustrating after '15 years of uninterrupted success'. He also expressed frustration at companies' insistence on resisting Hanson's takeover offers.

> Hanson Trust has been built up carefully to a pre-conceived plan that has not changed since the present top management team took charge 15 years ago. It was our intention then to build on a good existing business, continue its growth and enlarge it when we were sure that its success merited support. This has enabled us to develop internal growth over the years. At the same time, since we are innovators, we have actively sought growth by acquisition . . . We look for a good return on capital employed in our companies together with a positive cash flow. Our control of capital expenditure is strict. We have not only kept out of trouble that way but, as our record shows, have also achieved continuous solid growth.

There are different interpretations of Hanson's progress. Shareholders may not have understood what the pre-conceived plan was from the explanations which the chairman had produced over the years, and if the plan was based on organic growth of the existing businesses, then the actual growth of the group had little to do with that. In his first annual report as chairman, back in 1965, James Hanson had told shareholders about the policy of 'diversified expansion into areas where your management have specialised knowledge'. That would have restricted activities to transport, commercial vehicles, printing and publishing. By 1969 the explanation had become the three 'basic sectors' of transport, industrial and agricultural services, but by then the directors had already moved into an area they knew absolutely nothing about: brick-making. In the following year they sold the commercial vehicle business and moved into property development – another completely new area. By the end of the decade, when shareholders were presented with this rationale, most of the profits came from textiles, food manufacturing and service, and bricks. All of these areas were beyond the directors' 'specialised knowledge' and it would be difficult to describe any of them as 'industrial or agricultural services'.

So much for the 'pre-conceived plan'. What about the internal growth of the existing businesses, which was apparently part of that plan? The dismal performance of the early US acquisitions was mirrored by the UK operations. As well as the prompt disposal of the lacklustre fertiliser and sack-hire businesses, commercial vehicles were dispensed with in 1970. Gordon White's business, Welbecson, quickly disappeared into Northern Amalgamated Industries (NAI), which became part of the Industrial Services division. NAI's profit record is not inspiring: it made £1.2 million in 1979/80, a little lower than in the previous year and only the same as in 1976/7. Of the early acquisitions, only SLD showed any hint of internal growth. Profits peaked at £3.7 million in 1978/9, double what they had been in 1975/76, although helped by the addition of Rollalong. That level was never reached again. SLD, NAI and the UK agricultural business represented all that was left of the Wiles Group of ten years previously. Together, their profits in 1967/8 were about £900,000. Ten years later, when Sir James was boasting about internal growth, inflation would have made that figure £2.8 million. 'Internal growth', plus the addition of West of England Sack, Rollalong and a couple of smaller companies, pushed the figure up to £4.6 million, out of total group profits of £25 million. It is fairly clear what the balance was between internal growth and growth by acquisition.

The claim of 'continuous solid growth' was supported by the published figures, except for net assets per share, which had dipped in the slump of 1974. But in fact profits had been saved by property dealing in the early 1970s, and the process of conglomeratisation, which produces its own, sometimes notional, profits. In the year in which Sir James produced this homily, 1977/8, profits had increased from £24.6 million to £25.2 million, a rise of only £600,000. That growth was more than accounted for by the first contribution, of £4.7 million, from Interstate, illustrating both the importance of acquisitions to Hanson Trust's continuous growth record, and the difficulty of pinning down actual operating performance in a company like this.

The public relations campaign did eventually take effect, however, although it was not until 1979 that the share price took off again. The share price continued to languish and James Hanson continued to have very little success with acquisitions in the mid-1970s. In September 1975 it acquired from the declining Slater Walker empire a stake of 1.6 million shares in Whitecroft, a small conglomerate with interests in textiles and civil engineering. A bid for the rest of the shares eventually followed, valuing Whitecroft at £11 million. But it came to nothing when the board published optimistic forecasts and showed that they would recommend a bid only at levels which James Hanson did not regard as sensible. This was another example of the advantage of being a disinterested conglomerateur: there was nothing special about Whitecroft's businesses which James Hanson wanted, and which might have persuaded a determined bidder to pay too much. The attractions were all financial, so that those attractions disappeared once the financial equation swung in Whitecroft's favour. Another similar share stake that year did not even get as far as a bid. Hanson Trust had built up a 20 per cent shareholding in Charrington Gardner Lockett, but sold the shares gradually over the following year. The transaction was reported to have made Hanson a profit of £1.5 million, although this was not disclosed separately in the group's results for that year.

In 1976 Hanson paid £1.2 million for Rollalong, a private company making mobile cabins for use in the construction industry and elsewhere, and added to its agricultural interests with the purchase for £500,000 of Angus Milling – helping the Slater empire (by this time in the hands of James Goldsmith) once again, as Slater Walker's Estates House Investment Trust owned two-thirds of the shares of this small company. In the following year another small deal was completed, with the purchase of Hamlyn Group adding a little more to the Scottish agricultural interests. But these deals were tiny and irrelevant to the group's direction and progress.

More significant was a 'non-bid' in 1977 for Lindustries, which would eventually fall under Hanson's spell – but not yet. Lindustries was another small textiles and engineering conglomerate which was going nowhere. Hanson said it was prepared to make an offer valuing the company at £25 million, but only on condition that the Lindustries board recommended the offer to shareholders – given Hanson's subsequent reputation as an aggressive predator, it is surprising that Sir James, as he had now become, did not want to fight a takeover battle. The Lindustries board was not impressed by the offer, so no bid was actually made – until two years later. Before then Hanson Trust had mopped up a Northern Ireland textile company, the Henry Campbell group, for almost £5 million, and had abandoned an interest in textile group Selincourt, selling its 6 per cent stake.

Sir James eventually returned with a formal bid for Lindustries in August 1979, perhaps emboldened to make its first hostile UK bid for eight years by Mrs Thatcher's triumph at the polls which defeated the tottering Labour government of James (now Lord) Callaghan. Sir James's explanation was more mundane. Pointing out that Lindustries' share price had been sliding and the retiring chairman had warned at the previous week's annual meeting that profits were on the way down, Sir James commented: 'We've got to protect our investment.'[13] That disingenuous stance screened a typically opportunistic Hanson ambush. Here was a company in trouble – because effective action had not been taken to deal with problem companies while the chairman's succession was being sorted out. Here was Hanson, with a more impressive profit record, a burgeoning reputation, and cash in the bank following another rights issue of shares earlier that summer. The tactics, devised by Gordon White, became the standard Hanson approach: the company built up a shareholding and waited for an opportune moment to strike. In some cases, such as Selincourt, such a moment did not come, in which case the shares could be sold, usually at a profit. But with Lindustries the perfect moment arrived when the group's retiring chairman was too honest at the annual meeting. If he had hidden his gloom, his company might have survived. But having admitted to shareholders that profits would fall, it was no contest. As the *Observer* commented: 'The Hanson Trust chief has timed his new bid to perfection.'[14]

Lindustries' new chairman Peter Rippon was faced with the bid on his first day in the job. But he did not fancy being out for a duck, and put up as stiff a resistance as possible in the circumstances of poor results and poorer prospects. As all chairmen do when defending against takeover offers, he described the bid as 'totally inadequate'. He had a point: the £28 million bid was pitched at exactly the same price as when Hanson had approached the board informally two years previously; that price was more than a third below the value of Lindustries' assets, and it represented a multiple of earnings which was well below the stock market average for industrial companies. Mr Rippon was on shakier ground with the rest of his defence, however. On the company's prospects if it kept its independence, he could only promise that profits would not fall disastrously, that the dividend would probably be maintained and that the balance sheet was strong. And when it came to the fact that the bid had no 'industrial logic', it was clear that Lindustries was desperate. After all, the company itself had no industrial logic – there was no connection between its various businesses. Nor was there any industrial logic in Hanson Trust – any logic was purely financial.

In a style owing much to Gordon White's bravado, the group's brokers operated aggressively in the stock market during the bid period, buying up shares whenever and wherever possible. Hanson's ownership of Lindustries' shares rose steadily: 6 per cent at the start of the battle on 1 August, held since the earlier approach, 13 per cent by the 14th, 17 per cent by the 22nd, and 24 per cent by the end of August, when Lindustries' formal defence document went out to shareholders. A week later it was all over, without even needing to count the acceptances from shareholders who had responded formally to the bid. Hanson had bought just over 50 per cent of the shares in the stock market, despite the fact that several large financial institutions had held on in the hope that the bid might be increased or amended to include a share alternative to the original cash offer.

The success was important for Hanson. It erased the 1970s record of meandering disappointment in the United Kingdom. It confirmed the group's refurbished status in the City as a well-managed, purposeful enterprise which knew what it was about and was good at it. Thanks to the short time horizons of the financial community, the Slater era was now forgotten. No longer was Sir James described as a former Slater crony, nor was his company usually given the slightly pejorative 'conglomerate' label. Now he was the knighted head of a sizeable 'holding company' – well into the stock market's top 100, with a total share value of £100 million. Even when it emerged, shortly after Hanson won control of Lindustries, that Gordon White's 10 per cent of the US side had been bought out at a price of 4.3 million shares (worth $12 million or £5.5 million), previous critics had either left the scene or were silenced by the group's performance and public relations campaign. The Lex column was even moved to suggest that Sir Gordon had been cheated out of some of his dues because of the valuation method used.[15]

The Lindustries victory was an upbeat end to a lacklustre decade. It was in keeping with the advent of Thatcherism. Mrs Thatcher came to power in 1979 heading a government determined to cut trade unions down to size; to minimise the scale and presence of government in society at large but especially in the business world; and to reward those who were seen as being responsible for business success, notably by cutting taxes to let them keep more of those rewards. It was an approach and a government which Sir James, and more especially Gordon White, applauded vigorously.

Sir James had become more and more voluble in his denunciations of the Labour government. Under Harold Wilson's first administration in the 1960s, Hanson Trust had prospered and James Hanson had not found it necessary to make any political comments in his reports to shareholders, which concentrated exclusively on internal company matters. Likewise in the early 1970s, despite the chaos wrought by Heath's industrial relations policies, by the Barber boom and by the oil crisis, the chairman confined himself to company business, referring only to 'an air of uncertainty' in December 1973 as the three-day week loomed. This all changed, however, when Wilson returned to power once again in 1974, heading a party that now included a significant radical element which, for example, wanted to nationalise Britain's top 25 companies.[16] Hanson Trust was not yet in this élite but intended to be, and had no intention of becoming an arm of government when it got there. Having had the family business nationalised and thus been driven abroad, Sir James did not want the same thing to happen to his own creation. The Conservative Party also became more attractive to Sir James now it had been captured by Margaret Thatcher, offering a vigorous brand of free-market philosophy which was much more appealing to businessmen like Hanson and his friend John (later Lord) King – both of whom became staunch supporters of Thatcher. Hanson Trust had long supported the Conservative Party, or industrial organisations which fronted for it, but the usual £1000 donation shot up to £6000 in the election year of 1974, although quickly declined back to £1000 and ceased altogether for four years after James Hanson received his knighthood from Harold Wilson. But now that Wilson was back in Downing Street and his most radical minister, Tony Benn, was in charge of the Department of Industry, Sir James became more outspoken. Writing in December 1974, shortly after Wilson won his second election victory of that year, he told shareholders in the annual report: 'The free enterprise system, in which your board strongly believes, is under attack here, with a resultant decline in business confidence and a "don't know where we are going" attitude.' He returned to this theme in the following year's report, but was in more emollient mood:

> Following a period during which the free enterprise system has been under attack, there are now welcome signs that the government recognises the important contribution of profits and corporate success in providing jobs and investment, and that it intends to give greater encouragement to the growth of a healthy industrial sector.

In 1978, however, as Wilson's successor, James Callaghan, struggled to maintain an anti-inflationary wages policy, and as Thatcher's thinking became more focused and more attractive to Sir James, he regaled shareholders with a long homily on the merits of free enterprise:

> Against the overseas background of encouragement for the free enterprise system, particularly the financial rewards to all who work in it, the current scene in Britain is ripe for change and changed thinking by all who govern or have aspirations to govern.
>
> Our country cannot compete on many fronts against most of the giant industrial and agricultural nations, but where we are still at the top of the league is in our ability to innovate. All that is needed is a proper reward for *all* sections of our nation's workforce, through being able to keep more of what we *all* earn. The current confiscatory level of individual taxation here, compared, for example, with a top rate US federal tax on employment income of 50 per cent, is the most certain way to destroy forever the last sparks of business initiative that are keeping the flame flickering. The motivation for personal saving is removed and those in middle management and income groups are denied any prospect of accumulating capital. When the rigidities of pay control are added to the disincentive effect of penal taxation, the scope for mobility among management grades, an essential feature of a healthy economy, disappears. Similarly dividend control, for which there has never been any pretence of economic justification, distorts the pattern of investment. Successful and expanding companies are penalised for the benefit of those whose potential to contribute to future national well-being is much less. Bold thinking is required by our servants in government. It worked for us before, when the new government of the day in 1951 swept away virtually overnight all former war-time controls which had totally restricted our business way of life but which nobody had had the sense to abolish. They were never missed. All around us our way of life is slipping away under the rule of bureaucracy which cannot cope with day-to-day problems, let alone show us the one quality that is needed more than ever before . . . leadership.

This histrionic call to arms could almost have been an industrial and economic manifesto for the Conservative Party: remove controls, cut taxes on high earners and leave business to its own devices. It would become a familiar theme, not only in Hanson annual reports, but also from Mrs Thatcher and her supporters. But this essay was based on several myths – not least the notion that Britain was a highly taxed country by the standards of its industrial competitors. Most ironic was the idea that business had suffered from post-war controls, when, as we have seen in Chapter 2, the Hanson family business prospered during that period, and indeed benefited from working with the government.

The sentiments were nevertheless in tune with the Conservative Party, which was soon to form the new government – a government made for Hanson Trust just as Hanson Trust was made for that government. And when the going got tough for Mrs Thatcher in the early 1980s, as the severe monetarist approach resulted in a deep depression with unemployment soaring towards 3 million, Sir James was not shy of repeating these sentiments. In December 1981 – the year of the fiercely deflationary budget which ensured that Mrs Thatcher would not repeat Mr Heath's 1972 U-turn, and guaranteed that unemployment would breach 3 million; the year in which Britain's biggest manufacturer, ICI, shocked the financial community by cutting its dividend because business was so bad; the year in which 364 economists wrote to *The Times* expressing their horror at the government's economic policies – Sir James's loyalty to his new hero, Margaret Thatcher, did not crack. At the end of that horrendous year he wrote to his shareholders in relatively optimistic mood:

This has been a rough year for industry in the UK . . . leaner and more competitive than it has been for years, I believe that British industry generally recognises that the worst is over. Our government has made enormous efforts to bring back the spirit of free enterprise. In our turn we must support it in every way. Its record is impressive: inflation being tackled; direct tax rates cut to levels comparable with other European countries; bureaucratic controls over prices, pay, dividends and currency movements abolished; reductions in the numbers of civil servants and local government staff; and most of all, restrictions on uncontrolled government and local authority spending on worthless projects. Through it all, the encouragement to free enterprise shines bright and clear. Let us not fail to grasp this opportunity. If we lose it we may never see it again.

By the following year, with the economy slowly beginning to improve and the pound back down to more realistic levels, Sir James was equally outspoken in support of the government's efforts to cut public spending and taxation, and against calls for reflation. By that point, Sir James had joined the ranks of Mrs Thatcher's favourite business people, and was well on his way to becoming one of Britain's best-known and most feared business leaders. Hanson Trust was also well on its way towards the top ranks of British industry. If the 1970s had been disappointing for Sir James, despite his personal elevation and his group's establishment in the United States, the 1980s were to exceed all possible expectations. He was never in any doubt that he could continue expanding the group, because he was convinced, quite rightly, that there were still many companies led by poor managers that were ripe for exploitation. But even in his most optimistic moments Sir James could not have dreamt that the company which began the 1980s with one £25 million takeover under its belt (after the Lindustries success) would, within a few years, be paying £2.5 billion for the Imperial Group, and feel able to contemplate rescuing Midland Bank or helping the government over the sale of PowerGen.

It was not all plain sailing, however. During the Lindustries bid, Hanson was also busy on other fronts, none of which resulted in success. Sir James had takeover talks with a small Bristol-based conglomerate, John James Group, and bought 11 per cent of the shares in the engineers Central Manufacturing and Trading (CMT). The talks with John James came to nothing, and the CMT affair dragged on for a couple of years before the idea was abandoned, with Hanson Trust suffering a 30p a share loss. In the United States, it had acquired nearly 9 per cent of the shares in Barber Oil, a small oil and mining group. Victory seemed certain after the Barber Oil board agreed to a takeover, only for Hanson Trust to be defeated by the US shipping laws. At $163 million (£75 million) this would have been Hanson's biggest ever takeover, by a long way, upping the stakes dramatically and illustrating the group's new confidence. Barber owned a shipping fleet, however, which brought the bid within the scope of the rigorous US maritime laws, which prevent US ships being owned by foreign companies, and gave the oil company an excuse for wriggling out of the Hanson deal, refusing to give the British predator more time to find a buyer for the shipping activities. Hanson insisted that energy had become a new focus for its attentions, despite this defeat. Sir James told the annual meeting in January 1980 that he expected to make increased investment in 'energy and other basic commodities' during the new decade. It was another new direction, one which was actually not to be followed until right at the end of the 1980s, with the acquisition of the Peabody coal company.

Undismayed by his lack of success, Gordon White soon came up with a new target. This time it was McDonough, a company quoted on the New York stock exchange but representing the industrial interests of Bernard McDonough, a cavalier 76-year-old American businessman who owned 40 per cent of the shares and also owned separate businesses in the hotel and shipping industries. This was an agreed deal, so there was no room for last-minute slip-ups, and McDonough's cement, footwear and hand-tool businesses duly became part of the group late in 1980. It was Hanson Trust's biggest buy yet, at $185 million – rather more than Barber Oil would have been, although the strengthening of the pound in the meantime meant it was marginally less in sterling terms. In Gordon White's accustomed fashion, the group was putting up only $25 million of its own cash, the rest being borrowed from US banks against the assets of McDonough. And in what would become a familiar practice, Hanson quickly recouped that $25 million, and more, when it sold the cement and concrete operations back to Mr McDonough in June 1981, for $49 million (£25 million). The profit on that deal was not separately disclosed in the accounts, but must have been significant, since the cash recouped was a quarter of the purchase price for a business which had made about a tenth of McDonough's profits. It was a good start to the decade and it did not take long for Hanson to follow it up with another big deal, this time in the UK. For the first time the group also moved into more sensitive territory, with a takeover bid which raised issues of wider public interest than the usual narrow question of whether shareholders were best advised to support their company or sell out to Hanson. It was a difference which began once again to raise questions about the nature of conglomeracy and its impact on industrial performance, questions which had been forgotten during the gloomy 1970s, but which were to dog Sir James throughout the rest of his career.

Hanson Trust had just lost out in a small (£12 million) battle for brick and tile maker G.H. Downing, when its bid was topped by the building materials group Steetley. It was another disappointment, following soon after the defeat in the bid for CMT, but this was small beer compared with what was to come. On the morning of 10 July 1981, Hanson's stockbrokers, Hoare Govett, went to work in the stock market armed with £7 million of Hanson's money. After what was to become well-known in the 1980s as a 'dawn raid' they came away with 7.4 million shares in the battery company Berec, better known as British Ever Ready. Added to 2.4 million shares which Hanson had quietly been accumulating in blocks of 100,000 or so over the previous two months,[17] the dawn raid gave Hanson just short of 15 per cent of Berec's shares – the maximum permitted to be built up in this fashion under UK takeover rules. It was another aggressive Gordon White manoeuvre. He had begun to buy the shares when the battery company had announced a slump in profits to just £10 million – barely a third of its peak performance in 1977. The dawn raid came just two days after Berec's annual meeting had heard a gloomy prognosis from the chairman – a copy of the Lindustries scenario. Hanson's straight-bat spokesman, Martin Taylor, said the purchase represented 'a useful investment'[18] and said there was no immediate intention to increase the shareholding. Berec chairman Colin Stapleton attempted to project an air of calm, saying: 'There is no animosity . . . I am delighted that a company such as Hanson should be interested in us.'[19] But he can have fooled few people. He immediately called an emergency board meeting to plan a defence against the expected bid, and it was not long before hostilities broke out.

While Hanson Trust might be regarded as one part of the British disease, Berec was another. Hanson's short-termism and financial dominance was matched by Berec's arrogance, which led it to resist market changes. British Ever Ready, as the company had been until

1978, had prospered thanks to a virtual monopoly in Britain in the 1960s. This situation was a relic of the original sale of the UK company by its American parent, which had left the UK and US businesses with close ties, until forced separation after the Second World War under anti-trust pressures, but also with problems. The agreement following the original split prevented the UK arm from using the name Ever Ready outside the UK, so the company, realising that it was in a global market and needed a global brand, decided to change its name. In 1978 it became Berec. It was a justifiable move, but the abandonment of Ever Ready caused a storm of protest and there was little attempt to explain the rationale. Berec's comfortable position had also been undermined when the Monopolies Commission, in 1977, had ordered the sale of the group's stake in Mallory, the company which made Duracell alkaline batteries. The disposal of Mallory left Berec cut off from the new technology of longer-life products. Berec had known about alkaline batteries for a long time – the link with Mallory had existed since just after the war – but had preferred to concentrate instead on its traditional zinc–carbon product. The smaller and longer-lasting alkaline batteries were ideal for the rash of new consumer products – mostly made by Japanese companies with whom Berec had no links – but Berec insisted that this was a small, specialist niche market which was not worth pursuing. Instead it would continue to rely on its traditional mass markets, not only in Britain but also in South Africa and Nigeria, while also building a presence on the continent and in the Far East. By the late 1970s the company had begun to recognise the error of its ways. Duracell was making huge inroads into its UK base, attacking new distribution channels such as supermarkets as well as traditional outlets. Berec poured investment into new plant: £51 million between 1977 and 1980, doubling its fixed assets in that period. But it was bedevilled by the sort of management rivalries which stem from years of complacency, especially between competing research teams. And suddenly Nigeria cancelled the company's import licence.

Here was a company ripe for plucking by a group such as Hanson Trust. Berec's share value had slumped along with its profits, so that the share price failed to reflect the value of the new assets which had been installed, and the prospects for the company which would stem from those assets. But it was also a group whose top management inspired little confidence, allowing shareholders to sell out with a clear conscience to Hanson Trust – a group with a newly enhanced image for taking the tough decisions that Berec appeared to have ducked, for installing sound financial systems and leaving the managers who knew what to do to get on and do it, as profitably as possible. The takeover bid eventually arrived in September. Thanks to a resurgence in Hanson Trust's share price following the public relations campaign, Sir James was once again able to use Hanson shares to make acquisitions. He offered Berec shareholders three of his shares for every eight they owned, with an alternative of 105p per share for those who did not want to take Hanson Trust shares. This valued Berec at £73 million, which was only half the value of the group's shares in 1977, but was still more than the price they had been trading at, even buoyed up by takeover expectations. Berec directors put up as vigorous a defence as they could muster in the circumstances. They pointed out that the bid was a piece of financial opportunism, which was true but of little concern to shareholders. They also said it seriously undervalued the group's spanking new assets, which was also true and of rather more concern. Mr Stapleton additionally promised that profits, which had already begun to recover, would continue to improve and that the £20 million spent on developing alkaline batteries in the previous three years would soon start to bring returns. The company summed up its position in a press advertisement: 'Berec shareholders should not give away their company at the very moment when the tide is beginning to turn.'[20]

Former chairman L.W. Orchard also weighed in with a letter to the *Financial Times*, which provoked a stern riposte from Hanson Trust director John Pattison. Mr Orchard pointed out that Berec had great potential, which would not be aided by Hanson Trust:

> Berec is ready to take full advantage of increasing markets and further advances in the development and use of battery operated products. Both its markets, in the 110 different countries in which it trades, and its profits should show substantial increases without any assistance from Hanson. Hanson recognises this and that is why it is trying to acquire Berec while Berec's share price is low . . . I therefore say to my fellow shareholders in

Berec 'What can Hanson do for Berec that Berec cannot do for itself? Answer – nothing'. . . Do what I am doing. Drop the Hanson paper in the wastepaper basket where it belongs.

Mr Pattison responded by pointing out that Mr Orchard was largely responsible for Berec's predicament, having been chairman for ten years until 1979. He also refuted the suggestion that Hanson Trust owed its growth solely to acquisitions, and picked some holes in Mr Orchard's letter. And finally, he drew attention to Mr Orchard's Berec shareholding and asked him to disclose recent share sales. This irrelevant issue did nothing to divert attention from the central question, which subsequently arose time and time again in Hanson Trust takeovers, of whether Hanson was merely seeking to capitalise on the investment recently put into Berec, and whether Hanson's financial approach would be beneficial to such a company.

Nevertheless, these were not questions which concerned the financial community or the financial press, preoccupied with the short-term implications for shareholders in the two companies. On that basis, Berec shareholders had every reason to suppose that they would do better under Hanson Trust than under Mr Stapleton and his team, while the antics of Berec's management over the previous few years left them with little call on shareholders' loyalty. Hanson also leapt on some goings-on which seemed to show Berec directors exploiting their position even as their company struggled. Two directors had interest-free housing loans, while others owned property jointly with Berec, with an option to buy out the company at the original price at any time up to 1990. Further, directors had recently agreed new, better-paid, five-year service agreements. The lack of non-executives on the Berec board made these deals seem rather less just than shareholders might have been entitled to expect, and did not help to counter an image of a badly directed company which did not have shareholders' interests at heart.

Sir James was therefore expected to be victorious, unless Berec could come up with a 'white knight', which seemed to be its only hope of avoiding the clutches of the Hanson Trust takeover squad. And at the eleventh hour Berec did entice such a champion into the fray. Ironically, it was another conglomerate, Thomas Tilling, which came riding to the rescue, and even more ironically, one which would itself soon fall victim to takeover – by another young conglomerate, BTR. Thomas Tilling had been established rather longer than Hanson Trust, but was a very similar animal. It owned a diverse collection of businesses, including Cornhill insurance, Pretty Polly tights and the publisher Heinemann. Its philosophy was similar: letting local managers run their companies with a minimum of interference from the central team. But although it was twice as old and twice the size of Hanson Trust, it was hardly a match for Hanson corporate aggression; despite its position, this was only Tilling's second contested takeover battle. Tilling's offer, agreed with the Berec board, was worth almost 30 per cent more than the Hanson bid. But this gave an opening to Hanson. The Berec board would now not be able to turn down a Hanson Trust offer which more than matched the Tilling offer they had accepted. Sir James came back at the beginning of December with an offer which valued Berec at £95 million, marginally more than the Tilling bid.

Berec's directors had no room for manoeuvre. They effectively sued for peace, seeking to extract from Hanson Trust assurances about their future and the future of their company. By 19 December 1981 they had to admit defeat, telling shareholders to accept Hanson's offer, and that Sir James had given assurances 'that Hanson does not intend to make major changes to the Berec group'. That may have helped them to save face, but in fact Hanson had stated in its original offer document, back in October: 'Hanson does not intend to make major changes to the business of Berec Group.' The promise carried no greater weight in December than it had in October. By the middle of 1982 the first sales and closures were being made: head office, the loss-making Nigerian subsidiary, the disastrous Hong Kong factory, and the American operation. In August the Advanced Projects Group at Abingdon, one of Berec's research units, was sold to management. In December Hanson committed the ultimate sin, so far as old Berec hands were concerned: the European operations in Germany and Italy were not only sold, but sold to the great rival, Duracell. The sale raised £37 million, recouping almost two-fifths of the purchase price – in cash, whereas the acquisition had been made using loan stock subsequently convertible into shares. It reversed Berec's international strategy, justifying returning the company to its old name of British Ever Ready. Martin Taylor commented, with no hint of irony:

'The deal means that British Ever Ready is now able to concentrate on getting increasing returns from its interests in the UK and South Africa.'[21] In a business which was becoming increasingly global, however, it meant that those returns would not increase for long, as British Ever Ready's shrinking base left it seriously disadvantaged against global rivals. Berec was to be run for cash, allowed to shrink but because of that to keep contributing funds to the rest of the group, and producing the requisite return on capital. It was a familiar Hanson Trust tactic, first used in the 1960s with the purchase of West of England Sack, and it was highly profitable for the group.

While all this had been going on, Hanson Trust had also bought another UK company, the Berry Magicoal makers, United Gas Industries, but the price of £20 million, for so long in the 1970s a distant target, was now barely noticeable, so large had Hanson Trust become. It had now leapt into the UK's top 50 companies, with a total share value of almost £600 million. There were still blind alleys and disappointments: a stake in Gulf Resources which came to nothing, and thoughts of a merger with the retail giant Sears which got no further than thoughts. But Sir James was now a respected business leader, as well as feared. Gordon White had received his knighthood, balancing the transatlantic partnership as well as further elevating its status. Their company was treated with the respect its size deserved, rather than its tender age, especially as it continued to churn out apparently remarkable results regardless of the early 1980s recession. Its share price reflected the admiration of the City, maintaining an almost continuous climb from a trough in 1979 to a peak in 1985, consistently beating the stock market index despite the long advance in share prices during that period. In 1982 alone the Hanson share price almost doubled.

In 1982 James Hanson was 60 years old and Sir Gordon only slightly younger. In 16 years they had built a transatlantic empire which was feared and respected in more or less equal measure. Many other people would have felt the successful conclusion of the Berec takeover was a good time to bow out. Sir Gordon had his $12 million from the sale of his 10 per cent stake in the US business, Sir James's 3 million shares were then worth about £6 million. Instead, they were gathering their strength for an astonishing charge through the British and American industrial hierarchy which would leave their company even further up the ladder of business success, but by the 1990s would see the City beginning to question the style and achievements of the group.

CHAPTER 6

Megadeals: 1983–91

The Berec victory was a significant milestone for Sir James and for Hanson Trust. It was only about the same size as the acquisition of McDonough the year before, but it was by far the biggest UK deal to date – almost four times the value of Lindustries. More significantly, it was a different kind of target. Lindustries was a conglomerate, as was McDonough and most of the other US targets. There could be no objection in principle to one conglomerate being swallowed by another, no question of whether Sir James and his colleagues knew anything about the industry they were venturing into. But Berec did raise those sorts of questions for the first time: it was a very focused company in a very particular industry. Its defeat was a vote of confidence by the City in Hanson Trust's ability to run even such a specialised company in such an industry – a vote of confidence in Hanson Trust's perceived management ability. The perception that Sir James employed excellent managers who could run any industry may well have been misplaced, since the company's unique approach was not to attempt to run the companies it owned, in the accepted understanding of the term, but to leave the running of the companies largely to existing managers. Sir James sat at the centre, surrounded by accountants, attempting only to control the finances, not to be involved in, or even interested in, the business and operating issues which lay beneath the financial numbers.

This was not a widely recognised until much later in the 1980s. At this stage, observers and commentators continually looked for the kind of industrial logic which underpinned the strategic moves of most other large companies. Even Hanson Trust's alter ego, BTR, which was also essentially an acquisition-led conglomerate, did not buy just any company which met its financial criteria. It stuck largely to acquisitions of general manufacturing companies, where it felt its skills lay. Maintaining this belief that there was some underlying logic in Sir James's many moves was useful at the time. It helped the City to accept the huge leap in scale which the next takeover bid represented, and which set Sir James on his triumphant progress through the 1980s.

The next target was UDS, formerly United Drapery Stores, the store and property empire of the Lyons family. In fact there was no 'industrial logic' in the bid. Like almost all the others it was merely an opportunistic move because Hanson Trust rightly saw that it could make some money out of it. But there were shoe interests, an area the group was already involved in through the Endicott Johnson subsidiary of McDonough. This was enough for some commentators to allay worries about Hanson Trust moving into completely new areas.

UDS owned famous names such as the John Collier menswear chain, Richard Shops, Timpsons shoe shops and the Allders department stores. The battle for the group was a tortuous affair which involved some other famous 1980s names as well as that of Sir James. He intervened only on 16 February 1983, six weeks into a complex battle for control of the group. And it took a further two months before UDS was brought under the Hanson umbrella, despite the fact that this was another sitting-duck company, like Lindustries poorly served by an ageing chairman seeking to ensure a satisfactory family succession. In this case, however, so bad was the situation that the institutional shareholders had taken action. On 1 January the chairman, Bernard Lyons, had been replaced by Sir Robert Clark, chairman of Hill Samuel and coincidentally an old adversary of Sir James from his days as a director of Bowater in the early 1970s. Like Mr Rippon at Lindustries, he was faced with a takeover offer on his first day in the chairman's office – but in this case not from Sir James.

Sir Robert's first adversary at UDS was somebody else who would become a symbol of 1980s rapaciousness: Gerald Ronson, head of the private property-based empire, the Heron Corporation, and one of those who was convicted in 1990 over the Guinness affair. Mr Ronson had harnessed the unhappiness of several institutional investors following a sharp reduction in profits and a dividend cut, and had put together a consortium under the name Bassishaw, which had been amassing a share stake since the summer of 1982. Bassishaw presented Sir Robert with an offer of 100p per share, worth £191 million. It looked like a foregone conclusion. The poor profits record and boardroom antics of UDS had already lost it the support of many key shareholders, and there seemed little option but to try and push up the price. There was a complication, however. Also in the summer of 1982, UDS had been approached by another vigorous 1980s entrepreneur, Ralph (later Sir Ralph) Halpern. He was keen to expand the Burton group and had offered to buy not the whole of UDS, but the John Collier and Richard Shops chains. Early in February UDS agreed with Burton to sell these two chains for £78 million. Sir Robert's defence team also managed to rush out a property revaluation which showed that the remaining assets were worth 140p per share – well ahead of the Bassishaw offer. With a profits forecast also showing a substantial rebound in operating performance, there suddenly seemed some hope that UDS could retain its independence. On Valentine's Day, Bassishaw returned with a higher offer, but at only 114p per share it was significantly below the declared asset value. It was also above the UDS share price, however, and there seemed little more Sir Robert and his colleagues could do except haggle to try and extract a few extra pence, although he also attempted to boost the management team by the appointment of a top retailer, Tom MacAuliffe, formerly of Argos.

What were apparently the final throes of the battle were stalled by Sir James's intervention. He told Sir Robert Clark that Hanson Trust, which had a 15 per cent stake in UDS, would make a share offer worth 125p per UDS share, if the UDS board recommended the offer. UDS directors were initially in little doubt. 'They couldn't get their hands in the air fast enough,' Sir Robert later recalled.[1] But Mr Ronson was not beaten yet. He persuaded his consortium to increase its bid again, this time to 130p. That was not enough to deter Sir James, however, who returned within hours to add 20p per share in cash to his original share offer. Once again, the battle appeared to be almost over, but yet another twist emerged when the UDS executive directors revolted, and suggested that the board should back the Bassishaw offer after all, even though it was worth less than the mixture of shares and cash from Hanson. Significantly, for the first time, Sir James came up against fears that he would dismember the group were he to be successful. The UDS directors naturally feared for their jobs, as do all directors on the receiving end of a takeover bid. But they also feared for the break-up of the group, and justified their support for a lower offer by reference to the interests of employees. On 23 April, however, Hanson Trust won control: enough shareholders had accepted its offer. Five months later the fears of the UDS directors began to be justified when the break-up began. By the end of the 1980s none of the gigantic group remained within Hanson Trust.

In one respect, the UDS takeover was routine. It was a company in a poor state which could offer little resistance, especially to a predator like Hanson Trust which had a reputation for turning round such businesses. On the other hand, this was a milestone. The takeover was worth £260 million, almost three times the size of the Berec acquisition and almost ten times the size of the Lindustries deal. UDS, largely a retailing concern, was also another new business area. Despite the tenuous footwear connection, there was on the whole little pretence that UDS would have anything to do with Hanson Trust's existing businesses. The UDS affair therefore showed that the stock market was prepared to back Sir James with even bigger sums of money, and was not at all dismayed if the target of his attentions was in an industry where directors had no 'personal knowledge and wide management experience', to use Sir James's early strategic phrase. That paved the way for several years of astonishing takeover activity, not only by Hanson Trust.

Following the Conservative victory in the 1983 general election, with Nigel Lawson installed as Chancellor and Norman Tebbit in charge at Trade and Industry, the Thatcherite philosophy of deregulation, competition and ever lower direct taxes began to be put earnestly to the test. The level of sterling continued to slide, helping the competitiveness of British companies; unemployment finally began to fall as output took off; the stock market continued its climb, which had commenced following the sterling crisis and IMF rescue of 1976, and which would not end until the crash of 1987. It was like the 1960s once again. Memories of asset stripping and 'the unacceptable face of capitalism' were long faded. Instead there was official concern that inefficiencies should be stamped out – not this time, by the Industrial Reorganisation Corporation, but by competition. The City, too, was having to face up to competition. Under the threat of a reference to the Monopolies Commission, the stock exchange set about reforming its time-honoured restrictive practices, culminating in the 'Big Bang' of 1986. The early privatisations helped to stimulate interest in the stock market and the number of new companies being floated rose steadily, from only 35 in 1980 to 155 in 1987. Some of these were the hugely popular, high-profile companies such as Laura Ashley, Sock Shop and Body Shop. It was a time when the merger and acquisition departments of merchant banks were particularly busy.

These were ideal conditions for a company like Hanson Trust. During the recession it had developed a reputation for clever acquisition, international dealings and fiercely profit-oriented management. It had maintained a record of uninterrupted earnings and dividend growth, and in those days few people were worried about how that earnings growth had been achieved. Lord Hanson (as he became in 1983) was not slow to capitalise on these perfect conditions for his brand of industrial reorganisation. Over the next four years he made, or attempted to make, two major acquisitions each year, financed partly by what at the time was Britain's largest ever rights issue. The first of these had already been set in train even as Sir James was preparing to walk victorious into the UDS boardroom, intent on sacking the directors and selling the site. On 19 April 1983, three days before Hanson Trust won the battle for UDS, the group bought 3 million shares in London Brick (just over 2 per cent of the company). By October that had built up to a 9 per cent holding, which had to be publicly declared, and in December, shortly after publishing another set of record results, the bid was launched. This move was a little different to most Hanson attacks. It was essentially defensive, intended to head off London Brick's move into the market sector occupied by Hanson Trust's subsidiary, Butterley. That London Brick could be a feasible target showed how far Lord Hanson had come over the previous ten years. In 1973, Hanson's brick interests were insignificant when the Monopolies Commission investigated whether London Brick's dominance of the common, or 'fletton' brick market acted against the public interest. Yet now, the once-mighty London Brick went running to the Office of Fair Trading demanding protection under monopolies rules from takeover by Hanson Trust. In fact, it was a monopolies investigation prompted by London Brick's attempt to acquire Ibstock Johnsen (the loser to Hanson in the 1971 bid for National Star) which exposed the company to attack. The Commission concluded, in August 1983, that a combination of London Brick and Ibstock Johnsen would not be against the public interest, largely because they operated in different sectors of the brick market. In the meantime, however, London Brick had second thoughts. But the Monopolies Commission ruling had exposed it to attack by Sir James, who no longer had to worry about his bid being referred. The best that the besieged chairman, Jeremy Rowe, could make of it was to push up the price. This he succeeded in doing, not once but twice – the first time that the tight-fisted duo of Lord Hanson and Sir Gordon White had been forced to increase their offer twice to win a bid battle. They ended up paying £245 million, almost half as much again as the value of the first offer. Even then, the knife-edge battle went to the last moment before Hanson Trust snatched victory – when Lord Hanson's trusty stockbrokers, Hoare Govett, managed to buy a chunk of shares to push Hanson Trust over the 50 per cent mark. On 29 February 1984 they were able to announce that 59 per cent of London Brick shareholders had accepted the final offer. Butterley's position was protected, although at a hefty price.

Sir Gordon and Lord Hanson had little time to reflect on whether, for once, they may have been too eager to win the battle, and so persuaded to pay too much. Just two days previously, on 27 February, US Industries announced that it was planning a management buyout to take the company private. USI was an anonymous conglomerate, just like Hanson Trust, which Sir Gordon's acquisitions team had been keeping a close eye on for a couple of years. It seemed an ideal candidate for the Hanson treatment: a large number of smallish businesses in routine, unexciting industries, some of which could be sold to recoup part of the purchase price, others whose performance could briefly be boosted by better productivity and higher prices. Sir Gordon immediately began buying USI shares, amassing a holding of 1 million shares (5 per cent of the total) during

March. On 2 April, while a non-executive committee of USI directors was still considering the management buyout proposal, the group's chairman, Gordon Walker, received a letter from Sir Gordon offering to buy USI. Sir Gordon said Hanson Trust would pay more than the $20 a share which was contemplated by the buyout team. Mr Walker and his colleagues were not impressed. They upped their buyout bid to $24 a share, challenging Sir Gordon to match that price or, preferably, go away with a nice profit. It was Hanson Trust's first contested bid battle in the United States.

The predators did not match the planned buyout price, but Sir Gordon did increase his offer to $23 a share, at the same time abandoning the attempt at a negotiated deal and making a public offer for USI shares. As usual, Sir Gordon's judgement was right. The management team could not raise the finance to back their offer quickly enough, and at the beginning of May USI eventually went to Hanson Trust for $532 million. That was equivalent to £380 million at the time, making it another step up the size scale, exactly half as much again as UDS. The victory also restored the balance of the group between the US and the UK, something that Lord Hanson was always keen to maintain, and also helped promote the image of the chairman as a man who was not to be denied. Hanson Trust was now seen as a company which did not lose, despite its record of failures in the 1970s and even in the early 1980s. Defeats by Costain, Whitecroft, Barber Oil, CMT and G.H. Downing were all forgotten. Lord Hanson, it now seemed, would carry all before him.

Despite the run of victories, which now spanned the Atlantic, the next contest was to prove that Lord Hanson was not invincible – and that his insistence on resisting bankers' blandishments to 'just a pay a few pence more' was real enough. As so often, the move came in December, shortly after Hanson Trust had reported an astonishing 86 per cent increase in profits. The target was Powell Duffryn (PD), once the nation's largest coal company, which since nationalisation had become primarily a freight business. In 1984, PD was the market leader in short-haul bulk shipping, based on coal transportation, but it also had engineering interests, and like most companies which have seen their core ripped out by nationalisation, its history of finding something else to do was not without mistakes. Once again, Lord Hanson had been sitting on a shareholding for several months, and once again pounced after he had been able to announce another year of surging earnings, and after his target had hit trouble. This time, however, the trouble was not self-inflicted, as with many Hanson targets. It stemmed from the bitter miners' strike which had begun in spring 1984, and which had seriously damaged PD's fuel-distribution business. What was more, the company had already taken action to limit the damage, had reported a 42 per cent rise in profits in the previous year, and was able to predict a rise in the current year despite the coal troubles. Chief executive John Franklin was able to claim, with some justification, that Lord Hanson was merely trying to get the benefit of PD's heavy expenditure on restructuring over recent years. That has been true of many successful acquisitions, however, so it was not enough to persuade PD shareholders to resist Lord Hanson's offer. And in the early stages of the bid it looked like another foregone conclusion, especially as the Hanson Trust share price rose dramatically in early January 1985. Since the offer was in Hanson shares, not cash, any rise in the Hanson share price made the offer more valuable, and therefore more difficult for PD to counter. But the rise did not last. Before the end of the month share prices in general began to slide, carrying Hanson Trust's along with them. PD shareholders had also begun to believe their directors' claims that the strategy which had been implemented over the previous five years was correct and would be borne out by results. For once, Lord Hanson refused to increase his offer, attracting criticisms of arrogance which did not help his cause. 'Hanson Trust has displayed a nonchalance bordering on the supercilious in its dealings with the shareholders of Powell Duffryn,' commented the *Financial Times*'s Lex column. 'Faced with a take it or leave it offer, shareholders should leave it.'[2]

The end of January brought the end of the bid, and Lord Hanson's first defeat for four years. For once, Sir Gordon White's instincts seem to have been awry: this was not the usual helpless victim PD might have seemed. Also, his usually immaculate timing may have been wrong, allowing the PD management to show some evidence that they knew what they were doing, and to demonstrate that what they were doing was already working. While Lord Hanson insisted that the price was right,[3] and should not have been increased, this small episode – the bid was worth only £170 million, quite small by Hanson Trust standards then – may have evidenced the beginnings of an over-confidence which was to prove damaging later in the decade. Not that the bidding stopped there – far from it: 1985 was to see Lord Hanson launch his most audacious attack yet on the British business establishment. But while Hanson Trust continued to grow, the first slips in the previously sure-footed scramble up the corporate mountain can be seen in 1985, and the cracks in Lord Hanson's business reputation can be traced back to that year.

Lord Hanson had always been miserly in the issuing of new shares. He loved splitting the shares in 'scrip' issues which made them more affordable, and then watching the price creep back, on the new basis, to where it had been before the split. But because of the reduction in value to existing shareholders he did not like issuing wholly new shares, either to shareholders to raise cash, or in exchange for the shares of target companies. As one executive commented: 'We always felt that our shares were undervalued, even when they were very highly rated.'[4] That is why Hanson Trust was an enthusiastic and early user of convertible loan stock: loans which could be converted into shares at a later date, by which point a rise in the share price in the meantime would make the share issue much cheaper. Lord Hanson used to describe it as 'getting tomorrow's money today', a phrase he also used to justify selling a part of a group which had just been acquired, at a price which could be justified by the buyer only on the basis of superb future performance. But the phenomenal growth of Hanson Trust could not be financed entirely in this fashion. From time to time Lord Hanson had been forced to issue new shares in rights issues giving shareholders the right to buy in proportion to their existing holdings. The company's first rights issue had been made only months after it had been floated in 1964, to finance the acquisition of Tillotson and Commercial Motors (Hull). James Hanson's first issue came four years later, raising £721,000 to help finance the 1960s acquisition spree. Subsequent issues came in 1972 – raising £8 million and leaving the group in a happily liquid position to face the property and fringe bank crash – again in 1975, 1979 and 1981, by which time the issue raised £43 million.

On 10 June 1985, however, Lord Hanson asked shareholders to stump up £519 million, giving them the chance to buy one new share at 185p for every six they already held. It was the largest such request the London stock market had ever faced, apart from the part-nationalised BP, and the stock market did not like it. The gigantic scale of the offer made many investors pause for breath. True, Hanson Trust was much larger than it had been in 1981, but only about three times larger in terms of sales, profits and assets. Yet Lord Hanson was asking for 12 times the sum he had raised then. The £519 million was actually more than the total shareholders' funds at the end of the previous year, which stood at just £410 million. The flood of new shares also came to a market still struggling to cope with a recent influx as a result of the expiry on one of Hanson Trust's convertible loan stock issues. Another problem was the lack of a specific reason. Investors asked to put up more of their money like to know what that money is going to be spent on, even when they had done as well as Lord Hanson's shareholders had over the previous few years. Lord Hanson had said that more acquisitions were contemplated, but many shareholders would have preferred to wait and see what the target was before parting with their cash.

Some in the City were also beginning to worry about how much longer the Hanson machine could roll on. Merchant bank S. G. Warburg, in successfully defending Powell Duffryn, had raised the issue of Hanson's underlying performance. Warburg argued that Hanson Trust was merely an acquisition machine – and with remarkable prescience went on to suggest that to maintain his remarkable growth record, Lord Hanson would have to tilt at ICI by the end of the decade. The argument may have helped save PD, but it had also begun to sow some seeds of doubt about prospects for the thwarted predator. In April the *Economist* had observed: 'There is a suspicion that Hanson Trust may have lost its sparkle.' And a *Financial Times* reporter wrote: 'It seems inevitable that to maintain the company's formidable reputation for growth by acquisition, as the group gets larger Lord Hanson has to keep looking at bigger and bigger targets.'[5]

For once, Lord Hanson was also unlucky. First, the long slide of the pound against the dollar, which had begun in 1983 and had benefited companies like Hanson Trust with significant US earnings, was suddenly reversed early in 1985. In a rare display of unity, leaders of the Group of Five leading industrial countries, meeting at New York's Plaza Hotel, agreed that the dollar had been allowed to rise too far. In an even rarer display of cohesion, they worked together to make sure the dollar fell to more realistic levels. This action may have been helpful to the world's leading economies, but it did not help Lord Hanson. It made it much more difficult for Hanson's US businesses to continue reporting profits growth when their figures were converted into sterling for group reporting purposes.

Second, just as investors were contemplating the rights issue, the stock market was hit by a brief interruption in its long ascent to the silly summer of 1987. This combination of factors forced down the Hanson Trust share price, from 222p in June before the rights issue was announced, to a potentially disastrous 182p at the beginning of July. That was 3p below the price at which shareholders were being asked to buy their new shares, meaning they would be faced with an immediate loss and would therefore be sensible not to apply for the shares. In that event a huge proportion of the 200 million new shares would be left with the underwriting institutions, which would damage the Hanson Trust share price for many months and, even worse, damage Hanson Trust's reputation in the City. The company's merchant bank, N.M. Rothschild, and its stockbrokers, Hoare Govett, piled in with the heaviest selling effort they could muster. With some vigorously optimistic noises from Lord Hanson on the eve of the offer closing, they managed to edge the share price back above the magic 185p – but only by 1p.

It seemed at first that they had managed to avert disaster. On the evening of 5 July the word was that only a fifth of the shares had not been bought. But that proved optimistic – a rosy guess blamed on the quantity of applications from Lord Hanson's beloved small shareholders pouring in to the registrar's department of Lloyds Bank in Worthing. In fact, as the evening wore on it became apparent that underwriters would be left with about 100 million shares – a dismal 50 per cent success rate. With a distraught Lord Hanson on the phone from California panicking about the likely impact on his company's standing in the City, Hoare Govett and Rothschild put in a final, mighty effort. By the early hours of the morning of Friday 5 July they had managed to persuade the Kuwait Investment Office to take 100 million shares at fractionally above the 185p issue price. Later that morning, Rothschild's vice-chairman, Sir Michael Richardson, received a package from Hanson Trust. It was an oil painting of a dismounting hunter, a favourite of Lord Hanson's, which had hung behind his desk for many years and to which he was greatly attached. It was a mark of his immense gratitude for a job well done.

The reputations of Lord Hanson and of Hanson Trust were ostensibly intact. But further cracks had appeared in what had until 1985 seemed to be an indestructible veneer of success. With a stock market recovery following that jittery June, the Hanson Trust share price regained some of its losses. But it did not recover as fast as the market average. In fact the share price lost ground steadily, compared to the stock market index, from the beginning of 1985 until spring 1988. Only once since then have Lord Hanson's shares ever regained that early 1985 level – briefly, in the spring of 1990. It was not apparent at the time, however, that Hanson Trust had reached its peak, in share price terms, after a magnificent surge through the 1980s. And the rights issue difficulties did nothing to dent the bravado of Lord Hanson and Sir Gordon White. This was the peak of the 1980s takeover boom, which this duo had helped to create and which they were intent on continuing. The impossible had already happened, not only with Hanson Trust's victories over Berec, UDS and London Brick, but also BTR's acquisition of the once-mighty Thomas Tilling, the rise of Sir Terence Conran from the tiny Habitat to the brink of a merger with British Home Stores, and tobacco company BAT's move into financial services with the purchase of Eagle Star. In 1985, Burton bought Debenhams, Asda merged with MFI, and Guinness rode to the rescue of Distillers in the most extreme example of the period's acquisition over-exuberance. Lord Hanson was not going to be left out of this party.

The sceptics who had begun to point out that he would have to make ever-larger takeover bids were proved right not once, but twice, before the year was out. They were two of the most bitterly fought takeovers the business world has ever seen, however, and certainly the most vicious in which Lord Hanson has ever been involved. The targets used every weapon they could muster, including some which were barely within the scope of the business version of the Geneva Convention, and in doing so exposed the inner workings of Hanson Trust. US legal processes opened up Hanson Trust's procedures to public scrutiny, providing a rare insight into the minds of Sir Gordon White and Lord Hanson, and into the way they went about their business. Lord Hanson won both battles, which provided two of the most profitable acquisitions ever made. But the fierce fighting left wounds which would permanently weaken his defences. The defeat by Powell Duffryn had shown that Lord Hanson and Sir Gordon White were human after all. The rights issue affair had cracked the veneer of omnipotence. The two takeover battles, which saw Lord Hanson win control of Imperial Group and SCM, widened and deepened the crack, despite the fact that they both ended in victory.

The first move came in the US on 22 August 1985, when Hanson Trust made an initial $60 a share offer, worth $745 million (£536 million) for the typewriter, food and chemical conglomerate SCM. It was the beginning of a dramatic battle which perfectly represented the view of business life which had been painted by Sir Gordon White a few months previously:

It's like boarding a ship, robbing all the men and raping all the women. It's an adventure, as long as it's fun. It *has* to be fun if you're going to tilt against the Establishment or, and particularly in this country [the US] you're going into a very tough fight. Every time you have to gird up your loins to get in there and kill 'em because if not, they'll kill you.[6]

This depiction of corporate life might have seemed rather over-dramatic, even to many of Lord Hanson's staff back home in London, but it was a very accurate representation of the battle for SCM. The first skirmishes did not go Sir Gordon's way, and several times he looked as though he had been outmanoeuvred, but he eventually emerged victorious, if bloodied.

Despite the fact that SCM's shares had only recently risen from $45 the American company's shareholders were not too impressed with Sir Gordon's initial shot. The share price immediately rose above the offer price. Nor were SCM's managers very happy. They had fought off two previous predators and had no intention of making this third time unlucky. They got together with the mighty US investment bank Merrill Lynch and on 3 September announced that they were organising a management buyout, at $70 a share. As soon as the buyout plan was announced – within minutes – Hanson Trust topped that price with a revised offer of $72, but on condition that SCM did not grant any 'lock-up' options, giving special rights, to anybody else.

Merrill told the SCM board that it would be prepared to pay $74 a share, but only at a hefty price – in cash and conditions. The bank wanted $15 million in fees, $9 million of which would become payable if Hanson (or anybody else) acquired a third of SCM's shares. It also insisted on an option to buy the two key businesses – pigments and consumer foods. Merrill wanted to make sure it ended up with something at the end of the affair, even if it lost the battle for the whole group. The SCM board agonised, but eventually agreed to the option as the only way of keeping Merrill's bid alive. There followed some tough negotiations over a suitable price between Merrill and SCM's banker, Goldman Sachs. Goldman managed to push the price up to £430 million for these two businesses, but only by threatening to cancel the SCM board meeting to approve the agreement which was scheduled for the afternoon of 10 September. [7]

When this buyout deal was announced on the morning of the following day, Hanson Trust immediately withdrew its $72 offer. Instead it spent $230 million buying more than 3 million shares, at a price of $73.50, in an attempt to frustrate Merrill's condition of buying a minimum two-thirds of SCM's shares. At that point the battle moved into the courts. SCM won an injunction to prevent Hanson Trust buying more shares, or voting in shareholder meetings with those that it already owned. As well as appealing against this injunction, Hanson Trust also took to the courts with a writ seeking to block the buyout plan. At the end of September a New York court ruled that Hanson Trust could continue buying SCM shares, which it proceeded to do, up to a 37 per cent holding. That took Hanson Trust's stake past the point at which the lock-out option in the SCM – Merrill agreement was triggered, but at this stage Sir Gordon did not know of the trigger point. On 8 October Hanson returned with a formal offer, now raised above the level of the buyout bid, to $75 a share. But a day later, on 9 October, the $9 million fee was paid to Merrill and the asset option was exercised. At this point Hanson Trust returned to court, claiming that SCM directors had not acted in the best interests of shareholders by doing the deal with Merrill and selling the shares at less than the $75 per share now offered by Hanson. Hanson Trust lost the first round of this court case, but the decision was overturned by a majority decision in the Appeal Court early in the New Year. The arbitrageurs who now held large chunks of

SCM shares decided that SCM would not win another appeal, and the next morning Sir Gordon was able to buy a further 3 million shares, taking his stake to 66 per cent and effectively sealing victory.

It was the most profitable takeover of Sir Gordon White's career, despite the fact that the final price was two-thirds more than SCM's share price earlier in the year. The price of buying SCM may have been high, but so was the selling price of the parts which Hanson Trust did not want to keep. Stock markets on both sides of the Atlantic were in the run-up to the huge surge in 1987, business optimism was high, and the doctrine of deal-making was still unchallenged. There were plenty of buyers ready to pay handsomely for the surplus parts of SCM, and several examples of 'tomorrow's money today' as optimistic companies paid up for businesses which they felt were strategically important to them. Glidden Paints was sold to ICI – perhaps the first time that the British chemical company caused a twinkle in Sir Gordon's eye. Predictably, the lease on SCM's corporate headquarters, down Park Avenue from Gordon White's, home base, was sold. Durkee Famous Foods was bought by the English food and chemical group Reckitt & Colman, and the industrial food business sold to another British company, Unilever. The pulp and paper operations were disposed of. Along with a host of minor deals, and the eventual flotation of part of the SCM typewriter business, Hanson recouped a total of $1.6 billion from these sales. The group therefore made a profit on the deal of $650 million and was still left with SCM's titanium dioxide business and half the typewriter operations. The arithmetic is staggering. It testifies to the deal mentality of the mid-1980s, as well as to Sir Gordon's skill in buying and selling.

It was an unbelievably good start to 1986, but the victory had been expensive, not in financial terms but in exposing the way Sir Gordon worked. The attacks on Sir Gordon and Lord Hanson made in the lengthy court hearings would haunt the two men years later. SCM hired Bernard 'Mad Dog' Nussbaum, an aggressive New York lawyer. He elicited from Sir Gordon a picture of his predatory activities which was somewhat at odds with the image of careful analysis and meticulous calculation that was associated with Hanson Trust's success. Sir Gordon, in his typically laconic fashion, gave an account of how he came to offer $60 a share which owed more to

Where it all began: horse-drawn haulage up and down the Colne Valley and, later, motorised daily transport services from Huddersfield to London and beyond. (Huddersfield Daily Examiner)

TOP: *The wedding of Bill Hanson and Patricia Edge, 12 August 1953. Second and third from the right are Bob and Louisa Hanson, the parents of Bill and James.* (Topham)

BOTTOM: *Bill Hanson riding Monarch, the prizewinning mount bought for him by his father, clears the last jump in the Pennsylvania National Horse Show, 1953.* (Topham)

James Hanson with Jean Simmons, ringside at a light-heavyweight boxing match at Earl's Court, January 1950. Their romance was not to blossom. (Hulton Deutsch)

The photograph that accompanied the confident announcement of the intended wedding date, 30 September 1952, of Audrey Hepburn and James, but Roman Holiday *was to get in the way.* (Topham)

James with fiancée Audrey Hepburn, October 1952. The original caption to this photograph announced the postponement of their marriage; in fact pressure of their respective careers ensured that it would never take place, though they remained friends. (Topham)

LEFT: *James in 1967, aged 45, chairman of the Wiles Group, an emerging industrial conglomerate.* (Guardian)

RIGHT: *Robert Hanson, James's son, in 1992, the year he became a director of Hanson plc, aged 32 – the image of his father.* (The Press Agency (Yorkshire) Ltd, courtesy of *Huddersfield Daily Examiner*)

OPPOSITE: *James Hanson married Geraldine Kaelin at a Register Office on 17 January 1959. The press were informed after the event.* (The Press Agency (Yorkshire) Ltd, courtesy of *Huddersfield Daily Examiner*)

simple arithmetic than to complex analysis, more to whim than to strategy. Sir Gordon explained the process of stakeholding with a very English metaphor of making tea: 'our normal procedure, buying some shares in the company, and continuing to let it brew along a bit . . . If you make a cup of tea, you pour the water on the tea leaves and you let the tea brew, and then it becomes tea.'[8] He said he arrived at a value for the company through 'gut feeling' rather than detailed valuations from merchant banks, relying largely on his view of management: 'One of the major assessments that I make in my gut feeling on the value of the company is the manner in which it is managed.'[9] The $60 a share offer was justified thus: 'Well, it was above book value. The shares were standing at around $45 and that was the figure I felt was the right price to pay.'[10] On one thing he was perfectly clear, however: the whole thing was down to him. On this, as on everything else, Lord Hanson was in complete agreement. His only interest in SCM had been in studying the photographs in the annual report, and their quality was the only reason why Sir Gordon had sent him the report in the first place. On several occasions during his interrogation, Sir Gordon made it clear that he was the one, and the only one, who made decisions to proceed with stakebuilding. 'No one does anything in England. No one goes back to England . . . My method of approach is not to discuss with anyone what I am going to do until I do it . . . I am the one making the decisions.'[11] This total responsibility and control was not remarked on at the time. It seemed natural that Sir Gordon was in charge of takeovers, but it was to become an issue later, when questions began to be asked about why Sir Gordon was not a director of Hanson Trust, since he was clearly committing the company to spending huge sums of money, without the knowledge of those who actually were on the board, as Lord Hanson confirmed in his testimony.[12]

Mr Nussbaum was not solely concerned with the conduct of the SCM bid. With the excuse that Hanson Trust's writ questioned the integrity of SCM's directors, he did whatever he could to turn the tables, questioning the business ethics of Hanson Trust's two leaders. He was particularly interested in a legal action brought against Lord Hanson and Sir Gordon White three years previously by a former acquaintance of Sir Gordon's, Peter Bauer Mengelberg. Mengelberg was described by Lord Hanson as 'a percentage man'. He had brought various deals to Sir Gordon and had been involved in the 1970s in the purchase of share stakes in United Artists Theater Company, Gulf Resources and Barber Oil. His legal action had been for unpaid fees, in the course of which he had made several damaging allegations.

Lord Hanson's patience and temper were sorely tried by the questioning, on an incident which he had completely forgotten until presented with affidavits by Mr Nussbaum. At one point he exploded: 'I have never seen such a tissue of lies . . . This is a pack of lies here . . . I considered the charges to be beneath contempt.'[13] Stung by these allegations being given a public airing at such a critical time, Lord Hanson had his lawyer put the record straight the next day. An affidavit was filed which made it clear that, while the court had judged that Mr Mendelberg was owed $480,000, it had rejected his allegations of wrongdoing by Lord Hanson and Sir Gordon. This destroyed the potency of the accusations so far as the SCM case was concerned, but the mud had been flung, and future subjects of Hanson Trust's takeover attentions would fling it again in the hope that some might stick.

The next victim was the Imperial Group: as its name implies, one of Britain's grandest and oldest companies, though enfeebled by complacent, ineffective management and especially by the expensive acquisition of the Howard Johnson hotel chain (known as Hojo). Imperial Group had been in Sir Gordon White's sights for some time. He had first become interested when it bought Hojo, at a price which he regarded as wildly over-generous.[14] But Imperial's chairman, Malcolm Anson, had been replaced in July 1981 by Geoffrey Kent, who had immediately set about reshaping the group. There was still a long way to go, but financial results had improved, as had the company's reputation. In a confidential memo to Lord Hanson on 8 June 1984, copied to Sir Gordon, Martin Taylor and John Pattisson, acquisitions manager Philip Turner made it clear that Imperial would not be a soft target. Headed 'Strictly private and confidential', the memo summarised the latest situation.[15] It pointed out that Imperial's share price was near its high point over the previous year, based on a 26 per cent rise in pre-tax profits in 1983 and analysts' forecasts of a further 15 per cent rise for the current year. Mr Kent's reorganisation was proving expensive, but Turner – who was later to set up his own small conglomerate at Wassall – noted the £151 million extraordinary cost over the previous three years. That would be likely to help Imperial's reported profits in future, Turner said. Ironically, considering the fuss over Hanson's provisions in the 1990s, he warned: 'As with Courtaulds [another potential target] the sheer size of these below-the-line write-offs suggests scope to add back into future profits or into net assets.'

Imperial's businesses, on the other hand, faced significant risks. Tobacco, which provided almost half the profits, was a declining market, although Imperial Tobacco was believed to be the lowest-cost producer, and would be helped by the end of an attempted incursion into the UK market by British American Tobacco. Beer and wine, the other main business, was sensitive to weather and faced growing competition from supermarket sales. Hojo was now profitable but faced a $500 million bill to upgrade the hotels. 'That sounds like a lot of potatoes to me,' Turner wrote. The huge attraction to Hanson Trust, however, was the £272 million cash flow, described as 'stupendous'. And there would be plenty of scope for asset sales: Hojo, the foods division, UK hotels and off-licences. The City would want to give Mr Kent a chance to put things straight, however, and while Imperial's share rating was lower than Hanson Trust's, it was nevertheless quite high compared to other tobacco companies. The situation was finely balanced. Turner concluded: 'Could be extremely interesting if they hit a bad patch.'

The attractions were sufficient to make it worthwhile buying some shares, and then, as was the usual practice, waiting to see if an opportunity arose to make a takeover bid. Almost 12 million Imperial shares were picked up in 1984, through a Panamanian company called Olivet Enterprises. Such a large holding alerted Imperial Group, which made inquiries as to the ultimate owner of the shares. On 25 September 1984 Lord Hanson teased Geoffrey Kent: on personal, rather than Hanson Trust notepaper, headed 'Strictly confidential' and treated as 'Restricted' for internal purposes, he wrote: 'I thought I would cut through the usual channels to let you know direct that these shares are held by Hanson Trust. There is no association with any other party.' The letter was addressed, in Lord Hanson's own handwriting, 'Dear Geoffrey', and underneath the formally typed content he added this wry comment: 'I'm sure you share our pleasure in being shareholders!' before signing himself: 'As ever, James'.[16]

Hanson Trust had actually sold almost 4 million of these shares in December 1984, and with Sir Gordon distracted by, first, Powell Duffryn, then the SCM wrangling, nothing might have come of it for much longer. But, having sold Hojo in November 1985, Imperial announced on 2 December that it was making an agreed takeover of United Biscuits, the food group led by Sir Hector Laing. In effect this was a merger of the two groups, in pursuit of Sir Hector's dream of a British food group to rival the world's giants such as General Foods. From Imperial's point of view, the merger was also a defence against attack from Hanson Trust. In the event, however, it prompted just such an attack. Despite their entanglement in the US courts, Lord Hanson and Sir Gordon decided to go ahead with their own bid for the Imperial Group, which was announced on the morning of 6 December, the day after Hanson Trust had published yet another year's record profits.

Ironically, the decision pitted Lord Hanson against another of Mrs Thatcher's favourite businessmen, the UB chairman Sir (now Lord) Hector Laing. Sir Hector had been a personal friend of Mrs Thatcher ever since she won the Tory party leadership, but he was a very different business leader to Lord Hanson. Both men had started with family businesses, and both had done their fair share of merger and acquisition activity. But Sir Hector had pursued the classic approach of building his biscuit company into an international business by investing heavily and entering new markets, as well as acquiring competitors and other companies in the food industry. He believed fervently in cutting costs, just as Lord Hanson did, but he also believed in heavy investment and product development, and was more concerned with long-term strategy than short-term earnings per share. While an arch Tory – UB was one of the few companies to give more to the party than Hanson Trust – he was essentially an old-fashioned paternalist, very conscious of the duties and responsibilities of employers to their employees and their communities. He was, for example, one of the prime movers behind the business social action charity Business in the Community, and was its president for several years in the 1980s. Sir Hector may have been closer to Mrs Thatcher, but Lord Hanson was by now well plugged in to the Westminster political scene and he set about lobbying a variety of contacts. With the assistance now of the Prime Minister's favourite public relations adviser, Tim (later Sir Tim) Bell, he orchestrated a wide-ranging campaign to counter adverse comment on his bid for Imperial, and to lobby against a reference to the Monopolies Commission. Internal documents[17] show that he targeted a number of key politicians and others with access to the corridors of power, including Michael Portillo, then a backbench MP but a rising star of the Tory right wing. Another Thatcher favourite, Lord Hanson's old friend from the Slater era, Sir Jeffrey (later Lord) Sterling, was also lobbied, since he was known to be influential in the industrial policy area. Another target was Sir Brian Hayes, permanent secretary at the Department of Trade and Industry. His minister, Paul Channon, who took over as Secretary of State for Trade and Industry from Sir Leon Brittan when he was forced to go during the Westland affair, and junior DTI minister Michael Howard were also targeted. This activity did not go unnoticed. On 26 February, Mr Channon was forced to react to accusations from Members of Parliament that Lord Hanson's efforts had secured favourable treatment, not only because of effective lobbying but also because of his helpful intervention in the vexed Westland affair (which is described in detail in Chapter 8). Mr Channon insisted that the decision to allow Hanson's bid for Imperial but to refer the UB merger plan to the Monopolies Commission was based 'strictly on the merits of the individual cases'.[18]

The Imperial takeover was momentous in many respects. Its size, its ferocity and its benefit to Hanson Trust were all staggering, exceeded only by the SCM bid, the outcome of which was still in doubt when the assault on Imperial was launched. At almost £2 billion, the takeover attempt was Britain's largest ever. In other times it might have seemed over-ambitious, especially as it coincided with the SCM battle. Imperial had sales of £4.6 billion in 1984. Its balance sheet, even after the disposal of Hojo, showed total assets of well over £1 billion. Hanson's sales in 1984 were only £2.4 billion, although its assets, even before the 1985 rights issue and SCM purchase, were £1.4 billion. But despite its ambitious nature, the takeover attempt barely raised an eyebrow in the City or the financial press. This was the peak of the 1980s takeover extravaganza. At the beginning of the week in which Hanson Trust launched its attack on Imperial, GEC made its first attempt to acquire Plessey, and Argyll Group made its ill-fated bid for Distillers, which would then call in Guinness as a 'white knight' and thus spark the decade's most infamous takeover battle, resulting in the eventual imprisonment of several leading participants.

In that atmosphere Hanson Trust's move was met with equanimity, even enthusiasm. Despite the fact that success, even at the initial offer price, would see the issue of 100 million new Hanson Trust shares, so soon after the problems with the 1985 rights issue, investors seemed relieved that Sir Gordon had found another target, and one sizeable enough to make a big impact on the group's figures. There was a growing awareness, as had been asserted in the Powell Duffryn defence, that Hanson Trust needed to keep making big acquisitions if it was to keep growing at its accustomed rate. For example, the Lex column in *Financial Times* on the day the Imperial bid was announced carried an article stressing the need for Hanson Trust to succeed with SCM, or an alternative target:

> Hanson Trust would not just like to make a bid in the UK; it quite simply needs one. Yesterday's preliminary statement showed that the group is, by its own standards, overcapitalised . . . It is well over a year since Hanson made an acquisition of size and the consequences are starting to show. Pretax profits are unlikely to exceed £325 million this year in the absence of a deal; after a higher tax charge that could translate to single digit growth in earnings per share. And the shares . . . are discounting something a bit more special than that.

Imperial provided that 'something more special'. Alongside SCM, it was one of Sir Gordon's best deals, leaving Hanson Trust with the high cash generation of Imperial Tobacco for virtually no outlay once the rest of the group had been sold. The year of 1986 can be seen as the pinnacle of Sir Gordon's achievement, and indeed the pinnacle of Hanson Trust's progress. The group continued to grow after that, but never again managed to achieve such dramatic success or such a standing in the business world. Indeed, to date, Imperial Group was

Hanson Trust's last serious takeover battle. Lord Hanson and Sir Gordon continued to make acquisitions, but they were all achieved with the agreement of the target company. That may be because Imperial fought so tigerishly, not in the courts as SCM had done, but with diligent research into Hanson Trust, which was a useful model for ICI to follow five years later.

Imperial used every weapon at its disposal. It assigned its head of security, an ex-Scotland Yard detective, to try to discredit Lord Hanson and Sir Gordon White personally. In its attempt to destroy Hanson Trust's financial reputation Imperial used the consultants LEK. And it used financial advertising in the City pages of the newspapers to convey its attack – to great effect. The takeover rules were subsequently amended to prevent such advertising in future takeover battles: the vicious nature of the advertising copy was considered bad for the reputation of the City. The attacks on Hanson Trust were more successful than the attempts to undermine its leaders, and the financial analysis was rather more damning than the detective work. But neither was enough to save Imperial.

The detective work uncovered a private company in Guernsey linked to Sir Gordon White which had been used to facilitate a deal with Malcolm Horsman – who had last been in the Hanson picture with the aborted Bowater merger in 1973. The company, Brushwood Ltd, had been used in the sale of Talbott Group, a chain of shops acquired with USI. Talbott was sold to Pennine Resources, a company headed by Mr Horsman, in exchange for 15 per cent of Pennine. But the deal was not simply a straightforward swap between Pennine and Hanson Trust. The 2.3 million Pennine shares were exchanged for preference shares in Brushwood. The team working for Imperial hoped to show that there was something improper about this transaction. But they could not prove that it was anything other than a perfectly legitimate tax-saving operation.

Apart from this the Imperial investigators focused on three issues: criminal activities at the US vending and gaming machine company Interstate prior to its purchase by Hanson; the Gaming Board's refusal to grant a licence to Trident Television (chaired by Lord Hanson for two years in the early 1970s) after it acquired the Playboy Club; and investigations by the US Drug Enforcement Agency into the activities of the private Hanson transport operations in North

America. Despite extensive investigation, however, they found no evidence of wrongdoing in any of these three areas. The introduction to the confidential report summarising the investigation illustrated the weakness of the case, which it more or less admitted was based on unsubstantiated rumours:

> The results of enquiries conducted into corporate activities of the Hanson Trust and its subsidiaries in the UK and the US is such as to believe that if they were brought to the attention of the relevant authorities, a full investigation might have to be carried out before the bid for Imperial Group was allowed to proceed . . . We are in the possession of a lot of supposition, opinions of people in high places, and outright rumour. None of this is included. We have confined ourselves to the facts. Further investigation by outside authorities able to call on files from Scotland Yard and the drug enforcement agency should fill in the complete picture.[19]

The rumours were exciting. The facts, however, were not at all damning, as the report weakly showed.

On Interstate:

> Interstate and its employees have been involved in a series of investigations and law actions over a long period of years . . . Hanson Trust must have been aware of all this when they showed initial interest and throughout the negotiations.

On the Playboy affair:

> If a company is deemed to be unsuitable to operate gaming in Britain because of its connections, should it be seen as a suitable company to take over one of Britain's largest and most respected blue chip companies such as the Imperial Group?

In fact the investigation had come up with no hard evidence at all to support the rumours, and had not even managed to get important facts correct: for example, Hanson Trust never had an interest in Trident Television – it was a personal interest of Lord Hanson's. If it revealed anything, the huge effort put into this exercise showed only how the business establishment was prepared to believe ill of 'upstarts' such as Hanson and White.

Imperial's defence rested, therefore, on the kind of financial issues which were more usually associated with takeover battles, and the LEK analysis on this was rather more potent than the detective work had been. Imperial sought to show that Hanson Trust had not been successful at running companies, and that its success actually stemmed almost entirely from its acquisitions. The LEK analysis concluded that Sir Gordon would have to find a £10 billion target by 1990 if Hanson Trust was to maintain its growth record. In 1986, BP was valued at £10 billion, illustrating the scale of that task. The implication was clear: Hanson Trust would not be able to maintain its growth record. LEK backed up this view with detailed analysis of operating performances of the Hanson group companies. In Imperial's first formal defence document, sent to its shareholders in the middle of January, Imperial said that more than three-quarters of Hanson profits came from what it described as 'declining industries'. It added that growth from those businesses which had been part of the group throughout the previous five years was only 7 per cent. That was less than the rate of inflation, suggesting that these companies had actually been going backwards in real terms. And it was a stark contrast to the reported performance of the group: Hanson Trust profits rose from £31 million in 1979 to £169 million in 1984. Earnings per share, which adjusts for the fact that some of those profits were bought with share issues, grew by more than four times during that period, while the asset value had grown more than fivefold.

Imperial would naturally draw the most damaging conclusions, but the contrast between Hanson Trust's apparent growth and the rate suggested by LEK was so huge that it began to raise doubts in the City about the progress of Hanson Trust. This was one of the main issues raised in a confidential report from merchant bankers Schroder Wagg for a meeting of the Hanson acquisition team on 31 January.[20] The bankers had been talking to financial institutions – the shareholders who would determine the outcome of the takeover bid – and reported several concerns about Hanson Trust which threatened to swing the bid in favour of Imperial. They reported:

The financial institutions seem to have the following main areas of concern:

(a) How can Hanson sustain growth? Nearly all institutions asked whether Hanson needed to make larger and larger acquisitions, whether existing businesses could grow organically, and whether Hanson had plans/needed to divest.

(b) The question of management succession and lack of knowledge as to how Hanson management operated.

(c) On the consideration being offered, the drop in income and the inclusion of CULS [convertible loan stock] as part of the consideration are not popular.

(d) Why does Hanson want Imps? Will it be able to achieve growth with Imps? Has it the necessary expertise in the sectors in which Imps operates?

This summary was supported by specific questions which illustrated the unease in the investment community about the Hanson Trust phenomenon. Questions such as:

Does Hanson need larger and larger acquisitions to keep its share price up? Why is Hanson's management structure so hidden? And is it true that after Hanson acquires a company, good results are produced for two to three years and then there is a plateauing?

Aware that its assault was hitting home, Imperial continued to fight hard in a bitter advertising campaign that clearly touched a raw nerve. On 4 March 1986 Lord Hanson issued writs for defamation against the Imperial directors, the group and its advertising agency J. Walter Thompson. The full-page adverts, placed in all the leading quality national newspapers, dwelt on the poor performance of Hanson Trust's shares over the previous year and the operating performance of its companies. 'If you want to know what to do about Hanson's "paper", ask Hanson's shareholders', blazed one ad, over a picture of a 'thumbs down'. The copy drew attention to the 1200 million new Hanson Trust shares issued since January 1985, and the poor reception given to the rights issue which produced most of them, and contrasted the 20 per cent under-performance of Hanson Trust shares with the Imperial share record of beating the stock market index by 25 per cent. This theme was repeated in another ad consisting mainly of a chart showing the share price performance of the two opponents, but with the lines of the graph consisting of the two companies' slogans. The rising Imperial line read 'Famous brands doing famously', while the disappointing Hanson line read 'Continuing growth from basic businesses'. The copy suggested that Hanson Trust's shares had been suffering from a realisation that growth was dependent on acquisitions because three-quarters of its businesses were in declining industries. It also pointed out that Lord Hanson's attachment to convertible loans would mean that a third of the convertible loan stock market would consist of Hanson Trust paper if the Imperial bid was successful. Another assault on its attacker's share price performance showed a chart of Hanson Trust's price/earnings ratio, which had fallen from a figure of almost 19 to less than 14 since early 1985. The clever headline read: 'We always thought Hanson would climb down in the end.' The copy suggested that the high price/earnings ratio was not justified by the group's underlying business, and that Lord Hanson could sustain the high rating only by making further acquisitions. It concluded: 'Has Hanson's price/earnings ratio simply climbed down? Or could it be over the hill?'

Other attacks focused on operating performance. One consisted largely of a reproduction of a dollar bill, and examined Hanson Trust's US businesses. The first version calculated that organic growth (from existing businesses rather than acquisitions) was a mere 6 per cent between 1980 and 1985). Gleefully, Imperial re-ran this ad a little later, after protestations from Hanson Trust's lawyers. Now it said it had taken account of their information, and recalculated the growth as a mere 2 per cent. The same approach was used to analyse the profit forecast included in Lord Hanson's offer document. Again, the Imperial arithmetic concluded that Hanson Trust would achieve under 2 per cent organic growth in 1986, less than the 3.7 per cent rate of inflation.

One ad highlighted Ever Ready, Hanson Trust's last big UK acquisition and its only previous experience of consumer brands. The title read: 'Why Hanson shouldn't take over Imperial – a battery of evidence.' The copy, ranged round a picture of a leaking Blue Seal battery, referred to what Lord Hanson had described as his 'hands-off' management style. Then it detailed elements of Ever Ready's history under Hanson Trust: the disposals, the job losses, lower capital expenditure and higher selling prices. 'Given all this', the advert asked, 'it seems reasonable to ask whether Hanson's management philosophy was really "hands-off" or "sell-off"'.

For a long time, Lord Hanson resisted calls to fight back in similar fashion. Eventually he did sanction newspaper advertisements, but they were restrained. Rather than attacking Imperial, they concentrated on Hanson Trust's own performance.

The Imperial advertising campaign probably had a lasting impact on the City's perception of Hanson Trust, but it was not enough to save Imperial. In the end the battle hinged not on arguments about performance or strategy, but on the rather more prosaic issue of share prices and that was what the final ads from both sides focused on.

United Biscuits had entered the fray in February with its own offer for Imperial, following a Monopolies Commission decision that the two companies could get together if they agreed to dispose of Golden Wonder crisps, so avoiding monopoly problems from the combination of Golden Wonder and KP. As a result, Imperial shareholders were faced with a choice not between Imperial and Hanson Trust, but between Hanson Trust and United Biscuits. Much rested on the relative value of the two bids, which in turn depended on the share prices of Hanson Trust and United Biscuits. For a long time, it was neck and neck, with very little to choose financially between the two offers. By the end of March, both bidders had managed to buy about 15 per cent of Imperial's shares and seemed to be sharing the votes of the remaining shareholders fairly equally. On the closing date for UB's offer, 11 April, UB announced that, despite its offer being recommended by Imperial, it had managed to win control over only 34 per cent of the shares. Sir Hector Laing was forced to throw in the towel, leaving Imperial no option but to recommend the Hanson offer. It was a famous though narrow victory for the masters of the takeover battle, Lord Hanson and Sir Gordon White, and it was to be one of their most profitable. But while they had won the battle, they had also been wounded in the war for the hearts of the City.

Victory came in the same week as Distillers finally submitted to Guinness. Lord Hanson did not end up in prison, as did his opposite number at Guinness, Ernest Saunders, and there was no suggestion that he won Imperial through improper means, as was the case with Guinness snatching Distillers from the original bidder, Argyll Group. But Lord Hanson's victory, while purer, was ultimately less satisfactory. Once the trial was over and it was possible to concentrate on the business aspects, Guinness was seen to be a constructive influence on the Distillers group. It boosted the company's brands, improved their distribution, and in particular made huge inroads into the important Japanese market. The highly effective dismemberment of Imperial Group, on the other hand, emphasised that the skills of Lord Hanson and Sir Gordon lay in asset trading rather than running businesses. In fact the dismemberment was rather greater than had been anticipated within Hanson Trust. It had been intended to keep brewing and tobacco. They were good, basic, cash-generating businesses in low-risk, if low-growth industries – classic Hanson Trust characteristics. But John Elliott, head of the Australian brewer Elders, decided Courage could provide the UK base he had been looking for, and in September the sale was announced of the brewing and off-licence business. That sale raised £1.4 billion for Hanson Trust: another example of 'tomorrow's price today'. By the end of the year the busy team of accountants and lawyers had also raised £186 million from the sale of the UK hotel and restaurant business to Forte, and £87 million from Dalgety for Golden Wonder. Subsequently, Ross Young's frozen food business was sold for £335 million, ironically to United Biscuits, Lea & Perrins and HP sauces went to French group BSN for almost £200 million, and various smaller companies together raised about £120 million. The total bill for Imperial had been £2.5 billion, but these sales recouped more than £2.3 billion. Imperial Tobacco, which produced more than £200 million trading profit in its first full year for Hanson Trust, had been acquired for less than £200 million.

One sale which was not made, and which would have been expected on the basis of the previous takeover record, was of Imperial group's head office. The building itself was unimpressive – an anonymous concrete and glass structure with no character and little to commend it except perhaps functionalism. But it occupied a prime site, at the northern end of Grosvenor Place, just a stone's throw from Hyde Park Corner and overlooking the back garden of Buckingham Palace. The address itself, 1 Grosvenor Place, was valuable enough and signified the status of the site if not the grandeur of the building, which stands out like a sore thumb from the rest of the elegant terrace that heads down towards Victoria station. Instead of selling this building once the Imperial managers had been emptied out, as had happened with every takeover since Lindustries in 1979, Lord Hanson moved his own people in. He himself bagged a large office in the corner of the seventh floor, looking towards Hyde Park Corner in one direction and Buckingham Palace in the other. For some, this move was symbolic of a search for higher status. The office block may not have been opulent, but it was too big for the needs of Lord Hanson and his sparse head office staff. The move was tantamount to thumbing his nose at the business Establishment, showing in no uncertain terms that he had arrived at the top of the British business tree. But if Lord Hanson and head office were allowed such gestures, those in the operating companies might feel that they too deserved a little extra – that the ethos of grinding down on cost, of delivering the best possible result for head office, had been weakened a little.

The Imperial purchase was financially a staggeringly good deal for Hanson but there was precious little other satisfaction for many critics of the Hanson style in this extreme example of market trading in companies. And the cracks in Lord Hanson's image of being a brilliant industrial manager, which had first appeared in the Powell Duffryn bid, had become even more significant. There was much more overt questioning of how Hanson Trust kept managing to achieve such remarkable results, and more disquiet about its failure to come up with clear answers to those questions. For example, at the half-year stage in 1986, soon after the Imperial success, Lord Hanson was able to announce a leap in profits of 49 per cent thanks to the first profits from SCM and Imperial. Even for those concerned about the huge increase in the number of Hanson Trust shares, there was comfort in the growth of earnings per share as well. But for many investors and observers, joy was significantly not unconfined, as this acerbic comment in the *Financial Times* illustrates:

For a company that has underperformed the London market for a year and only just managed to push through its latest UK acquisition, Hanson Trust shows remarkably little desire to entice investors with information. In interim figures that show pretax profits rising by half and market capitalisation nearly three-fold on shrinking shareholders' equity, the number of divisions reporting has fallen from 12 to four. At this rate, the year end will probably show profits almost doubled but the divisions reduced to two: Bits and Pieces, perhaps. Those investors who swapped their Imperial holdings for Hanson paper presumably did so out of trust in the group's ability to manage both organic growth and new acquisitions. In these figures, which show pretax profits up by 49 per cent, they receive only modest comfort. Over here, UK profits are progressing slowly, with the falling rand wiping out growth at Ever Ready; what is happening at London Brick, which is forgoing price rises to rebuild market share, is anybody's guess. Over there, a tremendous performance by SCM's titanium dioxide business, and a return to profit by its typewriters, still left the old US acquisitions less than 10 per cent ahead in local currency terms.

The prime improvement comes, not at the operating level, but in the catchall line, which shows a £30 million sterling swing: the interest on the UK cash balances comfortably exceeded the payments of the US dollar acquisition debt, but that still leaves more than £10 million to be conjured out of dealing in helicopters or property or whatever.

It could be that with the sheer volume of Hanson equity and convertible paper about in London, its management consider the institutions need Hanson as much as vice versa; and that these must be content with a wrapped management package, which is said to be worth having and will not explode. However, there are enough troubling signals in these figures to suggest that this may be risky in London, never mind among ADR [American Depository Receipt – version of UK companies' shares sold in the US] investors in New York.[21]

Such scathing comment from such an influential source, and one which had been generally supportive of Hanson Trust, suggests that some of Imperial's mud may have stuck. Whatever the reason, the stock market paused only briefly in its steady downgrading of the company's shares. The fall, relative to the stock market index, had begun at the start of 1985. The end of 1986 saw a temporary respite, but then the decline continued until a low point in spring 1988. Over those three years Hanson Trust's shares fell by a third relative to the FT All-Share index.

Lord Hanson's problems were not helped by a huge row about the pension fund following the Imperial takeover. The row began quietly, but continued dogging the group, and Lord Hanson's reputation, for years. It began at the shareholder meeting called in October 1986 to approve the sale of the Courage brewing company to Elders. Normally such affairs are formalities. Few shareholders turn up – even the elderly, private shareholders who traditionally come to revere their chairman at annual general meetings seldom make these special meetings, which are usually over very quickly. But this meeting was different. It was used by Courage employees to protest about the treatment of the pension fund in the transfer of their company to the new Australian owner.

Worrying about the possible use of its pension assets if it were to lose the takeover battle, Imperial had altered the trust deeds to try to preserve the surplus in its schemes – worth £80 million – for the benefit of the scheme members and pensioners rather than the company's new owners. The High Court ruled early in December that Hanson Trust could not get its hands on the money. It was not the end of the pension controversy, however. In 1990, pensioners forced Imperial pension fund trustees back to the High Court once again. Still eyeing the huge surplus, which by now had grown to £130 million, Hanson Trust had attempted a new approach: making members an offer to move to a new scheme with the incentive of higher annual benefit increases. This time the judge, a senior Chancery Division figure, Sir Nicolas Browne-Wilkinson, ruled that Hanson could not limit increases in this way for members who refused to move to the new scheme. His comments also gave support to the pensioners' claims that Lord Hanson was merely attempting to get his hands on their money. In his judgment, he said:

Why is the company seeking to induce members of the fund to give up their rights and transfer to a new fund? I asked that question of the counsel for the company on a number of occasions, but received no answer. The pensioners suspect that the only reason is the company's wish to transfer the surplus to the new fund where it will belong to the company. In the absence of any other explanation, this is a fair inference.

The original clash, in 1986, had won for him the title of Capitalist of the Year from *The Times*. In other circumstances this would have been another award to delight Lord Hanson, to add to the many others which adorn the group's head office. But *The Times*'s award was made with a note of sarcasm, as the citation reveals:

> Lord Hanson has run away with it again . . . By brilliant dealing in the US his alter ego, Sir Gordon White, who shares the prize, rapidly recouped the $930 million cost of SCM and was still left with businesses making $120 million a year profit. In Britain, Lord Hanson finally won Imperial with a £2.8 billion takeover and quickly recouped £1.4 billion by selling Courage to Mr Elliott. What clinched the award, however, was Hanson's attempt to separate Courage employees from £70 million of surplus in their pension funds. It failed, but at Elders' expense, not Hanson's. This displayed the true lack of sentiment of the pure capitalist. For that, Lord Hanson receives a specially enhanced version of the Capitalist of the Year title, incorporating the rarely awarded Ebenezer Scrooge Star.[22]

Lord Hanson did win some rather more serious awards as well during this period. He had long been much admired in the business world – by those who did not feel too threatened by him. In 1984 he was voted one of the country's top ten industrialists in a poll for Channel 4's *Business Programme*. The top ten were an eclectic mixture, headed by Lord Weinstock of GEC but with the late Robert Maxwell in third place behind Sir Michael Edwardes of British Leyland. Lord Hanson was sandwiched between Sir Ernest Harrison of Racal – a true entrepreneur, who had built his company from scratch around its electronic skills – and Lord Sieff, the Marks & Spencer chairman. It was a sign of the times, in transition between the recessionary slog in which sound business skills were paramount, and the frothy mid-1980s when stock market skills came to the fore.

By 1988, however, Lord Hanson was clearly leader of the pack. He was voted 'most impressive businessman' in the annual Captains of Industry opinion poll conducted by the market research company, MORI. The poll of directors from Britain's top companies had been led by ICI's Sir John Harvey-Jones for the previous three years. But this year Lord Hanson beat him into second place. The following year Lord Hanson won the Hambro Businessman of the Year award. It was presented by his friend and fellow Thatcher acolyte Lord King, who praised his insight, determination and breadth of view. There may have been cracks in the Hanson façade so far as the financial community was concerned, but they were not apparent to many in the business world, to whom Hanson Trust was continuing in its accustomed fashion, clocking up ever higher earnings by dint of careful industrial management.

In some respects it was still business as usual. Sir Gordon and his team had been busy selling off most of SCM and Imperial, but also found time to continue buying. At the end of 1986 Hanson Trust made an agreed offer for Kaiser Cement, the fifth largest cement producer in the United States. Kaiser was well known to Hanson Trust's US managers. It had been in dispute with McDonough since Hanson Trust bought that company in 1981 – a dispute which was eventually settled, with a payment to Kaiser of $17.5 million, in the autumn of 1986. But now Kaiser was threatened by a growing share stake held by arbitrageur David Murdock and ran to Hanson Trust for safety. Agreement was soon reached at a price of $250 million – little more than petty cash now for Sir Gordon.

The next target, Kidde, was a little more substantial, costing $1.6 billion in 1987, at the peak of the stock market boom. It was another struggling conglomerate, originally a fire extinguisher company which now also had interests ranging from Grove cranes, through temporary employment services, to Jacuzzi pools. It was a classic Hanson Trust target, but the price agreed by Sir Gordon White was far from classic. Kidde's shares had been trading between $28 and $38 a share over the previous three years, and were actually lower in 1987 than they had been in the previous year, despite the stock market surge. But Sir Gordon agreed a price of $60.10 cash. The excess was not much different to the premium he had paid for SCM, but times had changed and this deal was nowhere near as profitable. Disposals over the years have recouped almost $1 billion of the $1.6 billion price. What is left is Grove cranes, Jacuzzi, Farberware cooking utensils, Rexair vacuum cleaners, Tommy Armour golf equipment, Bear and Valley sports goods, and Ertl toys (whose products include Thomas the Tank Engine diecast models). It is a motley collection, which together probably made profits (before interest charges) of about £130 million in 1993, about $200 million. Take off interest on the net price of $800 million, and that leaves about $150 million profit before tax: not one of Sir Gordon's better deals, as many people observed at the time.[23] One reason for the relatively poor return was that asset values crashed along with the stock market collapse in October 1987. But perhaps the unexpectedly high price was also a reflection of two other worrying factors: the need for Hanson Trust to keep buying something so that it could keep pushing up earnings; and the general hubris of 1987, which seemed to have caught out the normally cautious Sir Gordon as well as many other stock market operators.

In 1987, apart from buying Kidde, Sir Gordon made some strange share purchases which garnered nothing except adverse comment. In May, Lord Hanson broke a house rule of not commenting on stock market rumours by insisting there was no truth in suggestions that Hanson Trust had bought shares in GEC, the huge electrical group run by Lord Weinstock. The rumour reflected the wild state of the stock market, but also the feeling that Lord Hanson would have to do something significant soon. That feeling was confirmed in August when a shareholding was revealed in the merchant bank Morgan Grenfell – the bank which had been on the United Biscuits side in the battle for the Imperial Group. Observers had little time to speculate about a move into the heart of the City before an even more bizarre stake was revealed. This time the target was Midland Bank, the weakest of the Big Four British high street banks but nevertheless a huge institution with a wide spread of banking interests – and a solid member of the business and financial establishment. It was valued by the stock market at £2.3 billion – the kind of scale Hanson Trust needed to maintain its momentum, but nevertheless a formidable sum and a formidable target.

Hanson was not seen primarily as a potential bidder for Midland, however, although it was a more credible suitor than the advertising group Saatchi and Saatchi, which had also made an approach to Midland. Rather this was seen as a pure piece of stock market gambling: Sir Gordon hoping that somebody else would make a bid, and thus buy Hanson Trust's stake at a rather higher price than Sir Gordon had acquired the shares. Nevertheless, the Governor of the Bank of England, Robin Leigh-Pemberton, was moved to warn off both Lord Hanson and Maurice Saatchi. In a speech on the ownership of banks[24] he warned that non-banking groups would not be allowed to enter the banking system surreptitiously, nor would they be allowed to destabilise any major clearing bank by taking large share stakes. It was a gentle rap over the knuckles and an indication that Lord Hanson and Sir Gordon were outsiders to some and were perhaps overreaching themselves, believing they could assault not just the periphery of the business establishment, but its very heart – the City itself.

Another example of their self-confidence in 1987 was the pay packets the Hanson directors awarded themselves. In the early 1970s, the group's directors had earned fairly modest salaries, although they were supplemented by dividends on what in some cases were substantial shareholdings, as well as profits on share trading. Indeed, James Hanson's pay remained on £8000 for five years from 1969. When Hanson Trust moved into the United States in 1973, however, Lord Hanson's pay leapt from £8000 a year to £34,000 a year – equivalent to £200,000 in 1994 money. It was the first time that James Hanson had been the highest-paid director, which had presumably been Gordon White before then, on a salary of £13,000. The chairman's pay packet remained at around £34,000 for a further five years, but in the 1980s began to rise in response to the rapid growth of the group and the new spirit of Thatcherite enterprise. The sum almost doubled, to £66,000 in 1980, and took another large leap three years later, to £140,000. That would be worth only £230,000 in 1994, however, so Sir James had done little more than belatedly catch up with the inflation of the late 1970s.

The mid-1980s saw a boom in the pay not only of Lord Hanson but also of the rest of his board. The board had expanded from eight to 11 members in the early 1980s, but total board pay quadrupled in four years, to £800,000. That rise was nothing against what was to come, however. With a series of increases the figure reached £3 million in

1986, and even after that growth the directors doubled their pay in the following year. Lord Hanson's pay did not keep up with that rate of growth, until 1987. Then, while the total board pay doubled, his salary quadrupled to £1,263,000.

Lord Hanson had warned in his annual report for 1986 that there would be changes. 'We are strong believers in financial incentives for our management,' he had commented, reporting that consultants had been brought in to devise a new incentive scheme for the central management and directors. The results of this were seen in the 1987 accounts, and the chairman commented: 'Until now our senior UK executives have not had the benefit of global pay rates but this plan will begin to redress that differential.' It certainly did for Lord Hanson, but none of the other UK directors got anywhere near his £1.3 million pay packet, and even at that level he was outdone by his colleagues abroad. The highest paid UK director moved up from £230,000 to £315,000, with the other five main executive directors getting similar rises, though none of them was paid more than £200,000. Senior managers had similarly modest increases, by comparison with the chairman. The highest paid non-director rose from £115,000 to £170,000.

Analysis of the reported figures also reveals that the directors working in the United States were paid much more than their UK colleagues, and usually more even than Lord Hanson. Sir Gordon White's salary is not included in any of these figures, since he ceased to be a director of Hanson Trust when he went to New York. The US directors were Eddie Collins, who had helped Gordon White do his first deals from the Pierre hotel in New York, and who joined the board in 1982, and finance director Brian Hellings, who had worked in the US since the mid-1970s. In 1983, Eddie Collins and Brian Hellings shared £300,000, slightly more on average than Lord Hanson's £140,000. By 1986 this had risen to £1.6 million, more than a five-fold increase, while the UK directors had to settle for less than triple their 1983 pay. When they were joined by Derek Rosling in 1987, the three of them received £3.6 million, more than three times the sum shared by their six UK executive board colleagues. Sir Gordon White, as chairman of Hanson Industries and boss of the US side of the group, must be assumed to have earned significantly more than each of these three if the relationship between his salary and his fellow US directors matches that between Lord Hanson and the UK side of the board.

High pay levels were supplemented by some of the most generous share options in British industry. James Hanson and Gordon White had set out from the start with the view that it was essential to give managers financial incentives, and options on the company's shares had long been a key element of incentives for managers throughout the group. A study in 1990 found that six of Britain's top 20 option holders worked for Hanson.[25] Lord Hanson himself topped the table, with options worth £3.5 million. There were also two other Hanson option millionaires, while three others were just outside that threshold.

Reaction to the pay levels was muted in the late 1980s. This was before the growth in importance of corporate governance, which was fuelled by large increases in many major British companies. Hanson Trust spokesman Martin Taylor, in his usual deadpan fashion, explained that the increase was necessary 'to continue to motivate him [Lord Hanson] as he approached normal retiring age'.[26] Lord Hanson's motivation was less a concern to most City observers than the question of whether he would ever retire, or would, like his father, literally work until he dropped.

The hefty pay rises for Lord Hanson and his colleagues were not a scandal. Nor were any of the other issues described here. But they were all irritants, eating away at the famous reputation which had been built up in the first half of the 1980s. They did not prevent Lord Hanson winning the acclaim of his fellow company directors, but they damaged the company's standing in the City, each in a minor way, but collectively with some significance. By the end of 1987 it was commonplace for stockbrokers' analysts and financial journalists to wonder how Hanson Trust could keep finding sufficiently large targets to maintain its earnings growth.[27] And there were rumblings of concern about the eventual succession. The two men were so intrinsically part of the company and its success that investors worried what would happen when they were no longer around.[28]

Lord Hanson made strenuous attempts to counter these image problems, which had dogged him since the Powell Duffryn bid but which had grown significantly since the bitter battle for Imperial. His campaign included a series of television advertisements. Always one for a bit of showmanship, and ever eager to project the image and status of his company, Lord Hanson had previously sanctioned some TV adverts linked to the financial results. They supported the by now traditional press adverts proclaiming the group's unbroken earnings record. Now Hanson Trust appeared on television in general corporate adverts, not linked to specific results. The first had been intended to counter Imperial Group's vicious press campaign, but the takeover was completed before the advert ran. It ran nevertheless on British television in the summer of 1986, no longer as an encouragement to Imperial shareholders, merely as a way of promoting Hanson Trust. The advert featured the very British character actor Denholm Elliott and an aggressive American, Joe Don Baker, arguing about the merits of their separate companies. Ultimately they discover that in fact their companies, apparently from different sides of the Atlantic, are one and the same: Hanson Trust. This advert was a precursor of the more famous one featuring Glenda Jackson and George Segal, which ran early in 1988. The Jackson–Segal production was on a similar theme of discovering the diversity of the Hanson empire, and it introduced the notion of 'Over here, over there', a concept so successful that it was used by Prime Minister John Major many years later to promote the notion of British business being successful in the US. Despite its success, the theme was dropped for the third effort, which was much more in the mainstream of financial promotion. This advert, shown in the autumn of 1988, featured a steadily rising earnings line on an analyst's screen, as the screen depicted the many facets of Hanson Trust.

These promotional ventures helped to spread Lord Hanson's name further afield, but they did little to impress the City. Staff at stockbrokers James Capel, under instructions to wear sober clothing as they acted as a backdrop for the Segal–Jackson advert, provided rather more colour than was intended by inventing a funny tie competition to coincide with the filming. More seriously, some City observers were miffed at the spending on such general promotional activities at the same time as detailed information about the group was being reduced. *The Times* commented archly when the first adverts were running: 'Hanson Trust seems to think that corporate advertising on television is a substitute for detailed facts and figures',[29] echoing the *Financial Times*'s complaint that while the group had grown, the financial information was shrinking.

Advertising was not the only tactic to counter the negative sentiments about the group. Lord Hanson bowed to pressure from his public relations advisers to begin opening up the company to the financial community. In 1988 the company held two important briefings for analysts. The first took place at London's Guildhall, a grand City venue guaranteed to impress the audience of US analysts. Star guest at the bash was one of Lord Hanson's very good friends – none other than the Prime Minister, Margaret Thatcher, whom he continued to idolise in private and lionise in public. This event was followed by a similar, though more subdued, gathering in June. This time it was for UK analysts, and had a similar aim of stressing the quality of operating management in the group, as well as those in the centre who were presented as being ready to take over from the top team when they might eventually retire, which was suggested as being 1992, when Lord Hanson would reach 70.[30]

These efforts paid off to some extent. Hanson plc (the 'Trust' had been dropped in 1987) shares reached a low point in spring 1988, and from then performed better than the stock market as a whole until the beginning of 1990. However, this was more a matter of the very subdued stock market and a belief that an acquisitive, transatlantic company such as Hanson plc might fare less badly in the wake of the October 1987 crash, than any reconsideration of Hanson's potential. Its share rating remained subdued, at the same sort of level (measured by the price/earnings ratio) as in the early 1980s, before the megadeals began. Worries about the succession remained. Concern about the availability of suitable targets was still valid. And the stock market crash in 1987 had made matters worse. The market-induced acquisition hysteria was over. The Guinness affair and the other worst excesses such as Blue Arrow were heading for the courts. The first financial casualties, such as Coloroll, were about to signal the end of the boom years. In this much more restrained atmosphere, Sir Gordon was unable to find a significant acquisition in 1988 for the first year since 1977. Instead there was a stream of sales, including a Kaiser cement plant, Ross Young's frozen food to the old Imperial adversary, United Biscuits, Kidde's fire protection business, and Durkee Industrial Foods (an SCM company).

There was some speculation about the possible end of the empire. Some thought that Lord Hanson would split the group, either floating off the US side, or handing out separate shares in it to his shareholders. But others doubted whether Lord Hanson could ever bring himself to break up his empire, and felt that he would want to crown his career with a deal which would fit his self-image as a man of great significance and great benefit to the business world. The latter group was proved right, not once but twice in the next few years. In June 1989 it became apparent that the age of the megadeals was not yet over for Lord Hanson, even if the 1980s economic boom had followed the stock market boom into the history books. As recession began to bear down on British industry, Lord Hanson negotiated his biggest ever deal with the friendly purchase of Consolidated Gold Fields (ConsGold).

ConsGold was one of the world's largest mineral companies. Apart from the gold interests indicated in its title, it also mined other minerals and owned ARC, the UK's largest producer of crushed stone and other quarried products. The company had been under attack for years from the giant South African empire of the Oppenheimer family, whose twin pillars are De Beers and Anglo-American. Having built up a sizeable share stake, the takeover bid for ConsGold eventually came in 1988, via the Oppenheimers' Luxemburg-based vehicle, Minorco. Minorco was led by the former British Leyland boss Sir Michael Edwardes, but it was little more than a 'shell' company. Nevertheless it had managed to win sufficient shareholder support for its £3.5 billion offer, and had convinced the Monopolies Commission that the takeover would not be against the public interest. Despite these successes, however, its bid attempt was frustrated by the US courts. Then, in June 1989, Lord Hanson stepped in. Having escaped only on a technicality, it was clear that any other credible offer at around the same price would be successful. All that ConsGold chairman Rudolph Agnew could hope to do was to push up the price, and this he succeeded in doing. Hanson initially offered £3.1 billion, but after a couple of weeks of gentle negotiations this was increased. At £3.3 billion, it was nevertheless lower than the £3.5 billion which shareholders would have received from Minorco, a tribute to Lord Hanson's negotiating skills. It was Lord Hanson's biggest ever deal, and it was probably also the easiest. But the best part was yet to come.

Nobody expected Hanson to become a South African and Australian mining company, but the solution dreamed up by Sir Gordon and Lord Hanson was a surprise. Immediately he took control, Lord Hanson began selling assets to recoup some of his outlay. He again attempted to gain access to the victim's pension fund – and again he was thwarted by moves made by the target's board, precisely to prevent this. This time the affair did not get to court, as it became obvious that ConsGold's board had done too good a job. But the tenacity with which Lord Hanson personally pursued the possibility of getting his company's hands on the surplus pension cash astonished some observers especially since the surplus was relatively small, illustrating what one described as 'a peculiar, petty meanness'.[31] Lord Hanson was more successful with asset sales, at least in the beginning. The bulk of ConsGold's investment in the South African gold company, Gold Fields of South Africa, went first. Then in November, he surprised the City by selling the US operations of ARC, the company which had been considered the main attraction for Hanson in acquiring ConsGold. As usual, it went at an astonishingly high price. The Australian mining group CSR paid Hanson $670 million for the quarrying and building material business. It brought the total raised from sales out of ConsGold to a cool £1 billion, in just three months. After that, however, sales became more difficult. Recession was gathering on both sides of the Atlantic and buyers were hard to find at the kind of price which would satisfy Lord Hanson. The trickiest asset was ConsGold's 49 per cent share of the US gold company, Newmont. Once again, Sir Gordon came up with an unexpected answer. First, he spent $500 million to buy 45 per cent of the coal-mining company, Peabody. Then he spent a further $700 million buying the rest of the company – from Newmont. This left Newmont in a much healthier financial position, and in a position to be sold. The gold price, and hence Newmont's share price, was sliding, however. Then, suddenly, in October 1990, Sir Gordon agreed with his old friend Sir James Goldsmith to swap the Newmont stake for Goldsmith's timber interests, Cavenham Forest Products. It was an ingenious solution to a difficult problem, but it was not the kind of highly profitable deal which investors had hoped would replicate the amazing success of SCM's dismemberment.

This sequence of deals had also taken Hanson heavily into natural resources, an unusual area for the group and one which worried some investors. It did not have the usual cash-generative characteristics of Hanson activities – indeed, large amounts of capital investment were needed – and prices were subject to much greater uncertainty and less control than Hanson normally required. Along with Hanson's later attempt to buy PowerGen, these developments once again raised serious questions about the company's direction and its prospects. The doubters were given further ammunition by the flotation on the US stock exchange in 1989 of the typewriter business of SCM. Hanson Trust announced in June that it planned to sell half of Smith Corona, saying it had transformed the typewriter company's performance since acquiring it. At the last minute the issue price was cut from a planned $23–25 a share to only $21 in the face of weak demand and some criticism from US investing institutions. Dropping the price meant that Hanson would raise only $386 million from the sale compared to the $428 million it had originally targeted. But this lower figure included debt repayment by Smith Corona to the tune of $95 million, which would leave the newly independent company with significant debt levels, since none of the money raised from the flotation was going its way. 'Hanson is rewarding itself handsomely,' commented the respected credit-rating agency Standard & Poor's.

Dissatisfaction with the flotation soon ballooned as Hanson's reward seemed even more generous. Smith Corona's public life began badly when it announced a loss in the fourth quarter of its financial year, which was entirely due to bonus payments for senior managers amounting to more than $50 million. The planned payments had been clearly set out in the flotation prospectus, but it was not an auspicious start to the company's stock market quotation. Worse was to come, however. Barely two weeks after the new shares began trading, Smith Corona announced that it was cutting staff levels by a tenth because of falling sales. That had not been presaged in the prospectus, and the share prices fell by a fifth. Some investors found it hard to credit the claim by the chairman, Lee Thompson, that the poor sales picture had only emerged in August. Three aggrieved investors issued writs claiming that the company had misrepresented its financial condition.

The case was finally settled with a payment of $24 million to Smith Corona shareholders in 1991, the majority of which came from Hanson.

Regardless of the lawsuit, the affair had damaged Hanson's reputation with important US investors, and stalled plans to float other companies on the stock market. US investors were very unhappy. One said the announcement, issued by Smith Corona on a Friday evening after the stock market had closed, 'looked like an embarrassed company sneaking out from under a rock to drop a bombshell'. Another simply observed: 'They took me for a ride.'[32]

At the end of 1990, the flood of doubt burst through the crumbling dam of Hanson plc's public relations defences. It began with the Newmont–Cavenham asset swap, which the *Financial Times*'s Lex column summed up as resulting in 'a slightly puzzling lack of focus'.[33] Matters were made worse by the Imperial pensions case returning to the courts during that same dismal October. Economic conditions also seemed to be conspiring against Hanson, with the prospect of declining interest rates hitting the group's financial income as recession damaged its operating profits, and the whole made worse by the difficulty of finding buyers for businesses at profitable prices. The result was a flood of adverse comment, the like of which Lord Hanson had never been faced with before. The *Daily Telegraph* ran through the litany of woes, throwing in the question of succession to Lord Hanson and Sir Gordon as a further worry for long-term investors. 'There are doubts which are beginning to undermine the share price,' it commented, concluding that the dividend yield was the main attraction for buying the shares – highly unusual for Hanson shares, which had normally paid low dividends but had been bought by investors because of the prospects for growth in the share price.[34] In fact, from the beginning of 1990, the yield on Hanson's shares was significantly higher than the stock market average for the only sustained period in the company's existence, except for a couple of years at the end of the 1970s. That is a reflection of investors' sudden lack of faith in the company's growth prospects.

Doubts turned to fears as stockbrokers' analysts reassessed the company in the run-up to its annual results. Early in November 1990 two of the most respected analysts reduced their forecasts of Hanson's profits. 'The message is clear: not even the likes of Hanson are free from the effects of recession . . . the underlying business is expected to have deteriorated,' commented *The Times*.[35]

When the results were published at the beginning of December, the fears were duly realised. While Lord Hanson announced another year of record profits, in fact suitable adjustments[36] showed that earnings per share had fallen for the first time ever. This calamity – so far as Lord Hanson's carefully nurtured image of relentless success was concerned – was, however, obscured by a much more intricate, technical row about the balance sheet. Hanson had included a provision of £1.7 billion against future health claims by Peabody miners – to cover potential claims by miners suffering from diseases such as pneumoconiosis. Despite its significance, the huge sum was not openly announced as part of the presentation of the results. Instead it had to be winkled out of the company by alert analysts, who also discovered that the value of Peabody's coal reserves had been inflated to match this provision. For the first time the questions about Hanson's accounting which had featured in several takeover defences now surfaced as genuine doubts in respectable newspaper columns. The *Sunday Times* hinted at the scepticism concerning the neat matching of the two Peabody adjustments, joking: 'This is known as balancing the books',[37] while the *Financial Times* raised the more serious issue of the group's future prospects: 'It all prompts renewed questions about the quality of Hanson's earnings.'[38]

The Peabody provision was perfectly legitimate, as was the upgrading of its coal assets to something approaching their current value. The fuss about them symbolised the City's new-found disenchantment with Hanson, summed up by a lengthy analysis which must have dulled Lord Hanson's appetite as he prepared for his Christmas dinner. The *Sunday Times* commented that the City was beginning to think that 'the Hanson era is coming to a close'.[39] It quoted several leading analysts to the effect that the group's earnings were 'low quality', that is, not easily sustainable, largely because of the high proportion now coming from interest on the group's high cash balances held in the United Kingdom. A first fall in earnings, so proudly depicted in numerous advertisements over the years as an inexorably rising line, 'would dissolve the magic of the Hanson name'. Damningly, the writer observed: 'Without the magic, Hanson becomes just a humdrum group and the share price falls.'

Indeed, the share price had fallen dramatically, from 248p in June to under £2 by the end of the year. And this was during a period when the stock market as a whole had been fairly stable: Hanson's shares had fallen by about 15 per cent compared to the market index. As the article commented: 'In the City's eyes, Hanson needs a deal, another coup on the scale of Imperial or SCM, to secure its reputation.' The group clearly had the resources, in cash, to make a big acquisition, but the City doubted whether there were any suitable candidates, and even if there were, whether there were any buyers ready to help Hanson dismember the victim. It was a dismal end to a decade, the first half of which had been outstandingly successful for Lord Hanson and the now also ennobled Lord White. The decade had shot Lord Hanson to prominence. He no longer needed to introduce himself to important businessmen on Concorde; he now had first claim on his favourite seat 2A, so regular and important a passenger was he. Lord Hanson had always wanted the trappings of power and success, and felt they were important. Now he had them – VIP treatment, staff to attend to his every need, the respect of his peers. But over the last five years he had failed to deliver in the one area which he felt most important, and where he had been most successful in the past – the company's share price. Small shareholders still idolised him, and came in their hundreds to the annual meeting. But the professionals were beginning to wonder whether the show could go on. The doubts were still subdued, but would be fuelled by what was probably the two lords' greatest mistake: the attack on ICI, forced on them perhaps by the urgency of doing something dramatic to rescue the company's status and their own image as masterful businessmen. For the habitually high-flying Hanson, the 1990s were about to prove just as bumpy and troublesome as they would for his political idol and ideological fellow-traveller Margaret Thatcher, whose ousting was to deny Hanson the political support that might have proved so decisive.

CHAPTER 7

The Political Player

Margaret Thatcher's power as Prime Minister was already ebbing when on a bright May evening in 1990, more than 100 of Britain's opinion leaders – businessmen, politicians, analysts and the odd financial journalist – gathered at Cliveden, overlooking the Thames in Buckinghamshire, for a networking session hosted by the City brokers Smith New Court. Lord Astor's country home, a magnificent mansion built by the House of Commons architect Sir Charles Barry, has long been considered a place for political conspiracy. It fulfilled this role in the 1930s and more recently in the early 1960s when the elegant and promiscuous Cliveden set became associated with the Profumo scandal, which would play a key role in toppling the Conservative government of Harold Macmillan.

True to Cliveden's history and reputation, politics and intrigue were very much on the agenda on the night of 17 May 1990. Among the guests, brought together by Sir Michael Richardson, chairman of Smith New Court, one of the great financial fixers of the Thatcher years, were many of those associated with the Prime Minister's bold privatisation programmes – a model which would serve for the rest of the world. As the stockbroking arm of N.M. Rothschild, the favoured merchant bank in Whitehall, as well as advisers to Britain's most acquisitive-minded conglomerate Hanson plc, Smith New Court was at the interface between Thatcherism and business. Sir Michael Richardson is an urbane, charming fellow whose edges appear to have been smoothed by his well-bred training at Harrow, the Brigade of Guards and love of the foxhounds, but with the gentlemanly manner he is the premier operator in the financial world of the last two decades. Although a stockbroker by trade, he possesses all the real-world political skills of such illustrious financiers as Siegmund Warburg or J.P. Morgan. He has cultivated people from across the spectrum of opinion leaders – journalists, politicians and businessmen – and knows how to keep them on board by proffering advice, digging them out of holes and providing useful fragments of intelligence.

It was no accident that at the Cliveden gathering James Hanson was to be the leading business speaker and John (now Lord) Wakeham – Mrs Thatcher's Secretary of State for Energy – was among the guests. Hanson's speech was less that of the tycoon and more the rallying call to the faithful. With Mrs Thatcher's leadership of the Conservative Party under severe pressure as a result of the poll tax fiasco, the divisions in the Conservative Party over Europe and the deepening UK recession, the tall, blunt-speaking businessman placed himself full square behind the Prime Minister. The time had come 'to rally round the flag', he said. 'The only cloud on the horizon in Britain is the lack of faith here in this government. Britain has undoubtedly changed for the better but voters are fickle and ungrateful.'[1] While the Confederation of British Industry and more mainstream business organisations were starting to distance themselves from what they saw as a doomed administration which had run out of ideas, Hanson was loyal to a fault.

Hanson's loyalty was no act put on to deceive those present. He was then and remains now, some years after Mrs Thatcher's fall from power, immensely proud of the former Prime Minister, the changes she wrought in Britain, her admiration for entrepreneurship and the status she had conferred on the United Kingdom abroad. Moreover, it was Mrs Thatcher who had elevated James Hanson to the House of Lords and then, a few years later, after the intervention of Cecil Parkinson, did the same for Gordon White. But most significantly of all, for a shrewd businessman, the association with the Conservatives meant that when there was a business opportunity or deal involving the government, he was among the first to be consulted.

James Hanson was drawn from a small group of northern entrepreneurs with whom Mrs Thatcher could closely identify. These

The playboy lifestyle long behind him, Sir James none the less enjoyed visits to the Riviera, as here in 1977. (Rex Features)

OPPOSITE: *James in 1970, approaching the Pont Street Mews office which Hanson plc retains to this day as a London base.*

The Hanson plc senior executives. From top left: Derek Bonham, David H. Clarke, Anthony Alexander, Martin Taylor, Christopher Collins, Lord Hanson, Lord White, Derek Rosling and Robert Hanson. (Hanson plc)

Protesters against Hanson's proposed takeover of ICI in 1991 highlight concerns for the fate of the pension fund. (Martin Argles/*Guardian*)

Hanson charm offensive: Lord Hanson receives a kiss from the winner of a building-site safety competition, nine-year-old Elizabeth Micallef, who received her prize at the January 1994 Hanson annual general meeting. (Dylan Martinez/Popperphoto/Reuter)

Lord Hanson receives the Hambro Businessman of the Year Award, December 1989.

Gordon White and his wife, Victoria Tucker, at the races. (Rex Features)

The self-consciously adopted pose for the 1992 annual general meeting, in the immediate aftermath of the ICI share purchase: from their high stools Lords Hanson and White announced that they had decided upon their successors, though they did not name them. (Guardian)

were hard-working, self-made and confident business leaders in whose company the Prime Minister felt comfortable. Mrs Thatcher was likely to wince when approached at a Downing Street reception and asked by mainstream industrialists what the government was prepared to do to save the shipbuilding industry; but she delighted in being regaled with stories of Hanson's success in selling hamburgers to American housewives. She was also attracted to the pragmatic, 'can do' approach to business exemplified by such entrepreneurs as Lord Young, who was to serve in her Cabinet, and Sir Jeffrey Sterling.

Before the gathering at Cliveden, Sir Michael Richardson, as an adviser on privatisation, and John Wakeham had been pondering how best to deliver a good price for the government for the sale of PowerGen, one of the two English power companies carved out of the old Central Electricity Generating Board. Richardson saw Hanson plc as an ideal trade purchaser for PowerGen. Hanson's interests in low-tech basic industries from natural resources to bricks was legendary. His budding interests in coal, largely in North America, had brought him into close contact with the generating industry and he seemed the ideal person to shake away the cobwebs and to rationalise – part of the culture which came with public ownership. Spare land could be sold off, layers of management and bureaucracy wiped out and Hanson might even be able to bring about a degree of vertical integration – given his interest in coal. Richardson was greatly enthused by the idea and thought it was a genuine runner.

At the fringes of the assembly Richardson brought together Wakeham, the former chartered accountant, and Hanson, the businessman who never completed his accountancy training. The idea of selling PowerGen by private treaty, something which had not been attempted on such a large scale in the past, was briefly discussed. Hanson, who was returning to his own country house near Newbury that evening, agreed to come back the following morning – with Gordon White – to take the discussion further. It was realised from the outset that such a deal, which departed from the concepts of popular capitalism and wider share ownership, which were part of the creed of Thatcher's economics, could be politically awkward. It was made more so by the still swirling dispute over the terms under which Rover, Britain's last surviving large-scale motor manufacturer, had been sold to British Aerospace, with a helping of government and

European Community sweeteners. On the other hand, John Wakeham felt he had an obligation to obtain the best price for the government and the taxpayer. In the esoteric world of government finance, every penny raised through privatisation reduces the pressure on the public sector borrowing requirement, the amount the government has to raise on the financial markets through sales of gilt-edged stock. The view of PowerGen's less than ambitious management was that the company, in its current state, should be floated on the stock market; but it was worth only £700–800 millions. Wakeham was sceptical about the management assessment. 'I did not believe that was adequate and justified good value for the public purse',[2] the former Energy Secretary has argued.

The events surrounding Hanson's attempted purchase of Power-Gen provide a detailed illustration of the intrusion of political relationships in the business world in which Hanson operates. In an age of commercial diplomacy, in which governments through programmes such as trade and aid and export subsidies are becoming interposed in business transactions, political contacts become even more important. James Hanson personally has always believed that businessmen do not make enough effort to communicate with politicians, and that not enough resources have been allocated in this direction. In fact during Hanson's own siege of Imperial Chemical Industries in 1991, it found itself outmanoeuvred by Britain's leading manufacturer, which over the decades had cultivated an active lobby working inside the House of Commons itself on behalf of the chemical industry.

Hanson's belief that political parties can be useful to the businesses he runs has been most obviously reflected in the company's political contributions to the Conservative Party and to Mrs Thatcher's favourite think-tank, the Centre for Policy Studies. This was the intellectual driving force behind Thatcherism in the late 1970s as the Prime Minister-to-be sought to wrestle the debate away from the moderate, Butskellite wing of the party, exemplified by her more corporatist predecessor, Ted Heath, and to steer Conservatism in a new, more radical, direction.

James Hanson had learned from his father that making the right political judgements at the right time can be both useful and highly profitable. By accepting the economic realities of the situation in

1948, instead of mounting a hostile political campaign, Bob Hanson put himself in a better position to rebuild the family companies when the enthusiasm for a national transport network faded away.

Similarly, although conservative in his inclinations, James Hanson found he had few problems working with Harold Wilson after the Labour victory in 1964. The two men from Huddersfield, neither of whom can be described as connoisseurs of high culture, worked together to keep the D'Oyly Carte Opera Company, preservers of the Gilbert and Sullivan tradition, out of the hands of the receivers. If Hanson has any quarrels with modern British politicians they are with the Heath government of 1970–74. In quick succession Ted Heath is perceived by Hanson to have caved into the unions, strengthened exchange controls and intervened to refer Hanson Trust's plans to merge with paper-maker Bowater to the Monopolies Commission – thus halting the group's expansion in its tracks.

This series of events was among the factors that drove Gordon White to New York as a new base to expand the business. Once in the United States, Gordon White lost no time in developing the political contacts, establishing the Political Action Committees and hiring the lobbyists, which are such an integral part of the US way of doing business. Like his chairman, he recognised the importance of building alliances inside the political establishment. Gordon White also pulled off a rare trick among foreign investors in the United States: he managed to keep Hanson Industries as a low-profile and generally uncontroversial employer. That was until the United Mineworkers' Union penetrated the ownership structure during the prolonged 1993 strike at Peabody, targeting Hanson for the kind of hostile profile in the media, on both sides of the Atlantic, which it had studiously sought to avoid.

Playing the political game is an ingrained part of Hanson plc's corporate culture. It particularly developed during the Thatcher era and allowed Hanson, something of an outsider in the business world, into the inner sanctums of government. This privileged position opened the way for the Hanson bid for PowerGen. The morning after Michael Richardson and John Wakeham had initially discussed the trade sale possibility, a helicopter owned by Air Hanson and carrying Lords Hanson and White landed in the grounds of Cliveden soon after 8.30. Breakfast was over and the minister Wakeham, the acquisitors Hanson and White and the fixer Richardson gathered around a dining-room table to explore the concept of a trade sale. John Wakeham was an admirer of the Hanson approach to business, which he saw as being in the entrepreneurial traditions of the late Charles Clore, founder of the British Shoe Corporation. 'Hanson was one of the best imitators in the sense that he developed the techniques as it were of seeking to improve performance by acquisition and by pushing companies into the right slots and made a lot of money doing it,' Wakeham has observed.[3]

During the Cliveden meeting Wakeham briefed Hanson, White and Richardson on the issues involved: whether it was best to wait for a share floatation, which might produce less money and require some further restructuring of the power industry, or whether the matter could be wrapped up much more quickly as a trade sale. At this stage the financial aspects were not discussed, although White is understood to have raised the issue of whether Hanson might receive an arrangement/contingency fee should it become involved – with all its resources – and for some political reason the deal should fall through. White also suggested that the minister might do things the American way and have an auction for the company, which might attract generating companies from around the world.

With Michael Richardson having implanted the idea of a trade sale in the mind of John Wakeham, and the acquisition-minded brains of Hanson and White already engaged on the issue of price, the Energy Secretary and the two financiers clambered into the Hanson helicopter and returned to London. The flight itself, aboard the Hanson-owned aircraft, was symbolic in its own way of the informal and trusting nexus that existed between government and a small cadre of entrepreneurs during the Thatcher years.

Wakeham, who had brought some modern commercial ideas with him to the Energy Department, was fascinated with the idea of the trade sale. It would set a marker down for the rest of electricity privatisation, and the presence of Hanson, as an owner, would mean that the other players – the biggest generator National Power, the north of the border power firms Scottish Power and Hydro Electric, as well as the regional distribution companies – would know that privatisation was no soft option and that they were in for real competition. As far as James Hanson was concerned, if the price was right it was a good deal. PowerGen met his requirements of a strong cash flow, a good asset base and a generally proven technology – in addition it could purchase coal from Hanson's US mining operations. In the traditional style of Hanson plc it was Hanson who would have the final word on any deal, but Gordon White, brought to London especially, would handle the negotiations. The clincher, in White's mind, was the profits potential if the power industry in Britain could be updated. 'A station at the moment employs 850 people,' the financier noted once the talks had become public. 'You build a new power station and that can be run by 40,' he said.[4]

With the outlines of a deal under discussion, Hanson needed to know more about the animal it was considering buying. Although Hanson and White pride themselves on their intuitive way of doing business deals, in which price is largely subjective, PowerGen was slightly different. The price would partly be dependent on the debt which the privatised company would carry, and that required an agreement between John Wakeham and PowerGen's chairman Bob Malpas. Wakeham had wanted the company to carry £270 million of debt when it was sold off; Malpas argued that this would sink any possibility of a flotation. In the second week of July Hanson, through its merchant bankers N. M. Rothschild, and with the support of Wakeham, asked PowerGen to supply it with certain detailed balance sheet information. Armed with this it indicated to Wakeham that it would be prepared to pay £1.3–1.5 billion for PowerGen in a trade sale – around twice the figure which PowerGen believed it could obtain in a direct issues of shares to the public.

But the information request to Bob Malpas let the cat out of the bag. The last thing that PowerGen wanted was to become the newest subsidiary of a £10 billion empire, with a reputation for ruthlessly downgrading top management, closing down headquarters and reallocating surpluses in the pension fund. Within a week of the PowerGen board being informed, the Labour Party's then front-bench energy spokesman Frank Dobson, a burly, blunt-speaking northerner with a taste for the political jugular, received an anonymous telephone call which simply informed him that John Wakeham was considering a trade sale and James Hanson, one of Mrs Thatcher's favourite businessmen, was the likely purchaser. Dobson, a wily political operator sought to establish the facts by putting down a series of written questions in the House of Commons designed to flush into the open the trade sale proposal and the likelihood of Hanson being the favoured buyer.

At around the same time in mid-July the *Guardian*'s business correspondent, Simon Beavis, began to pick up the same speculation from Labour Party sources and by Friday 21 July felt confident enough to write a front-page article, disclosing Wakeham's new strategy. The Beavis account revealed that:

> The Government is considering turning its troubled electricity privatisation programme on its head by selling PowerGen, one of its two generating companies privately rather than floating it on the stock market . . . Ministers are thought to have investigated the possibility of selling PowerGen to Hanson, the conglomerate run by Lord Hanson, one of the Prime Minister's closest business allies.[5]

There was a predictable furore in the House of Commons where Hanson, because of his role as a big contributor to the Conservative Party and as a friend of the Prime Minister, was viewed with suspicion on the Labour benches. The leader of the Labour Party, Neil Kinnock, glaring across the dispatch box, excoriated Mrs Thatcher: 'The Prime Minister can twist and turn all she likes,' Kinnock shouted. 'The truth is that in breach of the promises she has already made, she is selling off at a fraction of its value a highly profitable company to a bosom chum and major contributor to the Tory party.'

The Shadow Energy Secretary Frank Dobson was even more vehement when he faced John Wakeham in the Commons. Mr Wakeham defended his decision to hold talks with Hanson and promised the Commons that: 'As the owners of PowerGen on behalf of the taxpayer, I would intend to lay down conditions which any singular purchaser must abide by. All of PowerGen's contractual rights and obligations would continue.'[6] But Mr Dobson was having none of it. He accused the Minister of 'Hawking PowerGen around the City, basically as a tax dodge. This is a disgraceful way to treat valuable assets that the public has paid for,' and claimed that Hanson Trust was a notorious asset-stripper. It wanted PowerGen because of its real estate portfolio and because they saw its potential as a high-tech tax haven against which to set its tax liabilities.[7]

The political attacks forced Wakeham into a partial retreat: he made it clear there would be a trade auction (an idea first raised by White anyway) in which Hanson would be just one potential buyer, and undertook that any underwriting fees paid to Hanson, for its role in valuing the company and arranging a trade sale, would have to be fully justified.

Richardson's ploy in bringing Hanson and Wakeham together was, however, starting to pay off handsomely for the government. The potential trade buyers, including Lord Weinstock's GEC and RTZ from Britain, Mitsubishi from Japan and West Germany's Veba, were now queuing up with Hanson plc for a share of the action. Now, however, the original Hanson bid of £1.5 billion was starting to run into the ground. Sir Gordon White, who had declared just a few weeks earlier that he would retire from business if he failed to bring PowerGen home for Hanson, raised a new set of issues. Drawing on his American experience he demanded assurances from the government that if Hanson went ahead with the trade purchase it would not be buying PowerGen's environmental liabilities, which could be potentially crippling. The merchant bankers approached the government with this request. The Treasury was deeply unhappy and the Hanson offer was withdrawn.

It was scuppered less by the political row and more by the caution of Hanson and White. But for the Energy Secretary John Wakeham the Hanson involvement had acted like magic:

Needless to say the board of PowerGen did not actually fancy starting their life in the public sector as a subsidiary of the Hanson Trust so they got cracking pretty well and what was around £700–800 million one day suddenly seemed to come fairly quickly to a figure not unadjacent to the £1500 million so I achieved my point, that was fine and the rest didn't matter . . . in the end of course the valuation for the business on flotation was £1.9 billion. So I reckon I earned in that transaction a billion pounds for the British taxpayer, which ought to secure my pension.[8]

The PowerGen deal was one of a series of transactions which the Hanson–White team failed to pull off in the early 1990s, leading to suggestions that they had lost their golden touch. Despite the protests of the Labour Party about sweetheart deals for Mrs Thatcher's friends, the strong bond which Hanson had forged with the government had been of mutual benefit. Hanson gained the first refusal on playing a role in the newly privatised power industry and John Wakeham gained breathing space and a better price for the power utilities. The other winner was the fixer supreme Michael Richardson: when privatisation took place Rothschild headed the list of merchant bankers and the higher price obtained meant better commissions for the issuing house and brokers.

The alliance forged between businessmen like James Hanson and Mrs Thatcher's government was part of the broader effort by the Prime Minister to overcome the corporatist trends in the British economy, in which deals were cosily fixed among government, the Trade Unions Congress and the Confederation of British Industry, and to develop an economy in which every individual had a stake. At the simplest level this meant extending the home-owning democracy through, for instance, the sale of local authority housing. But it also represented itself in the government's privatisation programme – still the most distinctive element of Thatcherism – and the wish to see individual stakeholders in the economy succeed. If this meant lifting the burden of government intervention, in the case for instance of large-scale mergers, then so be it. Similarly, if it meant reducing the tax burden on the better off, in the hope of unleashing some supply-side entrepreneurship, then that was a good development. The two pillars on which Thatcherism – as an economic concept – were to be built were tax cuts designed to unleash the supply side of the economy and privatisation.

In Mrs Thatcher's view, privatisation 'was one of the central means of reversing the corrosive and corrupting effects of socialism'.[9] She believed that if state ownership could be reversed, then 'the state's power is reduced and the power of the people enhanced'.[10] But this was only part of the argument. Corporations in state hands were protected from the ultimate competition – the threat of bankruptcy which 'is a discipline on privately owned firms'. Nothing made the

Prime Minister more happy than to watch her favourite business operators, the more self-made the better, slimming down bureaucracy and taming the power of the unions. 'Lord King turned around British Airways by a bold policy of slimming it down, improving its service to customers and giving its employees a stake in success,' the former Prime Minister would record in her memoirs.[11] In the private sector Lord Hanson appeared to be engaged in much the same activity: taking over seemingly moribund companies like Berec, London Brick and Imperial Group, slimming them down and making a more productive use of assets. Or that is how it looked, anyway.

There is a tendency, in some quarters, to see privatisation as simply an economic policy: one which would reduce the fiscal burdens of the government and bring about more competition in one swoop. But it was more than that. Part of the core ideology of Thatcherism was that in the marketplace, the individual rules. It is this principle which would lie behind a series of other measures and products designed to empower the individual financially, from Personal Equity Plans (PEPs) to the concept of a personal portable pension.

Much of this thinking had emerged from the Centre for Policy Studies (CPS), the right-wing think-tank originally founded by Sir Keith (Lord) Joseph and Mrs Thatcher in 1975, after two Conservative defeats at the polls. The aim was to develop a different kind of Tory Party. Sir Keith began a search for like-minded radicals, putting together thinkers such as (Sir) Alfred Sherman, a socialist turned *Daily Telegraph* leader writer, and (Sir) John Hoskyns, a wealthy business figure who identified the unions as the nation's biggest single problem. By the time Mrs Thatcher finally arrived in office in May 1979 the CPS had displaced the Conservative Research Department as the new Prime Minister's principal source of big ideas. Businessmen like James Hanson, who sought to make a contribution to the new economic thinking, did so by supporting the CPS. Throughout the 1980s the CPS – which provided expert advice for the Prime Minister's private office – received up to £20,000 per annum from Hanson plc. It was only with Mrs Thatcher gone from office, and her successor John Major installed as patron of the CPS, that Hanson began to wind down his support.

Of all the right-wing think-tanks which grew to prominence in the Thatcher years, such as the Institute of Economic Affairs and the

Adam Smith Institute, none was more influential than the CPS. Much of its thinking, such as the reinvention of pen and pencil tests at school, was to become government policy. Many of its thinkers and writers, such as the economist Professor Brian Griffiths, were to serve Mrs Thatcher at Downing Street. Its policy paper 'Monetarism is Not Enough',[12] to which Sir Keith Joseph wrote the introduction, came to be seen as the core document of Thatcherism. Although monetarism was part of the Thatcher approach, it was already part of economic conventional wisdom by the time she came to power in 1979, having been reintroduced to the British economy by Denis Healey under the tutelage of the International Monetary Fund. What Sir Keith Joseph argued was that unflinching monetarism needed to be supported by 'Substantial cuts in tax and public spending and bold encouragements to the wealth creators, without whose renewed efforts we shall all grow poorer.'[13]

James Hanson's support of the CPS did not mean he had any direct influence over its work. Hanson was introduced to the CPS by (Lord) Ralph Harris, better known for his economic work at the Institute of Economic Affairs. Hanson was attracted by the catholic range of views espoused, which were the more interesting for not always being pro-government. Nevertheless, because the CPS was so close to government in the Thatcher years it was one of those important levers on power on which Hanson liked to have a hand. It gave Hanson an amount of direct access to many of the prominent thinkers who throughout the 1980s were close to the seat of power, including Hanson's favoured outside public relations expert Sir Tim Bell – who would be Hanson's adviser during the siege of chemical group ICI in 1991. But Hanson also saw itself as a source of expertise and business personnel for the government. During the Thatcher period Hanson opened a revolving door to Whitehall, lending people to the civil service including the Home Office. At one point Alan Rosling, son of Hanson's veteran vice-chairman Derek Rosling, worked for the Prime Minister's private office at 10 Downing Street. The importance of the connection to the CPS was not to control or influence the flow of ideas, but indirectly to be part of the creative process of turning ideas into policy.

The main Hanson barometer of his commitment to the Conservative Party is his company's political contributions. As a publicly quoted company the Wiles Group, which became the Hanson Trust in 1969 and Hanson plc in 1987, is required by the Companies Acts to disclose its political contributions. In an age when the financing of political parties in Britain has come under close scrutiny, as a result of undercover payments from overseas financiers and plutocrats, the requirement to make such disclosures has been particularly useful. The Labour Party has often accused the Conservatives of aiding and abetting companies like Hanson which are large contributors to party coffers. Be that as it may, groups such as Hanson, which have been overt with their political contributions, cannot be accused of acting surreptitiously.

The issue of Hanson's political contributions, in fact, crops up at most of the company's annual meetings. The level of political payments was among the more contentious subjects at the 1994 meeting at the Barbican, at a time when the fortunes of the Conservative Party under John Major were at a low ebb as a result of a series of personal scandals surrounding second-line government ministers. One shareholder evoked laughter around the hall, including smiles from Hanson's partner Lord White, when he suggested that, as was the case with its investment in horses, the company was 'backing a loser'. This was a reference to the losses of the bloodstock companies which were revealed to the public during the heat of the 1991 struggle with ICI.

Lord Hanson was, however, unabashed in his praise of the Conservatives, as ever arguing that to back a Labour government would be 'entrepreneurial suicide' and it would be wrong to abandon the Tories just because they were going through a bad patch. Another shareholder won applause when he said the Tories 'were morally as well as financially bankrupt'. Such exchanges, which have been a regular feature of Hanson annual meetings, demonstrate how useful it is that corporate donations are there for all investors to question, even if smaller shareholders do not have the voting firepower to overturn them. Moreover, they illustrate Hanson's apparently intense loyalty to the post-Thatcher Conservative Party of John Major in its darkest hour.

James Hanson's prepared answer for the annual general meeting was as unequivocal as ever:

The Conservative party believes in encouraging business enterprise, which is more than can be said for the other two. Only the other day, after his posturing as a friend of business, John Smith [the then Labour Party leader] signed the European Socialist Manifesto which is as unfriendly a document to business as could be found. Why should we donate to commit entrepreneurial suicide? No, ladies and gentlemen, your board believes the way forward is through a party that truly believes in the creation of national wealth not spending it.[14]

Nevertheless, even as Hanson was attacking Labour policies in public, a Hanson envoy, veteran Hanson director Peter Harper, was launching a cocktail offensive with Labour's front-bench economic and industrial team. In the world of James Hanson, pragmatism dictates that business must be able to deal with both sides of the political spectrum.

Playing both sides of the table, however, does not mean that Hanson's financial support for the Conservatives ever weakens. From the Wiles Group's first political contributions to the Conservatives in 1968, soon after James acceded to the chair, when it donated a modest £550 to the Tories, the sum rose sharply until Hanson became one of the party's most dependable and largest contributors. By 1983 – an election year – the political contribution, including that to the CPS, had risen to £83,000 per annum, although it dropped back to £55,000 in 1994. In 1987, another election year, it surged to £117,000, a peak level which has not been surpassed since. The most recent 1993 annual report shows the donation holding steady at £115,000.[15] James Hanson, unlike John King of British Airways, has never sought to suspend political donations because of short-term differences with the government. Even during the early 1970s, when Hanson was finding it difficult to maintain the pace of expansion it wanted under the Heath government, the company's political contributions remained a constant.

The reasoning behind Hanson's generous policy of feeding Conservative Central Office is manifold. There can be no doubt that in the 1980s James Hanson bought the Thatcherite approach to economic management, hook, line and sinker. Unlike most of the business community he was a genuine supporter, who never failed during election campaigns to stand up and be counted. It was one of the Thatcher government's first moves, the first steps towards the abolition of exchange controls in Sir Geoffrey Howe's budget of June 1979, which helped to convince Hanson and White that the Thatcher government was on the right course. For a company like Hanson, which saw itself developing on both sides of the Atlantic, the presence of exchange controls – which required almost every transaction to be approved by the Bank of England – was an onerous requirement. It had been a problem for the Hanson family when, after nationalisation in 1948, it decided to invest in the Canadian trucking industry. It was also a severe problem for Gordon White when he left Britain in 1973, to plot Hanson's expansion in the United States. With exchange controls out of the way, Hanson would be able to transfer resources backwards and forwards across the Atlantic, and eventually take advantage of the chance to move vast assets to offshore financial centres such as Panama to launch raids on target companies, such as the Imperial Group, and to minimise its tax liabilities.

Hanson also took the view that Mrs Thatcher had restored Britain's global reputation. In a signed article in the *Observer* in May 1987, Lord Hanson could not find a critical word to say about the Thatcher administration: 'The business climate today is looking sunnier than at any time in post-war memory. Firm and stable policies – in stark contrast to the stop–go shambles of the Sixties and Seventies – have enabled business to develop beyond recognition.' He went on to add for good measure: 'The world recognises, even if we ourselves find it hard to see, that the process of rejuvenating and reinvigorating is well underway.'[16] As an entrepreneur who has always seen his company's future on both sides of the Atlantic, the overseas image of Britain and British business is very important to Hanson. Thus Thatcher's success reinforced the status of Hanson's North American activities, while the government's perceived reconstruction of industry and reshaping of the tax system chimed with Hanson's free-booting approach to business.

These factors, like the removal of exchange controls, were by no means of academic interest to Hanson. The rationalisation which came with privatisation and the reconstruction of UK businesses conferred a legitimacy on Hanson's acquisition formula which saw companies taken over and costs radically pruned. Even the presence of Hanson on the share register would force companies, including ICI in 1991 and beyond, to reform themselves. Sweating assets, as it became known, was seen as a respectable activity, not the asset stripping which earned such opprobrium in the late 1960s and early 1970s. Overseas, a strong image for Britain, which came with Mrs Thatcher and her soulmate relationship with Ronald Reagan, allowed UK firms to expand in North America without attracting the same level of hostility which accompanied Japanese investments, although there were to be flurries of anti-British sentiment during Sir James Goldsmith's assault on Goodyear in 1986 and Hanson's bitterly contested bid for SCM.

Above all, being a large fund-raiser for the Conservative Party confers on Hanson special privileges. These privileges operate on several levels. In the first instance Hanson found himself a political insider, courted by the Conservative Party's inner circle such as the former party chairmen Lord Parkinson and Kenneth Baker (Baker now sits on Hanson plc's board as a non-executive director), and those who counted themselves among Mrs Thatcher's greatest admirers such as the former Defence Minister Alan Clark. There was a less close relationship with ministers such as the former Chancellor Nigel Lawson – although he too would be expected to give the financier time in his schedule. On a second level, the act of donating up to £1 million to the party during the 1980s also meant that the patronage that governments can confer came the way of Hanson and his colleagues, including knighthoods and peerages and the power to command the presence even of the Prime Minister at corporate celebrations. Thirdly, and arguably most importantly for a business, Hanson could use his financial firepower to inject his company into the political process: this happened at PowerGen, as already described. But there was also a Hanson role in several other sensitive political situations including the Westland Helicopters affair, the privatisation of Rolls-Royce Motors, the BP share sale and, most recently, Canary Wharf.

It was axiomatic that James Hanson would have a good relationship with the Prime Minister and the people around Thatcher. The Prime Minister was a great admirer of successful business people – 'her husband had been a successful businessman after all,' Cecil Parkinson, a long-standing confidant of Mrs Thatcher, has observed.[17] She liked people who had become successful and was particularly fond of entrepreneurship. In her view to build up a company was a real achievement and deserved recognition. She particularly liked Hanson because he was a strong and visible supporter of the government, who was prepared to back his words with financial actions. He was not one of those conservative tycoons who preferred to do their political giving through front organisations such as British United Industrialists. This well-developed relationship with Mrs Thatcher meant that Lord Hanson could command the dinner tables of her aides and was able, on the twenty-fifth anniversary of the public company, to attract Mrs Thatcher herself as the star speaker. Tory ministers, including Lord Parkinson, would attend the annual seminar and dinners for executives which James would host immediately before the annual general meetings.

The intimacy with which Hanson was regarded in the upper echelons of the Tory Party comes through clearly from the accounts of a 1986 Sunday lunch at the then Deputy Prime Minister Willie (now Lord) Whitelaw's official residence at Dorneywood. Over the lunch, at which Willie presided, James Hanson and Alan Clark fell into a blunt conversation. 'He and I got on well, letting our hair down rapidly and using ' "fuck", "arsehole" and "shit" all too freely, although Celia [Whitelaw] gamely pretended not to hear,' Alan Clark recorded.[18] Later the after-lunch conversation would turn to the future of Rover and the proposed bid for the company from Ford. There was also some irreverent talk of the younger people working around the Prime Minister before Hanson made his customary disappearance by helicopter. Such occasions provide a flavour of the degree of fraternisation which had developed between James and the Conservative inner circle. When towards the end of the Thatcher era the Prime Minister's team were looking for a bolt-hole for Sir Charles Powell, her foreign policy adviser, it was to Hanson they turned. Alternatively when Lord Parkinson, as Transport Secretary, was looking for a new chairman of British Rail, Hanson felt confident enough to approach the government with a name from within his own group. In the Thatcher years the normally casual interplay between politicians and business was moving towards the symbiosis much more common in the American political system.

The privilege of being fêted at the highest levels of government was important for the self-esteem of James Hanson. His father Bob, who in many ways had lived a distinguished business career had never been recognised for his industrial achievements. Bob Hanson's belated CBE was awarded for his services to showjumping. In the 1950s James, despite his work in Canada, was seen as a less than serious figure because of his playboy tendencies. The idea of eventually reaching the House of Lords, and bringing his jet-set partner Gordon White with him, would have seemed preposterous. Yet that is exactly what his strong support of the Conservative Party delivered for him.

James's knighthood came in a slightly unexpected and almost tainted fashion. In 1976 that other famous Huddersfield son, Harold Wilson, resigned from office, while still at the peak of his powers. The custom on these occasions was that a Prime Minister would draw up a resignation honours list which would allow him to reward all those who had served with him in office. But present on the list were several business and showbusiness figures who had little direct connection to the Labour Party and could not even have been considered mainstream industrialists. These included Sir James Goldsmith, who was known to have exceptionally strong right-wing views; the showbusiness magnates Lew Grade and Bernard Delfont; Wilson's publisher George Weidenfeld; the maker of Wilson's trademark Gannex raincoat, Joseph Kagan; the property tycoon Eric Miller; and James Hanson, at that stage chairman of the Hanson Trust and Yorkshire Television.

These names caused a political outcry. The charge made by Wilson's press secretary, Joe Haines, who objected to several of the choices, was that the list had first been assembled by Harold Wilson's principal private secretary, Marcia Williams, on lavender paper. Wilson himself appeared generally agnostic about how the list was compiled, although Lady Falkender has consistently maintained that the paper was pale pink, not lavender and that the only reason it was on her private paper in her handwriting was because the slips of paper that Wilson had handed over were illegible.[19] The list was universally seen from the left to the right of the political spectrum as bringing the whole system of political patronage into disrepute.

So outlandish were some of the choices that the knighthood for James Hanson appeared relatively innocuous in the circumstances. Nevertheless, it ensured that Hanson, who had been missing from the gossip columns for almost 15 years came back with a vengeance. 'And now the Lord High Contributor,' declared the *Daily Express* in a reference to Hanson's support for the D'Oyly Carte Opera.[20] Other papers sought to portray Hanson as the mystery millionaire currently enjoying the St Tropez sunshine on his £700,000 yacht; not the kind of company one would expect to have seen on the honours list of a socialist Prime Minister. What much of the coverage appears to have missed is all the reasons why Hanson's presence was not that unexpected. Wilson and Hanson had become fast political friends because they hailed not just from Huddersfield but from Milnsbridge, the same corner of the West Riding. Moreover, as Lord Wilson has recalled, there was a family connection: 'D'you know his [Hanson's] aunt used to teach my sister Marjorie at Sunday School?'[21] As chairman of Yorkshire Television, Hanson was one of Yorkshire's most prominent businessmen; moreover it was Yorkshire TV which would be selected to broadcast Wilson's series on the Prime Ministers. Both Wilson and Hanson shared a fascination with Gilbert and Sullivan, and with the D'Oyly Carte, which was at the time on a three-month tour of the United States, confirming that: 'Mr Hanson has been instrumental in raising £30,000 towards the tour', while Wilson, who had joined the trustees at the same time, had helped with making the contacts for the tour with foreign embassies and consulates.[22] Moreover, despite his early associations with Slater Walker Securities, Hanson had emerged from the misadventure of the early 1970s intact as an industrialist, whereas many others associated with the City of those years had faded from view.

Hanson's eventual accession to the knighthood came via an entirely conventional route. Bill Black, the British Leyland chief, who was to become Lord Black, had written to Wilson recommending Hanson for a peerage for his services to industry. It had been Hanson, for instance, who had opened the North American market to Leyland trucks. When Wilson resigned, various government departments were asked if they had any recommendations they wanted passed on. Black's letter was handed on to Downing Street by the Department of Trade and Industry and was thus disassociated with the lavender list. Hanson was surprised and delighted with the honour when it came, regarding it as very romantic as well as recognising his wife. But he also saw it as politically important. It would enable him to gain more access to government thinking as well as to cultivate civil servants at a certain level.

After the public controversy over the knighthood, the peerage would come much more smoothly to Hanson. The businessman was first to meet Mrs Thatcher when she visited New York as leader of the opposition and was staying with the British Consul General Gordon Booth. At a dinner hosted by Emmanuel Kay, a fellow entrepreneur, the Labour-anointed knight found himself sitting next to Mrs Thatcher. It was mutual admiration at first sight. Mrs Thatcher, who always had a taste for good-looking men, was taken with the elegant industrialist with the trace of Yorkshire in his voice. She, quite naturally, asked Hanson about his American businesses. Hanson told her that among the companies the Hanson Trust had acquired was the Ball Park frankfurters business and pointed out that it was surprising that the American housewife spends ten cents of her shopping dollar on frankfurters. The would-be Prime Minister, who prides herself on her own good housekeeping skills, immediately observed that this was not possible. James quickly corrected himself, admitting he had meant a cent. Mrs Thatcher appeared pleased by her little victory. From that evening onwards, however, Hanson became a devout supporter of her political career, stepping up his company's political contributions.

The peerage which followed for Sir James Hanson in 1983 cannot be deemed unexpected. By then the Hanson Trust was on an acquisition roll on both sides of the Atlantic. The company's profits reached £58 million in 1982 on turnover of £1.1 billion and it had established itself among Britain's industrial leaders. As importantly, the company's political donation in 1983, an election year, had doubled from £40,000 to £83,000. Hanson's elevation to the House of Lords, where he could directly take part in the political debate, was part of a natural progression. His only disappointment was that the peerage arrived too late for his father to see what had become of his offspring.

It was not just Hanson who was to reap the benefits of patronage. In Mrs Thatcher's first year in office, 1979, Hanson's business partner Gordon White received his knighthood for his services to Britain's commercial and community interests in the United States, through his work for such organisations as the Anglo-American association and the International Committee of the US Congressional Award. White's knighthood caused concern in some quarters as a result of his tax exile status and a dispute with the Inland Revenue over his maintenance of a London residence which exposed him to some unpaid tax liabilities. White's tax status and residency was seen in parts of Whitehall as an obstacle to Sir Gordon joining his fellow Yorkshire industrialists, Hanson and King, in the House of Lords.

As the Hanson group expanded exponentially in the 1980s – its before tax profits reached £1.2 billion by 1990 – Lord Hanson conducted an active campaign to gain a peerage for Sir Gordon in the face of Whitehall opposition as a result of White's colourful personal life. In a succession of articles in the national press, between 1986 and 1990, Sir Gordon sought to establish his credibility as a serious commentator on public affairs, writing on a range of issues from crime in New York to the need for an easier takeover regime and in July 1990 on corporate governance, the issue which was to defeat the Hanson–White partnership in the 1991 ICI bid. White would argue cogently, and without irony given his own arrangements with Hanson, that the reward systems in the many boardrooms were out of hand. 'Stock options and incentive schemes are an appropriate and justifiable reward for the able, but rolling service contracts insulate the incompetent,' White wrote. 'Furthermore, underperforming companies are frequently typified by high top salaries, share options confined to a handful of apparatchiks and generous golden parachutes.'[23]

With the Thatcher era drawing to a close in the late 1980s, Lord Hanson became anxious that Sir Gordon had not received the recognition due to him for his role in building the group both in the United States and Britain. As a Conservative contributor he began to pull some strings. He called upon Cecil Parkinson, then Minister for Trade and Industry, whom Hanson knew well, and suggested that it was time that Gordon White had a peerage. Parkinson suggested that the best way of achieving this was for Hanson to go and see the Prime Minister himself. 'Let her know that he has done a hell of a job for Britain,' Parkinson suggested.[24] He also proposed that Hanson make the appointment on a Friday afternoon, when Mrs Thatcher would be in a relaxed mood before leaving Downing Street for a weekend at Chequers.

Hanson followed Parkinson's advice and called on Mrs Thatcher and explained to her Gordon White's role in the Hanson group, his community and charitable work in the United States and how he had been flying the flag for Britain. Lord Parkinson's advice did the trick. When the Prime Minister resigned in late 1990, Sir Gordon White, who had been a distant overseas player in the Thatcher years, was there among the 43 loyalists mentioned in her resignation honours list. He and three other loyal industrialists, with much stronger ties to Thatcherite policies – Sir Hector Laing, Sir Jeffrey Sterling and Sir David Wolfson – were also given life peerages. An overjoyed Hanson, who too had received his first honour in a resignation list, set about celebrating the occasion. A sumptuous dinner for more than 100 of Hanson's top executives and contacts was held under the glittering chandeliers at Claridges on 13 June 1991. The guest of honour was Lord Parkinson. Among the guests were Sir James Goldsmith and his wife Lady Annabel, Australia's richest citizen Kerry Packer, Princess Firyal of Jordan, Hanson and White's former business partner Jim Slater – and, of course, that other Thatcher favourite Lord King. When the tax-exiled Lord White of Hull was formally introduced to the House of Lords he came in on the arms of Lords Hanson and King.

As was the case with some of those on Harold Wilson's resignation list 14 years earlier, there were doubts as to whether White was a suitable choice. Unlike Lord Hanson, who has maintained a low public profile, White has frequently hit the headlines. He relishes the company of beautiful women and has been spotted in New York restaurants, his shirt unbuttoned to the waist, surrounded by women less than half his age. His personal life was to attract public attention in the winter of 1992 when White and his girlfriend, the 29-year-old model Victoria Tucker, were staying in actor George Hamilton's lodge in Aspen, Colorado. On 23 December 1991 Ms Tucker presented herself at the hospital with severe bruises and a statement was taken from her by two policemen in which she accused the noble peer of battering her. The charges were, however, dropped in January 1992 and the bruises were attributed to an accident on the piste. Soon afterwards the Tory peer married Ms Tucker, who is more than forty years his junior.

Lord White, who was known to have jaundiced views about Britain dating back to the early 1970s, caused a stir in February of the same year when he launched an attack on the National Health Service in Britain and bracketed Adolf Hitler and Franklin D. Roosevelt as 'the two great providers of work and developers of self-respect' of the twentieth century. 'Adolf Hitler created a workforce to build the autobahns. I am not an admirer of Adolf Hitler other than in his ability to revitalise a destroyed nation,' White told his hometown paper, the *Hull Daily Mail*.[25] No sooner had the remarks been published than the Hanson damage control machine roared into life. Sitting at an oval, veneered table in his study at the Pont Street Mews house, where Hanson and White had first set up office in the 1960s, Lord White said he wanted to apologise to anyone who believed he was an admirer of Hitler. He pointed out that he and his brother had fought against Hitler's armies and that his brother had been shot down and killed over München-Gladbach in 1943.[26] Despite the apology, the episode gave a brief insight into the views of the UK exile whom Mrs Thatcher had ennobled.

Lord Hanson delights in the respect and recognition which his peerage and that of Lord White have conferred upon them. But as importantly, Hanson's legendary closeness to the ideology espoused by Mrs Thatcher has given Hanson plc the opportunity to take a direct part in the political process. Hanson delighted in the role of the financial trouble-shooter, cantering to rescue the government from embarrassment – and in the process doing itself a favour at the same time. The Westland affair, which surfaced in late 1985, was just such a case. Westland was Britain's last surviving helicopter manufacturer and as a consequence regarded as important to Britain's cluster of defence industries and the range of expertise in the aerospace sector. In April 1985 it ran into financial difficulties and a number of spatchcock efforts were made to support it, including a failed £89 million bid from Alan Bristow, the former helicopter operator and self-made millionaire. In Mrs Thatcher's view the critical issue at Westland was whether a private sector company and its shareholders had the right to settle its own affairs, irrespective of whether it was heavily dependent on government orders. Others, including the

Defence Secretary, Michael Heseltine, saw it differently. Westland provided him with a chance to challenge the Prime Minister politically using Europe as the issue. In Heseltine's view the significant principle at stake in Westland was the preservation of a helicopter manufacturer which would fulfil Europe's defence needs. As those defence needs were not precisely in place he energetically set about creating them.

With the company in danger of going into receivership, after the Bristow bid had lapsed, the Bank of England was asked to intervene with the aim of pacifying the banking creditors while new management was brought in, in the shape of Sir John Cuckney, the industrial trouble-shooter. It would be his job to effect a reorganisation of Westland. As chairman, Cuckney determined a number of changes would be needed. These would include government underwriting of certain helicopter sales overseas, some launch aid for a new range of helicopters and the introduction of a wealthy minority shareholder. Sir John had in mind Sikorsky, the world's largest helicopter manufacturer, a subsidiary of America's United Technology.

It was the possibility of Sikorsky gaining a foothold in Westland that helped to galvanise Michael Heseltine into action. He frantically put together plans for a European alternative which would pull in two UK companies, British Aerospace and GEC. Heseltine argued that a Sikorsky deal would turn Westland into nothing more than a fabricator for the Americans. The Westland board favoured the American solution, while Heseltine worked frantically to keep a European option open. In the ensuing drama over Westland's future Mrs Thatcher lost two Cabinet ministers: Sir Leon Brittan, who was accused of misleading Parliament, and Michael Heseltine, who stalked out of Cabinet, after his case for a European solution was overruled. The Prime Minister herself appeared in danger as her veracity and judgement were challenged in the Commons.

Even as the political storm was erupting around Mrs Thatcher, one of Britain's foremost investors in the United States was to lend its financial firepower to the debate about Westland's future. On 17 January 1986, the eve of the extraordinary general meeting of Westland shareholders called to approve a joint rescue plan by Sikorsky and Fiat, Lord Hanson played his card. He announced to a stunned stock market that he had secretly acquired a 15 per cent stake in Westland to protect the interests of Air Hanson – the small Hanson Trust airline subsidiary, the main job of which is carrying James Hanson and his fellow executives around Britain and Europe.

Hanson's letter to Sir John Cuckney left no doubt on which side he was pitching into the battle over Westland. After wishing Sir John well in his endeavours he noted: 'Our subsidiary Air Hanson, the Weybridge-based helicopter operator formed in 1973, has for many years had operational arrangements with your company and with Sikorsky. It is hoped, by means of this investment, that Air Hanson will be able to strengthen these interests in the future.'[27] It was a politically astute intervention. As a rule Hanson was averse to stating why his company bought shares in another: in the Westland case this rule was broken, with Hanson plc committing some £10.5 million of shareholders' funds to protect the interests of its small, loss-making helicopter subsidiary. The reality was that Hanson was investing in Mrs Thatcher and the Anglo-American business alliance. His intervention ensured that, whatever the damage to the Prime Minister the Westland affair had caused, the private sector American solution she favoured would be victorious. The timing was useful to Hanson too. As the Westland affair was reaching its peak so was the battle for control of the Imperial Group: the most critical acquisition Hanson would ever make. James Hanson's shrewd decision to buy a stake in Westland and in effect sign up to the Prime Minister's cause would do the company no harm should there be any question of the Monopolies and Merger Commission looking at the £2.5 billion Imperial bid.

The possibility of buying a whole company such as PowerGen or a large government-owned stake in an enterprise clearly intrigued Hanson. Although the financier personally believes that being a known contributor to the Conservative Party makes doing deals with the government more difficult than it would otherwise be, this did not prevent him from getting involved in such transactions. Indeed, as far as can be told from the main financial events of the 1980s, there was no other business person who, like the character in the Woody Allen movie *Zelig*, would manage to insinuate himself into the main financial events of his time from the government's sell-off of its remaining share stake in British Petroleum, to the speculative purchase of a share stake in Midland Bank after the bank had incurred large, debilitating losses at its American subsidiary, Crocker National Bank.

James Hanson's supreme confidence about his ability to do any deal was demonstrated in May 1985 when he telephoned Peter Middleton, then Permanent Secretary at the Treasury, and requested a personal meeting with the Chancellor of Exchequer, Nigel (now Lord) Lawson, at 11 Downing Street. As would be the case when any major industrialist, but particularly one as loyal to the Tory cause as Lord Hanson phones, a secret appointment was arranged. The imposing, blunt-speaking Yorkshireman, who has appeared determined over the last decade to take over any company with imperial pretentions – Imperial Group and Imperial Chemical Industries – came straight to the point. His company, Hanson plc, was prepared to offer the government £6 billion for its 31.5 per cent remaining stake in British Petroleum. The deal would make good sense: as in the later case of PowerGen, the government would be spared the enormous costs of mounting what would be the largest share offer of all time and Hanson could bring its financial engineering skills to BP, which despite its private sector background was still being run like a commercial branch of the colonial service.

Nigel Lawson heard Hanson out, but gave him short shrift. While he listened patiently to what Hanson had to say, he basically regarded the approach as highly unusual, although the Chancellor could not help but be impressed by Hanson's ability to raise such an enormous sum of money, even more than the government had raised from British Gas, its biggest privatisation thus far. What Hanson did not know, but the Chancellor did, was that BP hoped to use the share sale as an opportunity to raise some £1.25 billion extra in the form of a rights issue to strengthen the company's capital base. When Wall Street crashed on Monday, 17 October 1987, just as the BP stake (after some delays) was being readied for a public sale in which the City was likely to take a bloodbath, the thought must have crossed the Chancellor's mind that the Hanson trade sale would have been far simpler. Moreover, subsequent events at BP, including a dramatic reduction in staff, a rationalisation of operations and a shakeup in the top management in June 1992 which saw the replacement of chief executive Bob Horton by David Simon, in some respects suggest that BP might have been turned around earlier had it received the Hanson treatment.

It was not just Hanson which was swept up by Mrs Thatcher's enterprise culture of the 1980s. The Canadian property developers Olympia & York, run by the Reichmann family, which in the 1970s had struggled through a maze of regulations and industrial disputes to complete a modest three-storey office block in Knightsbridge, were also impressed by the changes taking place in Britain. The Reichmanns thought on a grander scale than other developers, as their work on the World Financial Center in New York had demonstrated. The family recognised that the City of London was becoming over-crowded and that it was all but impossible to become involved in a property deal in the Square Mile, which preferred to do business with the developers they knew and trusted rather than outsiders. With this in mind the attention of the Reichmanns was drawn to Docklands, the vast tract of wasteland to the east of the City of London crying out for redevelopment. In July 1987 Paul Reichmann, the family head, announced that Olympia & York planned to turn Canary Wharf – a former tobacco dock on the banks of the Thames – into Wall Street on the water through a £3–4 billion office and shop development.[28] Reichmann anticipated that business could be drawn to the area by the creation of high-quality offices, equipped for modern data-processing systems in carefully landscaped surroundings. In throwing Olympia & York wholeheartedly into the project there was one aspect of the scheme with which the Reichmanns never fully came to grips – access. Two transport systems were being put into place: a new road structure and the Docklands Light Railway. However, the Jubilee Line which would directly connect Canary Wharf to the rest of London was a long way off being built, even though the Reichmanns pledged £400 million towards the cost. But like other grand projects conceived during enthusiasm for the enterprise culture, the nearly completed first stage of Canary Wharf came to grief during the recession as the devastating combination of high interest rates, collapsing property prices on both sides of the Atlantic and the failure to start work on the Jubilee Line led to the administrators being brought in and the Reichmanns being moved out by the banks. On 28 May 1992 the administrators Ernst & Young stepped in and the search began for a buyer willing to finance the project and rescue the prestige of the Conservative government, which had given it such strong backing.

As had so often been the case when the government's interest needed protecting, Hanson plc was quickly on the scene.[29] Although property was generally only a sideline for Hanson, it had the necessary cash resources to keep the Canary Wharf project going and, in the process, protect the government from embarrassment and a potential systemic collapse in the property market. Lord Hanson, who prides himself on an ability to read markets, took the view that the downward spiral of leasehold rentals and property values during the 1992–93 recession would soon bottom out. Thus Canary Wharf could be an opportunity to buy into recovery. Hanson, alert to tax opportunities, was also interested in Canary Wharf's £600 million of tax breaks.

Hanson pressed ahead with its exploration, holding a 'summit meeting' at its headquarters in mid-July attended by Olympia & York boss Paul Reichmann, John Ritblat of British Land (who was brought in as an adviser) and Gordon White. The session was inconclusive with Hanson holding out for the government to take steps to stabilise the climate in Docklands before going ahead. A month later, however, Hanson announced it was pulling out of the contest for control of the project. The company noted that the deal did not seem to be in the best interests of its shareholders: in other words its institutional investors opposed the deal. Once again a Hanson effort to intervene in a politically sensitive situation had been blown off course, this time, however, as a result of City rather than government concerns. It was interesting to note that the two main British bidders who had been in the running for Canary Wharf, Lord Sterling and Lord Hanson, were both Conservative stalwarts. Both were public supporters of the enterprise culture, whose business careers took off in the Thatcher years.

As someone who has been involved in business in North America for nearly five decades, James Hanson also recognises the value of political lobbying in the United States. Over the years Gordon White, as chairman of Hanson's US operations, has done a great deal in Washington and built up a good connection for Hanson plc. Nobody knows the importance of those connections as much as James Hanson himself. He particularly recognises the power which lies at state level where senators can be all powerful. Hanson takes the view that if you want something done in Louisiana it is imperative that the business person gets access to someone like Russell Long, the veteran senator from the state, who knows how to make sure a job is done, particularly if it involves his own constituents. Hanson contrasts the American attitude with that in Britain, where businessmen feel they know all that needs to be known.

In the Reagan–Bush years (1980–92), when many of Hanson's biggest acquisitions were made in the United States, the scale of lobbying by overseas companies in the US climbed steeply. Many foreign companies operating in the US formed Political Action Committees (PACs) whose job it was to funnel donations to the political campaigns of candidates favoured by the business lobby.

Essentially PACs are a means by which like-minded groups, employees of a company, members of a trade union or a trade association, such as the Bituminous Coal Operators' Association (to which the Hanson subsidiary Peabody belongs), band together to make voluntary political contributions. The PAC then pools the money and parcels it out to favoured candidates in federal elections. The rationale of most PACs is unmistakable: it is to support those candidates who will best advance the interests of their group. Alternatively, there are hostile PACs who see their job as attacking candidates and issues, which their contributors would wish to oppose. The power of the PAC has been seen by critics as detrimental to democracy. Small but influential groupings such as the car dealers and dairy producers have used their funding power to prevail in Congress, sometimes to the detriment of the wider population.

At the start of the Reagan years there were very few such foreign-controlled PACs. However, by the time President Reagan had settled into his second term more than 100 such PACs could be identified. These foreign PACs have been able to insert themselves into the domestic political process by lending their support to legislators who, for instance, oppose the contentious issue of unitary taxation – which can be detrimental to the interests of overseas investors like Hanson. Those who have expressed concern about the increasing influence of the foreign business lobby in the United States include the former Democrat chairman of the Senate Finance Committee, Senator Lloyd

Bentsen of Texas, who moved on to become Secretary of the Treasury in the 1992 Clinton Administration. 'You get an immediate reaction when you introduce a piece of legislation which affects these foreign investors in the United States,' Senator Bentsen observed. 'They don't just stop at the Washington level. You hear from their distributors and contractors back home right away.'[30] In the American political system the ideological boundaries between politicians from the two major parties, Democrats and Republicans, can often be blurred. Thus the PACs are as likely to target issues and the candidates which support them, than any one party. PACs also understand the political reality that in certain states, for instance Wyoming, there is no point in supporting anyone other than the incumbent Republican – because the Democrats have no clout. If you are a corporation which, like Hanson, happens to control the largest coal producer in the United States, the Peabody Coal Company, and that firm has extensive strip-mining interests in that state, then the incumbent senator is likely to receive support from your PAC. That becomes doubly true if that elected official happens to be Senator Malcolm Wallop of Wyoming, an influential member of the Energy and Natural Resources Committee. The PACs which support the senator in question can be reasonably assured that, in the event of new tax measures detrimental to the interests of the coal industry or a damaging coal strike, they can count on support on Capitol Hill from those legislators who over the years have received PAC support. America has the best Congress money can buy.

Official filings with the Federal Election Commission (FEC) and the US House of Representatives show that, as in Britain, Hanson subsidiaries have recognised the benefits of good political contacts. Over the years Hanson Industries, James Hanson's US holding company, has been consistently registered as a lobbyist on Capitol Hill. The purpose of these lobbying activities is in respect of legislation relating to: 'Tax, regulatory trade and other issues of interest to a diversified producer of industrial, food and consumer products.'[31] When legislation affecting Hanson's interests comes before committee the various law firms hired by Hanson will be in the corridors outside committee, buttonholing members and their staff to seek amendments, or in restaurants on Capitol Hill dining the politicians and officials who may be helpful. In much the same way

James Hanson personally conducts his own charm offensive with UK civil servants such as the Secretary to the Cabinet, Sir Robin Butler, a regular lunch guest at the company's lunch rooms above the headquarters of Melody Radio on Brompton Road in London.

The Peabody Coal Company, the coal-mining arm of Hanson Industries, is highly active both as a contributor to political campaigns and as a lobbyist on Capitol Hill. Political support has been particularly important for Peabody which has been at the forefront of the effort to lower the cost of coal production in United States by aggressively taking on the power of the United Mine Workers of America (UMWA). Peabody's goal has been to circumvent the union contracts, with their grandfathered health and safety benefits that had been inherited from previous generations, and replace UMWA members with non-union workers, with considerably lower payroll costs. In this expensive battle, which damaged Hanson's image as a coal-owner, lasted 200 days and cost Hanson shareholders over £100 million in foregone profits, Peabody was in need of political friends.

FEC returns show that through the Peabody PAC in the 1993–94 fiscal year the Hanson subsidiary distributed funds to no fewer than a dozen members of the Senate. Among the biggest recipients of funds were Senator Robert Byrd (Democrat) from West Virginia, where the Hanson-controlled Eastern Association Coal Company, with its deep mines, is among the ten largest employers in the state. Another recipient is Senator Malcolm Wallop (Republican) from Wyoming, a state in which Hanson subsidiaries operate large-scale non-union strip mining operations. In fact senators in almost every state in which Peabody does business are recipients of funds from the Peabody-controlled Political Action Committee. In the House of Representatives the Peabody PACs have targeted a further 19 members, including the powerful Democratic Majority Leader Senator Richard Gephardt, whose constituency includes St Louis, Missouri – headquarters to Peabody Holding Company Inc. The FEC returns show that in the first six months of 1993–94, a non-election year, the Peabody PAC dispensed $18,000 to Democratic political candidates and $17,050 to Republicans – thus helping both sides to rebuild their campaign war chests in time for the next confrontation at the polls.[32]

Meanwhile, back on Capitol Hill firms of lobbyists representing Peabody remain active on a number of fronts. Filings with the

Secretary of the Senate show that Peabody has been an active lobbyist in respect of: 'Legislative matters affecting the coal industry including: (a) environmental matters; (b) coal leasing; (c) coal research and development technology; (d) legislation affecting mining on Indian lands; (e) retiree health care; (f) energy and mineral taxation, and (g) mine safety.'[33] In the process of this lobbying, Peabody entertained Senate staff members and senators at some of Washington's finest restaurants. The submissions read like a critics' guide to the capital's eateries from Luigino's on H. Street in the downtown area to La Brasserie on Capitol Hill.[34] Peabody, like Hanson Industries and other subsidiaries of Hanson plc, knows as well as any American-owned company how best to play the political game. On Capitol Hill influence peddling is an art which knows no political colours. So even though Gordon White regards Democrats, like Bill Clinton, as espousing 'socialist principles'[35] his Peabody subsidiary channels funds to Representative Richard Gephardt, a Democratic leader in the Congress and a known protectionist. When it comes to winning commercial advantage, Hanson Industries is politically colour-blind.

On both sides of the Atlantic, Hanson-controlled companies have been pioneers in recognising the importance of political contacts to the modern, dynamic corporation. In the 1980s in particular, the triumph of the market economy in Britain and the United States and the decline of union power fitted in well with the driving political philosophy of the group's founder and chief executive, Lord Hanson. He has always recognised that being on the winning side of the political debate can be valuable.

When Hanson plc celebrated its twenty-fifth birthday on 19 January 1988, with a glittering dinner at the Guildhall in the City of London for its managers, investors and US analysts, the guest of honour was, appropriately, Mrs Thatcher. The Prime Minister was so enamoured with Lord Hanson and the success of his company that she put aside her prepared speech and launched into an embarrassing, near lachrymose paean of praise – more like that of a loving friend than a visitor from 10 Downing Street. It was during Mrs Thatcher's years in office that Hanson had graduated from being a relatively obscure survivor of the Slater Walker era to Britain's largest conglomerate with tentacles reaching deep into the UK and American economies. The laissez-faire atmosphere of the Thatcher–Reagan years had given James Hanson and Gordon White the confidence and the financial means to pull off a series of spectacular deals on both sides of the Atlantic, without raising the ire of the regulatory authorities as had been the case during the previous Conservative government of Ted Heath.

In making a presentation to a number of Hanson middle-managers then Prime Minister Mrs Thatcher, still at the peak of her powers, compared James Hanson's stewardship of Hanson plc to her own of the United Kingdom. 'A company, like a country, has to have good management, with clear goals and a strong sense of purpose,' she asserted.[36] It was James Hanson's debonair, can-do image and his loyal support of the Conservative Party which made him such a symbol of the Thatcher era.

When Mrs Thatcher fell from power and was succeeded by John Major on 28 November 1990 it was the end of an era for both the Prime Minister and Hanson plc. Hanson's relationship with Major would never be as warm, despite uninterrupted donations to the Conservative Party. James Hanson himself would recognise the lack of breadth in his company's British political contacts when it bought its 2.9 per cent share stake in Imperial Chemical Industries and found itself outmanoeuvred by the old established chemical giant, with its carefully cultivated political contacts in the House of Commons.

The Downing Street connection was no longer adequate for Hanson in the heat of a contested takeover battle. As the Conservative government of John Major became increasingly unpopular in 1993–94, James Hanson recognised that financial support for the Conservatives might not be enough and he should look at alternatives. As in the United States, where Hanson and its subsidiaries played both sides of the political fence with considerable aplomb, the company needed to reach out in different political directions, hence main board director Peter Harper, whose main responsibilities included political lobbying, was instructed to launch a charm offensive designed to bring Hanson closer to a potential Labour government. Hanson also became suspicious of ideas percolating in the Treasury, which was starting to change its attitudes towards the role of industry in the economy. A competitiveness White Paper published by the Major administration in May 1994 laid stress on the need for policies which encouraged longer-term attitudes towards industry. This was considered a significant intellectual shift from the cult of the dividend at which James Hanson had worshipped throughout his public company career. When the Treasury Financial Secretary, Stephen Dorrell, suggested that dividends might have become too high and inflexible, it provoked an immediate response from the Tory peer, who is never slow to rush to his word processor. He wrote to Dorrell at the Treasury accusing him of 'sounding like a socialist'.[37] In the modern world of global business, corporations must be able to work in all political conditions. James Hanson temporarily lost sight of this during his infatuation with Thatcherism and all it stood for. But a new age demanded a new political awareness, particularly if it meant that the party he had supported during his active business life was flirting with what Hanson perceived as dangerous, anti-business ideas.

CHAPTER 8

The Siege at Millbank

To the casual observer, by 1991 Lord Hanson and his American partner Lord White appeared, despite reservations from City insiders, to be at the peak of their financial, personal and political powers. The 1980s had been good for this pair of entrepreneurs who like the Masters of the Universe in *Bonfire of the Vanities*, Tom Wolfe's seminal novel of the New York of the 1980s, seemed all powerful. However, although the two elderly peers had pulled off some of their most spectacular deals in the 1980s, the frailties of some of their business techniques had been exposed to City analysts, institutional investors and financial commentators in the heat of the SCM battle in the US and the Imperial fight in Britain. Moreover, the company was finding it more difficult than in the past to keep earnings growing at the pace to which their shareholders had become accustomed.

Nevertheless, as the decade closed the deal-making went on. The £3.3 billion takeover of Consolidated Goldfields in 1989 was conducted with characteristic aplomb. Unusually, Lord Hanson showed great generosity to Consolidated Goldfields chairman Rudolph Agnew, allowing him to hang on personally to the accoutrements of his office and offering him a seat on the Hanson plc board – a move that would later be regretted.

Nothing perhaps characterised the unshaken confidence of Lord Hanson and Lord White better than the way in 1990 that White and his old gambling friend Sir James Goldsmith arranged an audacious swap of Hanson's 49 per cent minority stake in Newmont Mining (the largest gold producer in the United States) for 85 per cent of Cavenham, the Goldsmith-owned lumber company which is among the biggest operators in the Pacific north-west. Hanson had been preparing to float off its Newmont stake on the stock market when Goldsmith came up with his proposal. With a nonchalance which only comes with repeated success the Newmont float was called off and the assets swap fixed over a hectic weekend at White's Park Avenue office in New York. By Tuesday 17 October the deal was announced to stock markets on both sides of the Atlantic. It was the Goldsmith end of the deal which attracted media attention because of the accompanying declaration that this was Sir James's last deal. But what was really fascinating was the casual way in which Hanson plc could make a £1.3 billion transaction without convening its board or carrying out a full due diligence (a series of thorough checks undertaken by auditors, lawyers and other specialists to ensure the target company is as presented) of a company in an environmentally sensitive industry.

But by the early 1990s Hanson and White appeared to believe they were capable of anything. Both had been elevated to the peerage by Margaret Thatcher with whom they had managed to establish a special rapport. And although Mrs Thatcher had been dumped unceremoniously from office in November 1990 – much to the chagrin of James Hanson, who to this day regards her as the supreme statesperson of the post-war era – Hanson plc felt confident about its relationship with the new Tory administration of John Major. After a hefty programme of disposals and flotations, following the Consolidated Goldfields acquisition, the group was cash rich. The balance sheet was loaded with an estimated £7 billion of liquid assets: a war chest ready for the next takeover skirmish. Unlike most of British industry Hanson seemed to have come through the 1989–91 recession financially unscathed.

Takeovers were, however, a core element of the Hanson strategy: churning assets was seen as critical to keeping earnings per share and dividend income on a rising trend. In setting his sights on Imperial Chemical Industries, James Hanson saw the possibility of using Hanson plc's relative strength, compared to that of many of Britain's larger industrial companies, to make that one, last deal which would finally establish the company which he and Gordon White had developed at the top of Britain's corporate league. In so doing he hoped to create a legacy of business greatness which would extend beyond his own eventual retirement and on into the next century.

The model for Hanson plc's eventual assault on Britain's premier manufacturing company, ICI, was provided by three highly independent financiers: Sir James Goldsmith, the Australian Kerry Packer and (Lord) Jacob Rothschild, who operated from outside the citadel of the family firm of N.M. Rothschild. The target of this trio of opportunists was BAT (formerly British American Tobacco), a company which was as hidebound with tradition and bureaucracy as the Whitehall departments close by in Victoria. On 11 July 1989 the three entrepreneurs – Goldsmith, Packer and Rothschild – unsheathed a £13 billion takeover for BAT with Goldsmith declaring an intention to 'unbundle' the company. It was never to happen the way the trio saw it, because of the intervention of the insurance regulators in the United States. But every move in the battle had been monitored carefully at 1 Grosvenor Place – Hanson headquarters.

Hanson had first taken an interest in ICI in 1989, adding an expensive stake in the chemical giant to its portfolio. Hanson collected shares in top British companies throughout the 1980s, trading in and out on a regular basis and sometimes using them as leverage to seek a meeting with the chairman or to do a deal. The weekly transactions list, provided by his acquisitions department, were recorded on a sheet headed 'Top Secret' for the eyes of Lord Hanson and Lord White, and a small inner circle of Hanson executives. James had first broached ICI and met privately with its chairman, Sir Denys Henderson, with the idea of an alliance, some two years before he was to unleash his public fusillade.

Gordon White described the structure of ICI in very similar terms to Sir James Goldsmith, when he was promoting the unbundling of BAT.

The thing about the company [ICI] is what has happened to so many big companies. They've become bureaucratic, they have successive layers of management and those layers of management actually inhibit the growth of the business. When you think of something like Pan American, how can something go to nothing having been the greatest in the world. It's because the bureaucracy builds up.[1]

But as well as being a rich target for unbundling, ICI also represented for James Hanson something which had been a powerful motivation throughout his business career: the need to gain the ultimate respectability. Imperial Group, although it had been a large, establishment company, could never completely fulfil this role because it was a tobacco business – not something which James Hanson with his close eye on the cholesterol level of his staff, good diet and an interest in vitamins and sleek, healthy hair could ever be comfortable with as a Hanson plc flagship. ICI was different: it was the bell-wether of the stock market and British industry. Manufacturing leaders like British Leyland had reached the peaks and vanished along with the United Kingdom's edge as a manufacturing nation. However, ICI stood there fortress-like on Millbank, overlooking the Thames and the Houses of Parliament, a genuinely international chemical, pharmaceutical and biotechnology group, able to compete with the world's giants such as Hoechst of Germany and Du Pont of the United States.

Imperial Chemical Industries had been conceived as a national chemical grouping which would fly the flag for Britain in complex areas of research and development and in the global chemical market. The deal which hatched ICI was engineered by Sir Alfred Mond and hammered out aboard the great liner RMS *Aquitania*, on a crossing from New York in early October 1926. The deal brought together – through an exchange of shareholdings – four giants of the UK chemicals industry: Brunner–Mond, Nobel Industries, United Alkali and British Dyestuffs Corporation. It was planned that the new company would have a headquarters staff of 900 (some ten times what Hanson has in 1994). The agreement, drawn up on four sheets of Cunard headed paper, envisaged the creation of an enterprise with £100 million in assets, selling some 5000 products worldwide: the first chairman would be Sir Alfred Mond and the new company, with an authorised share capital of £65 million, became ICI.

Like much of British industry ICI prospered in the Thatcher years, moving from losses in the 1980/81 financial year, when chemical industries worldwide were still suffering the effects of the 1979 oil price shock, to a profit of £1 billion in 1984/5. The company's profitability had been transformed by John Harvey-Jones, who as chairman sought to strip out some layers of management and 'set the divisions free to operate as hard-edged businesses'.[2] Harvey-Jones shifted the company's strategy by breaking down the old tendency to spread itself thinly and instead focused on building ICI businesses around specific technologies, such as pharmaceuticals and agro-chemicals. He saw the opportunity to bring different sources of technology together to create products for the long term, such as new seeds, which would yield dividends in the year 2000 and beyond.

Harvey-Jones also looked for the widest possible marketing channels for ICI products, eventually stretching polyurethanes into 2000 different products from cavity insulation in houses to refrigeration on ships to soles of shoes. The group also expanded globally, becoming the biggest paint manufacturer in the United States through Glidden, bought for $580 million in 1986 from Hanson, and the purchase of the Stauffer group for $1.7 billion in 1987. In much the same period as Hanson was on its hostile takeover spree in the United States, buying SCM in 1986, ICI was making similar moves but with fewer waves. By 1989 when Sir Denys Henderson had moved to the helm, the company had become highly diversified, earning one-third of its revenue in the Americas, a quarter in continental Europe, a quarter in the United Kingdom and the rest in the Far East. At the start of the Thatcher years some 42 per cent of the revenues had been generated in the home market.

After this transformation, almost as impressive as that at Hanson, Henderson might have anticipated a period of quiet consolidation. But a whirlwind series of events, many of them unforeseeable, began to make the new-look ICI appear vulnerable. The bad patch began with the stock market crash of 1987 which sunk investor confidence around the world; this was followed in 1989–92 by the longest recession of the post-war era; the resignation of a Prime Minister; the chaos in the oil markets which followed Iraq's invasion of Kuwait in August of 1990; the restructuring of the defence industries at the end of the Cold War; and Britain's tumultuous entry and exit from the exchange rate mechanism. Much of British industry was bewildered, debt-ridden and short of markets in September 1992. ICI was no exception. In late 1989, as profits began to nosedive, ICI began a far-reaching look at itself which resulted, in February 1991, in a sweeping plan to reorganise ICI into seven core businesses: pharmaceuticals, agrochemicals, specialities such as Quorn and Biopol, paints, materials, explosives and industrial chemicals including titanium dioxide. The reorganisation plan would result in 11,000 job losses in year one, rising to 20,000 by 1993.

Lord Hanson and Lord White thought they could do better. Their big deals in 1990 had been on the other side of the Atlantic. It was time to redress the balance with a dazzling UK merger which would earn Hanson plc its rightful place at the top of British manufacturing's roll of honour. James Hanson's goal was to grab a strategic share stake in ICI without alerting the market to his intentions. Even the slightest sniff of Hanson's interest would send ICI shares soaring and cost Hanson and its shareholders millions of extra pounds. Without first consulting his board, Hanson approached his favoured financial adviser, Sir Michael Richardson of Smith New Court. It was to Richardson, whom he trusted implicitly, that James always turned when he had a tricky problem in the financial markets, just as he had in 1985, for instance, when the £500 million Hanson rights issue threatened to flop as a result of a sudden stock market reversal.

On the evening of 13 May 1991 Sir Michael and his two most senior executives, Michael Marks and Tony Abrahams, gathered at Smith New Court to review the day's events. Just a few hours earlier the stockbroker had made what one market insider was to describe as 'the most ballsiest ever roll of the dice ever made by a London investment house'.[3]

Smith had sold 20 million ICI shares to Hanson at a price of £11.93 per share – some 90p above the prevailing price on the stock market. This is what is known in the City as 'sold deal' and it meant that Smith New Court, if it was not to take a beating, had to buy the shares in the market before the end of the stock market account five days later, but without arousing any suspicion; if word got out the share price could be driven above what it had paid for the stock. Smith's dealers were primed for action and at mid-morning on 16 May they mounted a military-style operation, buying every ICI share they could put their hands on for an average price of £11.67 each. By early afternoon they had achieved their objective and had bought on Hanson's behalf some 3 per cent of Britain's largest manufacturer, picking up £4 million for the firm itself on the way. In effect Smith's had laid down the fodder for a siege.

Even as Smith New Court was conducting its audacious operation, James Hanson fulfilled his diary commitments as usual. At lunchtime on Tuesday, 14 May, shortly before details of the swoop on ICI shares began to register on the financial news wires, James was to be seen relaxed and confident, sharing the top table with Lord Stevens at a Savoy luncheon hosted by the United Newspapers chairman. It was a perfect feint. As details emerged later in the day that a mystery party had snatched a 2.8 stake in ICI, Hanson's name was barely in frame despite his close relationship with Smith New Court and Sir Michael Richardson. Much of the early speculation in the financial press was to focus on the German chemical giant Hoescht, seeking a broad European alliance, with only the city editor of the *Daily Mail*, Andrew Alexander, solving the riddle on day one under the headline 'Hanson presents a case for Holmes'.[4]

The mystery was short-lived. On Wednesday morning James Hanson phoned Sir Denys Henderson, to inform him that Hanson plc was now ICI's second biggest shareholder (after the Prudential) and was holding 2.82 per cent stake for 'investment purposes' and suggested they meet soon for talks. The call came as no great surprise to Henderson, who had known of Hanson's ambitions for ICI for some time. James Hanson had once told Henderson, in a friendly aside, that both companies had international positions and Hanson plc 'would quite like to get alongside you'. Henderson, a blunt Scotsman, replied sharply that he did not see much compatibility between bricks (one of Hanson's largest core activities) and pharmaceuticals. It was an assertion backed up by figures. In 1990 Hanson spent £34 million on research and development, or £1.59 for every household in Britain, while ICI spent £679 million, or £31.70 for every household. Despite Lord Hanson's claims of synergies – which are still being made some years after the siege – ICI and Hanson are culturally and industrially two very different enterprises.

In terms of the business cycle Hanson plc's move on ICI was as well timed as ever. The Anglo-Saxon economies of North America and Britain were slowly emerging from the shock of the Gulf War and recession. The demand for basic chemicals was close to its nadir – so shares in chemical companies could be bought at relatively cheap prices. The surge in ICI shares, in the hours after Hanson was revealed as the secret buyer – giving Hanson plc an instant profit of more than £20 million – was an indication that the market recognised that there was a great deal of hidden value in the shares. What had changed dramatically, however, was the political climate and the corporate mood in Britain. This was something not recognised by James Hanson and his inner core of executives, Gordon White and Derek Rosling, who were caught in a time warp – a point which James was later to recognise as a mistake.

The presence of John Major in Downing Street and the prolonged recession had altered the political balance inside the Conservative Party and the country. Many of the nostrums which were so fashionable during the Thatcher era, including the view that manufacturing does not matter, had been turned on their head. The collapse in prosperity of a series of new wave service and financial companies during the recession – from the Sock Shop, to Ratners and Next – had focused attention on how vulnerable the credit economy of the 1980s was to swings in the economic cycle. Making things and preserving high-value manufacturing jobs was now considered a priority. Moreover, John Major was starting to focus on when best to call a general election so that he could be confirmed in office in his own right. The prospect of a multi-billion-pound takeover battle, which divided his backbenches and the country, was not one to be relished in the run-up to the polls in October 1991 or the spring of 1992 – the eventual date selected.

The mood in the financial community had also shifted since the heady days of the 1980s. The ruination of a series of 1980s glamour companies including Asil Nadir's Polly Peck and British & Commonwealth, together with the collapse of the Bank of Credit Commerce International (BCCI) had put the practice and regulation of the financial community under the spotlight. Questions were being asked about the quality of financial advice; the state of accounting and auditing in Britain; the role of non-executive directors on the boards of the UK's largest enterprises; and the large salaries with which Britain's tycoons were rewarding themselves in the depths of recession. The warts in the boardroom, which shareholders tolerated in the good times, when the dividends were flowing easily, became an aggravation as conditions moved into reverse. The result was the establishment of the committee on corporate governance, under Sir

Adrian Cadbury, which was eventually to produce a final, ratified report in 1992.

However, at the time of the Hanson bid for ICI a new mood of reform was already sweeping through UK boardrooms at the instigation of institutional shareholders – arguably the most important players in the Cadbury process. They were demanding checks and balances in the boardroom by means of separation of power between chairman and chief executive, a strong cadre of non-executive directors, and independent auditing and remuneration committees designed to watch over the sensitive processes of accounting practices and pay to the top executives. Much of this practice – which required the board to take into account the interests of a broader range of stakeholders – was outside the experience of James Hanson, who had never seen his board as much more than a monthly talking shop where he was seldom challenged.

It was Lord Hanson through his skilled purchase of ICI stock and his careful manipulation of his favoured business sections in the Sunday press who drew the first blood in the siege of ICI, attracting fawning headlines such as the 'ICI: The Grand Design of Hanson',[5] 'Dynamic Duo Strikes Again'[6] and 'Hanson's World-class Power Play'.[7] It seemed for a brief few days that it was not a matter of whether Hanson and White would succeed in making a full takeover or a forced merger with ICI, but when. The overweight, overstaffed, feather-bedded chemical giant, with its imperial pretensions, was in no position to put up any real resistance. Even the normally sane *Wall Street Journal* – especially interested in the deal because of Hanson's large American holdings – joined the phony war, noting that Hanson had the financial resources – some £7.4 billion of liquid assets and borrowing facilities – necessary to finance a full bid for ICI.[8]

Breaking with the Hanson tradition of keeping the target company guessing, Lord Hanson took the opportunity for an early get-together with ICI, which took place at the chemical company's private executive office suite at Smith Square, behind the Millbank head-quarters. Hanson spent a great deal of the meeting outlining possible joint activities between the two companies, but at no time went as far to suggest that he wanted a full merger or to become chairman of ICI. This ambition was, however, publicly unsheathed ten days after the initial share purchase when the prospect of Imperial Hanson

Industries was first broached with the *Financial Times* and Hanson declared himself no longer interested in hostile takeovers. 'We have become so successful financially', he told the FT, 'that we are now able to look at other ways and means of making money for our shareholders.'[9]

But while Hanson was preaching the new softly-softly, more establishment approach to ICI from the Hanson plc head offices at Grosvenor Place, a different message came from Gordon White, in the Hanson hideaway executive offices behind Harrods. The 69-year-old White, who is a fitness fanatic, chose to round personally on the culture of Britain's boardrooms: 'So many managers are overweight, drink too much and smoke too much, they have to give up when they get into their sixties,' he claimed. The remark was not designed to win White, already distrusted in the UK, many friends.[10]

The assumption by Hanson and his close advisers and their media supporters that ICI was like the Imperial Group – heavy with sleepy management which could easily be picked off – was a wrong one. While Hanson and his advisers Smith New Court were enjoying the first favourable burst of publicity, ICI was putting its board on a war footing. This would be no gentle establishment defence, in which the campaign would be restricted to heavily edited material that could be placed in formal rejection documents or newspaper advertisements. It would be cut-throat defence which would aim at the highest levels: the apparently invincible reputations of James Hanson and Gordon White.

Hanson and White were to find they had a worthy adversary in the shape of Sir Denys Henderson who had become ICI's eleventh chairman in 1987 at the age of 55, taking over from the charismatic John Harvey-Jones. Henderson was a Scottish solicitor from Aberdeen whose generally genial demeanour masked a pugnacious character and, as in James Hanson, a short temper. The ICI chairman had spent much of his life preparing for battle. His favourite reading was the Lewis Grassic Gibbon trilogy *A Scots Quair*, which told of the grinding struggle to make a living in rural Scotland in the depressed 1920s. The books, which the young Henderson reread while studying at Aberdeen University, ingrained in him the psychological need to counter adversity with every means at his disposal.

Like some of the top officials at Hanson, including Alan Hagdrup, one of James Hanson's closest associates, Henderson began his corporate career as a lawyer in the company secretary's office, a good training ground in the legally complex world of takeovers. From there he moved through the agriculture, explosives and paints divisions before, in the 1980s, setting up ICI's acquisitions team, which was responsible for the bold globalisation of group activities. In contrast to his flamboyant predecessor, Henderson had a predilection for conservative grey suits, quiet ties and a neat haircut. During the most intense part of the ICI siege there was nothing that Sir Denys would enjoy more than sharing a bottle of whisky with his chief executive, Ronnie Hempel, and journalists in his elegant office overlooking the Thames. He took such opportunities to explore the weak spots in the Hanson armour and draw attention to the unrecognised strengths in ICI. This was intimate, forward-looking, carefully targeted and hard-nosed briefing at its best. It was a relatively relaxed technique which James Hanson, when put on the defensive, found hard to match.

With the outbreak of hostilities in May 1991 when Hanson had first purchased shares, ICI headquarters at Millbank went on red alert and Henderson formed a war cabinet consisting of himself, deputy chairman Frank Whiteley, Ronnie Hempel and finance director Colin Short, who had been blooded in the harsh world of US takeovers. It was Short who Lord Hanson would blame for what he regarded as ICI's vigilance – their preparedness to contest the Hanson bid. Henderson, however, was personally well prepared for what was coming with a large grey binder-file with his plans for defence against predators. At the first meeting of the war cabinet on 15 May he told colleagues: 'We will make four assumptions. One, that he [Hanson] will bid. Two, that if it is referred to Brussels we will not be let off the hook. Three, you should not assume the institutional investors would not be interested. And four, that we will win.'[11]

But Henderson was not to rely simply on his own wisdom and knowledge of the takeover game to defend ICI. He recruited arguably the most powerful group of financial advisers ever involved in a British takeover battle. The communications aspects of the bid, critical when the newspapers play such a strong role in forming the public perception of politicians and institutions, was entrusted to

Alan Parker, the energetic son of former British Rail chairman Peter Parker, who with his firm Brunswick had experience of opposing Hanson in a series of takeovers including the Imperial Group in 1986 and SCM. But the real stroke was bringing together, on one ticket, the two most aggressive and feared merchant banking houses. Warburgs, whose City-based mergers and acquisitions department is considered second to none, threw John Walker-Haworth, a former director-general of the Takeover Panel – the City's neutral referee on the conduct of bids – into the bout alongside a London newcomer, Goldman Sachs of New York, with a reputation for taking no prisoners in its conduct of takeovers. The more blue-blooded merchant bankers Schroder Wagg, under a team of a dozen headed by John Reynolds, was also brought aboard to advise on how best ICI should unbundle itself (in the manner of BAT) should it become necessary.

James Hanson was mistaken in his belief that ICI was a slumbering giant, unfit to deal with the guerrilla tactics so deftly deployed by Gordon White in takeover situations. In fact, ICI's war cabinet held its first meeting on Wednesday 15 May 1991, the day that Hanson's share purchase made the front-page headlines on almost all the national newspapers – including the tabloids. In a pattern that would be repeated daily throughout the battle, the cabinet gathered before 8 a.m. in ICI's sixth-floor boardroom and broke up between 9 and 9.30 a.m. having formulated an action plan for that day. This directorial group would work closely with a committee of advisers, headed by John Thornton, the youthful 37-year-old head of the mergers and acquisitions department at Goldman Sachs' London office. Thornton, who is routinely described as the brightest corporate financier in Britain, was quickly to develop a healthy disdain for Hanson and its methods.

Under Thornton's guidance the team of ICI advisers launched a barrage of research projects. KMPG/Peat Marwick were called in as investigating accountants to scrutinise the Hanson accounts; they embarked on a trail at Companies House which would eventually uncover hundreds of subsidiary companies and lead them to offshore tax havens in Bermuda and Panama in search of the financial and tax engineering which drove Hanson's profits base. Initially, the US management consultants McKinseys were called in to study the performance and flaws in Hanson's underlying business, on the advice of Warburg's. But when Thornton became disappointed at the work being done the defence group turned to the UK-based consultants LEK, who had done some skilled work on the Hanson business at the time of the Imperial Group bid. As if this were not enough, the private detective agency Jacob Kroll, whose speciality is uncovering the underside of corporate life, was brought in and assigned the relatively routine but important task of checking out Hanson's potential environmental liabilities in the United States – in case they could be shown to be higher than disclosed in the published American accounts. The net effect of putting together such an impressive bunch of defenders was not only to expose Hanson's softer underbelly to the world but to conduct a scorched-earth policy which meant that much of the best advice was unavailable to Hanson – even if he wanted it. The net effect of the decisions taken by Henderson and his advisers in the first forty-eight hours of the bid was to put up the ramparts, long before Hanson could even consider climbing them.

It was in those early strategy sessions that one of the most critical decisions – which would be a key element of the siege – was established. The best way of attacking James Hanson was to go for the weakest link in his organisation: Gordon White. Even in the first few days after the share raid, ICI's defence team recognised that there was a difference between the approaches of Hanson and White. As James had indicated, in his private conversation with Henderson, it was Imperial Hanson Industries he was interested in heading. Gordon White's strategy was far clearer: in his view ICI was simply another group ripe for the kind of dismemberment that the Hanson team had engineered on both sides of the Atlantic. But White was also vulnerable. His anomalous position as chairman of Hanson Industries but an absentee on the Hanson plc main board was at last put under severe scrutiny. The company White chaired, Hanson Industries, was merely a branch of Tillotson Commercial Motors. It was the vehicle which allowed Gordon White to claim an important title, for the consumption of the US business community.

Moreover, White had never fully abandoned the playboy lifestyle which James Hanson had buried with his marriage and his family. It was also felt, by Alan Parker and John Thornton, that White and to a lesser extent his top aide in the United States, David Clarke, were paid excessive salaries and used the group to back associated companies. In many ways Lord Hanson, trusting the same small group of advisers which had stood with him in the 1980s, was unprepared for the onslaught which followed. On the political front Lord Hanson took the view that Hanson plc's contributions to the Conservative Party – £852,000 in the period 1979–92 – would minimise the risk of opposition to an ICI merger.

Hanson now acknowledges that he misread the level of his political clout, particularly after the departure of Mrs Thatcher from office. Similarly, he thought that the battle would be conducted by the normal rules in which the sharp criticism was aimed at the underlying businesses and accounts, rather than those who ran them. But John Thornton of Goldman Sachs brought a different approach to the game: he was determined to establish if the group was treating the shareholders, whom it claimed to serve, unfairly.

A team of advisers was put together by James Hanson too but remained convinced through much of May and early June, as the media explored almost every aspect of the prospective bid, that White and Hanson's small cadre of executives including vice-chairman Martin Taylor, could generally deal with matters themselves. It was James's son Robert and his nephew Chris Collins who were put in charge of the campaign. The chief executive, Derek Bonham, and Hanson's acquisitions manager, Andrew Arends, were largely excluded from the deliberations. At the sharp end among Hanson's advisers was Sir Michael Richardson, who had directed the daring raid on ICI shares from his Smith New Court offices and like James was well connected in the Conservative Party. He worked in tandem with Smith New Court's patron N.M. Rothschild, the Tory government's favoured merchant bank for many privatisations, where Russell Edey was the main adviser. On the public relations front, Hanson's main adviser was Sir Tim Bell, Mrs Thatcher's chosen communications adviser, who was meant to be responsible for ensuring that Westminster was on the Huddersfield businessman's side.

Among the City experts in the Hanson camp were Roddy Dewe of Dewe Rogerson, which joined the establishment in the 1980s through its work on the advertising and public relations of privatisation issues. The most realistic operator on the Hanson payroll was expert firefighter Brian Basham, who knew instinctively how to play the game by the rough-house rules deployed by Thornton and Alan Parker. Basham would in later years win notoriety for his exploits on behalf of Hanson's close friend Lord King, in besmirching the reputation of Richard Branson's Virgin Airways. By 1991, however, the strong Thatcher connection in the Hanson advisory team was starting to look passé with the advent of the Major administration and the strength of the opposition parties in the opinion polls. When compared to the professional skills assembled by the ICI team and the quality of the outside work commissioned, the Hanson group had a slightly tired feel – a view which Lord Hanson himself was to share as the siege entered its second month when he personally sought to take more control of the agenda.

While ICI waited for its 'attack' material to emerge, from its extensive research exercise involving KMPG/Peat Marwick and LEK, it aimed to secure its own employment and political base. This meant recruiting the support of its trade union officials, taking steps to secure its pension funds (a major source of conflict in previous Hanson takeovers) and furious political lobbying in both Houses of Parliament. Within a week of the Hanson share purchase ICI's six largest unions – the general union TGWU and GMB, the EETPU electricians' union, the MSF general technical union and the construction union Uncatt – launched an offensive with the aim of preventing a takeover. The unions lobbied the Office of Fair Trading for a Monopolies Commission referral in the case of a full takeover as well as the European Commission in Brussels (the competent competition authority) and the members of the European Parliament. As Fred Higgs, secretary of the coalition of unions put it: 'We're confident that if Hanson decides to go ahead with a full blown takeover he's going to discover he's bitten off more than he can chew.'[12] When one union official made careless allegations about Hanson's management philosophy, Lord Hanson angrily intervened, threatening legal action against the individual concerned and personally demanding and receiving an apology from the *Guardian* which had quoted the comment. The incident provides a good illustration of Lord Hanson's short fuse when the image of his company appears threatened in the eyes of the British establishment.

On the political front, where ICI had over the years established good relations through the chemical industry group of MPs, the prospect of a Hanson bid brought forth an immediate outcry. With a workforce of some 53,000 people in the UK spread among 70 sites – 30 of which employ more than 200 people – ICI had a presence in no fewer than 42 constituencies, several of them Conservative marginals which would have been crucial had John Major called a general election. Among those speaking out against the bid was Nicholas Winterton, the Conservative MP for Macclesfield where ICI plants employed some 1200 workers: 'I am absolutely appalled at the prospect of a bid for ICI,' Winterton fumed. 'I cannot see that Hanson can do anything for ICI that ICI could not do for itself.' Winterton and others vowed that they would put pressure on the party and ministers to ensure that a Hanson bid would not succeed.[13] Ministers central to the issue, such as Peter Lilley, then Secretary of State for Trade and Industry, found themselves under pressure from the company, its advisers, the trade unions and fellow MPs to intervene in Brussels should the expected takeover offer come along.

It was no coincidence that when Sir Denys Henderson decided to make his first public comments on the prospects of a Hanson bid that he chose the largely friendly, well organised and cross-party chemical industry group. The plain-speaking Aberdonian told the assembled MPs: 'ICI is not a plaything for those unfamiliar with the chemical industry.' In a direct allusion to James Hanson's informal offer to create Imperial Hanson Industries out of the two companies, Sir Denys told the generally sympathetic group of MPs: 'It is hard to imagine anyone, however successful in their own field, who can aspire to run ICI without the relevant skills, knowledge and experience.'[14]

In an effort to counter the Henderson blitz and to go over the head of the national newspapers, who tend to filter bid developments through their own lens, Lord Hanson – an experienced broadcaster from his wartime days – reached for the airwaves. In a series of radio and television interviews his message was more or less the same: Hanson was not, as ICI was portraying it, an aggressive shareholder. If only ICI would cooperate, then Hanson would bring a great deal to the party. 'I think we come with a great deal of experience, a lot of funds, a very strong balance sheet to them, as a principal shareholder, where we could achieve something'.[15]

The difficulty with Hanson's personal broadcast intervention was that in almost every case his message was counterbalanced with words from Sir Denys Henderson, which muffled the message. Moreover, as Hanson and his PR advisers Sir Tim Bell and Brian Basham ought to have realised, the media battle during takeovers is fought on the financial pages of newspapers, which are read carefully by the institutions, analysts, politicians and the main players, not in brief bursts on news bulletins which are aimed at a wider public. Nevertheless, Hanson's airtime blitz showed that ICI's aggressive defence was starting to become more than an irritant.

In an outburst on ITV, James accused ICI of 'totally overreacting' to Hanson plc's investment and 'stirring up the unions, pensioners and others, which I think is very wrong for them to do'.[16] Hanson's increasing indignation also spilled over in Parliament. In a letter to a dozen Tory MPs from his internal public relations chief Michael Shea (former press secretary to the Queen), Hanson plc warned them that some of the comments they were making may have been based on 'inaccurate information'.[17] The letter was a further indication that the new experience, of less than adulatory treatment in the media, was proving hurtful.

The political timetable was also starting to intrude on Hanson's plans, if he were minded (as Gordon White was urging) to make a hostile bid. The ICI intelligence on the sixth floor of Millbank was that Conservative Central Office had informed Hanson that it would be extremely concerned should a full-scale offer be launched during the run-up to John Major's intended decision to call a general election in the spring of 1992. Sir Denys Henderson and his team of advisers had drawn the conclusion that a bid, if it were to come, would have to be made before the end of the summer of 1991 so the political ructions could die down and the regulatory hurdles be crossed well before the election. The fear at Central Office was that an industrialist/ financier with as close ties to the Tory Party as Lord Hanson could cause the Tories considerable damage in marginal constituencies where jobs could be put at risk. Moreover, the sight of the big battalions of business arm-wrestling in public as the country was struggling to pull out of recession would not be very edifying. Any bid so momentous was viewed as a likely gift to the Labour Party.

Another area which allowed ICI at a stroke to score some useful points with both its workforce and the public at large was its steps to protect the ICI pension funds, some of the best resourced in the British private sector. Over the years Hanson, largely following practice in the United States, was one of the financiers who recognised there was hidden value in the valuation surpluses held by many older pension funds. Legally the ownership of those surpluses in UK pension funds has been unclear, although the Goode Committee, which reviewed pension-fund law following the Robert Maxwell scandal in late 1991, leaned towards the view that such funds did belong to employers, rather than employees.

In ICI's case the surplus was very large. The ICI pension fund, at the time Hanson acquired his 2.82 per cent stake, had assets worth £5.9 billion – almost half the value of ICI itself at prevailing stock market prices. The surplus was estimated to be of the order of £500 million. From the point of view of Sir Denys Henderson and ICI, protecting the pension fund would have three advantages: it would be supported by the whole ICI workforce and pensioners, sealing the bond between them and the company; the impression would be created, rightly or wrongly, that Hanson plc was not a company to be entrusted with pensioners' funds; and it would secure the pension fund for future generations should ICI reorganise or split, as was eventually to happen.

Thus in mid-June, just a month after Hanson's share purchase, ICI moved to put the £5.9 billion of pension funds with the Law Debenture Trust, the same group which had been given the management and responsibility of the Consolidated Goldfields pension funds. As was the case throughout much of the phony war for ICI, in the summer of 1991, ICI and its communications adviser Alan Parker went to great lengths to ensure that dissemination of important moves in the takeover arena went to those newspapers showing most interest in the issue.

While the headlines and airwaves were filled with the political ramifications of the siege, the KPMG/Peat Marwick teams of accountants were beavering away in the files at Companies House in

Cardiff, at the Securities and Exchange Commission in Washington and in locations as far afield as Bermuda and Panama – which was to prove to be pivotal. KMPG had split its task in two: Gerry Acher was given responsibility for investigating Hanson's accounting practices, which had drawn some heat during the Imperial Group bid some eight years earlier. Another smart KMPG accountant, Robert Berg, was put in charge of the tax investigation. Working at breakneck speed through the accounts of every Hanson subsidiary Berg's team could put its hands on, KMPG conducted literally hundreds of searches using public documents which were eventually to fill more than 40 crates.

So enthusiastic were the KMPG team that on one occasion they unwittingly crossed the borderline of propriety. When one of the tax trails led to a brass plate, far-flung Hanson office in Bermuda, KMPG sent a junior associate on the island to this office in search of public record documents. According to the KMPG version of events, a legal clerk at the Hanson offices more or less opened the files to the accountants, perhaps mistakenly believing they were working for Hanson rather than ICI. The result was that the KMPG clerk left with some highly confidential documents, which were not public. Lord Hanson was furious when he heard what had happened. During a luncheon at his favourite restaurant, Santini, in south-west London, Hanson expressed outrage at the way that ICI and its paid hands were behaving. He alleged that the KMPG officials had misrepresented themselves at the Bermuda offices and had thus been able to obtain confidential company documents under false pretences.

The Berg investigation of KMPG had, however, come closer to identifying Hanson's sophisticated tax strategies than had ever previously been achieved by an outsider. On the morning of 7 June 1991 Berg was invited to join the ICI war cabinet and its senior advisers to provide a preliminary briefing. He described how, by working back from a series of subsidiary accounts at Companies House, KMPG had been led to a network of some 20 lowly capitalised companies in Panama, which had been formed for tax purposes to filter through the proceeds of Hanson plc's American acquisitions. In some years several billion pounds of cash had passed through this highly unusual structure. Those present were mesmerised. After the meeting ICI's voluble communications consultant could hardly contain his excitement and emerged from the room uttering a series of expletives and declaring that Christmas had arrived early.

The ICI war cabinet and its advisers knew they now had some valuable material which would be fully exploited should the Hanson siege become a full-scale assault. But it was also realised that to release the information during the phony war would be a mistake, since there would be less decisive matter in the armoury should the battle proper be enjoined. Since some of this material lay close to the surface in the public accounts, inquiring journalists would be gently steered in its direction. Enough would be uncovered to stimulate curiosity and to allow questions to be raised, but it was unlikely that any media outlet would be able to draw on the resources or time to conduct the kind of root and branch investigation which was being conducted and assembled at KMPG/ Peat Marwick.

A week after Berg had delivered his fascinating report to ICI's war cabinet, the first fingerprints of its findings appeared in the press. It was revealed in *The Times* that Hanson plc had embarked on a restructuring in 1989, involving the valuation and internal purchase of £9.5 billion of group assets, mostly held in Panamanian and Bermudan subsidiaries.[18] Some of the detail of what took place, through a company called Hanson Overseas Holdings, was available, if one knew where to look, at Companies House.

Hanson's vice-chairman, Martin Taylor, described the transactions, which had not been explained in the annual report, as part of a 'major reorganisation of the ownership of the business, because we had found that the management of various parts of the group did not match the organisation'.[19] Mr Taylor declined to comment on the tax implications. Senior Hanson officials have acknowledged that all the transactions, involving Bermudan and Panamanian companies, were in connection with sophisticated tax strategies. The disclosure of huge asset transfers, and reports along similar lines which followed, were another public relations coup for ICI. Hanson's tax transactions had been exposed not by ICI itself, but more credibly by a third party. Nevertheless, the well-documented research by *The Times* might never have taken place had not KMPG done the groundwork in the first instance.

The next orchestrated leak from the accountants' study was more accessible than Panamanian tax straddles. And as importantly for

John Thornton of Goldman Sachs, marshalling the ICI defence forces, it aimed directly at what he perceived as the soft target in Hanson plc's armour: the anomalous position of Gordon White. Timed exquisitely to coincide with Ascot week – the premier summer season event for royalty, the gentry and business sponsors – it emerged from Companies House searches that some of the horses running in the colours of Lord White were not owned by him at all but by Hanson plc shareholders. Acting through three subsidiary companies, Cheval One, Cheval Two and Cheval Three, it was disclosed that Hanson plc (which owned 80 per cent of the shares) together with Lord White and two highly placed racing friends, Robert Sangster and Simon Fraser (who owned the remaining 20 per cent between them), had invested some £10 million of Hanson company funds in bloodstock.

The racing partnership was not without its highlights. In 1989 Legal Case, wearing Sir Gordon White's colours, romped home in the Champion Stakes. White was registered as the sole owner with the Jockey Club. Unfortunately for Lord White's prestige as a bloodstock owner and for Hanson shareholders, not all the horses in the string performed as well as Legal Case, and Hanson plc initially had to take a £7.72 million write-off. Cheval has never made a profit. The company is still part of Hanson plc, but has been wound down and is now dormant. Among the surprising aspects of the case was that Hanson plc was already known for its involvement in racing through the high-profile sponsorship of the Derby by its Ever Ready subsidiary; thus in the racing context there seemed little reason not to publicise the Cheval operation. In fact White was enormously proud of the Ever Ready sponsorship of the Derby, noting it was an extremely effective way of projecting the company's name. It also gave Lord Hanson and Lord White the opportunity on Derby Day to entertain grandly more than 200 invited guests.

The Cheval disclosures, which spread from the financial pages to the social columns and the *Sporting Life*, were, however, embarrassing. It reinforced the impression that Hanson plc operated in some respects like a private company. The unpublicised nature of the operation (although the up-to-date accounts were available at Companies House) raised questions as to whether there were other such enterprises in the Hanson locker. Moreover, as a joint venture between Hanson plc and one of its principal executives (even if he was not a main board director), it would have been desirable if it had been disclosed in the audited accounts because of potential conflicts of interest. The incident added to the concerns that had already been voiced about Lord White's status within Hanson, although Lord Hanson would personally maintain, to anyone who would listen, that Cheval was an immaterial operation in the context of Hanson plc's large worldwide interests.

Despite the embarrassment which the Cheval companies caused Hanson plc, in the first heat of the ICI siege, Lord White has never really accepted that there was anything awkward about the arrangement. Sitting in his study at Pont Street Mews, surrounded by horseracing oil paintings and fine prints from the winners' enclosure, White was adamant that there had been no need for disclosure even though his boss, James Hanson, had conceded that disclosure would have been preferable. 'All I can say is that if I had wanted a perk, I wouldn't have taken horses racing in my colours. I've had 300 horses in my racing career, excluding the ones that went into Cheval.'[20]

Lord White disclaimed responsibility for setting up Cheval, arguing that the idea was Simon Fraser's, whose father, Lord Lovat, was a longstanding friend of horseracing, and that he had simply decided to go along. He had been advised: 'If you're buying a percentage of bloodstock, if you've got a chance of buying one champion, one champion pays for all the mistakes. The one thing missing from the scenario was luck and luck I'm afraid is something that business cannot rely upon.'

As for providing details of Cheval operations in the Hanson plc accounts, White was adamant it was not necessary to do so because to provide information of every deal would have meant 'just reams and reams of paper'. In Lord White's view the Cheval losses have to be looked at in the context of Hanson Industries – the American arm of Hanson plc which he founded: 'It was created from nothing and it's worth about $7 billion and it belongs to the shareholders and it's never cost them a penny.'[21]

But it had diminished the business credibility of Lord Hanson's lifelong business associate – a point which the ICI hit team had been determined to bring into the open from the outset. Throughout June and July 1991 the onslaught on White continued. There were puzzles over his status and the scale of his remuneration. Lord White's ability to make decisions with large financial consequences, such as the conduct of the $930 million bid for SCM (as well as his role in the campaign against ICI), at a time when he had no place on the main board of Hanson plc was seen as incongruous. Other work at Companies House revealed that White was a director of just one Hanson plc subsidiary, the Guernsey-registered Hanson International Management Services. Hanson Industries did not exist as a British company and it was hard not to reach the conclusion that the mystique surrounding his position shielded White from scrutiny.

It also emerged that Lord White had at his disposal a mansion in Beverly Hills, California, bought by a Hanson subsidiary for $7 million. White explained that the property 'is used as an office and it has accommodation as a house'.[22] Nevertheless, the estate in the Beverly Park district had often been referred to in published reports (not corrected) as White's home. In planning applications for expansion of the property, including a new swimming pool with solar heating, the owner was described as Lord White. This, like the Cheval affair, made it seem that few distinctions existed inside Hanson plc and its US subsidiary Hanson Industries between what was corporate business and what was private. Such vagaries simply served to create the impression that Lords Hanson and White saw the vast empire they had created with their vision, drive and style to some extent as a personal fiefdom rather than a public property.

The issue of Lord White's status was more fully explored by the Channel 4 documentary programme *Dispatches* in early 1992, after the initial excitement which followed Hanson's ICI share purchases had died away. In a specially commissioned opinion Alan Newman QC (based partly on the depositions of Lord Hanson and Lord White in the SCM case in New York) found: 'There is a powerful case for stating that Lord White is indeed a shadow/de facto director of Hanson plc.' As such Lord White, like other directors of the main company, would be required under the Companies Act of 1985 to fulfil several obligations, including the disclosure of any loan relationship with the company, any personal interest in contracts, any service contracts, any employment and any substantial transactions in which he was involved.[23]

As the driving force behind Hanson plc's acquisition and expansion, during an era in which there was less scrutiny of company boardrooms, Lord White found it difficult to come to terms with the confining nature of the contemporary board and the power which comes with being a full director. 'Power doesn't excite me, it doesn't interest me, I hate people to be afraid of me,' he maintains. 'I've got a bloody good life over there and I don't want to come back here for board meetings . . . if you are going to be on board, you've got to be steeped in what's going on to make a contribution.'[24]

The media exposure of the unconventional side of Hanson's corporate life served the ICI defence team admirably. It placed the whole issue of the group's corporate governance, including the succession when the two 70-year-old leaders step down, in the public arena for the first time. And all of this was achieved without having to buy advertising space or to put out the formal defence documents which are *de rigueur* once a formal merger offer has been made. But it also gave ICI and its advisers an opportunity to follow a further defence strategy: that of unbundling. If Hanson was not to be allowed inside Millbank to do the job for the ICI management, it became increasingly clear that it would have to do the job itself. This in a sense would be victory for Lord Hanson's strategy, but the punishment which Hanson plc had taken along the way gave it a hollow quality.

As 1991 drew to a close the possibility of a Hanson bid had receded into the distance. With the strong prospect of a spring election, eventually held on 10 April 1992, Lord Hanson – ever the Conservative loyalist – did not want to rock the Tory boat. As the second largest holder of ICI shares, Hanson looked for opportunities to harry, comment and criticise the moves made by Sir Denys Henderson and his team. Without doubt this continuous scrutiny, together with the strain on executives caused by operating on a war footing, led ICI towards a more radical restructuring. At the end of 1991 Sir Denys put in a personal call to Sir David Scholey, the highly respected chairman of Warburg's, and asked for someone on his staff to take a fresh look at the restructuring of ICI from a City and stock market view. The job was given to John Mayo, a 36-year-old corporate finance wunderkind, who after six weeks came up with a proposal: splitting ICI down the middle into two. Henderson was hesitant, knowing the time, explaining and work it would require in the build up to his proposed retirement in 1995 – but he still decided to go ahead.

With Hanson still sitting on his shoulder, Henderson put together a small taskforce at the highest level of ICI which began to develop the Warburg proposal (based around the demerger model at Courtaulds in March 1990), code-named Project Dawn (later renamed Project Mortar), as the team of support staff swelled. The 'hive-down', as it was called in ICI, involved more than 400 companies within the group, working in 150 different countries. There was something of a race against the clock because of concern that if the Conservatives won the election Lord Hanson might end his siege and move in for the kill. On 10 April John Major surprised the pundits and the pollsters by winning the general election with a majority of some twenty-one seats. Psychologically, however, the game was up for Hanson. The battle for ICI had been too costly and the noble Lords no longer appeared to have the appetite for an all-out battle. As the stock market soared to a post-election peak on 8 May 1992, Hanson quietly disposed of his stake, taking a £42 million investment profit for shareholders. At ICI the excitement was just beginning: on 29 July 1992 the board decided formally to create a new company, later to be named Zeneca, to take over ICI's pharmaceutical and biotechnology businesses. Hanson had been a force for change, but from the outside rather than the inside, as he had intended when he picked up the stake.

The whole exercise was a salutary one for the master tactician Lord Hanson. In the view of his closest associates he had made three crucial errors: his ICI mission was ill defined; he lost the war of the media (vitally important in hostile takeover bids); and he had failed to dominate the market. With the benefit of hindsight Lord Hanson now claims that the demerger at ICI was his achievement. He is probably right although arguably Sir Denys Henderson and his team may have eventually reached the same conclusion on their own. What Hanson never appeared to appreciate was how different his own conglomerate, a collection of established, basic businesses, was to ICI's largely research-driven culture. The concept of Imperial Hanson Industries was a mismatch designed to create a legacy for Lord Hanson: it was marriage with little industrial logic.

In the process, however, of pressing his case James Hanson found his own business methods put under the microscope in a more ruthless way than he had encountered in the 30-year history of Hanson plc. The decibel level of criticism and his inability to counter it were extraordinarily frustrating. The drumbeat of revelations about Gordon White, the surrogate for his own lost brother Bill, put the financier on the defensive. It was almost as if his own family was being attacked. Instead of being able to press the Hanson plc case for moving in or merging with ICI and creating his dream of Imperial Hanson Industries, he found himself beleaguered in the traditionally supportive financial press, in the House of Commons and on the airwaves. In the searing heat of June and July 1991 in London Hanson sought to conduct his own personal charm offensive, taking on all criticism directly.

A column written by this author (Alex Brummer) commenting on corporate governance lapses was countered line for line by Hanson. At the same encounter Hanson, who had failed to inform his board at the outset of the ICI share purchase (forcing the resignation of non-executive Rudolph Agnew on this precise point), promised he would be bringing non-executive directors and modern corporate governance to Hanson plc. Among those he was trying to persuade to join the company was the American corporate guru Warren Buffett. It was a vintage Hanson performance. The tall businessman, courtly in his beige suit, charmed and cajoled, cavilled and chaffed, but left this author feeling he had become a friend and had been granted some confidences. Had Hanson personally had the time, the energy and the ability to deal with all the media lined up against him in this manner, there can be little doubt that the Hanson case would have been dealt with more sympathetically.

But in many ways it was too late. All the Hanson methods from its taxation practices to its remuneration and succession – including the position of Robert Hanson – were now in open court and James recognised that he had fallen behind in the vital communications war. In a famous memorandum to his PR consultant Sir Tim Bell (copied to his other adviser, Brian Basham), written after the height of the siege but before the ICI share stake was sold in spring 1992, Hanson vented his spleen. Lord Hanson wrote that he was 'disappointed with the press recently', adding that Alan Parker, ICI's outside consultant, 'shows himself to be running circles around us'.

'I think we're entitled to better results. Weekly strategy meetings are a waste of time. We've put our faith in your ability to SELL Hanson . You know what a great story is out there, but it's not getting through,' he added.[25] The leaked memorandum, with its highly charged sentiments, provided a close insight to how let down James felt. The charmed run which Hanson plc and its two bosses had enjoyed through the 1980s was over. Even those who Hanson had considered his friends in the press had turned against him in a feeding frenzy.

White was being humiliated. Even his own son Robert, designated business heir, had been caught in the crossfire. Robert's conduct of the bid was seen as naïve in that the declaration that the ICI share stake was for investment purposes made it more difficult to bid under US takeover codes as laid out in the Hart–Scott–Rodino act. (Such a declaration precludes a bid being made in the United States for 90 days. Given that both companies had extensive US interests, ICI would certainly have challenged Hanson in the US courts.) Moreover, Robert's own seat at the top table at Hanson plc had been questioned. The siege at Millbank had in some respects become the siege of 1 Grosvenor Place. Hanson may have scored a moral victory when ICI split and took the opportunity for a £1 billion-plus refinancing of its debts through a large rights issue, but the damage to James's self-esteem and the reputation of Hanson plc had been costly. The empire James had founded would never be quite the same again.

CHAPTER 9

Seeking a New Identity

At one moment the group of burly, bearded men, dressed from head to toe in camouflage fatigues, stand calmly in the bright early-morning sunlight, chatting proudly and amiably about their lives as miners in south-western Indiana and their fears for the future. Then, without warning, the atmosphere changes. The familiar crunch of a large service truck on the unfinished gravel track can be heard; the pickets grab their signs and bullhorns and march briskly up and down at the entrance to the Lynnville colliery bellowing 'Scabs, scabs', at the top of their voices and sounding klaxons.

As the driver looks down at the pickets contemptuously, security guards, deployed behind barbed wire in sentry posts and in a high tower by the mine-owners – the Peabody Coal Company – focus their video cameras on the mêlée and switch on their listening devices. When the driver edges his way forward, one striker presses close to his cab shouting, 'You're going next, you're going next' as he becomes more angry and frustrated. The truck is chased to the no-go territory of the mine entrance (proscribed by the courts) with the trailing cry of 'asshole, asshole' ringing through the still air, laced lightly with coal dust and sulphur.

The events at the entrance to the Lynnville pit – then one of 18 Midwestern mines operated by Peabody Coal Company in Indiana, Kentucky and Illinois – were a microcosm of the bitterness, disruption and brutality that characterised the 1993 selective strikes of the United Mine Workers of America (UMWA) against the

Bituminous Coal Operators' Association (BCOA). It was a battle fought largely against America's largest coal-owner, the Hanson subsidiary Peabody, for a new, secure and enduring union contract, and involved issues of labour market flexibility, health care, foreign ownership and protectionism which are at the core of the global economic debate. In essence it was a dispute which mirrored Margaret Thatcher's titanic struggle with the National Union of Mineworkers in 1982, which was to herald the ruthless rationalisation of the British coal-mining industry and the breakdown of union ascendancy in the United Kingdom. It was the kind of tough stand which industrialists like James Hanson and Gordon White admired.

Clashes at the entrance to the pit or the factory gate, even violent confrontations in which people are maimed or killed, were nothing new in the history of US labour unions. It was part of popular culture as seen in Jack Nicholson's 1992 portrayal of Jimmy Hoffa and in the classic West Virginia coal-strike movie, *Matewan*. What was different in the Peabody strike were the tactics deployed by both sides and James Hanson's determination, like Mrs Thatcher just over a decade earlier, not to give in to the union battalions even if it meant millions of tons of lost production.

Instead of bringing all his 70,000 or so unionised miners out on strike, the UMWA president, Richard Trumka, considered by some to be the most exciting and innovative labour leader in the United States, brought out 17,500 at selected pits that best represented aspects of the contract worries and erosion of economic power which faced the mineworkers. Moreover, by keeping most of the miners at work it was possible to sustain the stoppage with strike pay. Rather than focus the strikes purely on the mine operators themselves – more often than not the subsidiaries of international conglomerates – the strikers set about targeting the ultimate owners and their share-holders, wherever they happened to be. In the case of Peabody, the largest privately owned group of coal companies in the United States, the target had become Hanson plc and its American subsidiary, Hanson Industries, Lords Hanson and White as respective chairmen of the two companies, and other stakeholders in these companies. In many respects the US mining unions sought to emulate the success of ICI in defending itself against the Hanson siege of 1991, by turning the dispute into a fight about image, communications and corporate governance; the unions knew full well Hanson's sensitivities in this area. The UMWA may have learnt more from ICI's Sir Denys Henderson about how to take on an Anglo-American conglomerate of Hanson's size than from the traditions of violence, sabotage and mass activism associated with the feared US miners' leader of the mid-twentieth century, John L. Lewis.

The UMWA even embraced modern public relations by engaging Frank Greer, the media strategist who helped propel President Clinton to the White House in 1992, to produce television and radio commercials designed to appeal to a non-union audience. It also set up a network of personable and articulate miners – one at each striking pit – to provide instant responses to local, national and international media questions and to ensure that regional organisers were constantly available for comment. This was a break with the tight-lipped approach to previous strikes.

Similarly, the mine operators also strove to modernise their armoury. Anyone travelling along the public roads which surround Peabody's Squaw Creek colliery in Warrick County, Indiana – a sprawling mix of cornfields, reclaimed land and deep creeks, gouged out of the countryside by massive shovels and dragline machinery – was shadowed by beefy red-helmeted security guards equipped at each checkpoint with cameras. The coal operators also scoured the public airwaves for film footage which they perceived to be damaging to the cause or image of the strikers.

A video provided by Peabody Coal Company, at their Henderson, Kentucky, headquarters, strung together what they considered the golden highlights of the strike up until September 1993. In this smoothly edited production every minor incident has been cut into a piece of exciting action, and the word 'violence' is repeatedly used until it becomes a mantra of the strike; also included was an allegation that the miners murdered a non-union employee. At the centre of this allegation was the killing of Eddie York, a contract worker in Logan County, West Virginia, who was, in the words of the video, shot in the 'back of the head' as he approached a mine operated by a non-Hanson coal company. The video, distributed to some 600 media outlets across the US and regularly updated (it even includes BBC footage of a lachrymose interview with the slain worker's daughter), seeks to recast the union miners in their historic role as murderous thugs and terrorists.

The Peabody dispute had started on 1 February 1993 when the UMWA called an 'unfair labour practice' strike against Peabody and its affiliate, Eastern Associated Coal Company, based in West Virginia. In many ways it was an economic fight for the survival of the coal unions which have seen their numbers dwindle from 120,000 to 70,000 over the last ten years in a period in which union power in the US was seriously weakened by the 1982 decision of President Reagan to sack the organised air traffic controllers and replace them with non-union workers. That said, despite the long history of labour disputes in the coal industry in general, Peabody had enjoyed a relatively stable relationship between union and operator prior to Hanson's purchase of the company. Perhaps the most infuriating aspect for the striking miners was that their job security was threatened at a time when their working practices had responded to management demands. The union members had accepted more mechanism and downsizing resulting in a substantial increase in productivity – up from less than 2 tons per man-hour in 1992 to 3.1 tons in 1993. That in turn had been hugely profitable to Peabody, which saw earnings rise from $100 million in 1986 to $300 million in the peak year of 1991, the year after Lord Hanson had acquired Peabody for $1.2 billion. By 1993, however, union miners were considered too expensive by Peabody. At the time of the 1993 strike they were earning $16 per hour, while their non-union counterparts could command $18 an hour. However, when the union benefits package of health and pensions is added in the UMWA employee could cost an estimated $29 an hour. This was the kind of cost-cutting which Hanson, with its reputation for ruthlessly pruning the costs of businesses it has taken over, could understand perfectly.

As part of the Hanson/Peabody effort to wriggle out from this cost structure, Peabody and the other coal operators used what is known as 'double breasting' – whereby the coal-owners from a new, non-union, company exploit the seam previously mined by union staff from a different pit-head – as a means of putting additional pressure on the rump of the union. The existing contracts between the mineworkers and the operators guaranteed that the employers filled three out of five jobs at new mines with union members. According to the

UMWA, Peabody Holding Company, the 100 per cent owned subsidiary of Hanson Industries, avoided this contractual obligation by establishing new subsidiaries (next door to the old) with non-union labour. They could thus circumvent the coal agreement and the health and benefit costs of using non-union labour.

Nevertheless, the confrontation in the coalfields was to cost Hanson dearly. By the end of the 1993 calendar year the coal strike had resulted in some £182 million of lost profits, with a further small loss to come in the early months of 1994. This was an embarrassment for Hanson in a period in which earnings failed to increase, and in which the dividend to shareholders had to be held. But the fight, in Hanson's view, was one worth winning since the cost savings made at its existing coalfields would increase its bargaining power as it acquired further coal holdings. On 25 June 1993 the company swapped its remaining US gold operations, which came with the Consolidated Goldfields purchase, for Santa Fe's mining and quarrying operations – acquiring in the process a further 700 million tons of coal reserves. Together with its Australian coal interests, finally bought from Costain in 1993 after a protracted legal dispute, Hanson with some 3220.9 million short tons of proven coal reserves (and 5001 tons of probable reserves) had become the world's largest private-sector coal company.

But the bitter coal dispute did nothing in the United States to enhance Hanson plc's reputation, which had also suffered in 1989 as a result of the SCM flotation, which saw the share price fall after a profits forecast was missed, to the anger of shareholders and workers, whose jobs were pruned as a result. Lords Hanson and White, in typical style, did not get involved in the Peabody dispute at local level. Instead all the main decisions were left to Peabody Holding Company chairman Ira Engelhardt, whose tough tactics made him and the company he ultimately worked for, Hanson, a feared entity at the coalfields. Hanson's attitude served to reinforce a negative image of foreign investment in the United States.

The mining culture is deeply embedded in Midwestern towns like Boonville, Indiana, a community founded by a relative of the legendary Daniel Boone and whose historic courthouse played host to a young Abraham Lincoln. The town, its houses and businesses, from banks to hairdressing salons, remain deeply committed to the mineworkers and festooned with posters and placards of support – 'Pensioners for the UMW', 'United we stand', 'UMW forever'. At Jeremiah's café, a local hangout, the reaction of Debbie Polk, a miner's wife, was typical: 'Someone should tell Hanson he has put us under a lot of stress. I don't think someone from another country should be controlling our economy.' In the minds of many of the activists Lord Hanson was seen as the modern equivalent of the nineteenth-century English coal-owner. A picket outside Peabody Coal's suburban headquarters in Henderson, Kentucky, declared: 'Bring that Mr Hanson here will you. I would love to meet him, and dunk his head.' The picket notes with some passion that the American people fought a revolutionary war to rid themselves of 'British kings and lords'.

Union activists like David Hadley, a tall figure with a red beard, believe that the attitude of management at the Warrick County mines started to change with the Hanson takeover of the Newmont mining properties. Supervisors and foremen who had been with the company for years, and had a good and flexible working relationship with the miners, left, undoing the old values in the coalfields. In Hadley's view there has been a reversion to the days when the mine operators regarded the mineworkers simply as work fodder, rather than being involved in what amounts to a business partnership. Peabody Coal, during the course of the strike, rejected such criticism. It argued that the reasons for the current dispute were nothing to do with the Hanson ownership or any effort to squeeze every last cent of profits but everything to do with the UMWA's own problems

'The double breasting issue, the decline in UMWA membership and other demands by the union are all related to the needs of the UMWA as an institution,' it maintained during the course of the strike. 'They have no impact on the job security or the economic welfare of the individual worker,' the company asserted. That may well be the case. The removal of structual impediments in the labour market was one of the issues high on the agenda at the Detroit jobs summit in March 1994. Lord Hanson, although he had distanced himself personally from the coal dispute, was determined to win the fight, despite the cost of the strike, because of the need to lower the cost of production. Hanson was absolutely clear about this at a luncheon held at his Brompton Road dining suite in south-west

London on 5 August 1993. He told the assembled company, which included his son Robert Hanson and the Cabinet Secretary Sir Robin Butler, that there could be 'no compromise' because it was essential to control the cost of production if Peabody was to remain as profitable as it had been.[1]

But there had been risks attached to Hanson plc's ruthless tactics. Popular opinion in the United States, its most important market-place, had been alienated and there was some angst on Wall Street about Hanson plc as a company. But it also raised new questions in the United States about the good sense of allowing foreign investors such easy access to America's corporate heritage. For a group like Hanson, with up to 60 per cent of its assets in the United States, that may potentially have been the most serious long-term effect of the confrontation in the coalfields.

The Peabody strike provides a useful metaphor for events at Hanson after the siege of ICI. With the benefit of hindsight Lord Hanson now recognises that in many ways the spat with ICI was a turning point for his company. 'I still feel bitter about the incident,' he observed in late 1993. 'It is unfortunate not to be believed. My word is one of the greatest assets I have got in business. I take the blame for making a decision which turned out to be wrong, but we did make £40 million out of it though, which is not nowt.'[2] In the wake of the failed ICI merger attempt there was a change of philosophy at the top. 'Hansonisation', which had been the watchword for the company's activities in the 1980s, was displaced by normalisation – an effort to remake the company as an industrial trading group. The change was partly brought on by necessity. Gordon White, who for so long had been the creative genius behind Hanson's audacious bids, was fading into the background. A prolonged bout of ill-health in 1993 had left him enfeebled.

The process of normalisation would affect every aspect of the company's structure. At the main board level there would be thinning out of the old guard, which had run Hanson as a family business. In 1991 Alan Hagdrup, who had been the lawyer to the Wiles Group, departed. Then, most notably, came the final departure in May 1994 of Derek Rosling, who along with James Hanson and Gordon White had been with the company since its earliest days. In response to criticism from the corporate governance lobby, the main board was expanded to include an improved range of non-executive directors, with an enhanced ability to monitor the activities of the executive chairman. But most importantly of all Hanson and White, having both crossed into their eighth decade, designated successors.

Derek Bonham, a tall, quiet accountant in the Hanson financial mould, stepped up to become chief executive of Hanson plc, deputy chairman and the designated successor to Lord Hanson himself – who announced his intention to retire at the end of 1997, at the age of 75. In the United States, David Clarke, long-time business partner of Gordon White and one of the best remunerated executives in the Hanson group, was designated successor at Hanson Industries and later appointed vice-chairman of Hanson plc. With a spin-off of US Industries, a collection of some 34 non-core Hanson US businesses in February 1995, David Clarke became chairman and chief executive officer of the newly quoted company severing his executive role at Hanson plc. Other younger directors also joined the board, including finance director William Landuyt, 38, brought in from Hanson Industries in 1992, and Graham Dransfield, 42, an Oxford-educated solicitor who stepped up to become legal director in 1992. The age profile and style of the Hanson executive directors were changing rapidly. The ageing loyalists who had been at James Hanson's side since he began building the enterprise were gradually being displaced by a new, more professional cadre.

Normalisation also meant a less aggressive takeover style: Hanson was to take on the mantle of the kinder and gentler 1990s. The big transactions, such as the 1991 takeover of Beazer – the Anglo-American housebuilding, construction and aggregates business – would effectively be a rescue operation. The same would be the case in Hanson's £1.7 billion takeover of the US Quantum chemical concern in 1993 – in which Hanson would use its high credit ratings to relieve the burden of Quantum debt. The company would embark on a campaign to dispose of surplus smaller businesses. This policy would culminate in the de-merger of US Industries in 1995 with revenues of more than $3 billion and a quotation on the New York Stock Exchange. Improving the shape of the underlying businesses by the purchase of complementary companies, such as Watt Housing, which enhanced the position of Beazer in the US house-building market, would be part of this strategy, as would be the effort to underpin the profitability of the vast coal investments through the contract confrontation at Peabody. Hanson shares would be marketed in a different way with the company's brokers, Hoare Govett, putting out circulars focusing on particular sectors such as Hanson's role in leading the US construction sector out of recession.[3]

Lord Hanson's first indication that he was considering normalising his board, so that it conformed to the higher standards of corporate governance demanded by the investing institutions, came in the summer of 1991 – while the ICI siege was still underway. Hanson had reluctantly agreed it was time that he added some fresh non-executives to his board. At the time James, who feels strongly about his public image, was also starting to think that it might be time to follow the recommendations of the institutions and establish a better line of succession within the Hanson group, with a clear division between the posts of chairman and chief executive. He revealed that he had asked Sir Gordon Booth, the former diplomat and adviser to the group, to draw up a potential list of non-executive directors. The initial list, drawn from both sides of the Atlantic, contained some 80 names from business, politics and communications. Of the original 80 possibilities a short-list of some 20 people were approached to see if they would be interested in working in a non-executive capacity for Hanson.[4]

The team of three new non-executive directors, which eventually emerged in September 1991, was considered to be lacklustre given the size, importance and transatlantic nature of Hanson plc. The first of the trio, Jonathan Scott-Barrett, senior executive of a small publishing group, Centaur Communications, was a virtual unknown but was thought by Lord Hanson to be a sensible choice because of the media and entrepreneurial skills he brought with him. The company's 1993 corporate governance statement, which forms part of the annual report, showed that Scott-Barrett had been elected as chairman of the communications committee which 'reviews all aspects of the company's public relations activities'.[5] More conventional choices were Simon Keswick, a director of the Far Eastern trading house Jardine Matheson, and (Sir) David Hardy of the London Docklands Development Corporation – who would be a useful sounding board in 1992 when Hanson showed an interest in acquiring Canary Wharf, in London docklands, from the receivers. Hardy, an accountant, with a

City job at Bankers Trust Investment Management, would eventually take on a critical role as chairman of Hanson plc's audit committee.

The knowledge, contact and skills of Keswick would be particularly useful to Lord Hanson in 1994 when he asked his son Robert, by then a main board director, to take charge of exploring the business opportunities for Hanson in the fast-growing region of East Asia. Having crossed the Rubicon, Lord Hanson took the opportunity to strengthen the board further whenever possible. The former Home Secretary and chairman of the Conservative Party Kenneth Baker would follow in 1992, after he stepped down from the Cabinet following Prime Minister John Major's post-election reshuffle. The appointment re-emphasised Hanson's deep commitment to the Conservative Party and in particular the Thatcherite wing, of which Mr Baker is part.

Despite the appointment of independent directors in September 1991, institutional investors – including the Prudential Portfolio managers, Norwich Union Life Insurance Society and Standard Life Assurance – would press Lord Hanson for further changes. They demanded clarification of Lord White's role in the group and most significantly sought information on the succession, given the age profile of Hanson plc's two leading lights, both in their seventies. At the company's annual general meeting at the Barbican, in the City of London, on 28 January 1992, Hanson acknowledged to shareholders that he recognised the issue. 'We have the succession,' he informed shareholders, 'we just don't plan to name it at this time.' Hanson plc, the chairman asserted, had 'a galaxy of management talent', adding that others would take on responsibility 'as some of us fade away'.[6] As the chairman had not revealed his hand, one niggling concern among the institutions was that he was planning to hang on long enough so that he could eventually hand over the reins to his son Robert.

The shareholders would not have to wait too long for more detailed information. Lord White demonstrated his continued capacity to surprise when he told a February 1992 meeting of Hanson's analysts and divisional executives that David Clarke, the president of Hanson Industries, would be his successor when White retired in 1997. Clarke had been a close confidant of White since 1973 when Hanson Industries offered him some $32 million for the family company,

Seacoast. The two men would develop an extraordinarily close relationship, with White almost regarding Clarke as his own son. As White had become older, and less interested in the day-to-day running of the business, it was Clarke who took up the slack. The anointed US successor, however, saw development of the group differently to his mentor – whose main interest had been doing deals. 'If people are saying that Hanson needs another mega-bid to grow, they are looking at it the wrong way,' he asserted on being singled out by White. 'Commentators should start to look at Hanson as an operating business. I would guess that the bulk of our profits this year [1992] will come from running our own businesses, such as Cavenham Forests, Peabody Coal and Beazer.'[7]

The announcement and attendant publicity surrounding David Clarke's elevation as White's successor may have been satisfying for White and Clarke, but it was not pleasing to James Hanson. It gave the impression that someone other than the group's executive chairman was making important personnel changes, without considering their implications. Moreover, Lord Hanson was not a great fan of Clarke. He is understood to have been less than comfortable with Clarke's rather unsubtle American approach to business problems and had little respect for his communications skills. Moreover, Hanson and his senior executives in London had become increasingly concerned about Clarke's continued role in Marine Harvest International, an associate company in which Clarke had a personal stake. The dealings of Marine Harvest – an enterprise with a financial history as intricate as the history of its trading name: MariFarms brought Marine Harvest and adopted the new company's name as its own – was taking up an increasing amount of space in Hanson's annual report.

The events which led to the Marine Harvest entry in the annual report also illustrate, however, Hanson plc's unusual approach to the role and involvements of the group's directors. They stem from the fact that Clarke, the operational boss of the US empire became the chairman and chief executive of a publicly quoted US company – the Ground Round restaurant chain – in 1987. It bought assets from Hanson and for which Hanson guaranteed borrowings, and in which Clarke, as well as other senior Hanson US executives, held shares. There was nothing illegal about these arrangements, but they were entered into with some misgivings among senior Hanson staff as a way of retaining Mr Clarke's services. The various transactions were also properly reported, where necessary, to Hanson shareholders.

Few company chairmen would be prepared to contemplate such arrangements, which involved senior Hanson executives and the Hanson group in the financial affairs of a quite separate quoted company, and raised questions over conflicts of interests. This was clearly not one of Hanson's usual investments, since it offered zero returns. In their annual report for 1991, the Ground Round directors warned that the company had not paid a dividend since 1980, did not intend to pay a dividend in the foreseeable future, and was indeed prevented from so doing under the terms of its lending agreements.

A former Hanson executive, confusingly called J. Eric Hanson, but no relation to the Hanson family, was central to the web of deals which developed. Mr Hanson was an Englishman who had been sent to work on acquisitions in the United States in the early 1980s, but departed to join Revlon in 1986. He left Revlon the following year when one of the Clarke family businesses – a property company called Great South Beach Sales – was acquired by a publicly quoted but insubstantial company, International Proteins. This company was a fish processor, similar to Mr Clarke's original company, Seacoast. It seemed that Clarke wanted to go back to his roots and run his own company again and Eric Hanson had helped him find a vehicle to do so. This was effectively a 'reverse takeover' which left Clarke owning more than a quarter of the shares and in control of the company as its chief executive. Eric Hanson became 'senior vice-president corporate development' and a director of the company, and executives who still worked for Hanson Industries also joined the board. No mention was made of all this in Hanson's annual report until, in a bid to prevent Clarke leaving the group to run this business, Hanson in 1987 invested \$3.5 million in International Proteins shares.

Two years later a brief report appeared in some UK newspapers noting that Hanson had sold one of the relics of the Imperial acquisition to International Proteins. The company concerned was the Ground Round restaurant chain, which Imperial had acquired as part of the ill-fated Howard Johnson hotels deal. What the press reports did not reveal was that David Clarke was chief executive of this company, while his deputy and current Hanson main board member, John Raos, and a senior Hanson lawyer, George Hempstead, were also shareholders. The Hanson annual report for 1989 disclosed that before this transaction Clarke had owned more than a quarter of International Proteins and Raos owned rather less than 1 per cent of the shares. Their holdings fell, however, because, most unusually, Hanson took shares instead of cash for Ground Round. Hanson's shareholding therefore rose to 49 per cent of the company, which had changed its name first to GR Foods, and eventually to Ground Round Restaurants.

As part of the Ground Round deal, Hanson had the right to nominate two directors to the board. John Raos and George Hempstead were duly elected, although since they were also personal shareholders in the company they were faced with carrying out a dual role: their fiduciary duty as directors of a public company was to the Ground Round shareholders but they were responsible to Hanson for the strategy of Ground Round. The Hanson connection was enhanced in 1990 when Diana Burton, who had been Clarke's personal assistant since 1982, became Ground Round's company secretary. Ground Round also agreed to manage some other restaurants owned by Hanson in the United States, although this agreement soon wound down, so that only two sites were covered by the end of 1990. These restaurants were sold to Ground Round in 1991.

But in that year the Hanson plc executives began to concentrate on Ground Round's non-restaurant interests. Clarke resigned as a director of Ground Round in September 1991, after his company, GSB, had raised $1.4 million by selling a quarter of its shareholding. Hempstead and Raos also resigned, joining Clarke (as chairman) in a separate company called MariFarms, which was created by handing out shares in the new company to the existing Ground Round shareholders. Clarke's former assistant, Diana Burton, became company secretary, having left Ground Round. Only Eric Hanson remained as a Ground Round director, on a part-time contract worth $12,000 a year for five years, although in fact he was paid $36,000 in 1993. Eric Hanson also had a consultancy agreement with Great South Beach, the Clarke family company, under which he was paid a one-off sum of $135,000 in compensation for waiving his right to 60,000 MariFarm shares. And he had a two-year consultancy agreement with MariFarms, worth $90,000 a year.

MariFarms also further sucked in Hanson plc. In 1992 it bought Unilever's salmon farming interests – Marine Harvest, which would be adopted by MariFarms as their company name following the purchase – for $39 million, the bulk of which was provided by Prudential of America which bought $32 million of MariFarms preference stock. This finance was effectively guaranteed by MariFarm's main shareholders: the Hanson plc subsidiary HMI, the Clarke family company Great South Beach, and Richard Dowling, a financier who had also been involved in Ground Round. In consideration for these three shareholders making these guarantees, MariFarms was to pay them a total of $1.1 million a year – in direct proportion to their liability. In fact the company raised cash in the following year which enabled it to repay the Prudential loan, and the amounts actually paid for the period of less than a year were $749,000 to Hanson plc (through HMI), $118,000 for Mr Clarke's company, while Mr Dowling's share was $46,000, paid to his estate following his death in June 1993.

By this point Mr Clarke had stepped down from the chair, though remaining on the board. But the Hanson connection was actually strengthened. Clarke was replaced as chairman by John Mistretta, who had previously chaired Hanson Industries' recreation and leisure group. Brian Beazer, former boss of the Beazer construction group, which had been acquired by Hanson plc in 1991, also joined the board, although George Hempstead resigned, and Marine Harvest recruited Frank Reilly as chief financial officer. Mr Reilly had been with Hanson since 1988, first as assistant treasurer and ultimately as director of acquisitions.

The involvement of so many current and former Hanson Industries executives was a continuing embarrassment to several senior executives of the Hanson group. It was a telling example of the way in which Hanson plc's view of the executive as entrepreneur resulted in complications which many other company chairmen would not have been prepared to contemplate, and which could place some senior executives in difficult positions where they may be liable to face conflicts of interest.

But the most far-reaching implication of all in the premature disclosure of David Clarke's promotion by Lord White was the belief that it had given Clarke a leg-up in the race to succeed James Hanson himself. Suddenly, Clarke had leapfrogged above other Hanson executives, including Tony Alexander, the chief operating officer in the UK since 1986, and Derek Bonham, who had been a director since 1981 and was in charge of the most important group function – finance. Hanson, who was angered and confused by White's audacious promotion of Clarke, formalised when he was appointed deputy chairman of Hanson Industries in March 1993, moved quickly to redress the balance of power between New York and London, as well as to resolve the institutional shareholders' anxiety.

After consulting with his colleagues, including vice-chairman Martin Taylor, who would have to explain the changes, and his son Robert – who had become James's closest confidant – Lord Hanson made his move early on 20 April 1992, ahead of a scheduled meeting of analysts. Derek Bonham would fulfil the newly created role of chief executive officer. Hanson was effusive in his praise for Bonham, noting his 'pivotal role' for over two decades in the group and his 'intelligence, creativity and energy'. The chief financial officer of Hanson Industries, William Landuyt, would become finance director and, pointedly, the person passed over, Tony Alexander, would remain as chief operating officer in the UK.[8] The news release announcing Bonham's new post also contained the ritual encomium from Lord White regarding the new appointments, and added that 'everyone in the company will share my pleasure that these vital posts have been filled from within Hanson'.

Everyone, it seemed, was pleased except David Clarke, who according to close associates felt he had been outmanoeuvred in London. His first public comments on the Bonham elevation reflected this disdain and Clarke's determination that Bonham would not roll his tanks on to American turf. 'There is no conceivable way that Derek Bonham would have anything to do with these matters outside Lord Hanson's control,' he told the *Financial Times*.[9] The succession struggle had served to heighten long-standing tensions between the UK and US operations and in 1993 would lead to public suggestions – from US stockbrokers Smith Barney – that the best way forward for the group might be to split it into two separate enterprises: one covering Britain and Europe and the other North America.[10]

The new chief executive officer, Derek Bonham, has none of the personal élan which has made Lords Hanson and White such fascinating public figures. Yet those who have worked with Bonham see him as even tougher than Lord Hanson, and certainly a stronger figure than Tony Alexander who had been tipped for the post. Bonham was also thought to have the nerves of steel which might eventually be required if David Clarke was to be challenged in his own domain. As someone recruited by Brian Hellings, the long-time Hanson plc director and acknowledged tax wizard within the group, Bonham brought an abundance of financial skills which are such an essential part of Hanson plc's makeup. He showed an immediate willingness to tackle the US operation if necessary. 'Just as James is chairman of the group, so am I chief executive of Hanson plc,' he declared in his first round of public interviews.[11] In Lord Hanson's company, including corporate lunches, Bonham would still, however, tend to fade into the background as his chairman would fire the questions and lead the debate.

With the pecking order at the top established, Lord Hanson promulgated a further advancement for Derek Bonham in November 1993, elevating him to deputy chairman. David Clarke was also promoted as 'a vice-chairman', following the departure of Derek Rosling from the senior posting. James, who until the end of 1993 insisted that all statements to shareholders went out in his name, is now starting to work on improving Derek Bonham's visibility, gradually easing Bonham into the post of chairman: 'We want the world to know Derek Bonham, *Derek Bonham*.'[12] Hanson is fully aware that his name is over the door, but it is also now certain that he has the successor he wants. All Lord Hanson is now seeking is a greater awareness in the world of business that it is Bonham who is taking the major decisions about the running of Hanson plc. The reality is that Hanson, although he is in constant touch by fax and other means from Palm Springs, has increasingly become an absent landlord at 1 Grosvenor Place, spending fewer than 90 days a year in his London office, coming to the United Kingdom for the quarterly financial results, annual meetings with staff and shareholders, and the Epsom Derby.

The establishment of the succession in the spring of 1992 may have cleared away part of the legacy of poor corporate governance which had served Hanson so badly during the ICI siege, but it would not be the end of the chairman's difficulties with his larger investors. Just as it seemed as if a new era of *glasnost* had arrived at the company, Lord Hanson dug in his heels. In a move designed to throttle dissent at the company's general meetings, Hanson proposed five changes which would give greater powers to the chair. The effort was partly designed to silence the expected protests of the UMWA, which had targeted American institutional shareholders as a means of addressing its grievances against the Peabody Coal Company. In the UMWA president, Richard Trumka, and its Washington-based master of public relations activism, Kenneth Zinn, Hanson had opponents prepared to fight union battles differently.

If approved, the changes at Hanson plc, which were to be put to an extraordinary general meeting on 25 June 1993, would have severely restricted debate at annual meetings. The proposals denied shareholders the right to nominate a director unless they spoke for 10 per cent of the company's shares; denied shareholders the right to pass resolutions unless they held 5 per cent of the shares; gave the chairman, Lord Hanson, the right to refuse a poll of shareholders if he considered the issue 'irrelevant' or 'vexatious'; allowed matters to stand even if the chairman gave an incorrect ruling; and granted the chairman the right to stop any single shareholder speaking more than once. Veterans of Hanson annual and extraordinary meetings, which had never in the past been known for the level of noisy protests, were puzzled. Lord Hanson's annual meetings were far more renowned for their razzmatazz, slickness and video technology than for the effectiveness of dissidents in challenging the chairman.

For institutional shareholders, on both sides of the Atlantic, the proposed changes were a red rag to a bull. The Hanson company secretary Yves Newbold, sensing the dangers, promised that the measures would be reviewed at a future meeting of shareholders, if it was felt they were too intrusive. But opinion was mobilising strongly against the company. As Ms Newbold herself was later to acknowledge, the changing shape of the Hanson share register made it more vulnerable to pressure from the US institutions. In the wake of the completion of the Quantum purchase on 30 October 1993, some 27 per cent of Hanson plc shareholders would be represented by American depository receipts (ADR) – foreign shares quoted on the New York Stock Exchange. The effect of this was quite acute, in that some 60 per cent of US institutional shareholders are generally considered activist as against 20–30 per cent in the United Kingdom.

In the event the pressure from the ADR shareholders in the United

States, fired up by the striking American mineworkers' union, together with a campaign by the Pensions & Investments Research Consultants (PIRC) in Britain, produced an extraordinary climbdown by Hanson plc which abandoned the proposals in a formal letter to shareholders. Derek Bonham sought to put the best gloss on the affair, arguing that Lord Hanson 'didn't want to give the impression of undermining shareholders'.[13] PIRC, which has long been active in efforts to alter Hanson's corporate governance, was delighted by the outcome, arguing that if the measures had gone ahead shareholders' rights would have been curtailed. But the bullets which led to the retreat had been fired by the US shareholders – including the State of Wisconsin Investment Board – who had been persuaded to oppose the measures by the US mineworkers. The fight in the coalfields had produced a change of direction for Hanson. It was a battle for which the UK institutions may not have had the stomach without the uncompromising support of their American cousins.

In the takeover field the 1990s would also produce a different style from Hanson. This change in tactics, which followed the attempt to merge Hanson plc with ICI, reflected a number of broader cultural changes. As the early 1980s drew to a close, a different style of political leadership emerged. The election in the United States of George Bush in 1989, followed by Democrat Bill Clinton, produced a less red-blooded form of capitalism than that which existed during President Ronald Reagan's eight years in office. The new decade was less hospitable to the hostile takeovers and laissez-faire style economics of the 1980s. Similarly, in the United Kingdom the arrival of John Major in Downing Street produced a partial retreat from the free enterprise dominated culture represented by Mrs Thatcher. This new era also brought with it changes in the financial markets. Many companies which had expanded too fast in the 1980s entered the new decade burdened with debt which offered a company like Hanson, with its cash resources and ability to obtain credit on fine terms, an opportunity to pick off debt-ridden companies at a relatively low equity cost. This more friendly approach to takeovers could partly be justified by the sharp increase in share value which took place in 1992–93 – on both sides of the Atlantic – which made hostile takeovers using the company's own shares that much more difficult. As serious a factor was the changing nature of Hanson's management.

Gordon White, who had conducted so many takeover campaigns, was a sidelined figure and, as a result, James Hanson was not being fed with the same volume of potential targets by his staff. Both David Clarke in the US and Derek Bonham in the UK seemed more concerned with consolidating and tidying up existing businesses before embarking on a more aggressive path.

The September 1991 bid for Beazer, an Anglo-American construction, housebuilding and aggregates business, was to provide a model for a different Hanson. Beazer with its strong interests in basic businesses was a Hanson-style company, although it had fallen foul of the recession on both sides of the Atlantic. Beazer would also allow Hanson to increase its dominance in the aggregates market in addition to the holding it had gained through its Consolidated Goldfields deal in 1988. The Beazer company was also a victim of the 1980s takeover wars, having burdened itself with huge debts in the United States to outbid American rivals for control of the aggregates producer Koppers in 1988.

It was the combination of the $1.72 billion debt from the 1988 deal together with the collapse of markets which caused Beazer to fall into Hanson's arms. The Beazer deal was also a useful feint for Lord Hanson as he decided the future of his stake in ICI. It showed that the new Hanson of the 1990s was a less aggressive company, interested in rescue bids and market position and not just churning assets, whereby newly acquired assets were sold off quickly for profits that would be directed towards the next takeover. Lord Hanson was also to argue that it was a timely deal since the US construction industry had reached the bottom of its current cycle of recession. After the ICI onslaught James Hanson recognised that he needed to work harder to underpin the reputation and share price of his company.

In many respects the substance of the Beazer deal and its lasting impact on Hanson accounts went unrecognised. Although the equity offer price was a relatively modest £391 million, the actual cost was far higher. In buying Beazer, Hanson also took on some £1.497 billion of debt and added to its balance sheet some £1.286 billion of provisions. This included £889 million of provisions for potential environmental liabilities related to Beazer's Chemical & Allied Products business. When this was sold via a management buyout, Hanson agreed to pick up the responsibility for 120 waste sites being investigated and monitored by the US authorities. Calculations by brokers Barclays de Zoete Wedd put the total cost of Beazer at £3.1 billion, making it just behind Consolidated Goldfields in terms of size. What had appeared in initial news reports to be some clever trawling in the recession by Hanson, actually turned out to be one of the most expensive purchases the group had ever made in terms of the relationship between price and earnings.[14] The Hanson accounts had also acquired for themselves a fresh scar in the shape of a note showing that the potential costs of the Beazer environmental commitments could stretch over 30 years.

Nevertheless, Hanson and Lord White were almost certainly correct in seeing Beazer as an important beneficiary of the clumsily named US 'Intermodal Surface Transportation Efficiency Act 1991', which was charged by President Bush and Congress with a major repair and renovation programme for interstate highways and bridges. Routine road repairs had all but been neglected in the Reagan years when the budgetary focus was on increasing defence spending in a final push to win the Cold War. Beazer's four largest construction markets – California, Texas, New York and Pennsylvania – received the largest allocation of the approved federal funds. With 60 per cent of Beazer's construction activities based around public works, the company was particularly well placed. Hanson and White, the arch exponents of free markets and 'small' government were to benefit from a large-scale government programme. The company was also able to meet the challenge more cheaply after a ruthless exercise in Hansonisation at Beaver which reduced overhead and administrative costs by an estimated $30 million.

After the ugly confrontation with ICI, the Beazer deal was therapeutic for Hanson. Even if the price had been high, it demonstrated that the company had lost none of its skills in cost-cutting, refinancing and repackaging. There remained serious questions, however, after the lacklustre conduct of the ICI campaign, as to whether James Hanson still had the killer instincts necessary to carry through a hostile takeover. His handling of the October 1992 action to take over Ranks Hovis McDougall (RHM) suggested that he had run out of firepower. In many ways RHM, which a few years earlier had come under attack from Sir James Goldsmith, resembled in its structure the deal which did more to create Hanson as a multi-billion sterling player than any other – the Imperial Group takeover of 1986. At £780 million the cash bid for RHM was clearly smaller than the £2.5 billion offer for Imperial. Nevertheless, RHM was a combination of ill-fitting businesses including a large range of consumer products such as Robertson's jam, Mr Kipling cakes, Chesswood mushrooms, Rombout's coffee and Sharwood's sauces. As at Imperial there was a core business at the centre, in this case of RHM flour milling and bread production. There were serious questions as to whether this activity – even with Hansonisation – could be turned into the cash cow which tobacco became. However, with Hanson profits apparently becalmed, and a recession-hit Beazer unable to produce the kind of increase in profits and asset churning which Hanson needed, RHM appeared to be a good bet. Having made his offer, Lord Hanson followed his customary practice and called on his target the following day, 6 October 1992, in the hope of discussing terms of surrender. However, RHM chairman Stanley Metcalf wanted none of it, simply arguing that Hanson's bid of 220p per share seriously undervalued the company.

In the 1980s this would have been an excuse for Lord Hanson to dive into the stock market and seek a position in RHM shares. A senior adviser who worked with Lord Hanson on many of the 1980s bids has argued: 'James made the fatal error of not dominating the market in the RHM bid . . . He lost out to his old pupil Greg Hutchings who followed precisely that technique.'[15]

It was perhaps inevitable, given the number of successful exiles from the Hanson school of management, that eventually one of them would come up against the master in a takeover bid. The challenger turned out to be Greg Hutchings at Tomkins – an aesthetic, sensitive figure, who prefers drinking hot chocolate with his meals rather than coffee. But his demeanour is somewhat deceptive. A series of large deals in the late 1980s, many of them in the United States, had thrust Tomkins into the forefront among the Hanson graduates: among its bolder moves had been the eyecatching $112.5 million purchase of gunmaker Smith & Wesson in the summer of 1986.

After the Hanson bid for RHM the food company's first response was to deploy the BAT and ICI defences, hoping to convince institutional shareholders that it would be better split up into three separate businesses: milling and baking, grocery/speciality products and Mr Kipling's cakes. Stanley Metcalf claimed that the proposal to divide the company had been planned for some time: 'While it might be true to say that Lord Hanson has provided the stimulus for these proposals, I would not wish to dent his modesty by overstating the case,' he asserted.[16] Lord Hanson, for his part, rejected the breakup plan, arguing that his company intended to run it as a stand-alone business. That this suggestion should have been made at all shows the extent to which the culture had changed at Hanson. This debate was quickly to prove irrelevant when Greg Hutchings appeared on the scene. In talks with RHM a price worth 260p per share (40p more than Hanson) was recommended to shareholders, valuing RHM at £925 million. For a few days Hanson discussed with his advisers the possibility of a higher cash alternative, before walking away from the deal. In the past, as Hanson and White had demonstrated in their US battle with SCM, they had been willing to fight hard for victory. But in RHM they showed hesitation from the start as the more cautious counsel of Derek Bonham made an impact. There was also fear at Grosvenor Place that a prolonged, hostile bid might lead to some repetition by RHM of the Goldman Sachs style ICI defence – with some further embarrassment to Hanson.

If being seen off by a protégé at RHM proved a salutary experience, then the Beazer exercise provided a useful rehearsal for a different kind of Hanson bid: the rescue purchase of Quantum chemicals. Like Beazer, Quantum was a large loss-maker, which had become overburdened by near junk-bond quality debt in the heady atmosphere of the 1980s. The company, which was highly dependent on the polyethylene market, had also been affected by the slump in the price of its principal product during the US recession, which had ended in 1992. As with Beazer the equity element of the purchase, which was formally agreed by Quantum shareholders on 30 September 1993, was relatively modest at £500 million. But Hanson, which had picked up a great deal of debt with Beazer, was also taking a further £1.7 billion on to its books, making an official purchase price of £2.2 billion. Although relatively simple to execute, the deal was the biggest to date for Hanson in the United States. Lord White was plainly pleased with his new acquisition and left no doubt with Quantum's management as to what was likely to happen: 'We will proceed with Quantum's cost-reduction programme and seek further saving by refinancing Quantum's debt,' he announced. However, as work on the Quantum deal proceeded, White, battered by ill-health, found himself sidelined as James, at the age of 71 but still in rude health, spent an increasing amount of time in the US bedding down Quantum.

The immediate task was to bring down Quantum's debt stock. Within 24 hours of moving into the chemical company, Hanson disclosed it was to redeem some $1.15 billion of debt, on which the weighted interest cost was 10 per cent. Essentially, Hanson was using its own borrowing powers and strong credit standing to give Quantum some immediate breathing space – this was much the path it had followed at Beazer too. Hanson was fully aware that if it could bring Quantum's cost structure down and restore its pricing structure, there were potentially strong profits gains to be had from both the basic chemicals business and the propane gas distribution company. Before the onset of recession in 1988 Quantum had managed to turn in profits of $711 million, which had swung into a loss of $10 million in 1993 – the year that Hanson plc added it to its portfolio. Hanson techniques were quickly applied to Quantum: sharp cost-cutting at headquarters would produce some $15 million of savings in 1993/4, rising to $60 billion by 1995/6; the size of the workforce was slashed and uneconomic plants closed down; some $25 million was quickly squeezed out of Quantum's technology centre – cutting R&D is a typical Hanson practice. James Hanson was obviously pleased at the swift way in which he was able to refinance Quantum's debt, and a 'tombstone', to commemorate the achievement now rests in an honoured position on the mantelpiece of his westward-facing office, overlooking Buckingham Palace.

As well as becoming a more normal company, Hanson became an ordinary company too. In his 1993 annual report to shareholders Lord Hanson had to find words which glossed over a sharp fall in after-tax profits to £734 million from £1.1 billion and a dividend income which had been held: the claims of unbroken years of earnings and dividends increases since the earliest days of the Wiles Group looked less impressive. Hanson also found itself embarking on a rapid-fire series of disposals and flotations in an effort to clear up a balance sheet which had become heavily geared by its own historic standards, and to disentangle itself from surplus activities – which had been hung on to out of habit. Although the upturn in the housing market might have provided Hanson with some useful profits in the mid-1990s, it chose instead to sell off its housebuilding companies on both sides of the Atlantic.

In the United States Beazer Homes USA which had seemed to be a permanent fixture of the Hanson empire after it bought luxury home-builder Watt Housing for $116 million in April 1993 as part of an enhancement operation, was rapidly floated off, raising some $184 million of cash. A parallel flotation was arranged in the United Kingdom which raised a further £412.5 million in March 1994. In the US and UK the Beazer aggregates businesses were kept by Hanson and put together with others owned by the company. The objective of these cash-raising exercises was primarily to reduce net debts of some £2.5 billion and thus perhaps prepare Hanson plc for a further major acquisition should one come along. By the summer of 1994 net debt had been steadily reduced, bringing the gearing – the level of debt expressed as a percentage of shareholders' equity– down from a peak of 86 per cent in 1993 to 69 per cent. Hanson, which had long been considered by its detractors as a financial engineering group churning assets, sought to lay the emphasis on its role as an industrial group.

This image was pursued with a highly creative and effective new corporate advertising campaign in the national media, on both sides of the Atlantic, aimed at stressing a new identity for Hanson. The company now sought to portray itself 'As an industrial management company with major investments in basic industries. Coal, chemicals, building materials, forest products, tobacco and material handling', with a stress on the group's strong brand names such as Jacuzzi.[17] James Hanson, with his lifelong interest in photography, played a personal role in the selection and approval of the television campaign, which drew its inspiration from the opening scenes of the 1941 Orson Welles classic, *Citizen Kane*. The Hanson pastiche opens with the tale of Charles Forsyte King, who ruled Wall Street. Or, as he once put it, 'Ruled Wall Street? I am Wall Street.' After King's death, his associates, filmed in monochrome, sit around discussing where King had gone wrong. One says: 'King's mistake was in preferring paper money to paper itself – he should have invested in timber.' One of the grey figures in the commercial goes on to suggest he should have gone for other basics, like bricks. Finally, another figure points out that the clue to the failure of the financier's life lay in his dying word . . . Hanson.

The purpose of the commercial, put together by Lowe Howard-Spink in London, was to underpin Hanson's new, more open image and prop up its reputation as a solid industrial enterprise. The group which Hanson and White built in the 1970s and 1980s was no longer the slick financial operation but a group deeply involved in basic industries on both sides of the Atlantic. Financiers such as Jim Slater in the early 1970s in Britain and Carl Icahn in the New York of the 1990s come and go. The permanence and solidity that were the main themes of Hanson's 1994 corporate advertising campaign led to suggestions that even in his seventh decade James still nurtured dynastic ambitions. The same drive, which added Hansonisation to the lexicon of the business analyst, remains alive and well.

Much of Lord Hanson's lofty ambition for perpetuation of the Hanson name has been invested in his son Robert. His adopted son Brook has been relegated to the second division, working for the private family company, Hanson Transport, from its modest Huddersfield offices. His step-daughter Karen is an interior designer, although his son-in-law Cheever Hardwick did have a spell working inside Hanson plc. In September 1992, shortly before Lord Hanson launched his unsuccessful run at RHM, the group announced that Robert Hanson, then aged 31, would be moving up from his associate director role to become a main board director. The appointment was contentious. Robert Hanson would be the youngest director of a FTSE-100 company and a full 11 years younger than the next youngest Hanson plc director John Raos, the chief operating officer of Hanson Industries. The younger Hanson's appointment caused some consternation among institutional shareholders who argued that there was no track record by which it was possible to assess his abilities. Scenting difficulty the younger Hanson – whose privacy remains carefully shielded by his father – was offered to the *Financial Times* for interview. He told the paper: 'Life may not always be fair and other executives here may feel they should be on the board. But Mr Bonham [the chief executive] wanted me on the board which approved my appointment. There will be no dynasty here, because Hanson is a meritocracy.'[18]

The younger Hanson enjoyed a more privileged education than his father, who had never made the public school he had hoped to attend, and was in the services when he might have been at university or finishing his accountancy training. Eton was the chosen school for the Hanson heir and from there he moved to St Peter's College, Oxford, developing along the way the same kind of liking for the high life that his father had enjoyed after his army career. At Oxford the young Robert Hanson was involved in the rowdy and sometimes distasteful Assassins dining club and he celebrated his thirtieth birthday with a party to end all parties at his Berkshire home. The younger Hanson inherited the family interest in horses and has his own polo team, the Bulldogs.

Following his initial spell at Hanson plc, in 1991 Robert was put in charge of the acquisitions and mergers team where he worked alongside Lord Hanson's nephew Chris Collins. This may, however, have been one of the least successful periods for the company in terms of mergers – which for decades had been the group's lifeblood. Robert was closely involved in the possible trade purchase of PowerGen, although significantly it was Lords Hanson and White who conducted the negotiations. Similarly, he was part of the team which investigated the possibility of a rescue offer for Canary Wharf. As a former N.M. Rothschild merchant banker, Robert Hanson also worked closely with Smith New Court in developing the strategy for the 1991 assault on ICI. None of these deals came to fruition. With the UK proving more difficult than in the past and the onset of the single market in Europe, Robert and Chris Collins set their sights on a European acquisition. But although Europe appeared the right place to look for expansion, the younger Hanson was finding it difficult to deliver.

Lord Hanson was now regularly inviting Robert, along with Derek Bonham, to his high-powered Brompton Road lunches. But these occasions remained dominated by the greater personality of Lord Hanson. Robert, an unimpressive personality in the presence of his father, made little impact. It was during one of these occasions, in the summer of 1993, that Robert began to express the view that Europe – with its tightly held cross-shareholdings, in which a small group of companies own equity in each other that constitutes a defensive web, and high price-earnings values for companies – was proving a difficult nut to crack. It was a view which Hanson's real acquisitions chief, Gordon White, after taking a year out in Europe, had reached some years earlier. White recalls:

After I started in America I went and lived in Paris for a year and I couldn't get anywhere. I couldn't get anywhere because of the system of bankers and interlocking shares. Frankly, I believe that the owner never plays the same way as exists in the United States and United Kingdom.[19]

By the spring of 1994 Europe was starting to look less seductive. In the summer of 1993 the exchange rate mechanism imploded under the weight of the failure of the Europe economies to develop converging economic policies. A prolonged recession in Germany, as the Bundesbank bore down heavily on the money supply, spread to most of Europe where interest rates remained unexpectedly high and unemployment ratcheted upwards. In Britain John Major's government was as riven by Conservative divisions over the future of Europe and the single currency as Mrs Thatcher's had been before it. The continent, with its economic sclerosis, restrictive labour practices and obstacles to takeover, began to look less alluring to Hanson.

It was becoming increasingly likely that the 1990s and beyond would be the era of East Asia. As the world enters the final half-decade of the twentieth century many of the Western economies are plagued by sluggish growth, structural unemployment and social dissonance. While the Western economies are barely growing, the East Asian economies have moved into overdrive with the combined economies of the Chinese Economic Area – Taiwan, Hong Kong and Southern China – stronger in terms of exports than those of Britain and France within Europe. Investment pours into China from the Group of Seven industrial countries, attracted by a highly competitive labour market, a vibrant domestic market and the sophisticated financial services offered by Hong Kong.

In March 1994, some time after many US, Japanese and British commercial concerns had expanded in Asia, Hanson decided to join the rush. Lord Hanson's son Robert, now aged 33, seemed a sensible choice. Despite his trumpeted European ambitions the younger Hanson had not discovered or consummated one major takeover in Britain or Europe since taking over as acquisitions chief. But Robert, who had worked for N.M. Rothschild in Hong Kong in 1986–88, was the obvious candidate to head up the new Asian operation from London. It was emphasised that the new Hanson Hong Kong office would seek to solicit joint ventures for Hanson's major areas of enterprise including Peabody Coal, SCM Chemicals, Cavenham Forest Products and Imperial Tobacco – which was already looking to China's vast population as a market for its products. Although the operation would be headed by Robert Hanson, who would chair Asia Pacific, it was to be run by two new group appointees: Simon Hsu, a former investment banker, and Cheng Ng, a US-trained lawyer. But even this enterprise would break an old Hanson family rule of business: that it was important for the person responsible for running the enterprise to be on the spot. This had been true for the young James Hanson, when he left for Hamilton, Ontario, after nationalisation. It was also true of Gordon White's phenomenal success in setting up and establishing Hanson Industries.

In many ways, however, the Hong Kong office could be regarded as part of the process of normalisation. Hanson in the 1990s, with a younger board, more non-executive directors and its stress on developing business, was not quite the takeover machine it had once been. Although Beazer and Quantum were, in their own terms, large deals – among the top rank in Hanson's acquisitions – they were essentially rescues utilising the financial reputation Hanson plc had built up in the 1980s. Similarly, the opening of the Hong Kong office by the younger Robert Hanson was part of a process of extending and developing existing businesses rather than taking on new activities. All of these reflected the personality of Derek Bonham, as chief executive, who saw the new Hanson as a global industrial holding company.

The deal which has most come to symbolise the new Hanson, with its focus on core businesses, came early in 1995. A joint statement from Lords Hanson and White revealed that the company was bundling together 34 of its non-core American businesses – including such famous brand names as Jacuzzi, Faberware and Tommy Armour sports gear – into a separate enterprise, US Industries. The deal would yield some £855 million for Hanson plc shareholders and create a new quoted company in the United States which would rank number 160 among the Fortune 500 list of America's largest corporations. This spin-off fell short of the grand split which had been looked at by Lord Hanson in the early 1990s, but could not be done efficiently for tax reasons. By no means was Hanson abandoning the US; but, by concentrating on basic businesses like chemicals, through Quantum, and coal through Peabody, it was taking on a new, less quirky profile.

The period after the ICI bid also saw the beginnings of a less arrogant Hanson plc. Although James's effort to silence critics at general meetings was seen as anti-democratic, it taught the group that wanted to be a global company an important lesson: the need to open itself up to the world. The company began to hold press conferences to present its quarterly results instead of relying upon a quiet word with the chosen few; analysts' meetings became less of a triumph of style over substance and concentrated more on detail. The establishment of a communications committee of the board was designed to improve investor relations, to reach out to political parties beyond the Conservatives and to put across the group's message in a more accessible manner. James Hanson personally remained sceptical about improved corporate governance and greater openness, but was persuaded to go along by the corporate modernisers Bonham and his son Robert Hanson. He was looking to a less involved role as perhaps president of the company, like Lord King at British Airways and Lord Forte at the company which bears his name. James, still more active and involved than colleagues many years his junior, was preparing slowly, but carefully, to begin fading into the background as he approached his 1997 retirement date. 'I will retire knowing the company is in safe hands but I expect to be kept on in some advisory capacity,' Lord Hanson told an interviewer.[20] But in a company where the cult of the personality had been so strong for many decades, it will be an extraordinarily difficult transition and lingering doubts will remain as to whether the designated successor Derek Bonham will move up the batting order until the day Hanson finally retires.

CHAPTER 10

The Reckoning

In less than thirty years, the company over which Lord Hanson presided grew to be one of the ten largest in the United Kingdom. It is undoubtedly a remarkable personal success story: it has made Lord Hanson extremely rich – number 230 in the *Sunday Times* rankings with an estimated wealth of £55 million. It has also elevated him from the status of ex-playboy not only to royal circles, the House of Lords and the innermost sanctums of government, but also to the business pantheon. He has been a role model for many businessmen, as shown by the collection of various personal awards which are proudly displayed on the office walls of the Hanson headquarters. The Hanson approach to business has gone out of fashion in the 1990s but is still, for some in the business world, a supreme paradigm for the pursuit of shareholder value, which is regarded as the overriding purpose of the capitalist company in the Anglo-American model.

For many on the left of British politics Lord Hanson is an arch example of uncaring capitalism: exploiting political connections, buying and selling companies as though they were pieces in a board game, throwing people out of work in the interests of shareholders' profits, and damaging industry by a reluctance to invest. Such views are inevitable from a political position which challenges many of the fundamentals of the capitalist model, and because of that political motivation they would not trouble Lord Hanson for a moment. But there are many others, whose approbation he would hope for, who also have serious misgivings about Lord Hanson's impact on the business world. As one senior merchant banker put it: 'Within his objectives he runs companies particularly well. But I think the objectives are wrong. It is one of the reasons for the British industrial base being destroyed.'[1] Such misgivings give rise to serious questions about how successful Lord Hanson's business empire has actually been, about the impact its growth and style of operations have had on other companies, and about the manner in which Lord Hanson has presided over this public company. This chapter is concerned with answering those questions.

Lord Hanson was feted in the 1980s, especially by Mrs Thatcher. Along with Lord Sterling of P&O and Lord King of British Airways, he was the kind of businessman she admired: tough, single-minded and above all successful. But these were qualities admired far beyond Number 10. Of these three business lords, Lord Hanson stands out as an icon of the 1980s, 'the first and the finest casting to emerge from the Thatcherite mould'.[2] He was the swashbuckling symbol of the 1980s business approach: shaking sleepy, Establishment figures out of their complacent lethargy, and taking the financial and political rewards for doing so. What is more, this approach represented the government's industrial policy. Mrs Thatcher's abhorrence of government intervention made the notion of industrial policy almost absurd. But insofar as she had an industrial policy, it was influenced substantially by people such as these three business lords. And it was to allow businessmen like Lord Hanson to dismember the weakest companies, arguably making their constituent parts stronger in the process. That was in stark contrast to the views of many Tory businessmen, who favoured a traditional approach of building businesses of sufficient scale and expertise that they would be strong enough to compete in the world. As another Thatcher favourite, and Lord Hanson's opponent in the battle for Imperial Group, Lord Laing, observed: 'She was in too much of a hurry for that. It would have taken too long.'[3]

The recession at the turn of the decade suggested that the 1980s style of industrial policy had failed, and provoked serious questions about the short-term, financially dominant nature of British capitalism. Both business people[4] and politicians[5] began to argue that a more sober, co-operative, long-term approach was needed for Britain to compete in the twenty-first century global market. These views had been formed partly from a belief that any success which Lord Hanson and his imitators had achieved in the 1980s had been shallow and temporary. While it may have been success in a personal sense, and for Hanson as a company, the argument was that it did not help, and could well have been a contributory factor in the competitive decline of British industry. Hanson emerged in the growing recovery of the mid-1990s in much stronger shape than many of the other takeover artists of the 1980s – indeed several of them did not emerge, but fell victim to their own over-enthusiasm and the ravages of recession. But Lord Hanson also emerged with his reputation dented. If it could be shown, however, that the jaundiced view of Hanson was mistaken, and that Lord Hanson had indeed created some sustainable successes, that would be an argument against the rubbishing of the 1980s business ideology, and Lord Hanson could look forward to retirement knowing that the mark he had left on late twentieth-century Britain would not be depicted as a trail of destruction.

On the face of it, it might seem preposterous even to question the success of Lord Hanson's company. Sales of almost £10 billion, 80,000 employees and a stock market value of almost £14 billion put Hanson plc in the top division of any corporate league table. It is a long way from the Wiles Group when James Hanson took the chair in 1965: a tiny, uncelebrated agricultural and vehicle company whose statistics, even adjusting for inflation in the intervening years, would undoubtedly place it in a minor league. In 1994 money, Wiles Group had sales of little more than £70 million when James Hanson took the chair. It employed barely 1000 people and was valued by the stock market at the 1994 equivalent of about £30 million. Apart from the phenomenal growth from that meagre base there is Lord Hanson's proud boast of 25 years of unbroken advance in profits. And from the point of view of shareholders – and in Lord Hanson's view that is the only point of view that matters – there have been enormous returns on their investments.

Surprisingly, however, returns for shareholders have not been as consistently excellent as is often assumed. It is true that an investor who originally bought £1000 worth of Wiles Group shares in June 1965 and invested in all the rights issues along the way would now have a holding worth more than £350,000. But the real test of how well a share has performed must include comparison with the stock market as a whole, as expressed in an index of share prices. This comparison excludes general influences which may have boosted or depressed all shares, not just those being examined, such as economic boom or slump. Comparison with a stock market index concentrates attention on the specific performance of the individual share. Comparison of the performance of Hanson shares with the FT All-Share index shows that there has been significant underperformance since spring 1990. In fact the 1990 high point for Hanson shares only just matched their standing at the beginning of 1985, before the defeat by Powell Duffryn and the fateful rights issue. In the spring of 1995 Hanson shares were a quarter lower, relative to the All-Share index, than those two peaks. In other words, shareholders who bought at the peaks would be more than 25 per cent worse off than if they had invested in a broad basket of shares, or in a fund which tracks the index. There has only been a brief period since 1984 when somebody could have bought Hanson shares and found that they were better off in spring 1994 than if they had merely followed the index. So for ten years Lord Hanson failed to deliver on his overriding objective – delivering value for shareholders in the form of shares which perform better than the pack.

There have been other periods over the years when the same would be true. The peak of 1968 was not surpassed until 1975 – seven years during which share buyers at the peak would have lost out. Similarly there was a five-year spell in the 1970s when unlucky buyers would have found themselves worse off than investing in the All-Share index. Only at the beginning of 1981 did Hanson Trust's share standing relative to the index pass where it had been in 1976. This is far from the picture of steady progress and returns which has been painted over the years, although it must be said that those who bought Hanson shares in 1966, 1970 and 1979 will have been handsomely rewarded.

Share price performance is ultimately a reflection of the past progress and expected future prospects, however. And it is this actual performance of the company, rather than its shares, which casts most doubt on Lord Hanson's achievement, and the claim that industrial management has transformed the performance of the companies he has taken over.

Hanson's performance owed much more to dealing than to managing, but it is not a simple matter to assess the financial performance of the company. The many acquisitions and disposals mean that one year's results can never be compared directly with another. The impact of fluctuations in the sterling/dollar exchange rate confuse the picture further. Finally, the vagaries of accounting procedures inevitably distort the underlying business performance of a group such as Hanson. But it is possible to examine the performance of some individual operating units. The battery business is a good example, because unlike most Hanson acquisitions it has been through the Hanson wringer and emerged into new ownership in a similar, though not identical, form. If the Hanson approach is indeed the way to reinvigorate British business, then British Ever Ready should have left the Hanson group in world-beating condition. Sadly, that was not the case.

In 1992 Hanson sold Ever Ready for £132 million to the US conglomerate Ralson Purina, which also owns the US Eveready Company – thus reuniting the group which had been split up after the First World War. Taking account of inflation, that is about £20 million less than Hanson paid for Berec in 1982. Nevertheless it was a good deal for Hanson: the group still retains the South African operations, and reduced the original cost substantially by the swift sale of the battery company's business on the Continent, and by the sale of properties. Hanson also received handsome profits from Ever Ready. When Ralston Purina took over, however, they found a company 'a number of years behind the times . . . a business in decline . . . the whole infrastructure was pretty thin'.[6]

Hanson's defence is that Berec would have gone bust without the Hanson medicine.[7] That may be true, although as in so many takeovers, remedial action had already begun by the time Hanson pounced. Berec had not been a case of exemplary management before its takeover. It exemplified some of the worst traits of British business: comfortable dominance of the UK market, extravagant bureaucracy and political infighting among top managers. But there were two important strands to its strategy which have now been vindicated. First, it was attempting to build a global business; and second, it believed research and development were crucial to success. Those are key elements of the strategy now being followed by Ralston Purina, and indeed Hanson had acknowledged the need to internationalise Ever Ready. Twice during the 1980s it attempted to acquire an international companion company, but failed to buy Duracell and US Eveready. Berec's management had implemented its strategy badly – its heavy research spending in particular was badly focused and lacked an understanding of how the market was changing. But Hanson Trust's strategy was misguided because it abandoned internationalism – except for the lucrative South African market – and the much smaller research budget was used in a purely defensive way. Berec pursued the right strategy badly; Hanson pursued the wrong strategy well.

In fact 'strategy' is not a word which fits easily with Lord Hanson's approach to business. He is interested only in return on capital and cash flow, not in how those financial demands are met. One way in which Lord Hanson was ahead of his time was in believing that managers of subsidiaries should be left to get on with their business, because they knew it better than anyone else. But company chairmen are crucial in setting the culture within which such managers operate. And Lord Hanson has commanded a culture of safe non-adventure. He has not been interested in ambitious plans with uncertain outcomes – which require strategic thinking – to develop businesses he owns. In fact Berec was unusual, and probably a mistake, because it required such thinking. Most businesses which Lords Hanson and White have been interested in are not in that kind of competitive position. Cigarettes and brick – the main remaining UK businesses - are much more typical. They are stable industries, in the sense that there is a small number of established competitors, with no new entrants, and there is very little change in these markets. These are the famous 'basic industries' which Lord Hanson has always said he is interested in. The battery industry probably looked like that, too, in 1982, but in fact it was a rapidly changing market, and so far as the UK was concerned there was also a powerful new competitor in the shape of Duracell. The thinking which Lord Hanson has instilled in his company was unable to deal with that kind of market. It led, for example, to the crucial mistake of selling continental European businesses to Duracell and abandoning other international prospects.

The deal gave Hanson Trust 'tomorrow's money today' but it left Ever Ready short of money, and short of markets, when tomorrow came.

Bricks and tobacco, like most of the US businesses, have been much more suited to the Hanson treatment, which is essentially to ignore strategic thinking and to concentrate on operational efficiency. And Ron Fulford represents the ultimate operational manager. Mr Fulford was acquired by Hanson along with United Gas Industries in 1982, and has proved himself to be highly effective in this limited role of running factories well, first at Ever Ready, then at Imperial. He is widely respected both inside and outside the company for his ability to keep squeezing more productivity out of mass manufacturing plants. He has been rewarded with the title of 'senior associate director', but knows that under Lord Hanson's approach to running the company he cannot expect a seat on the board. Board seats are not available to operational managers, no matter how good or how senior they become.

The experience of Imperial Tobacco under Mr Fulford illustrates both the positive and negative aspects of Lord Hanson's approach. The immediate post-acquisition reorganisation slashed the number of managers by 50 per cent. A subsequent production reorganisation dramatically improved operating efficiency, reportedly by as much as 90 per cent.[8] This cost improvement has been reflected in Imperial's reported profits, which grew from £225 million in 1990 to £307 million in 1993 – although care must be taken with interpreting such trends when there has been heavy reorganisation expenditure. That is the positive aspect of Hansonisation. The negative side presented at Imperial, however, is a lack of interest in new markets. Like US Eveready, most cigarette manufacturers see the newly liberated markets of Eastern Europe, China and other developing countries as a major opportunity. They are a means of offsetting growing pressure on domestic profitability as a result of health concerns. Hanson's view of such prospects has typically been short term and financial: 'many companies are currently selling their product into these markets at a loss in order to build up relationships.'[9] Exactly the same view was taken at Ever Ready when competitors were moving into Russia and China.[10] At the end of 1993, however, there was a hint of the changes which were beginning to take place as Lord Hanson started to take a less dominant role in the group. His designated successor, Derek Bonham, wondered aloud about the possibility of Imperial's venturing into overseas markets,[11] and a joint venture in China was announced in June 1994. Imperial is behind its competitors in such ventures, however.

The Imperial experience – where production reorganisation cost £40 million – shows that Lord Hanson is prepared to sanction heavy capital expenditure. But the emphasis on such spending has always been protection of existing products or markets, and the pursuit of lower costs. The crucial requirement has always been that the investment would produce a payback (recoup the spending in higher profits) within four years – a period which was relaxed to five years when Derek Bonham took over. New ventures which carry a higher risk that they will not achieve such a payback are not attractive to the chairman, and operational managers, who must seek head office approval for spending above £1000 in the UK, naturally follow this lead. Managers know what is expected of them, much more clearly than in most large companies, and that is not to ask for large sums to spend on speculative ventures. 'It's too complicated to get approval, so they won't even try.'[12] Most are not strong-willed or determined enough to push for such investment, as a small example showed in the early 1990s. Smith Meters, one of the smaller UK industrial interests which was not sold to management in the clear-out at the end of 1993, has produced steady profits as a result of a long-term contract with British Gas. But its products are based on old technology. Several years ago, according to internal Hanson sources, its managers, realising this, put forward a project to develop the new technology which would be required to sustain the company. 'What is the payback?' was the only question that interested the accountants at 1 Grosvenor Place. Smith Meters' managers were unable to say, so the project was turned down.

As a result of these dispiritingly narrow horizons, Hanson has a miserable investment record. Just to maintain a company at its existing base level, it can be expected that capital spending should exceed depreciation. Depreciation spreads the cost of equipment over its useful life, so it represents the consumption of previous investment. But it represents consumption at previous price levels as well. Given inflation of, say, 5 per cent, new spending would be required at

5 per cent above the previous level to maintain a plant's productive capacity, assuming replacement with identical equipment. Yet as far as can be deduced from figures which are confused by many acquisitions and disposals, Hanson has managed to invest more than its depreciation in only five of the last ten years. Indeed, this is hardly surprising, since heavy capital spending in target companies is one of the things which brings a gleam to Lord White's eye. 'The first thing I do is look back and see what a company has spent and also at its depreciation. If they've spent in excess of their depreciation, I might be interested,' he has said.[13]

Of course, investment is no good unless it produces satisfactory returns, but in many businesses it is impossible to achieve satisfactory returns without making risky investments. That is the essence of business, especially the essence of entrepreneurial business which was supposed to be the heart of the 1980s free-market, free-wheeling philosophy. It has never been Lord Hanson's style, however. He has always aimed to buy safe companies in low-risk industries and to run them conservatively. Lord White has made it clear that risky ventures are not at all attractive. 'I'm only interested in what we can lose. The down-side risk is something that I constantly hammer home to any of my people involved in a smaller way in acquisitions. I say: "Don't worry about how much you can make, how much you can lose?"'[14]

According to conventional financial theory, low risk should bring relatively low returns. However, Lord Hanson has been said to have delivered exceptional returns. But this claim, like others about his business success, is open to dispute. Ostensibly Lord Hanson presided over a company which produced more than his target 20 per cent return on capital employed in every year until recession began to bite in 1991. This ratio has been severely distorted by acquisitions, however, and especially the writing-off of goodwill, that part of the purchase price of a company which does not relate to the value of physical assets. Writing off goodwill reduces the capital, which results in an increase in the return on capital. In other words, the more acquisitions there are, and the more goodwill that is written off as a result, the higher will be the return on capital. US accounting practice adopts a different approach, which does not result in goodwill being written-off shareholders' funds, and so provides a more realistic measure of capital employed. Using the US-style accounts, which have been available since 1985, presents a very different picture to the soaring results shown under UK accounting. With profit also calculated according to US principles, the after-tax return on shareholders' funds rose to a phenomenal level in 1988, but has plunged swiftly since then. As the benefits of the Imperial and SCM deals flowed through, the return on shareholders' capital reached 25 per cent in 1988 – and that is after tax. But by 1992 it was only half that level and slumped to just 8 per cent in 1993. Nor was it above 20 per cent in the years immediately before 1988 rising to that peak from 17 per cent in 1986. That still represents exceptional after-tax returns, but there are serious question marks over some of the profit figures in these calculations.

These are aggregate figures. Another way of looking at Hanson's performance is to examine individual purchases. It is difficult to assess the returns on most specific acquisitions, because few have remained in one piece long enough for reported profits to be matched to the investment made. But some estimates can be made. SCM and Imperial were by any standards incredibly lucrative deals. SCM in particular is a testimony to Lord White's skills, leaving a net profit on the transaction of more than $600 million, even before counting the contribution from the remaining assets: SCM chemicals and the 49 per cent share of Smith Corona typewriters. Imperial was not as profitable as that, but Imperial Tobacco's £300 million profits (in 1993) were acquired at a net cost of just £200 million. None of the other major acquisitions has come near this standard, however, and many have produced relatively poor returns. For Kidde, a string of small sales reduced the investment to about $600 million, but Grove cranes, the main legacy, produced profit of only about $100 million even before the recession started to bite. It is not the only example in which the outlay produced meagre returns. The net cost of what is left from ConsGold, for example, is about £1 billion. Yet what is left – essentially ARC UK – appears to generate profits of only about £50 million before tax. That represents a return on capital of only 5 per cent. USI, bought for $532 million in 1984, now shows a net cost after a string of disposals of about $180 million – excluding any carrying cost to allow for the interest on that sum. Yet all that is left is a handful of peripheral businesses: USI Lighting, office equipment companies

United Chair and Anderson Hickey, and a couple of suppliers to the auto industry.

These different ways of looking at Hanson's financial performance all suggest that it does not live up to the company's reputation. Shareholder returns were brilliant in the first half of the 1980s, but have been pedestrian since. The performance of key companies within the group has also left much to be desired, while some of the major acquisitions also seem to have produced disappointing returns. But if all this is true, the question arises as to how the group managed to report continuing growth in profits for 25 years. And looking at the record in the 1980s, the answer appears to be that a combination of accounting and tax skills has been largely responsible.

Concern about Hanson's accounting has been heightened by Lord Hanson's close and enduring relationship with his auditor, which was considered unusual by other leading firms of accountants but is another example of Hanson's loyalty to long-standing business associates. At the annual general meeting in 1994 Lord Hanson took the surprising step of asking the auditor, Iain Bryce, to stand and receive on his retirement the acclaim of shareholders for his long and excellent service to the company. In fact that association was longer than most shareholders will have realised. Mr Bryce acted as company secretary to the Wiles Group when its shares were first floated on the stock exchange in 1964. He worked for the Yorkshire firm of Buckley, Hall, Devin & Co., which was the Wiles Group's auditor. The firm also supplied a company secretarial service, as many small firms do to small clients, and Mr Bryce was responsible for this service. The firm also audited the motor vehicle companies belonging to Jack Brignall, and it was from Mr Hall that James Hanson first heard that his proposed takeover of that company was endangered by a similar interest from George Wiles.

Buckley, Hall, Devin was eventually taken over by Whinney Murray, which subsequently became part of Ernst & Young. For ten years from 1983 Mr Bryce was the partner in charge of the audit. Ernst & Young is one of the world's top firms, but unusually for a huge multinational such as Hanson, the audit is still handled from the firm's office in Hull, where Mr Bryce is based. This is a slightly larger office than might be expected for such a town, since it also serves Northern Foods and a few smaller public companies. But the allocation of such a large audit to a partner in such a relatively small office is regarded as highly unusual by leading auditors from other top firms. The concern in such situations, expressed clearly in the profession's ethical guidance to members, is that the audit income might represent too large a portion of that office's income for the audit team to maintain the necessary professional objectivity. That concern is heightened by the fact that the senior audit partner had such a long association with Lord Hanson's company.

There has never been any suggestion that Mr Bryce has breached ethical standards or other professional guidelines but the dangers in such close and long-lasting relationships between auditors and clients have long been recognised by the accountancy profession. Accounting is an inexact science and auditing a matter of judgement. In 1993 the Institute of Chartered Accountants introduced new, tighter ethical guidelines because of growing concern that auditors' independence was less than it should be.[15] The new guidance toughens previous suggestions that an audit partner should not work for the same client for long periods. From 1 February 1994, an audit partner is not allowed to be responsible for the same client for longer than seven years.

For most of Lord Hanson's chairmanship, technical accounting matters were largely ignored by the investment community. But a number of scandals in the late 1980s, such as Maxwell Communications and Polly Peck, brought home to investment analysts the importance of purely technical accounting matters. At the end of the 1980s it came to be realised that distortions, crucial to the evaluation of share prices, affected many other companies, especially those involved in takeover bids. 'We felt that much of the apparent growth in profits which had occurred in the 1980s was the result of accounting sleight of hand rather than genuine economic growth,' one analyst wrote of the 1980s phenomenon.[16] Conglomerates were generally most heavily involved in the accounting practices which worried analysts, because many of those practices were associated with takeovers. And Hanson provided a prime example: 'Two features of Hanson's provisioning cause concern. The size of the provisions, which exceed capital and reserves, and utilisation of provisions, which can continue long after acquisition, with consequent question marks over underlying profitability.'[17]

Takeover accounting, which is extremely significant for highly acquisitive companies such as Hanson, is a nightmare. A number of issues make it difficult to present a clear picture of the resulting combination, and make it easy for acquisitive companies to flatter their figures. The most subtle of these acquisition issues is the effect on the earnings per share. It is a natural consequence of share-based acquisitions and is important because of the stock market's attachment to earnings per share as a measure of performance, and to the price/earnings ratio as a measure of share value.* The effect on earnings per share is a purely arithmetical matter, which is why it is so subtle – it requires no accounting adjustments. It means that a takeover financed by shares and made on the right terms inevitably improves the acquirer's earnings per share, even without any subsequent improvement in the performance of either company. It is like pouring either water or squash into an already diluted mixture. Adding more squash makes the mixture stronger. Adding more water dilutes it further.

'Dilution' of an acquirer's earnings per share occurs if a takeover is made at a price which represents a higher p/e ratio than that attached to the acquirer's shares which have been used in the takeover. On the other hand, if the takeover price is a lower multiple of the target's earnings than the p/e ratio of the shares issued to finance the takeover, the acquirer's earnings per share are automatically enhanced. This means that companies with highly valued shares (high p/e ratios) can afford to pay higher prices for acquisitions than companies with low share ratings. But the process is also self-reinforcing: being able to make such a takeover helps to push up earnings per share and so sustains or even increases the share rating – thus enabling more acquisitions to be made.

The earnings per share effect has been significant for Hanson over the years, but it is not something which could be avoided: it is an automatic factor of share-based takeovers. Despite concerns about this distorting effect and demands for figures that clarify the impact

*The price/earnings (p/e) ratio is the ratio of a company's share price to the earnings per share.

281

on earnings of a takeover – thus revealing the movement in earnings due to operational management – having been voiced as early as 1969,[18] accounting standards and stock exchange rules do not require such information to be published, so it is not done. In common with other companies, Hanson even stopped showing the amount of profit which had come from new acquisitions. This was detailed in the profit and loss account from 1971 to 1975, but was then abandoned, until required again by new accounting standards in 1993.

The other means of boosting earnings following a takeover are less indiscriminate. Indeed, they require management decision. They are entirely financial, accounting practices. Again, they apply to all companies making a takeover, although the extent to which they are applied, and thus the extent to which subsequent earnings are affected, varies considerably from company to company. The scope for such adjustments has been lessened considerably over the years by the accounting profession's attempts at standardisation, now represented by the Accounting Standards Board. But in the early 1990s there was still plenty of leeway for companies to choose accounting treatments which suited them best, and so to flatter their financial performance. Using an example from the early days, following the acquisition of West of England Sack Holdings in 1968, Wiles Group decided to change the acquired company's depreciation policy on its sacks, by lengthening their expected life and reducing the depreciation charge.[19] Such policies were not required to be disclosed in the accounts of Wiles Group at the time, so readers of the accounts would have been none the wiser, even though the effect would have been to increase Wiles Group's profits above what they would have been under the previous depreciation policies.

Accounting for the acquisition itself also confuses the profit picture because reorganisation costs are not reflected in the profits of the acquirer. For example, it is usual to make any provisions for anticipated reorganisation costs and losses at the time of an acquisition, and to treat them as part of the acquisition cost. Similarly, it is normal for a potential owner to assess the value of assets which have been acquired – usually the value is lower than the target company's valuation figure, in which case the adjustment is normally made, once again, as part of the takeover accounting. That can have a double effect: any loss does not trouble the acquiring group's profits, while if the reduction in value has been overdone, the group realises a profit (which is included in its profits) when the assets are subsequently sold. This gives acquiring companies a crucial advantage over their targets, which cannot avoid charging reorganisation costs and asset write-downs against profits. In another early example, Wiles Group's results for 1967/68 showed that almost £62,000 was provided for 'terminal and other non-recurring losses applicable to subsidiary companies acquired during the year'. These losses were removed in arriving at the net profit available for shareholders. In the following year, £577,000 of losses 'on sales of net assets in subsidiaries and properties' were excluded from the profit calculation. Such accounting treatments were normal practice at the time, but it made it difficult, if not impossible, for shareholders to gauge the managerial performance of the new whizz-kids who were so actively transforming the Wiles Group.

Calculating the profit or loss on the subsequent sale of acquired companies – a common event throughout Hanson's history – is another problem. In the early days, the cost of the acquisition was calculated using the 'nominal' value of the shares. But that figure is meaningless. The effective value of a share is its price on the stock exchange, not the nominal value given to it when the company was formed. For example, in 1969 West of England Sack and Butterley were included in Hanson Trust's balance sheet at a cost based on the nominal value of the shares issued to buy them, of 5 shillings each, which resulted in the acquisition cost being £835,000 lower than the value attributed to the assets acquired. The actual value of shares is the price at which they are trading, which in this case was around £1 each. That was the value of the shares issued to the shareholders of these companies – the actual amount paid. The accounts noted that this actual value was £3.5 million higher than the figure used on the balance sheet. That £3.5 million leeway was an instant profit. The companies could be sold immediately for the same price at which they had been bought, but a profit of £3.5 million would have been declared. While the nominal basis of valuing acquisitions was ended in the 1970s, the problem continued until 1993, when the Accounting Standards Board decreed that the profit or loss on selling a company should be based on the actual cost when it was acquired, including any goodwill which arose at the time. These same issues applied throughout Hanson's growth. By 1989, following the ConsGold acquisition, provisions in the balance sheet for liabilities other than tax and pensions were £758 million, compared to only just over £1 billion in shareholders' funds (share capital plus undistributed profit). The reason why the funds figure was so low was that more than £2 billion of goodwill had been written off on acquiring ConsGold. This is normal accounting practice in Britain: goodwill is eliminated as soon as the acquisition is made, rather than including it in the balance sheet and depreciating it over several years. By 1993 Hanson had written off in this way almost £5 billion of goodwill, a sum described by one leading accountant as 'a quite extraordinary figure'.[20]

The scale of these figures began to worry stockbrokers' analysts by the beginning of the 1990s,[21] and it is easy to see why. Assume that the provisions are for spending which is spread over 20 years. In 1993 such provisions had grown to £2.3 billion. That would have meant that, if an average is taken, £115 million of provisions was used – that is, £115 million of actual spending was not charged against profits. Yet Hanson's operating profit from continuing operations was only £930 million. In other words, if the provision had not existed, operating profit would have been reduced by one-eighth on these assumptions. The figures are even more significant when taken in the context of the individual operating companies concerned. An estimated £200 million provision was made on the Imperial acquisition. Yet in 1990, the first year in which tobacco profits were reported separately, the profit was only £225 million. The Peabody figures were even more dramatic. Provisions of £1.7 billion were made when the coal company was acquired, which can be assumed to represent £85 million a year. And Peabody's profits in the early 1990s were around £160 million – they actually fell from 1991 to 1992 and then in the following year were badly hit by the prolonged UMWA strike. Without the acquisition provisions it can be assumed that Peabody's profits record would have been much worse.

Of course, it is not permissible to charge any costs indiscriminately against such provisions: the costs must relate to the purpose for which the provision was established. But it is nevertheless true that such provisions can be made without affecting profits only by acquiring companies. If the target company had wished to make allowance for such future costs, the sum would have hit its reported profits in the year in which the provision was made. This gives a huge advantage to acquirers such as Hanson when comparing their profit performance against companies which have not made large acquisitions. It has also become widely accepted in the 1990s that it is impossible for auditors to police such provisions properly, ensuring that only appropriate costs are charged against the provision. It is now assumed that companies in general do abuse such acquisition provisions.[22] The Accounting Standards Board developed a new approach to the issue during 1994 because of this disquiet.

While Lord Hanson's accountants, led by Brian Hellings, and the designated successor as chairman, Derek Bonham, had long been accused by target companies of making the most of accounting rules, a number of specific examples at the outset of the 1990s made the investment community take these issues more seriously, and so eventually question the sustainability, or quality, of Hanson's earnings. It was not merely a matter of accounting debate. The problem for investors was that the size of the questionable items had become so important compared to the operating profits that the sustainability of profits was in doubt – as analysts put it: the quality of the earnings was poor. This was one of the main reasons for the City falling out of love with Hanson at the start of the 1990s. A key year was 1990, when Hanson plc was struggling to maintain its unbroken growth record. Ironically, although the company's published accounts did achieve that aim, the restatement by the financial database company Datastream showed that earnings per share had fallen for the first time – only marginally, from 20.55p per share to 20.32p per share, but that was enough to break the record. And indeed, when Hanson itself restated its financial record in 1992 to take account of the latest accounting standards, the new trend showed a substantial fall in profits and earnings in 1990. In the restated figures, 1989 profits were boosted to £1406 million, compared with just over £1064 million originally. But 1990 profits were reduced from £1,285 million to £1164 million. As a result, the increase in profits between the two years, which was originally reported as a 21 per cent rise, turned out to be a fall of 17 per cent. Earnings per share, which had been shown to have risen by 8 per cent, had now fallen by almost a quarter. This dramatic effect shows just how important accounting treatments can be in assessing performance.

Even after these adjustments are made, however, there are further question marks about the 1990 profits. Of the reported £1285 million profit before tax, a staggering £290 million (more than a fifth) came from non-trading items. This was shown separately from the operating profits and described as 'net interest, property and other income, less central expenses'. Separately, the net interest income was revealed to be £186 million, and assuming central expenses of about £25 million, this left unexplained a sum of about £130 million. In the following year's accounts the presentation had changed. Now an item of £101 million was separated out, described as 'profit on disposal of natural resources assets'. This explained the bulk of the mysterious £130 million, but it did not explain the treatment. Such a profit on disposal of a business or major asset would normally have been treated as an extraordinary item, rather than being included, as in this case, in pretax profits, and the earnings per share calculation. Without the inclusion of this £101 million special profit, the 1990 accounts would not have been able to show an increase in earnings per share.

The subsequent abolition of the notion of extraordinary items, as recognised in Hanson's subsequent restatement of these figures, makes this argument somewhat academic. There is, however, a much more substantive question about this £101 million profit – a question of whether it was really a profit at all. The profit would have been calculated by reference to the value of the shares in Hanson's balance sheet. But unusually, it appears from careful reading of both the UK accounts and the version filed in the US that the amount included in Hanson's balance sheet was not the 'fair value', based on the current share price, but the original cost included in ConsGold's accounts. In other words, the profit which was recorded had not arisen while the assets had been in Hanson's ownership, and under a more usual accounting treatment it would have been incorporated in the asset value on acquisition. A similar problem arose with the swap of the 49 per cent stake in Newmont the following year, 1991. This registered a profit of £170 million, based on a swap value of $1.3 billion. But that asset value of $1.3 billion was a rather more variable number than usual, since this was not a direct sale but a swap for the Cavenham forestry assets of Lord White's old friend, Sir James Goldsmith. A high asset value on this deal might have suited both sides, since the higher the value, the higher the profit on the deal for both sides. And since no cash changed hands, the value put on the transaction did not affect either party's financial position.

The size of these individual profits emphasises that these technical accounting issues have been much more important than might be imagined in Hanson's profit performance, and in trying to assess that performance. It is clear from this analysis that Hanson's profit record had rather less to do with the skills of the operating managers than with the small team of accountants at head office, who were clearly significant profit contributors. And this is also obvious from an examination of the group's tax bills.

Hanson has a record of paying very little tax, measured as a percentage of profits. Indeed, over six years in the early 1980s, despite declaring total European profits of £569 million, almost entirely from the UK in that period, cumulatively the company paid no mainstream UK tax at all – that is, excluding the proportion of Advance Corporation Tax (ACT) which had to be deducted from gross dividends and could not be set against UK profits. Looking at the total tax bill in the early 1990s, and taking a three-year average to smooth out the lumpiness of some tax payments, figures from the Datastream database show that the company came near the bottom of the commercial and industrial companies in the UK top 100. In other words there were few companies charged a lower proportion of profits in tax. Hanson has typically been charged just under 22 per cent tax rate in the early 1990s. This compares to almost 30 per cent for other leading industrial and commercial companies.

Lord Hanson's tax experts seem not only to have kept the tax charge unusually low for many years, it has also remained at a remarkably steady level. This occurred because the amount of ACT that has been charged has varied significantly from year to year. For example, between 1985 and 1989 the ACT element of the tax charge was twice negative – in other words, it reduced the total tax bill – then soared to £81 million and fell back again to just £14 million. Without this volatility the total tax charge would have bobbed about between 13 per cent and 26 per cent. The smoothing effect of the ACT charge left the tax charge at around 24 per cent throughout the period. That resulted in a smooth progression of earnings per share during those years.

The low tax charge is a tribute to Brian Hellings in particular, and the group's small team of tax accountants whose job it has been to search out new ways that will ensure the US and UK tax authorities get as small a share of the group's profits as possible. Hellings has been with the group since 1968, when he was recruited as financial comptroller. His previous employer was P. B. Cow, maker of Cow Gum and other rubber products. That company was acquired by Slater Walker as part of its attempt to reorganise the British rubber industry, and subsequently refloated as part of Allied Polymer. As a result, Hellings developed a deep dislike of Jim Slater – an anomalous attitude given his new employer's links with Slater and use of his methods.

Hellings was Lord Hanson's second financial comptroller but his predecessor, Douglas Oliphant, quickly moved to run the miscellaneous industrial businesses described as Northern Amalgamated Industries. Hellings was therefore responsible for creating the financial structures which drove the group, and for recruiting the men who made those systems work. He recruited Peter Harper as his first deputy in 1970, who eventually joined the board 20 years later after running various operating units. Even more importantly, he recruited Derek Bonham in 1971 to replace Harper. In 1974 Hellings joined the board and Bonham became financial comptroller, finally also becoming a director in 1981. Two years after joining the board, Hellings moved to the US. This move was partly to control Lord White's exuberant activities there, but also because Hellings and Hanson clashed continually. Unlike the other directors, who form a closely-knit group around Lord Hanson, Hellings was not prepared to mollify the tempestuous chairman, and as a result the two found it impossible to work together. Despite moving to the United States, he has not been an integral part of the US business operation – either the management operation run by David Clarke, or the acquisitions team headed by Gordon White. He has remained primarily responsible for the financial structure of the group, and even after Derek Bonham was appointed as finance director Hellings was described, until 1992, as 'senior director responsible for finance'. Hellings might be described as an accountant's accountant, unlike other members of the profession on the board, such as Derek Rosling, Martin Taylor or Tony Alexander, who soon became more rounded businessmen. Hellings, on the other hand, remained a pure accountant, concerned with the minutiae of accounting practice much more than with the broader sweep of deals and reorganisations. He has been happy with very few of the group's many acquisitions. And those he has liked, such as Butterley Brick in the early days and ConsGold more recently, have pleased him because of the accounting opportunities to increase the value of the assets acquired rather than write off huge amounts of goodwill.

Hellings has been highly rewarded since his transatlantic move but he has also been remarkably successful in minimising the group's tax bill. The impact on the group's earnings of Hanson's exceptionally low tax charge has been formidable. It can be quantified by calculating what the tax charge would have been if the standard company tax rate had applied to profits. In the early 1980s, even taking the lower of the UK and US tax rates, the earnings on a full tax charge would have been less than two-thirds of the figure which was actually reported. In the second half of the decade the earnings on this basis would have typically been about three-quarters of the reported level. But the saving in tax also generated other savings in the form of interest income on the cash which stayed in Hanson's bank accounts. If interest is assumed to have been worth 10 per cent on these sums the total impact on earnings is even greater than under the original calculations. At the extreme, in 1983 and 1993 the adjusted earnings would be less than 60 per cent of the reported figure, falling from £734 million to £436 million in 1993. Cumulatively, beginning in 1980, these tax and interest savings amount to a staggering £2.2 billion by 1993, with the benefit running at between £300 million and £400 million in the early 1990s. It must be said that few major UK companies have regularly been charged tax at the standard rate, but even if Hanson had been charged an average rate its earnings would have been reduced significantly.

As the 1980s wore on, it appears that Hanson adopted increasingly aggressive methods to maintain the savings, and thus the earnings growth record. Hanson has not broken any laws in pursuing every company's duty to pay as little tax as is legitimate within the rules. But as the tax rules have changed, Hanson has found itself nearer to the boundary of what is acceptable to the tax authorities. One leading tax accountant described the situation like this: 'The tax rules are hurdles which have to be jumped. In the mid-1980s they were jumping them well, but as the rules changed the hurdles became higher.'[23]

A key tax-saving technique used in the early 1980s was the use of what are known as dual-resident companies. For example, HM Anglo-American, a Hanson Trust subsidiary used in the acquisition of SCM and Kidde, was incorporated in the US but it had a trading address in Britain. Before this possibility was blocked, in a 1987 Finance Act, this meant that it was possible for Hanson to claim tax relief on the company's interest costs both in the US and in the UK. Without the use of such dual-resident companies the tax charge in 1984 and 1985 would have been well over 30 per cent, instead of around 25 per cent. This represented a tax saving – which is actual cash, unlike some of the accounting savings – of at least £20 million a year. That was 16 per cent of the declared after-tax profits in 1984.

Dual residence was not the only tax-reducing mechanism, and others became more important once the dual-residence schemes were blocked. Brian Hellings and the three top tax accountants who work in Hanson's London headquarters had to use their skill to maintain the unusually low rate of tax. For having benefited from such a low rate for several years, any significant increase would endanger the continued growth of earnings per share at a time when the lack of lucrative takeovers and the unhelpful trading environment made it difficult enough anyway to maintain the record of earnings growth. They turned to Panama, which offered companies tax-free profits and secrecy, and to complex corporate structures to make the US acquisitions of the 1980s.

In the 1980s, Lord Hanson's responsibilities indirectly included more than twenty companies incorporated in Panama. Some had exotic names such as Yesin, Yenhal, Makara International, Cherrelyn Holdings, Zurfran Capital Corporation and Kilbirnie. Some made huge losses: for example in 1984 Yesin Holdings lost £161 million through its subsidiary, Yenhal, which had lost that sum on selling assets. In 1987 a company called Gainor made a loss of £854 million on the disposal of assets. These were not the kind of results expected by the Hanson group when buying and selling assets, but clearly these transactions were not the kind of headline-grabbing deals that so fascinated the financial community. The transactions were carried out not by the high-profile company chiefs, but by the expert accounting staff. The assets on which these Panamanian companies made such losses were in fact the assets which Sir Gordon had bought in various takeovers – from SCM, Kidde and others – and which were then shuffled round the group. The loss made by Yesin and its subsidiary Yenhal, for example, stemmed from transfers of assets of the UDS group. Gainor's losses were made on Imperial assets.

Gainor, and another Panamanian company, Ramsey, were used by Hanson as repositories of the assets of Imperial Group. The tobacco business went into Gainor while most of the other assets, other than Courage, which was sold to Elders, were put into Ramsey. Both these companies were then acquired by a Hanson subsidiary called Lloyd Litho, which was subsequently renamed Imperial Group. Gainor and Ramsey then proceeded to sell the Imperial assets they had acquired to their own subsidiaries. In the case of Gainor, the tobacco business was sold to a new subsidiary, renamed Imperial Tobacco Ltd. Ramsey made the sale of other assets to a company called Bickleylake. Losses of £854 million and £149 million respectively were made by the two Panamanian companies.

The US acquisitions of the 1980s were even more complex. SCM was actually acquired, not by Hanson Trust or Hanson Industries, but by two joint bidders: HSCM Industries and a Dutch company based in Curaçao, Hanson Holdings Netherlands. This is one of the few Hanson subsidiaries of which Brian Hellings is a director, perhaps illustrating its significance in the group's financial planning. Hanson Trust directly owned 70 per cent of the Dutch company, with the other 30 per cent owned by a UK company called Marnee which was itself owned by Hanson Trust. HSCM Industries was ultimately also owned by Hanson Trust, but through a long and complex chain. HSCM Industries had 19 shareholders, called HSCM1 to HSCM19, some owning only 1 per cent but the first four owning 15 per cent each. These companies were in turn owned by HSCM20, which was owned by HM Holdings. All these were US companies. They were eventually owned by Hanson Trust through HM Anglo-American, which had the benefit of dual residence.

The structure became even more labyrinthine with the purchase of Kaiser Cement and Kidde. Lloyd Litho, Ramsey and Bickleylake again featured in the Kaiser purchase, as they had with Imperial, while as many as 62 companies were shareholders in the company, HIMP-2, which owned one of the bidders for Kidde. The other bidder was again Hanson Holdings Netherlands (HHN). But ownership of the HHN shares had now passed from Marnee to another Hanson Trust subsidiary, Morebeat. Both Marnee and Morebeat are registered in the UK. But while Morebeat was not based in the exotic location of Panama, it certainly had unusual finances. In 1988 it had a share capital of £2, but an accumulated loss of £420 million and loans from another group company of £2.5 billion. In the following year it made sales of £248,940, which resulted in a pretax loss of £261 million. But a £715 million extraordinary gain, in the accounting and literal sense, turned that loss into a profit.

Morebeat and Marnee were significant elements of the network of companies through which Hanson Trust managed its tax affairs. In the late 1980s they were instrumental in a huge legal reorganisation which helped to solve Hanson's balance-sheet problems. Throughout the 1970s and early 1980s the group continually had low reserves in the balance sheet of the holding company, Hanson Trust plc. This was an entirely technical problem, unrelated to the availability of cash, but it was nevertheless crucial to the group's dividend potential. For most purposes the distinction between the holding company of a group such as Hanson and the group as a whole is insignificant. But it matters enormously for dividend purposes. Company law prevents a company paying a dividend unless it has sufficient 'reserves' in its balance sheet. In this case, 'reserves' does not refer to cash sums, but to the accumulated profits over the company's life which remain after paying dividends. So far as the Hanson group as a whole is concerned, availability of cash has not been a problem. But the group's dividend is technically paid out of the holding company, and Hanson's accounts reveal that the holding company has frequently been close to having insufficient accumulated profits. This situation arose because, from the early 1970s, little of the group's growing profits fed through to the holding company's profit and loss account.

The reorganisation which corrected this situation involved the transfer of the 20 Panamanian companies referred to earlier. Morebeat, active in the context of the Kidde acquisition, began to acquire the Panamanian companies in 1986. It also bought Hanson Holdings Netherlands and an Isle of Man company, United Handcraft Insurance. The purchases were completed in 1987, bringing the total acquisition cost to £2.7 billion. In the following year Morebeat sold these companies to a subsidiary, Hanson Industrial Services (HIS), once again for £2.7 billion. In 1989 HIS also purchased two other Panamanian companies, pushing its total acquisition cost to £3.2 billion. Interestingly, Morebeat also acquired half the share capital of Tillotson Commercial Motors – the company with which Lords Hanson and White had first come into the Wiles Group almost 25 years previously.

In 1989 HIS began to sell these overseas companies, either directly or indirectly to Hanson Overseas Holdings (HOH) for shares. These shares were then exchanged for shares in Hanson Holdings (I) Ltd, which owned HOH, and eventually those shares were sold to Hanson plc. All these transactions were valued at £4.3 billion. The culmination of these transactions came in 1990. Morebeat, HM Anglo-American and 50 per cent of another US company had been acquired by HK Holdings (No. 2) Ltd (HK2) and HK2 now proceeded to exchange HM Anglo-American for shares in HOH. And just as HOH had eventually sold its investment to Hanson plc, the same thing happened with HK2. As before, the HOH shares were exchanged for shares in HHI, which were then sold to Hanson plc, in this case for £3.2 billion, most of which was then paid as a dividend – ultimately to Hanson plc, it can be presumed.

The complexity of these transactions shows the extent to which Brian Hellings and his associates had to go in pursuit of their objective of effective group structure. Hanson executives have said that the purpose of these transactions was merely to reorganise the group structure after years of acquisitions and to remove anomalies which had grown up during the 1980s. But they have also said that there were tax benefits.[24]

The tax implications were clearly recognised when Marnee was established in 1984. Its Memorandum of Association – the company's constitution – states that its primary object is to acquire investments and goes on to stress that Marnee does not have the power to deal in such investments, merely to hold them for the purpose of receiving income. If it sells investments, any profit on the sale 'shall be dealt with as capital surplus, and not available for the payment of dividends'. Such a clause has been used by other groups with subsidiaries which they want to treat as investment rather than trading companies. The distinction can be crucial because a transaction within a group which is not considered an investment would be subject to tax on what would be regarded as dealing profits.

As well as their role in the reorganisation, Morebeat and Marnee were also important in another respect. Despite being small companies in terms of sales or capital employed – Morebeat had a share capital of only £2 and sales of only £35,000 in 1988 – these companies were involved in huge financial transactions, notably loans of more than £2 billion bearing interest at 10.5 per cent. The crucial aspect of these deals is that Marnee's accounting year ends on 31 March, unlike most of the Hanson group which has 30 September as a year end. The importance of this is that the loan interest paid by Morebeat would be available for tax relief against Hanson's profits in the year to September – for the first time in the 1987/88 financial year. But Marnee's interest income would probably have been taxed for the first time in the following financial year. Thus Hanson would have received a one-off benefit of tax relief worth tens of millions of pounds in 1987/88, with no impact in the following years as the interest income from Marnee would then cancel the interest cost from Morebeat.

It is clear from these illustrations that the skills of Hanson's accountants were important in the group's continued earnings growth during the 1980s. The group's treasury team also played their part by delivering high levels of interest income. By the end of the 1980s the interest figures were substantial even by Hanson's standards. Net interest – that is, the difference between interest income and interest cost – rose to almost £200 million, and contributed between 15 and 20 per cent of total profit before interest had been taken into account. But these net interest figures are the differences between the much larger separate elements: interest receivable was more than £800 million in 1990, 1991 and 1992. At the same time, in each of those three years the group paid interest of more than £600 million. The group's explanation for these huge sums was that it kept large cash balances in Europe, benefiting from high interest rates there, while borrowings were largely in the US where interest rates were low. The interest income represented an excellent return on the cash which Hanson had lying around. But at an average rate of 12.6 per cent this return was not particularly dramatic, considering that deposits of billions of pounds do attract top rates, and UK interest rates began 1990/91 at 15 per cent.

Much more dramatic was the interest rate apparently earned in 1986 and 1987. The sums involved were much smaller: cash balances were only £1.1 billion in September 1985, rising to about £3 billion two years later. But the interest rate earned on these balances seems to have been phenomenal, if the cash balance at the year ends reflected levels throughout the year. At a time when UK rates were falling from a temporary 14 per cent at the start of 1985 to just 8.5 per cent following the stock market crash of 1987, the rate of interest earned by Hanson shot up from 11 per cent in 1985 to 20 per cent the following year and remained at 16 per cent in 1987.

The group's cash balances appear to relate closely to the assets in the Panamanian empire. Because accounts are not publicly available for Panamanian companies, it is impossible to know from public records what their activities are and how they impact on the Hanson group. But it *is* possible from analysis of the UK companies which owned the Panamanian subsidiaries to track the value of those offshore companies. And the value of these Panamanian companies in Hanson's accounts matched closely the group's cash balances in the mid- to late 1980s. In the four years 1986–89 the total cash balances were in each case rather larger than the value of the offshore companies but the growth in each is very similar, rising in total from about £1.5 billion in 1985 to around £5 billion in 1989. One implication is – although the lack of information in Panama means that we cannot know for certain – that Hanson's cash mountain was invested in or through Panama.

None of these tax-saving measures contravened the tax rules. To a large extent, the low tax charge is a reflection of the expertise of Hanson's tax accountants. Indeed, when some of the details of the group's tax practices emerged during the ICI affair, tax managers in other companies were berated by their bosses for not being as effective as their Hanson counterparts. But the tax story nevertheless raises questions about the quality of Hanson's earnings. It is clear that a significant element of the group's earnings stems from its tax-management activities. It also seems that Hanson's tax experts were driven to use increasingly innovative and skilful measures which in some cases delivered only one-off benefits, and which involved huge investments in and by Panamanian companies. This has never been fully explained to shareholders, although the practices brought them significant gains.

On a purely financial basis, these tax methods are risky. Hanson received legal opinions to the effect that all the practices used were in accordance with tax rules. But tax law is uncertain. What is within the law according to legal opinion may turn out not to work after a challenge by the Inland Revenue. Such challenges often materialise years after the accounting year which benefited from the scheme in question. So when the profits are declared, it is impossible to be certain that the tax savings will eventually materialise. Like many companies, Hanson has had several years of tax computations 'open' at one time – that is, still to be agreed by the Inland Revenue.

The lack of disclosure of these important transactions in the annual reports and the lack of explanation of the profits arising from Hanson's accounting, tax and treasury skills, clashes with current thinking on corporate governance. For example, in 1989 Hanson Holdings (I) bought £14 billion of assets as part of the internal reorganisation. That was double the value of the Hanson group as shown in its balance sheet and in excess of its £11 billion stock market value. Yet shareholders remained ignorant of the transaction until it was reported in the press.[25] And even now they remain ignorant of the assets which the Panamanian companies own, because of the secrecy involved. This analysis of Hanson's financial performance finds little evidence that Lord Hanson or Lord White or the rest of the team which built up the company, deserved their 1980s reputations as highly skilled industrialists.

Clearly, they were successful in building a huge empire, in making themselves and many shareholders rich. But that success was very narrow. It did not stem from creating new businesses or from building existing ones through the classic pattern of investment, product development and similar risk-taking actions which are the stuff of entrepreneurship. Indeed there is plenty of evidence in this chapter that Hanson's custody left companies weaker, not stronger, and that the Hanson style has actually been negative for British industry, despite the impetus it may have given to greater operating efficiency.

Operating efficiency is a minor victory compared to the greater defeats suffered from a lack of vision beyond the next set of financial results. But Hanson's very success in generating the kind of results which pleased the financial markets made it more difficult for other companies to adopt such vision and pursue long-term strategies to build businesses for the future. Hanson's success heavily influenced the investing culture during the 1980s, leading to over-emphasis on steadily rising earnings per share, and a lack of interest in new products, new projects and the potential for earnings in the next decade. Companies tempted to pursue such strategies knew they would be punished for short-term declines in earnings, at the very least by finding difficulty in raising capital, and at worst being taken over – by a company such as Hanson.

CHAPTER 11

The Legacy

Hanson was a company formed in the freewheeling, lightly regulated atmosphere of the 1960s, when it seemed that financial market forces could shake up moribund British industry, and it came into its own in the heat of the Thatcherite revolution, when once again government's hopes for an economic leap forward were invested in the fire of market forces.

Hanson the man and Mrs Thatcher, Hanson the company and the 1980s, were made for each other. The individuals shared a belief in the power and rights of money and the value of economic liberalism, together with an impatience which demanded swift action rather than slow reform, investment and gradual improvement. The company was founded on a dealing philosophy which came to prominence again in the 1980s and was fed by the liberalisation of financial markets.

'Big bang' summed up the company's approach to doing business as it did the upheavals in London's stock market which helped to feed the dealing frenzy of 1986–88.

By the beginning of the 1990s, however, the backwash from that frenzy, in the form of collapsed companies and disappointed investors, together with the vicious recession in the early years of the decade, had created a very different atmosphere, one which Lord Hanson and his company were completely uncomfortable with. The financial conditions of a lacklustre stock market and a depressed economy were unsuitable for the torrent of takeovers which had characterised Hanson's most successful period, while the group had grown so large that only a target such as ICI would add the required impetus to earnings per share. But the attitudes which came to the fore in the early 1990s were also unsuited to Hanson. The responsibilities of business – to the environment, local communities and society at large – once again became prominent. The simple notion that business was merely a vehicle for making money receded, overtaken by the belief that how the money is made is important.

Such ideas were reflected in the deliberations of senior industrialists taking part in the RSA's Tomorrow's Company Inquiry, and the new approach to corporate governance under the aegis of the Cadbury Committee.

The development of the Cadbury Code highlighted how far from the mainstream Hanson had become. Corporate governance has never been one of Lord Hanson's enthusiasms. His bad-tempered response to the new rules on company board operations brought in by the Cadbury Code on corporate governance illustrates his impatience with external interference in company affairs: 'Much has been said recently about corporate governance, but most of the advice *has been long on accountability and short on encouraging efficiency and enterprise*' (his italics).[1]

The Ground Round/MariFarms case described in chapter nine is an example of the way in which Lord Hanson sometimes seems to have thought of himself as chairman of a private rather than a public company. He seems to have continued to operate Hanson plc as though he were chairing the family company, but that attitude is far from the collegiate attitudes of the 1990s, as represented by the Cadbury Committee. Lord Hanson's view of the role of directors and of the board is not just at odds with the views of the Cadbury Committee; it also clashes with the approach of many other chairmen of public companies. For many years the Hanson board consisted of the small group of people who came together in the early 1970s. There were some outsiders but they were friends of Lord Hanson rather than independent appointees: Robert Dean of Pearl and Dean was a director between 1975 and 1981; Sir Christopher Harding has been a director since 1979; merchant banker Hugh Ashton joined the board briefly during the mid-1980s. But until the early 1990s there was no attempt to create a strong independent non-executive presence. Even in 1991 a number of the appointees fell more into the category of personal friends than figures who might challenge the orthodoxies of the executive directors. From time to time some directors were designated in the annual accounts as non-executive. But this was frequently more a matter of Lord Hanson's preference than any reflection of their status or contribution.

Even executive directors, however, were barely involved in some policy decisions. The company's investment in Melody Radio, for example, was merely announced to the board, and can be seen to be a personal initiative of Lord Hanson's. Much more significantly, some directors learned of the company's purchase of ICI shares through the newspapers rather than through a board meeting. Such meetings are largely concerned with very detailed reviews of operating units, but with little questioning, and only brief attention paid to accounting and tax issues, despite their importance; nor do they deal with the perks available in particular to Lords Hanson and White, or to the other US-based directors. Lord Hanson's top directors operated as a cabinet, rather than a traditional board, but with Lord Hanson very clearly in the role of a dominant Thatcher-like prime minister. But they have generally been a cabinet with few portfolios, in the usually accepted business sense. Martin Taylor has been the public face of Lord Hanson, the man who dealt with press inquiries – usually with a 'no comment' – and has been a member of the CBI council, the Takeover Panel and similar bodies. Derek Rosling was initially important in the financial aspects of takeovers but has never had the kind of formal responsibilities which might be expected in a more conventional group. Tony Alexander has been the link with the operating companies, while Brian Hellings, as previously described, has been responsible primarily for the financial structure of the group. Derek Bonham has come closest to a constitutional role as finance director.

These five accountants, plus lawyer Alan Hagdrup, constituted Lord Hanson's top team for the key years of its dramatic growth, from the late 1970s to the late 1980s. The preponderance of accountants in this group illustrates the company's approach to business; the absence from it of the second most powerful person in the business, Lord White, illustrates the quixotic nature of the board: the members had many privileges, but not the privilege of power. Lord White usually has had the ultimate say over acquisitions, and to a lesser extent disposals. And his involvement has been on both sides of the Atlantic, not just in the US, where he has not usually been closely involved in any operational detail. That has been the responsibility of David Clarke from the earliest days. This illustrates another misconception about the group – that it is divided geographically, primarily between the US and the UK, with one Lord for each half. In practice the group is divided into operating companies, which stand largely alone. For example, SCM's UK titanium dioxide plants are managed from the US, responsible ultimately to David Clarke, not to the UK director responsible for operating companies, Tony Alexander.

Lord Hanson's personal inclinations have always been important, but never as much as Lord White's gut feel. Thus, when Lord King, approaching retirement, came to persuade Lord Hanson to make a bid for British Airways, Lord Hanson's sense of loyalty to his old friend did not override his respect for his partner's common-sense view, which said this would be an expensive, controversial and risky investment. When it came to disposals, a certain amount of personal whim has always been involved. For example, Boots has attempted to acquire the Seven Seas vitamin company on several occasions. But this is one of Lord Hanson's personal interests, and he has refused to sell, despite several offers.

Lord Hanson has chaired his company for almost thirty years in the style of a personal fiefdom. The boardroom is his court, in which decisions are often handed down, rather than the pinnacle of collective decision-making and control, where opinions are tested and orthodoxies challenged. Indeed some of the board changes of the early 1990s seem to have been defensive, protecting Lord Hanson's position of authority on the board at a time when he may have felt unsettled by the departure or imminent departure of many of the old guard such as Alan Hagdrup, John Pattison and Derek Rosling. The appointment, in 1990, of his son, Robert Hanson, and his nephew, Chris Collins, to manage acquisitions enhanced the family nature of the board.

Clearly the relationship between Lords Hanson and White has been crucial to the group's development and success. It has been depicted as remarkably close, with Lord White playing the part of James's lost younger brother, sometimes rather disdainful of Lord Hanson. Lord White has been the only other person in the group whose opinion Lord Hanson automatically respects, and the only one who never receives the sharp edge of his tongue, although he has often been impatient with Lord White's dilettante approach to business. One early colleague said, 'Hanson is a perfectionist. He was very serious about the business. He really wanted to grow it and run it properly.'[2] Lord White's whimsical, disinterested approach was therefore annoying from the earliest days, just as his later antics with women and horses caused Lord Hanson great anger and embarrassment. The anger was controlled, however, unlike with other long-serving associates. Lord Hanson's temper has often been expended on even his oldest colleagues, such as Derek Rosling, who has often been treated with less respect than might be expected considering his long association with, and elevated status in, the company. Lord White could get away with much more, because of his special relationship with Lord Hanson. One colleague explained the horse-racing venture which emerged during the ICI affair: 'Hanson would never had done it himself, but he would never have stopped Gordon doing it.'[3]

The two Lords have always been more equal than other directors, including the earliest recruits such as Rosling, Taylor, Hagdrup and Hellings. It is part of Lord Hanson's style to remain slightly aloof. At Christmas parties, even in the 1970s when the head office staff was very small, he would always leave fairly early, rather than remaining and letting his hair down like the other directors. It is also useful and perhaps necessary for him to remain above his colleagues, in order to exercise control and continue to command the enormous respect within the company. And there is no doubt that Lord Hanson is a much more elevated person within this group than are most company chairmen. The company's organisational style has been described as being like a universe rather than the conventional pyramid: 'The management system is a solar system, with everyone circling round the sun in the middle, James Hanson. Everyone is in elliptical orbit. Suddenly you are at the centre of the universe and the next moment you are hurtling into outer space.'[4]

Lord Hanson's dominance of the company by far outstrips that of even long-standing colleagues. The reasons for his enormous authority lie in the role he played in building the enterprise, and the fact that it bears his name. And at least part of the answer must also lie in his personality, his almost patrician assumption of power, based on an upbringing as part of Yorkshire's powerful business élite, but also his remarkable aura. Despite the fact that his younger brother, not James, was originally destined to take over from their father, James Hanson grew up used to exercising power, and thus expert at leading a team and instilling intense loyalty. But he has also constantly needed the reassurance of power to prove to himself that he has indeed achieved at least as much success as his brother would have.

Hanson's strong personality is expressed tangibly by the multitude of photographs of himself (and Lord White) which adorn the group's offices and which are given to staff in recognition of achievement or on occasions such as their leaving the company. It is also expressed in his painstaking preparation for the annual meeting – *his* annual meeting with his loyal shareholders. And a certain vanity is expressed in a concern for his physical appearance. His image of himself is of a great businessman and representative of the business class. He was that to Mrs Thatcher, and for a time many businessmen in the 1980s would have been happy to nominate him as their role model. But few chief executives in even so exalted a position would have had the assurance to send a personal letter to a senior minister, as he did to Stephen Dorrell in June 1994, purporting to represent not just his own company but British industry in general – especially when he has rarely been involved in any representative organisations such as the Confederation of British Industry or the Institute of Directors.

But that self-assurance has also been part of Hanson's undoing – it has helped to prevent his recognising that the times have changed, that in the 1980s business mores are outdated, and that Hanson plc needed to change with the times. A more sensitive person might have realised that Hanson corporate attitudes would not be suited to the 1990s, and that the 1990s kind of investment community – especially in the United States – would not be prepared to accept the creation of a Hanson dynasty.

Lord Hanson's persona is thrown into relief by comparison with Sir Owen Green, the boss for a similar period of the other great conglomerate of the 1970s and 1980s, BTR. Sir Owen has always hated the comparison, because he believes the two companies have been very different and BTR's achievements to have been more solid.

But the differences are most marked in comparison of the two leaders. Sir Owen has largely been an anonymous industrialist. Despite his success, at least as great as Lord Hanson's, he has received very little publicity. Despite his own long reign as BTR's chief executive, his personality was by no means stamped on the company, and his fellow directors were active participants in group decision-making, as in most companies. And most crucially of all, Sir Owen left the company with a sounder reputation for solid business achievements, despite similar difficulties over acquisition accounting, and with a respected management team in charge. It remains to be seen whether Lord Hanson will ever truly leave the bridge of his company, but if he does, the team he leaves behind will not stand comparison with that at BTR.

Lord Hanson's high opinion of himself has often been tempered by a desire to reflect some of the glory on others. He has been keen to assuage Lord White's irritation at having been upstaged by James himself in the 1970s and early 1980s, by promoting Lord White's contribution to the group's success at his own expense. But that is part of his very keen sense of understanding and managing people, which has also helped him to move very easily in political circles. Lord Hanson was one of the pre-eminent business politicians of the 1980s. His personal convictions put him very close politically to Mrs Thatcher and he enjoyed translating that political proximity into personal closeness – something which also fed his vanity and so completed a circle. Lord Hanson moved smoothly through the corridors of power, at ease with the country's most powerful civil servants, just as he was with the most powerful politicians. But his touch was not always adroit, and sometimes did not help his company, as the Westland and PowerGen affairs showed. Westland also showed that Lord Hanson was prepared to put politics before business, but as the Thatcher era receded it also became apparent that there was a limit to such idealism. By the mid-1990s, Lord Hanson was launching a charm offensive to cultivate the Labour Party, pragmatically recognising the likelihood that it could soon be in power again. To Lord Hanson, it seems that power is as important as party politics.

Charm and temper are Lord Hanson's other main personal traits, both of which have proved useful in political dealings as well as business affairs. The charm cloaks a steely determination. 'He has a terrible smile. He smiles at you and you know he's fucking you, you can feel him fucking you,' as one former colleague observed.[5]

Most importantly, he has been the leader of the company for almost 30 years. He has been responsible for choosing key members of the team, for motivating them, and for building and retaining their loyalty. In that he has been exceptional. Many feel intense loyalty, to the extent even of feeling that they are letting him down by retiring. Some of that loyalty stems from the fact that many people owe Lord Hanson an enormous amount. He has stood by his early colleagues, not all of whom would otherwise have found themselves running the huge organisation which Hanson plc has become. It could be argued that some of that loyalty has been bought with high salaries and generous share options. But many companies have found that their incentive schemes have failed to generate loyalty to the corporate body, but have instead generated destructive manipulation and intra-group competition. Lord Hanson must take credit for having made his incentives work for the benefit of the Hanson group. But this places his main contribution as an administrator rather than a manager or industrialist.

It is clearly as a leader and orchestrator that Lord Hanson has been most effective. And yet his approach has been far from the classic role of insight and vision which might be expected of such a person. This chairman of a multi-billion-pound corporation is responsible for some of the most mundane of the group's affairs, such as the car parking spaces at head office, the minutiae of the annual report and the tidiness of the offices. He has been an administrator, someone for whom no detail has been too small, who cares passionately about the appearance of his staff as well as himself, who would personally ensure that the office of a new recruit to head office was suitably decorated (usually with photographs of himself and Lord White) and that the pictures were absolutely straight on the walls. That is not a notable contribution; it is the work of an office manager rather than a chairman.

Lord Hanson has never attempted to be a 'manager' in the usual sense of the word in an industrial context. His company has never really been an industrial company, or even a conglomerate, as the term is now understood. The description 'industrial management company', coined by Lord Hanson as long ago as 1969, is more than merely a euphemism for the unfashionable 'conglomerate' label. It describes more accurately than has often been realised what the company has always been about. That purpose has been the management of industrial investments rather than the management of industrial operations. A financial business such as the US leveraged buyout specialists KKR is a much closer parallel to Hanson than any industrial group – the focus is on buying and selling companies rather than on running factories. This was revealed very early on in his progress. In an unguarded moment, which echoed a famous remark of Jim Slater's about making money, not things, James Hanson said: 'I'm not interested in making things and I'm not interested in building companies up from scratch.'[6] In reality, Hanson plc is actually a rather small company, and that also explains the intense bond between Lord Hanson and many of the hundred or so people who work at 1 Grosvenor Place. The other 80,000 and the companies they work for, are almost incidental. They are investments, no different in substance from the myriad other investments which the group holds at any time in companies large and small – the difference is only in the size of the investment, which determines which line of the balance sheet it appears on, and whether it is formally considered part of the Hanson whole.

Just as Hanson plc is really a small investment bank and not a huge industrial empire, so it is a mistake to view Lord Hanson as an 'industrialist', as he has so often been described. It is probably an accident of birth that he has ever been regarded as an 'industrialist' rather than a financier. The fact that he came from the North of England, and spoke with a Yorkshire accent, helped project the image of a down-to-earth businessman who knew what life was like on the shop-floor – an image he has always been careful not to destroy. If James Hanson had been born in Havant, Hove or Hemel Hempstead rather than in Huddersfield, perceptions might have been a little different. He might then have been seen more clearly as the rich financier which he was and which he has remained: a member of the county set, pampered by a retinue of personal and business support staff and an expensive web of houses, cars and planes, someone thrust reluctantly into the business world because of his brother's early death and his father's dynastic ambitions.

Nevertheless, there have been plenty such rich young men who remained at best anonymous, at worst bankrupt. James Hanson has had remarkable success in building a group which is bigger than he or any of his early associates would ever have dreamed. Looking at what became of most other conglomerates from the 1960s, 1970s or 1980s shows that it is not easy to win at Lord Hanson's game. Much of the credit for that success, as Lord Hanson readily admits, must go to Lord White, the man mainly responsible during the 1970s and 1980s for the buying and selling. If Lord Hanson has been Lord of the detail, Lord White has been the Lord of the deal. And deal-making, while in many respects much easier than building companies from the ground, is fraught with pitfalls. Above all, the price must be right. That requires luck, judgement and negotiating skills. Lords Hanson and White have had all three. They were lucky to find West of England Sack, waiting to be pillaged. They were lucky not to get too heavily involved in property, and to enter the 1970s recession with plenty of cash because of the failure of the transport, Costain and Bowater deals. They were lucky to make money from Seacoast in its first year even if subsequently it disappointed. But judgement has also been crucial, in identifying SCM and the price it was worth, in the stock market operations which won several takeover battles, and in walking away from others. Walking away is relatively easy, especially for the disinterested conglomerateur. But a deal-making company can only afford to lose a limited number of battles, otherwise its reputation, so crucial to its success, becomes in danger of collapse. Bad judgement in picking targets would have meant walking away from too many of them, thus making it more difficult to mount the next attack.

This combination of ingredients has left Lord Hanson at the head of a huge empire when many others have seen their similar approaches disintegrate. But the success seems shallow when examined in detail. Lord Hanson's business escaped the fate of others who followed Slater's approach, partly through the luck already referred to, partly because he stuck with the original Slater notion of investing in industrial companies rather than being tempted by the fool's gold of financial operations. Hanson entered the Thatcher era with an enhanced reputation because of Lord White's early US deals and the naïvety of investors in the face of takeover accounting. And he capitalised on the freedoms of the Thatcher era, with help from tax and accounting skills and the benefit of high interest rates.

All that, however, has left precious little of substance as Lord Hanson's legacy. In the narrowest sense, his legacy is Hanson plc, although it remains to be seen how long that remains in the form which he built. But the legacy must also include the 'little Hansons' which he has spawned, and the more general impact on British industry of his enormous success during the 1980s. The ICI affair can be seen to have marked the end of the buccaneering White era. His health unreliable, and his mind no longer fixed on the chase, Lord White played a decreasing part in the affairs of the group thereafter. David Clarke, for a long time the operational head in the United States, became more prominent, and began to make it clear to investors that he wanted Hanson Industries to become a more conventional company, based on its key resource interests in North America: coal, timber and chemicals. In the UK, Lord Hanson's looming presence remained more substantial, even though he was spending more and more time in the US, but Derek Bonham's influence could be seen creeping over the group in various ways. Taking the advice of public relations supremo Sir Tim Bell, he began to open up the company to City analysts and financial journalists. In December 1993 the company held its first ever press briefing for journalists on its financial results, instead of the usual practice of Martin Taylor fending off requests for more information than was included in the brief press announcement. Journalists were also invited to the annual meeting, including the associated exhibition of the subsidiaries. Also in December, Bonham presided over the management buyout of a package of companies which included some of the group's earliest acquisitions: SLD Pumps and Dufaylite. This sale, raising £90 million, was overshadowed by the flotation of Beazer Homes, but it was of greater significance for the future of the group. It signified that in the UK, as in the US, Hanson was becoming a more normal company, following the fashion for focus on core activities – primarily Imperial Tobacco in the UK. This reorientation was also having an effect at head office. For the first time ever, staff began to undertake tasks more normally associated with a head office function, such as long-term planning.

Perhaps they were also working on another task unfamiliar to

Hanson staff: preparing defences against a potential takeover bid. The group's **poor** share price performance since 1985, and especially since 1990, and its uncertain financial prospects in the immediate future, made it a potential target. In many ways it is a classic Hanson target. It is not difficult to imagine a bidder painting a picture of a company dominated by elderly old-fashioned management which has not moved with the times, and has pursued pet projects such as Melody Radio and enjoyed personal comforts such as the use of company assets and other corporate support. While Lords Hanson and White were still in the saddle, it is difficult to imagine anybody brave enough to try to unseat them. But with the two Lords taking a less prominent role, the opportunity for an ambitious bid becomes more credible. Hanson playing the same role as Thomas Tilling (the conglomerate defeated in the bid for Berec and subsequently acquired by BTR) is a plausible scenario, especially after several years in which earnings per share had fallen, and a number of tactical errors ranging from Lord White's investment in the bloodstock to the bungled attempt to change the company's constitution in 1993.

One potential defence could have been a division of the group between the US and UK components. This had been much talked about throughout the early 1990s, although ostensibly ruled out on tax grounds. It would have made considerable organisational and managerial sense: there is virtually no overlap between the businesses on the two sides of the Atlantic. Despite their being shoe-horned into the three reporting categories of Industrial, Consumer and Building Products, following the sale of housebuilding the only common operation is the aggregates business. Some companies such as SCM chemicals operate in the UK and the US, but it is managed entirely from the US. There would therefore be no difficulty managerially in splitting the group into two.

But this option was ruled out by the demerger of 1995. Hiving off the new USI rid Hanson of virtually all its smaller businesses, as well as ridding Derek Bonham of the difficult relationship with David Clarke. It left a group with seven substantial businesses, mostly oriented towards resources. But while the move tidied up the empire, it did not change its nature as a conglomerate where there was no rational link between each business, for example tobacco and bricks in the UK or coal and chemicals in the US.

Such businesses can only justify their existence in the financial markets if they produce excellent financial performance. And that did appear likely in 1995, as the resource-based businesses, particularly Quantum Chemicals, were poised to benefit from surging demand as the economic cycle turned upwards. Focusing on these activities left Hanson peculiarly exposed to general economic trends, which had never been the case previously. Just as the economic cycle was expected to boost Quantum's profits in the years 1994–96, so it seemed likely that they would inevitably decline in subsequent years when the economy turned down.

This was a new phenomenon for Hanson, which had always been able to beat the cycles by choosing stable industries and by boosting profits through deal-making. It created pressure to make a substantial acquisition in an industry which experienced a balancing economic cycle – probably one exposed to consumer spending rather than a capital-intensive business such as chemicals. But this carries its own dangers. Part of Hanson's success was due to the fact that it could always walk away from targets. There was never a need to acquire a particular business, since there was no underlying rationale for the acquisition, except to make money. Now Hanson finds itself in the position of any ordinary company seeking to grow in a particular field, with the accompanying difficulty of doing so at the right price and without the ability to sell off huge chunks of the purchase.

This is another part of the normalisation of the group as Derek Bonham's influence over it strengthened. And like any normal business, it also leaves the group exposed unless it can produce the earnings growth demanded by investors. One option might be a friendly merger, perhaps with one of the 'little Hansons' which emerged during the 1980s. Tomkins is the largest of the three companies run by former Hanson staff largely on the Hanson principles, the others being TT Group and Wassall. Indeed Tomkins showed that it had well and truly escaped from Hanson's shadow when it succeeded in winning the takeover battle for RHM against Hanson in 1992. In fact Tomkins is more like BTR in that it has indulged only marginally in the classic Hanson activity of selling parts of its victims to recoup part of the purchase price and to make significant dealing profits. These three companies are another part of the Hanson legacy and are an illustration of the wider impact Lord

Hanson's success has had on the British industrial scene. The success of Hanson Trust in the 1980s spawned not only these three companies. They are a tangible representation of a much greater influence: a strengthening of the financial orientation of British business, of the attention to short-term financial results which many believe to have damaged the long-term performance of British industry. When Lords Hanson and White were rampaging through the stock market, no company director could sleep safe in bed unless he was secure in the knowledge that his company could deliver consistent increases in earnings per share. And that knowledge must have led many companies to defer or abandon risky investments which might have had a short-term negative impact on earnings, even if they would have been beneficial in the long term. Companies which were known to be targets of Lord Hanson or a similar raider have also found the recruitment of top staff extremely difficult. Few people want to take a new job in a company which might not be in existence for very long.

Supporters of the Hanson style argue that the predatory impetus has not only prevented company directors from sleeping in their beds, but also from sleeping in their boardrooms. The threat of a letter from Lord Hanson announcing his ownership of a share stake must have helped many directors to take difficult decisions which they might otherwise have ducked. ICI directors accept that while they might have opted to split the group without Lord Hanson's intervention, his action helped them to convince other executives that floating off Zeneca was the right strategy to follow. And there is no doubt that companies such as Lindustries, Berec and Imperial Group had made mistakes. In many cases, however, Lord Hanson's victims had already begun to remedy errors, making it easy for him to collect the benefits without having to incur all of the effort or pain. In any case, if shareholders decided that a company's management needed changing, that could have been done without control passing to another company. There is little evidence that Lord Hanson and his team have demonstrated a good record of running businesses, except in the areas of accounting and taxation, and in the narrow sense of squeezing cost and capital out of manufacturing operations. The predatory impact of Lord Hanson and his imitators must have had some positive effects. But it is difficult to believe that they have not been outweighed by the negative impact of short-term financial thinking, which permeated British industry in the 1980s, just as it had in the 1960s, when James Hanson and Gordon White first began to copy Jim Slater's approach.

Lord Hanson can therefore be said to have built an empire, but in Slater's image and relying hugely on the dealing skills of Lord White. In the mid-1990s, however, the empire appears to be in decline. It has little inherent logic and therefore seems unlikely to grow to become, as Lord Hanson would wish, one of the great business dynasties in the same league as the Rockefellers. In the time he has led the company, others have built enduring empires: Lord Weinstock's GEC, Grand Metropolitan, the retail groups and advertising agencies. Some of these have struggled, such as Saatchi & Saatchi, but they nevertheless seem likely to survive and grow, because the businesses that have been built have the creative flair that is not obvious in the collection of companies that is Hanson.

Beyond the confines of Hanson plc, Lord Hanson also built a financial style of doing business which was in keeping with the extravagant 1980s. But it has fallen out of fashion, along with the other components of the superficial, unsustainable boom of that decade. If Lord Hanson had retired at 60 following the Berec takeover, or even at 65 after the best ever but acrimonious deals of Imperial and SCM, he could have taken with him an intact reputation as a successful empire builder. By hanging on past his 70th birthday, however, he became vulnerable to the fate of so many empire builders who wish to turn their success into a dynasty.

Appendix 1: Table of main UK bids, failed bids and disposals, with value where known (excluding initial deals bringing in Tillotson, Commercial Motors (Hull) and Welbecson)

Year	Share stakes which came to nothing	Failed bids	Agreed takeovers	Successful contested bids	Significant disposals
1966					C Wiles £0.4m
1967			SLD £0.7m		
1968			West of England Sack £3.2m Nathaniel Lloyd Dufaylite Butterley £2.8m		
1969			Provincial Traction Jack Olding		
1970		Steels Garages	City & St James (50%)		Motor businesses £4m
1971					
1972		Thomas Cook Costain £30m	British Steel brickworks £2.7m	National Star & Brick £2.1m	
1973		Gable Industries Bowater (merger) Sykes Lacy Hulbert Rolls-Royce motors (consortium bid)	BHD £12.2m NCB's Midland Brick £2.2m J Howard Smith $32m (Seacoast)		Holset £13.6m
1974	UATC				
1975	Charrington Gardener Lockett		Indian Head textiles $36m (Carisbrook)		
1976		Whitecroft	Hygrade $32m Rollalong £1.2m Angus Milling £0.5m		
1977		Bluebird Foods	Hamlyn & Co £0.9m		Bucilla $16m (ex Carisbrook)

Appendix 1

Year	Share stakes which came to nothing	Failed bids	Agreed takeovers	Successful contested bids	Significant disposals
1978	Selincourt		Interstate $30m Henry Campbell Group £4.9m Templon spinning mills $7.3m		
1979	John James Group	Barber Oil		Lindustries £28m	Natural Casings $11m (ex Hygrade)
1980					
1981	Gulf Resources	CMT GH Downing	McDonough $185m	Berec £95m	McDonough cement and concrete $49m
1982	Avondale Mills Dan River		UGI £19m		
1983	Tate & Lyle			UDS £260m	UDS shops £152m: John Collier, Timpson, Orbit, Richard Shops. Berec units $60m
1984	Charter Consolidated		USI $532m	London Brick £245m	Seacoast $32m USI unit $22m
1985	Bowater Babcock	Powell Duffryn			USI units $36m Interstate $93m
1986	Goodyear Westland	Eveready (US)		SCM $930m Imperial Group $2,500m	USI units $142m SCM paper $160m Glidden $580m Durkee $120m other SCM units $75m Imps hotels, restaurants £186m Courage £1,400m Golden Wonder £87m

Appendix 1

Year	Share stakes which came to nothing	Failed bids	Agreed takeovers	Successful contested bids	Significant disposals
1987	Midland Bank Morgan Grenfell		Kaiser Cement $250m Kidde $1,600m		Kaiser units $63m
1988	Cummins Engine Armitage Blue Circle				Kaiser units $185m Ross Young's £335m Lea & Perrins £199 Kidde units $402m Durkee Industrial $185m
1989	Thomson T-Line		ConsGold £3,300m		Hygrade $140m Allders £210m Smith Corona $309m (part float) S African gold £608m
1990		PowerGen	Cavenham Peabody $1,200m —— share swap with ——		Newmont $1,300m Arc America $650m
1991		ICI	Beazer £391m		
1992		RHM	Southern Ohio coal $165m		Ever Ready £132m
1993			Costain coal $299m Watt housing $116m Quantum Chemical Corp $3,400m Santa Fe coal & quarry assets —— swap for ——		Axelson $83m Stationery companies $162m SLD etc £90m ConsGold gold assets

Appendix 2: Profit record of Hanson units 1975/6 to 1982/3

(Operating profit in £ millions)

UK Divisions	1975/6	1976/7	1977/8	1978/9	1979/80	1980/1	1981/2	1982/3
Agriculture	0.6	0.7	1.3	0.7	0.8	0.6	included in NAI	
Butterley	3.5	3.0	3.7	5.0	5.8	5.5	5.9	7.8
SLD	1.9	2.1	2.3	3.7	3.1	1.9	3.4	3.0
Nthn Amalgamated Industries	0.6	1.2	1.0	1.3	6.6*	4.9	7.7	18.3**

* including Lindustries from this year
**including United Gas Industries

(Operating profit in $ millions)

US companies	1975/6	1976/7	1977/8	1978/9	1979/80	1980/1	1981/2	1982/3
Seacoast	9.1	10.3	7.3	13.0	9.8	3.2	−3.6	1.8
Hygrade	4.1†	11.0	7.3	11.4	11.2*	9.7	10.4	10.3
Carisbrook	7.5	9.5	9.5*	11.0	18.6***	23.3	21.8	17.5
Interstate	–	–	9.3**	11.7*	10.3	10.9	13.1	12.1

* disposals of some units occurred during years marked thus
** 9 months only
***Lindustries unit included from this year
† 6 months only

Source: Company accounts

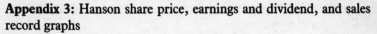

Appendix 3: Hanson share price, earnings and dividend, and sales record graphs

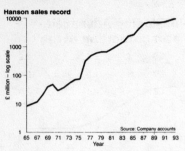

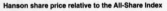

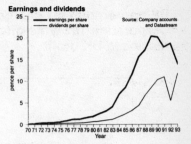

The graph simply shows how the Hanson share price compares to the All-Share Index. When the line of the graph rises it indicates that the Hanson shares are out-performing the Index; when the line falls it shows the Hanson shares under-performing the Index.

Appendix 4: The effect of advanced corporation tax write-offs and UK corporation tax graphs

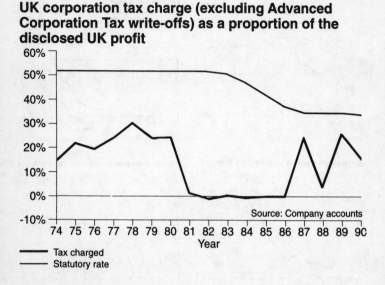

UK corporation tax charge (excluding Advanced Corporation Tax write-offs) as a proportion of the disclosed UK profit

Source: Company accounts

— Tax charged
— Statutory rate

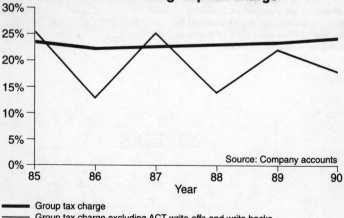

The smoothing effect of Advanced Corporation Tax write-offs on the Hanson group tax charge

Source: Company accounts

— Group tax charge
— Group tax charge excluding ACT write-offs and write backs

Appendix 5

Appendix 5: Sample ownership structure of a Hanson subsidiary: Kidde

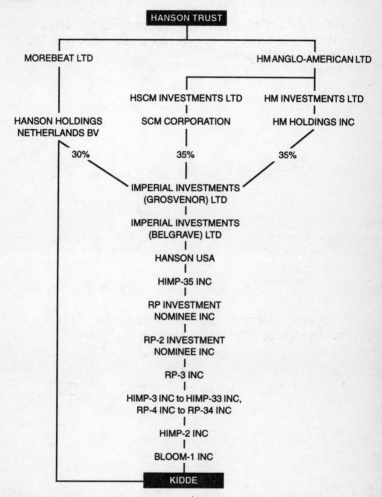

The purchase of Kidde was made by Hanson Holdings Netherlands BV and Bloom-1 Inc. As the diagram shows, the ownership of Kidde by the various Hanson companies is complex – Bloom-1 Inc is several tiers distant from the ultimate owner: Hanson Trust.

Source: Offer document for Kidde purchase, 25/9/87

Note: Only Hanson Trust and Morebeat were English companies. HSCM Investments, HM Investments, HM Anglo-American had as their principal business addresses the Hanson Group Headquarters: 1 Grosvenor Place.

Notes

Chapter 1: The Private Potentate

1. 'Hanson Backs Wilson Statue', *Huddersfield Examiner*, 21 December 1989.
2. Hugo Young, *One of Us* (Macmillan, 1989).
3. Confidential interview with the authors, October 1993.
4. Lord Hanson, interview with the authors, 16 February 1994.
5. United States District Court, Southern District of New York. Hanson plc against SCM Corporation. Ref: 85 CIV 6667 RLC.
6. Philip Ziegler, *Wilson: The Authorised Life* (Weidenfeld & Nicolson, 1993).
7. John Campbell, *Edward Heath: A Biography* (Jonathan Cape, 1993).
8. Alan Clark, *Diaries* (Weidenfeld & Nicolson, 1993).
9. Lord Parkinson, interview with the authors, 11 October 1993.

Chapter 2: Packhorses, Charabancs and Trucking

1. 'Big Fire at Milnsbridge', *Colne Valley Guardian*, 22 August 1919.
2. Advertisement: Joseph Hanson & Son, *Colne Valley Guardian*, 22 August 1919.
3. 'The Milnsbridge Fire Case: An Award of £500', *Colne Valley Guardian*, 6 August 1920.
4. Property in the Market/Auction Notices, *Huddersfield Examiner*, 21 August 1920.
5. 'Echo of Furniture Fire: Milnsbridge Bankruptcy Case', *Colne Valley Guardian*, 18 January 1924.
6. 'Offer Lord Hanson's Groom Couldn't Refuse', *Daily Mail*, 22 February 1994.
7. Una Stothard Smith *The Bridge* (a history of Milnsbridge), private monograph.
8. Letter dated 11 February 1916. G. Lumb transport archives, Huddersfield.
9. 'A Busmen's Holiday', *Huddersfield Daily Examiner*, 13 October 1947.
10. 'Partners in Profit', *Sunday Times Magazine*, 8 December 1991.

11. Eaton Smith & Downey, invoice to Hanson's Buses Ltd, December 1935–July 1936. G. Lumb transport archives, Huddersfield.
12. Confidential interview with the authors, 1993.
13. 'Hanson's Progress', Robert Cockcroft, *Yorkshire Post*, 21 February 1989.
14. Wilbert Morris, interview with the authors, 1993.
15. 'A Microphone and a Frequency', Doreen Taylor, Heinemann, London, 1983 pp. 14–15.
16. Lord Hanson, letter to Mrs Betty Bruce, 1 March 1989.

Chapter 3: Prosperity, Playboys and Partners
1. 'Seventy-five Years in Road Haulage. I. W. Holdsworth's Anniversary', *Motor Transport*, December 1945.
2. *Hanson Transport: A Brief History*, published by Hanson Transport, Huddersfield, p. 6.
3. Peter Hennessy *'Never Again': Britain 1945–51* (Jonathan Cape, 1992), p. 183.
4. Ibid., p. 207.
5. 'New Company', *Colne Valley Guardian*, 20 December 1946.
6. '£3,000,000 Road Transport Deal', *Huddersfield Daily Examiner*, 6 August 1948.
7. 'Transport Chief in Huddersfield', *Huddersfield Daily Examiner*, 20 January 1949.
8. *The Rockwood Harriers* (Reid-Hamilton, 1954–55), p. 17.
9. 'Unique – Finest Middle-Weight Hunter!', *Huddersfield Daily Examiner*, 13 July 1951.
10. Jean Stead, interview with the authors, 1993.
11. Ibid.
12. 'Man with £100,000 off to Win Dollars', *Sunday Express*, 28 August 1949.
13. 'Transport Firm Building New $750,000 Terminal', *Hamilton Spectator*, 17 January 1957.
14. 'British Capital Goes West', *Commercial Motor*, 17 May 1957, p. 532.
15. 'Partners in Profit', *Sunday Times Magazine*, 8 December 1991, p. 24.
16. Confidential interview with authors, 1993.
17. 'James Home, as Jean Steps Out', *Daily Express*, 1 February 1950.
18. Sheridan Morley, *Audrey Hepburn: A Celebration* (Pavilion Books, 1993), pp. 8–10.
19. David Shipman, *The Great Movie Stars* (Angus & Robertson, 1972), pp. 216–19.

20. *Daily Mail*, 22 January 1993.
21. Charles Higham, *Audrey* (New English Library, 1984), p. 41.
22. 'Mr J. E. Hanson and Miss A. Hepburn', *The Times*, 4 December 1951.
23. 'It Should Have Been a Wedding Smile', *Daily Herald*, 1 October 1952.
24. 'Star Date', *Woman's Sunday Mirror*, 15 April 1956.
25. 'Third Time Unlucky for Playboy Bachelor', *Daily Mail*, 21 November 1956.
26. James Hanson, letter to *Huddersfield Examiner*, 31 January 1959.
27. 'Mr James Hanson is Married in Secret', *Huddersfield Daily Examiner*, 2 February 1959.
28. 'Meet the Girl who Caught the Bachelor', *Daily Express*, 4 March 1959.
29. *Daily Express*, 11 October 1960.
30. 'Lord Brabazon Opens Hanson Haulage New Freight Terminal at Huddersfield', *Huddersfield Daily Examiner*, 12 April 1962.
31. Lord Hanson, interview with authors, April 1994.

Chapter 4: The Slater Years: 1964–73

1. Wiles Group flotation document, 5 March 1964.
2. 'Wiles of an Ex-playboy', *Sunday Mirror*, 3 November 1968.
3. Jim Slater, *Return to GO* (Weidenfeld & Nicolson, 1977), p. 15.
4. Charles Raw, *Slater Walker* (André Deutsch, 1977), p. 132.
5. Slater, *Return to GO*, p. 98.
6. Alan Whicker, *Whicker's New World* (Weidenfeld & Nicolson, 1985), p. 111.
7. 'Wiles Chief's £20 Million Deal', *Daily Telegraph*, 1969.
8. 'An Insider Speaks', John Gilmore, *Guardian*, 10 February 1967.
9. Confidential interview with the authors, 30 September 1993.
10. 'Handsome Hanson on the Rebound', *Daily Express*, 20 January 1970.
11. Whicker, *Whicker's New World*, p. 99.
12. 'We Must Expand, says Trident TV's New Chief', *Campaign*, 28 April 1972.
13. *Financial Times*, 1 December 1971.
14. Slater, *Return to GO*, p. 178.
15. 'Bowater Bid £51m for Hanson', Kenneth Gooding, *Financial Times*, 16 June 1973.
16. Ibid.
17. News analysis, Terry Dodsworth, *Financial Times*, 16 June 1973.

18. 'Why Bowater's Bid for Hanson is Ill-conceived', *The Times*, 25 June 1973.
19. 'Bowater Drops Hanson Bid', *Financial Times*, 26 July 1973.
20. *The Mergers Handbook: A Guide to Board of Trade Practice* (HMSO, 1969). See also Raw, *Slater Walker*, pp. 224, 225.

Chapter 5: Up and Away: 1973–83
1. Alan Whicker, *Whicker's New World* (Weidenfeld & Nicholson, 1985), p. 98.
2. 'Sir Gordon Dares . . . and Wins', *Observer*, 13 May 1984.
3. Whicker, *Whicker's New World*, p. 106.
4. 'Interstate United Vending Deals Hit', Chuck Heschmeyer and Jeff Rundles, *Rocky Mountain Journal*, 7 December 1977.
5. 'Food Service Firm Bares Bribes', James Strong and Ronald Koziol, *Chicago Tribune*, 19 March 1977.
6. 'Food Exec Guilty in Labor Exortion', Thomas Powers, *Chicago Tribune*, 28 May 1978.
7. 'Hanson Trust: The Strange Interstate Tale', Lorana Sullivan, *Observer*, 16 January 1983.
8. Lex column, *Financial Times*, March 1976.
9. Lex column, *Financial Times*, December 1976.
10. Financial Editor, *The Times*, 17 December 1974.
11. Questor column, *Daily Telegraph*, 17 December 1974.
12. Confidential interview with the authors, 14 October 1993.
13. *Financial Times*, 2 August 1979.
14. *Observer*, 5 August 1979.
15. Lex column, *Financial Times*, 29 September 1979.
16. Labour Party National Executive Committee resolution, 1974.
17. Hanson Trust offer document for Berec Group, 1 October 1981.
18. 'Hanson Dawn Raid Catches Ever Ready by Surprise', *Guardian*, 11 July 1981.
19. 'Hanson Buys £7 million Stake in Berec', *Financial Times*, 11 July 1981.
20. Advertisement in the *Financial Times*, 29 October 1981.
21. 'Hanson up on Sale of Subsidiaries', *The Times*, 18 December 1982.

Chapter 6: Megadeals 1983–91
1. 'The Battle for UDS', *Financial Times*, 16 April 1983.
2. Lex column, *Financial Times*, 29 January 1985.
3. 'Hanson Bid for Powell Duffryn Fails', Martin Dickson, *Financial Times*, 30 January 1985.
4. Confidential interview with the authors.

5. 'Hanson Trust, Low Tech, High Profit' *Economist*, 20 April 1985; 'Call that Brought the City to Life', Stefan Wagstyl, *Financial Times*, 11 June 1985.

6. Alan Whicker, *Whicker's New World* (Weidenfeld & Nicolson, 1985), p. 111.

7. Findings of fact in case of Hanson Trust etc. v SCM etc., Southern District Court of New York, November 1985.

8. Sir Gordon White's deposition in the same case, p. 9.

9. Ibid., p. 14.

10. Ibid., p. 15.

11. Ibid., various pages.

12. Lord Hanson's deposition, p. 82.

13. Lord Hanson's deposition, pp. 122, 148.

14. Whicker, *Whicker's New World*, p. 103.

15. Obtained privately by the authors.

16. Obtained privately by the authors.

17. Obtained privately by the authors.

18. Statement by Trade and Industry Secretary Channon on Hanson Trust, *The Times*, 27 February 1986.

19. Obtained privately by the authors.

20. Obtained privately by the authors.

21. Lex column, *Financial Times*, 4 June 1986.

22. 'A Scrooge Star for Hanson', *The Times*, 29 December 1986.

23. For example, 'Hanson–Kidde – Nice Price, Shame about the Company', Chris Blackhurst, *Business Magazine*, January 1988.

24. Speech to Northern Ireland Chamber of Commerce, 13 October 1987.

25. 'Hanson Bosses Dominate Share Option League, Research Shows', Lisa Buckingham, *Guardian*, 22 January 1990.

26. 'Hanson Quadruples Chairman's Salary', David Waller, *Financial Times*, 18 December 1987.

27. For example, 'Hanson Fears', Tempus column, *The Times*, 4 December 1987.

28. Surprises Ahead at Hanson', City Comment, *Daily Telegraph*, 29 November 1988.

29. Tempus column, *The Times*, 4 June 1986.

30. 'I'll Still Be Running the Show at 75, Vows Lord Hanson', Dan Atkinson, *Guardian*, 31 January 1991.

31. Confidential interview with the authors.

32. 'Did Hanson Hide Bad News?', Todd Vogel and Christopher Tucher, *Business Week*, 28 August 1988.

33. Lex column, *Financial Times*, 17 October 1990.

34. Questor column, *Daily Telegraph*, 29 October 1990.

35. 'Warburg Blow for Hanson', Michael Clark, *The Times*, 10 November 1990.
36. Analysis by Datastream, the financial and economic database company.
37. Contango column, *Sunday Times*, 9 December 1990.
38. Lex column, *Financial Times*, 15 December 1990.
39. 'Hanson Loses Magic Touch', David Brierley, *Sunday Times*, 23 December 1990.

Chapter 7: The Political Player
1. 'Power Struggle', Michael Jones and Andrew Lorenz, *Sunday Times*, 29 July 1990.
2. Lord Wakeham, interview with the authors, January 1994.
3. Ibid.
4. 'Sir Gordon White: Profile', Robert Peston, *Independent on Sunday*, 29 July 1990.
5. 'PowerGen Sale May Go Private', Simon Beavis, *Guardian*, 21 July 1990.
6. 'Labour Claims Electricity Sale a Sleazy Shambles', Nikki Knewstub, *Guardian*, 24 July 1990.
7. Ibid.
8. Lord Wakeham, interview with the authors, January 1994.
9. Margaret Thatcher, *The Downing Street Years* (HarperCollins, 1993), p. 676.
10. Ibid.
11. Ibid., p. 677.
12. 'Monetarism is Not Enough', Introduction by Sir Keith Joseph, (Centre for Policy Studies, 1976).
13. Sir Keith Joseph quoted in Shirley Robin Letwin, *The Anatomy of Thatcherism* (Fontana, 1992), p. 116.
14. 'Political Donations', prepared answer supplied by Lord Hanson, 16 January 1994.
15. Annual reports of Wiles Group, Hanson Trust and Hanson plc 1968–1993.
16. 'Hanson's Choice', Lord Hanson, *Observer*, 24 May 1987, p. 36.
17. Lord Parkinson, interview with the authors, October 1993.
18. Alan Clark, *Diaries* (Weidenfeld & Nicolson, 1993), pp. 140–42.
19. Philip Ziegler, *Wilson* (Weidenfeld & Nicolson, 1993), pp. 494–501.
20. 'And Now the Lord High Contributor', *Daily Express*, 21 May 1976.
21. 'Out of the Shadows the New Mr Playboy', Geoffrey Levy, *Daily Express*, 5 November 1981.

22. 'And Now the Lord High Contributor', *Daily Express*, 21 May 1976.
23. 'Why Management Must be Accountable', Sir Gordon White, *Financial Times*, 12 July 1990.
24. Lord Parkinson, interview with authors, 11 October 1993.
25. 'Lord White Praises Hitler', Ben Laurance, *Guardian*, 11 February 1992.
26. 'Lord White Apologises Over his Praise for Hitler', Alex Brummer, *Guardian*, 12 February 1992.
27. 'The Mystery Buyer is Hanson', *London Standard*, 16 January 1986.
28. Peter Foster, *Towers of Debt: The Rise and Fall of the Reichmanns* (Hodder & Stoughton, 1993), pp. 194–9.
29. 'Hanson in the Hunt for Purchase of Canary Wharf', Alex Brummer and Mark Milner, *Guardian*, 1 June 1992.
30. Martin and Susan Tolchin, *Buying into America* (Times Books, 1988), pp. 16–17.
31. US House of Representatives Lobbying Act Report Identification Number 04045026, 12 January 1987.
32. Federal Election Commission Index of Candidates Supported/ Opposed 1993/4 Peabody Political Action Committee Reference C00110478.
33. US Senate Lobbying Act Report Identification Number 17977000, 14 October 1993.
34. Ibid.
35. Lord White, interview with authors, 1992.
36. 'Prime Minister Presents Hanson Management Achievement Award', Hanson press release, 19 January 1988.
37. 'Hanson Angered by Dorrell Query Over Too High Dividends', Roland Rudd, *Financial Times*, 4–5 June 1994.

Chapter 8: The Siege at Millbank

1. Lord White, interview with the authors, February 1992.
2. Carol Kennedy, *ICI: The Company that Changed our Lives* (Paul Chapman, 1993), p. 188.
3. 'Hanson Lights the Fuse', Jeff Randall, *Sunday Times*, 19 May 1991.
4. 'Hanson Presents a Case for Holmes', Andrew Alexander, *Daily Mail*, 15 May 1991.
5. 'ICI: The Grand Design of Hanson', *Sunday Telegraph*, 19 May 1991.
6. 'Dynamic Duo Strikes Again', *Mail on Sunday*, 19 May 1991.
7. 'Hanson's World-class Power Play', *Observer*, 19 May 1991.

8. 'Hanson plc Discloses it Bought ICI Stake of 2.82% as "Investment"', Craig Forman, *Wall Street Journal*, 16 May 1991.

9. 'Corporate Crusaders', Charles Leadbeater and Roland Rudd, *Financial Times*, 25 May 1991.

10. Ibid.

11. Kennedy, *ICI*, p. 193.

12. 'Unions Warn of Fight on a Scale Never Seen Before', *Financial Times*, 21 May 1991.

13. 'MPs Unite in Possible Opposition to Bid', *Financial Times*, 21 May 1991.

14. 'ICI not a Play-thing says Chairman Hanson', Ben Laurance, *Guardian*, 20 June 1991.

15. 'Hanson Takeover Bid', *Financial World Tonight*, BBC Radio 4, 19 June 1991.

16. 'Hanson Bid', *ITN News at Ten*, 19 June 1991.

17. 'Hanson Writes to MPs to Correct "Inaccurate" Bias', Ralph Atkins, *Financial Times*, 11 June 1991.

18. 'Hanson Moved £9.5 Billions of Assets in Secret Restructuring', Angela Mackay, *The Times*, 14 June 1991.

19. Ibid.

20. Gordon White, interview with the authors, February 1992.

21. Ibid.

22. 'Hanson's $7m Beverly Hills White House', Michael Gillard, *Observer*, 7 July 1991.

23. 'Opinion: In the Matter of a Television Programme Provisionally Entitled "Dispatches Hanson"', Alan Newman QC, 15 January 1992.

24. Gordon White, interview with the authors, February 1992.

25. 'Lord Hanson's Tiff with Sir Tim', *Observer*, 13 October 1991.

Chapter 9: Seeking a New Identity

1. Lord Hanson, at a luncheon attended by the author, 5 August 1993.

2. 'Hanson', West Riding News Service, 19 December 1993.

3. 'Hanson: US Construction', published by Hoare Govett & Co., July 1993.

4. 'Hanson to strengthen its board', Alex Brummer, *Guardian*, 28 June 1991.

5. Hanson 1993 Annual Report, p. 29.

6. 'Secret Grooming for Successors', Dan Atkinson, *Guardian*, 29 January 1992.

7. 'White Heir is Promised the Crown', Roland Rudd, *Financial Times*, 15 February 1992.

8. 'Hanson Names Bonham CEO', news release Hanson plc, 20 April 1992.
9. 'Hanson May Opt for Part-time Position', *Financial Times*, 22 April 1992.
10. H. Lloyd Kanev and Solin Cho, *Hanson plc* (Smith Barney, 1993), p. 6.
11. 'The Hanson Price', Lindsay Vincent, *Observer*, 26 April 1992.
12. Lord Hanson, interview with the authors, 16 February 1994.
13. 'Hanson Bows to Investors' Campaign', Ben Laurance, *Guardian*, 18 June 1993.
14. 'Hanson: At the Crossroads', Barclays de Zoete Wedd, March 1993.
15. Confidential interview with the authors, December 1993.
16. 'Rank Plans Split to Beat Hanson', Karen Cooper, *Daily Telegraph*, 17 October 1992.
17. Hanson Interim Report, 17 May 1994.
18. 'A Time to Test the Strengths of the Rising Son', *Financial Times*, 3 October 1992.
19. Gordon White, interview with the authors, 1992.
20. Hanson interview, West Riding News Service, 19 December 1993.

Chapter 10: The Reckoning

1. Confidential interview with the authors, 13 October 1993.
2. 'Predator Game to the End', *The Times*, 3 December 1990.
3. Sir Hector Laing, interview with the authors, 13 October 1993.
4. Tomorrow's Company, Royal Society for Arts, Manufactures and Commerce, 11 February 1994.
5. House of Commons Trade and Industry Select Committee Report on Competitiveness of UK Manufacturing Industry (HMSO), 20 April 1994.
6. 'Assault and Battery', David Bowen, *Independent on Sunday*, 27 June 1993.
7. 'Hanson Trust's Predatory Peer', Stella Shamoon, *Observer*, 22 December 1985.
8. Stockbroker's circular, Smith Barney, July 1993, p. 88.
9. Ibid., p. 90.
10. Bowen, ibid.
11. Financial results press conference, December 1993.
12. 'Hanson: The Dangers of Living by Takeover Alone', John Byrne and Mark Maremont, *Business Week*, 15 August 1988.
13. Jeffrey Robinson, *The Risk Takers*, (George Allen & Unwin, 1985), p. 188.

14. Alan Whicker, *Whicker's New World*, (Weidenfeld & Nicolson, 1985), p. 104.
15. Institute of Chartered Accountants in England and Wales, members' handbook, 1994.
16. Terry Smith, *Accounting for Growth* (Century Business, 1992), p. 4.
17. 'Accounting Matters', James Capel & Co., September 1992.
18. *The Mergers Handbook: A Guide to Board of Trade Practice* (HMSO, 1969).
19. 'The Operators', Stephen Aris, *Sunday Times*, 14 July 1968.
20. Confidential interview with the authors.
21. 'Hanson: Quality of Earnings Strained', Barclays de Zoete Wedd, 3 April 1991.
22. Smith, *Accounting for Growth*, p. 23.
23. Confidential interview with the authors.
24. 'Why Hanson Tidy-up Came after 10 Years of Growth', Angela Mackay, *The Times*, 27 June 1991.
25. 'Hanson Paid £14 billion for Own Assets', Angela Mackay, *The Times*, 17 June 1991.

Chapter 11: The Legacy

1. Hanson annual report, 1992.
2. Confidential interview with the authors.
3. Confidential interview with the authors.
4. 'What Drives the Lords of the Deal?', Charles Leadbeater and Roland Rudd, *Financial Times*, 20 July 1991.
5. Confidential interview with the authors.
6. Aris, ibid.

Index

Index

Index